YO-DJO-631

...Pacience is an heigh vertu certeyn...
...Trouthe is the hyeste thing that men may kepe...

THE FRANKELEYNS TALE
by Geoffrey Chaucer, 1388

FRANKLIN- REVOLUTIONARY SCIENTIST

Roy Meador

ANN ARBOR SCIENCE
PUBLISHERS INC
P.O. BOX 1425 • ANN ARBOR, MICH. 48106

Preface

Franklin—Revolutionary Scientist began when Edward Lewis, the publisher, sought an appropriate project in honor of the U.S. Bicentennial. Taking a close look at the life and science of Benjamin Franklin was quickly recognized as an ideal answer, with potential significance through and beyond 1976. Sharing a fresh acquaintance with the most versatile of America's Founding Fathers provided a particularly rewarding way for Americans to start a third century.

The original intention was to concentrate on science, but Franklin often refused to collaborate with such a cramping arrangement. A commitment to science was a central fact of his life, but Franklin's many-sided intellect and skills sent his talents and energies capering in sundry directions. America's all-purpose Renaissance man, he was the first, indeed *only* American to earn international renown as scientist, statesman, author, wit, inventor, tradesman, philosopher, philanthropist, sage, &c. In this study, all of Franklin's identities insist on and receive attention, though his personal wish was to be known as a *Natural Philosopher* (eighteenth century terminology synonymous with scientist or research scientist today).

A country and a people can be judged by the heroes they keep.

v

It speaks hopefully for America that an all-time hero is still this cheerful, near-sighted, broad-visioned genius who believed in asking questions without fear until truth was determined, who counselled "moderation amid the passions of a fierce controversy," and who considered reason the surest weapon against falsehood, ignorance, and inhumanity. He stressed individual freedom, working to achieve the common good, and justice for all as obligations to be cherished. Such extraordinary concepts became fixed American rights, thanks in large measure to this printer-scientist from Boston by way of Philadelphia.

Are Benjamin Franklin's "basics of democracy" still healthy and on the job? An encroaching fear today is that modern complexities and anxieties may be eating away at them. Neglect, alarm, and suspicion can form an eroding drip-drip-drip of time. In his *Reflections on the Human Condition*, Eric Hoffer wrote, "It is the malady of our age that the young are so busy teaching us that they have no time left to learn." Haven't many Americans, not just the young, stopped learning and remembering clearly about the American past and spirit? The story needs frequent retelling, since looking back prepares for a wiser look ahead. Hence one eminent and practical reason for revisiting Benjamin Franklin. Pleasure, vivacity, and good-humored instruction are others.

Bifocals in place, Doctor Franklin can help us discover it is never too late to learn about America. He makes an ideal teacher, and a Bicentennial makes an ideal time. Franklin understood the premise and the promise of this land perhaps first and best. For him the promise was bound up with the progress of science and the rich continent science would help develop. He trusted future generations ...us... to preserve freedom. He knew that freedom was the ideal environment in which human minds could grow and science could work to liberate men from material want. Franklin expected the benefits of science to be enjoyed by everyone, not simply a privileged few.

At the end of this book hopefully you will find yourself mentally saluting Benjamin Franklin, champion of truth and reason, while thinking realistically and optimistically about the country he helped shape from eighteenth century clay. Resurrecting the mind and heart of Benjamin Franklin should be excellent Bicentennial therapy for what ails us. Happy Anniversary.

Ann Arbor, Michigan   Roy Meador
October, 1975

SPECIAL ACKNOWLEDGMENT

From my Mother and Father, I first learned the deeper meaning and hope of Benjamin Franklin's country. With work and faith, they embodied the meaning and served the hope. In free and stormy Oklahoma, they had reason to respect the man who signed their Constitution . . . and explained lightning. She was born on the treeless plains of New Mexico, he in Indian Territory before Statehood. They lived on America's frontier, helping extend the horizons of liberty.

This book was completed on my father's 75th birthday. He lived to see America enter an era of troubled greatness. His confidence was as enduring as Franklin's that trouble could be left behind and the promise of this land fulfilled.

DEDICATED TO
THE LADY OF THE LILIES WHO
FOUND AND OPENED A SILENT
DOOR OF TRUTH

Contents

Preface   *v*

I.   The Sage   1
Doctor Franklin Attends a Birth 1 · Councils
Unconfounded 6 · The Signing Hour 8 · Whither
the Sun? 11

II. Home is the Traveller   17
Scientist at Sea Again 17 · The House That Franklin
Built 22 · Two-Headed Curiosity 24

III. The Making of an American Scientist   29
Coming of the Father 29 · A Tradesman's Son 32 ·
Scholar Days in Boston 35 · Apprentice in a Shop of
Letters 37 · Books and the Boy 40 · The Benign
Queerness 45

IV. Philadelphia, Here I Come   49
New Citizen for Athens on the Schuylkill 49 · Three Penny
Bread and a Future Wife 52 · A Philosopher's
Hometown 55 · Stoop, Stoop! 58 · The Water American
and an Interlude of London 60

V.   Aquatic Sciences   67
Doctor Franklin, Swimmer   67   •   Mind Over Water   69

VI.   "Rational Creature"   75
A Surfeit of Flour in the Pudding   75   •   Fine Printing to
Order   79   •   The Printer Takes a Wife   85   •   Scientific
Virtue   89   •   Educating a President   92

VII.   Gazette Galley Proofs   97
Editor at the Type Case of Power   97   •   The "Foolishness"
of Truth   101   •   Equations for a Rational Creature   105

VIII.   Toolmaker   115
Two Ways of Science   115   •   Heat Riddles   118   •   Word
Doctor Versus Tool Doctor   123   •   Fire Alert in
Philadelphia   127   •   The Franklin Stove   128   •   An End to
Being "Scorched Before & Froze Behind"   132   •   The
Sweetness of Iron   136   •   Earthbound with Wings   139

IX.   A Club of Ingenious Acquaintance   145
"You Should Form a Small Junto"   145   •   Queries   149   •
Plain Truth Starts Something   157

X.   Games of a Scientist   163
Leisure for Studies and Amusements   163   •   A Tonic Bath
Without Water   166   •   Madam Gout's "Abominable Game
of Chess"   169   •   The Most Magically Magic of Any Magic
Square   171   •   Miss Polly Baker, the Prosecuted Matron   177

XI.   Medicine Man   183
Patient, Heal Thyself   183   •   Inoculation and the Mathers of
Boston   186   •   Acting Editor of the *New-England
Courant*   188   •   The Oldest Disease in the World   190   •
Fearless of Air and Water   193   •   The Dry-Belly-Ache and
Other Aggravations   195   •   Electrical Medicine   197   •
The Friedrich Anton Mesmer Controversy   198   •   A Very
Beneficent Design   202

XII.   Music Maker   227
Romance in G   227   •   They Laughed When I Sat Down
at the Armonica   231   •   Armonica Directions (Rainwater
a Must)   235

XIII.   Ingenious Men   241
Founders, Keepers   241   •   The Philosopher Said, Let
There Be Books   242   •   And There Are Books   245   •
Books Instead of Bells   251   •   Correcting a Misfortune
to Youth   252   •   Several Meetings to Mutual
Satisfaction   255   •   First Pool of American Brains   258

XIV.   Strange Fires   265
The Electrical Secrets of Matter   265   •   Some Particular
Phenomena That We Look Upon To Be New   269   •   Queen
Elizabeth's Doctor, &c.   274   •   The New Science of

Points 276 · Positive and Negative 278 ·
M. Musschenbroek's Wonderful Bottle 281 · An Electrical
Battery 284 · Electrical Conspirators and a Feast 289

XV. Lightning: An Extreme Subtle Fluid   293
Let the Experiment Be Made 293 · Ten Thousand Acres
of Electrified Sky 297 · Lightning Points 301 ·
Publication of the Electrical Letters 305 · Proof on Three
Wine Bottles 310 · Reaching for the Fire 312 · The Bell
and the Rod 314 · Rod of Fear or Rod of Reason 318 ·
Pointed Rodders Versus Round Rodders 321 · Inventors
Beware 326

XVI. Living Usefully   331
The Vocations of Leisure 331 · Another Feud with a
Nonexistent Ben 333 · How "Benjamin" Was "Poor
Richard?" 336

XVII. A New Scientific Star   341
The Royal Society 341 · The Stars Applaud When
Philosophers Embrace 345 · Newton and Franklin in the
Guest Book 348 · Common Friends to Mankind 348 ·
End of a Crisis 351

XVIII. The Long Arm of Science   357
Quoi Bon L'Enfant? 357 · Cast Your Oil Upon the
Waters 359 · Whirlwinds and Waterspouts 361 ·
Shooting Stars 366 · Bifocals 366 · Daylight Saving
Time 368 · Corn 372 · Sea Shells on Mountains and
the Gift of a Tooth 374 · The Long Arm 375 ·
Without Boundaries 377

XIX. The Lasting Revolution   381
The Friends of Franklin 381 · The Press of Steam 384
Bugle Boy 385 · Electrifying 388

XX. A Lasting Revolutionist   393
Ablutions in an Era of Fleas 393 · Come with Me to
Philadelphia, and We Will Make Beautiful Experiments
Together 396 · A Cane with the Cap of Liberty 399

An Afterword on Sources   407

Bibliography   411

Index   417

Dear Doctor Franklin, Sir,

You are cordially invited to attend a birthday celebration, time and circumstances allowing. The infant nation you helped father is celebrating its two hundredth year. Without you, the celebration just wouldn't be complete. Please come.

You're probably busy wherever you are, humming cheerfully and performing elaborate scientific experiments that need ages to finish. In the old days they kept interrupting your experiments with public enterprises . . . the Declaration of Independence, leading and financing a Revolution, a Constitution for a new nation, &c. But now perhaps you're making up for lost time, exploring the Higher Sciences with curiosity free to roam, and relishing every new adventure of the mind.

This time we promise not to keep you from your work, but we want you at the party. Bring the bifocals you invented and look us over carefully. We think you'd like to see how we're turning out after our two hundred year start. We could benefit from a frank dose of that calm good sense in which you specialized. Your gift of humor won't be unwelcome either. We'll need a good laugh at our two hundredth birthday party, a Ben Franklin laugh.

Sir, here's a curious fact that may interest and amuse you. In a recent public poll, the majority of Americans indicated that Benjamin Franklin was one of the great, early Presidents of the United States. History has elected you to George Washington's office, ignoring the fact that you truly never wanted public position. You simply wanted to stay home and spend your time deciphering nature's secrets.

Each of your old friends will be asked to the party, of course: General Washington to whom you left your crabtree walking-stick, Thomas Jefferson who succeeded you in Paris, Thomas Paine who carried your letter of introduction, Marie Antoinette who questioned you about electricity, scientists such as Ebenezer Kinnersley who helped with the electrical experiments, Cadwallader Colden, James Logan, and many others. If they know you're expected, all will appear. You had a genius not only for maneuvering through oceans of data to reach scientific truth, but also for rallying people to support everything from the first successful scientific club in America to the longest surviving republic in the world.

Help us do our party right, Sir. You'll be a special guest of honor.

We Are, &c.,

YOURS, THE PEOPLE

I. The Sage

DOCTOR FRANKLIN ATTENDS A BIRTH

> WE, THE PEOPLE of the United States, in Order to form a more per-
> fect Union, establish Justice, insure domestic Tranquility, provide for
> the common defence, promote the general Welfare...

Shall we be assertive and insist that never has a nation been
more dramatically ushered into the world.

Monday, the 17th day of September, 1787. Important events
were taking place in Philadelphia, the largest city in North America. For the delegates, the day began early and moved slowly, but
it was not to be the same as other days, some of which had seemed
interminably long during the hot summer months, as the Federal
Convention to draft a Constitution met at the State House on
Chestnut Street in Philadelphia. The delegates were tired after
protracted debates, bickering, and sometimes angry quarrels over
the various articles of the document they were struggling to put

1

together. All of them wanted to get it done, and no one questioned the importance of finishing as soon as possible. But it was equally true that impulses to hurry were suppressed. What they were doing was too critical. It had to be done right.

All the delegates that Monday seemed clear-headed and alert. There were no visible signs of excessive meditation at the Bunch of Grapes tavern or inordinate dining at the City tavern. Each knew what might be taking place that day, and wanted to be ready.

Did any of the delegates feel the presence of the future that morning as they walked toward the State House? Were there any intimations of coming times when the old State House would be called Independence Hall and the hurrying feet of many generations would have reason and reverence to enter it? If such reflections occurred, no mention was made of them. They were hard-headed, practical soldiers, planters, lawyers, and businessmen. They met in a time that would later be called the age of reason and also the age of revolution, ignoring the contradiction, as if sometimes reason and revolution could cohabit the same century and make beautiful sense together: A new nation perhaps with tranquillity and even justice . . . For all?

The delegates had a vital job to do for themselves and posterity. They were aware of both obligations. They had to plan for and build for the future or there might not be one. But while serving the future, most were also consciously and conscientiously serving themselves and their followers at home. Many different points of view were represented. They had to weld those points of view together somehow in a workable compromise. Maybe they were getting closer. . .

There was one delegate among them with a reputation for being the greatest philosopher in America and probably the world. Since the death of *Voltaire* nine years earlier, there had been no other of a comparable stature. Being a philosopher and a delegate representing no particular faction . . . he was there because of who he was, not because of what was expected from him . . . he more than the others could be said to represent and to speak for the future. He had given that impression more than once during the proceedings. He was in a strange but genuine way a voluntary delegate from the nineteenth and twentieth centuries, and farther times still, too distant for imagining.

Undoubtedly the philosopher spared a thought for those to come later. His years notwithstanding, the fertility and variety of his thoughts matched those of most other delegates, including such brainy young gentlemen as *James Madison* and *Alexander Hamilton*. Often they disagreed about interior decoration for the structure of government they were trying to erect, but they could agree on the value of America's chief intellectual and scientific ornament. In France and other parts of the world, America was beginning to be seen as a legitimate country and a civilized one as well chiefly because the natural philosopher claimed it for his own.

He wasn't in the best of health, and it was painful to stand or try to walk, but there was nothing faltering or slow about *Benjamin Franklin's mind*. He was as sharp as he had ever been, which meant a razor edge. He "possesses an activity of mind equal to a youth of twenty-five," wrote *William Pierce*, delegate from Georgia.

Doctor Franklin's fidelity to the convention had also been an inspiration through the hot summer. They knew what it cost him in pain to be present. But there he was. Genial as ever, listening, watching, counseling, always available.

George Washington, President of the Convention, wrote in his diary that it took "not less than five, for a large part of the time six, and sometimes even seven hours sitting every day, except Sundays, and the ten days adjournment to give a committee opportunity and time to arrange the business, for more than four months."

That Monday morning, *James Wilson*, delegate from Pennsylvania, read a speech to the convention written by his colleague, Benjamin Franklin. The delegates conscientiously attended the words. Franklin had served more as a conciliator, a presence, an architect of compromise during the Federal Convention than in any other capacity. He was not a politician and had not tried very seriously to force his political views on the delegates. Franklin was present for another reason: to make certain that the foundations of a viable government emerged and that there was no disastrous epidemic of factionalism or hothead squabbles. He had not found occasion to address the convention often, but when he did, the words usually read by Wilson, his international renown as scientist-statesman-philosopher assured a respectful audience.

His comments that morning, the third Monday in September, were typical of the man, thoughtful and sometimes playful. Humor was inevitable in anything penned by Benjamin Franklin, and the delegates cheerfully accepted whatever levity he offered. A sense of fun was still one of his most conspicuous traits, as indispensable for identification as his glasses or amused smile.

The story was told that Franklin had not been asked to write the Declaration of Independence eleven summers earlier because he would have found it congenitally impossible to resist inserting a sly jest at some solemn moment. His fondness for wit might have wounded with levity the serene solemnity of that rococo document, with the Doctor certain that a worthy jest could never fail to benefit any declaration, whether of independence or love.

But if amusement was inevitable from Franklin, so was good sense. The delegates knew that from reading and experience embracing much more than one summer in Philadelphia. His Monday speech for the 17th began with admission that he couldn't approve of the Constitution in all its aspects. Then continued:

> Sir, I am not sure I shall never approve it; for having lived long, I have experienced many instances of being obliged, by better information or fuller consideration, to change opinions even on important subjects, which I once thought right, but found to be otherwise. It is, therefore, that the older I grow the more apt I am to doubt my own judgment, and to pay more respect to the judgment of others.

There were appreciative smiles. Doctor Franklin's long career had often furnished evidence of his ability to change his mind. Hating war and loving England, he had invested a decade before the Revolution in trying to prevent hostilities. Failing that, he had altered course, informed his friends in England that George III and Parliament had made peace impossible, and supported the cause of American independence without reservations. He went much further than mere support. The full force of his intelligence, energy, and cunning were put to work making certain the cause of independence became a reality. The Federal Convention was proof of that reality, and the responsibility of the delegates was to make certain they didn't lose it.

There was something more behind Franklin's words. Accepting the views of others when they proved out experimentally was a necessity of what the Doctor liked to consider and describe as his true profession: Natural Philosophy, or science. Franklin had earned worldwide fame as a scientist through his own experiments and papers. He knew much better than the non-scientist delegates the vital importance of adjusting opinions to accommodate new findings. "If you will not hear Reason," Franklin had warned in the guise of Poor Richard, "she'll surely rap your knuckles." Science was a humbling mistress, since fuzzy opinions couldn't wish an experiment into succeeding. Only truth could do that. However many of Franklin's associates at the convention were politicians, and *they*, surely, were members of a curious species. They possessed the remarkable ability in spite of evidence to conclude that what they wanted to be true, *must* be true. Where their own convenience was involved, they could be blindly positive. Completely unscientific, of course. Often during his lifetime, and even more frequently during the convention, Benjamin Franklin had reflected that politicians could benefit from the disciplines of science. Though it was accurate that occasionally during his lifetime, he had himself been a politician, some said the consummate political artisan of his age, during the Federal Convention, he was trying to go straight. Perhaps he was succeeding. Observing Franklin's continuous diplomatic efforts to reconcile differences among the delegates rather than arguing strenuously for his own positions, William Pierce decided that "what claim he has to the politician; posterity must determine," adding that he did not "seem to let politics engage his attention." The evidence suggests that what chiefly engaged Benjamin Franklin's attention during the Constitutional Convention was the future. The first step into that future was a Constitution the states would ratify and the citizens agree to respect.

> Though many private persons think almost as highly of their own infallibility as that of their sect, few express it so naturally as a certain French lady, who, in a little dispute with her sister, said, 'I don't know how it happens, sister, but I meet with nobody but myself that is always in the right!

As Wilson read, several laughed. Even Hamilton of New York and *Governor Randolph* of Virginia smiled. Franklin's arguments were with those inclined to imitate the French lady. Each delegate automatically assumed that someone other than himself was targeted.

The Doctor's expertise on French ladies would, of course, not be challenged. He was known as *the* outstanding American for many more reasons than one. And part of his genius, charm, or amiable rascality was that the American public had nearly always let him live the way he wished and say what he pleased, then loved him for it. The Doctor was a special man all right, earning admiration for behavior that might have caused another man, Thomas Paine, for instance, to be pilloried. But, of course, well, Doctor Franklin was

... uh ... Doctor Franklin, so it was all right that the American sage, though of advanced years, had as *John Adams* critically observed in Paris neither lost his love of beauty nor his taste for it.

COUNCILS UNCONFOUNDED

As the morning advanced, it became warm in the chamber, and the flies swarmed. Some delegates fanned themselves as James Wilson read on. It wouldn't be a long speech. Benjamin Franklin could be trusted to say the needful with dispatch, and with his familiar nimble grace that made them enjoy listening while learning.

> I doubt too, whether any other convention we can obtain, may be able to make a better Constitution: for when you assemble a number of men, to have the advantage of their joint wisdom, you inevitably assemble with those men all their prejudices, their passions, their errors of opinion, their local interests, and their selfish views. From such an assembly can a perfect production be expected? It therefore astonishes me, Sir, to find this system approaching so near to perfection as it does; and I think it will astonish our enemies, who are waiting with confidence to hear that our councils are confounded.

Astounding their enemies would not be a new experience. Most of the listening delegates had participated variously in the long adventure of the Revolution. Together with their countrymen they had persuaded the British it was impossible to hold the Colonies or win their allegiance. So the British, discouraged if not exhausted, finally went home. The Americans had won with determination to hang on whatever the setbacks, and with patient strategy. General Washington had waited and picked times to fight when there was a reasonable chance of winning. The British hadn't expected such tenacity. In the end the only rational thing to do was what they did: board ship and go home.

The British government had been slow to learn, but they had finally been convinced by the obvious, that they had a great deal more to lose than to gain through a forced continuation of hostilities. The victory of the colonies had surprised and impressed other governments, but the years after that victory proved even more astonishing. Civil war had frankly been anticipated among the colonies after the British departure, but more than three years had passed since *Franklin, John Jay, and John Adams successfully negotiated the final peace treaty with Britain,* and the colonies had remained loosely organized under the Articles of Confederation. A key purpose of the Federal Convention was to see the formation of a more effective American government, and thus, as Franklin put it in his address, "astonish" their enemies, the various governments of Europe with unappeased territorial ambitions in North America.

Many men had helped convince the British and the governments of Europe. Two were especially esteemed for their parts. One was the general, of course. And there he was, calm, sober, not much changed from Valley Forge, sitting as the presiding officer of the Federal Convention and even credited with its existence, since there were those convinced that George Washington could have been named King George the First of America with only nominal opposition. The other was the man whose words were being read aloud, Doctor Franklin. Before the Revolution, Franklin had given up the leisure he hoped to devote to science, and struggled to keep Great Britain from pursuing vindictive and narrow policies. Failing in his struggle with the Parliament and the King, Franklin helped Jefferson refine the document that made it final:

"... The good people of these states reject and renounce all allegiance and subjection to the kings of Great Britain."

Then Franklin had crossed the ocean again, indulging his long practice of using the time at sea for scientific observations, a habit begun decades earlier when he first sailed from one continent to another at the age of nineteen. France, not England, was his destination for the later crossing. Franklin had gone to Paris with fellow commissioners *Silas Deane* and *Arthur Lee* to reason and charm the governors of France at the Court of Versailles into financing with money, men, and arms, the struggle of George Washington's rabble and colonial farmers.

And it ended as Franklin had always warned the government of Britain, then the most powerful of nations, that it would have to end. He found support in England from *William Pitt, Edmund Burke*, and his fellow scientists such as *Joseph Priestley*, but these voices could not prevail at first over the entrenched king and hereditary lords of Parliament. It was the unyielding pig-headedness of the British government that persuaded Franklin allowing Parliament sovereignty over the three million people of America was "the greatest of absurdities, since they appeared to have scarce discretion enough to govern a herd of swine. Hereditary legislators! ...

There would be more propriety, because less hazard of mischief in having ... hereditary professors of mathematics." He could be patient with mental obtuseness, but didn't want to be governed by it.

So Franklin told the blind men of Britain what would happen. He even used his old satirical weapon, first tried as a boy in his brother's newspaper, of speaking in the guise of another person. Franklin pretended to be a remarkably changed George III who had faced realities at last and who could warn Parliament about its course rather than spurring the members on to greater follies.

> If I were to give you a word of advice it should be to remind you of the Italian epitaph upon a poor fool that killed himself with quacking. *Stava bene, per star meglio, sto qui.* That is to say: I was well, I would be better, I took physic and died.

But the real George III was unable to match the wisdom and the wit of Franklin's imaginary king. Great Britain took physic (forced the colonies to fight) and lost the colonies just as the printer-electrician from Boston by way of Philadelphia had insisted. Franklin had been compelled to postpone the natural experiments he wanted to perform for the purpose of leading a great political experiment in freedom. That summer of 1787 Britain and the rest of the world were watching closely to see how the experiment would end.

Doctor Franklin was determined the experiment in freedom would not end but would go on and on, confounding the cynics of Europe. Franklin's determination and the hope that nourished it were plainly written into the speech he had asked James Wilson to read. Slowly, for greater emphasis, Wilson read the scientist's final words to the Federal Convention:

> I hope, therefore, that for our own sakes, as a part of the people, and for the sake of our posterity, we shall act heartily and unanimously in recommending this constitution, wherever our influence may extend, and turn our future thoughts and endeavors to the means of having it well administered. On the whole, Sir, I cannot help expressing a wish that every member of the Convention, who may still have objections, would with me, on this occasion, doubt a little of his own infallibility, and, to make manifest our unanimity, put his name to this instrument.

THE SIGNING HOUR

When Wilson sat down, Franklin moved that the execution form prepared by *Gouverneur Morris* to confirm approval of the Constitution should be unanimously signed. Franklin's move was pre-arranged. It was thought appropriate for the oldest man among them to do so, and Benjamin Franklin's personal prestige might also be persuasive with delegates finding it difficult to make up their minds. There were many doubts among the delegates, and Franklin had anticipated them by admitting his own. *James Mc-Henry* of Maryland, for instance, rationalizing his vote in favor, made careful notes at his desk paraphrasing Franklin: "... I have had already frequent occasions to be convinced that I have not always judged right..."

Franklin had achieved what it was hoped he might, convince uncertain delegates that they should approve the Constitution even if they could not bring one hundred per cent conviction and support. This was a critical service at a critical moment, possible only to Benjamin Franklin. During the convention, his contributions had been few, but those few were crucial. The main work had been done by younger men because of his age and enfeeblement. But he was conscientiously there, and when the authority earned by six decades of service was needed, it was supplied.

In urging the delegates to sign, Franklin was asking the Founding Fathers to allow their infant nation to be born. But a diversity of opinions still had to be reconciled. Those who opposed signing wished to explain why. Others disposed to sign but with reservations wanted their doubts on the official record. Alexander Hamilton from New York, who considered many ideas in the Constitution alien to his own, nevertheless was anxious "that every member should sign." He sensed the public's readiness and feared the future consequences of delay. Gouverneur Morris from Pennsylvania also voiced reasons to hesitate, but he was ready to accept the plan as the best they could then achieve. It was vital, he emphasized, for security and survival, to establish a national government.

Doctor Franklin listened with pleasure. He sensed that after a generation of struggle, the United States of America was ready to enter the world, be patted on the rump, and sent kicking and squealing into the future. He remained in his seat while debate centered on whether the word "forty" should be changed to "thirty" as *Nathaniel Gorham* of Massachusetts proposed. George Washington speaking from the chair approved the change, and it went through without opposition. So the number of citizens in a state warranting a member in the House of Representatives would be 30,000 rather than 40,000.

There was no intensity or bitterness in the discussions that

Monday. There had been ample demonstrations of both, often through the summer. Well, pain was one of the concomitants of birth, willingly borne in hopeful anticipation. Pain is borne that we may be born. It wasn't up to Poor Richard's old standard, but suitable perhaps for the last anxious hours of a Constitutional Convention.

The day was relatively peaceful. Positions were essentially established. The necessary compromises had been made. It was nit-picking time, tidying up day, and *soon, the signing hour at the Federal Convention.*

Two months before in July, close to the eleventh anniversary of the Declaration of Independence, Doctor Franklin had made a compromise recommendation at a crucial time to reconcile those favoring equal representation in both bodies of congress and those favoring proportional representation. The compromise was simple and obvious. The Senate would give each state an equal vote, and the other house would be based on proportional representation determined by state population. Later the delegates would wonder why that hadn't seemed an obvious compromise until Franklin advocated it. Franklin the scientist could have told them it was often the nature of great truths to be simple and obvious once they were found and exposed to light. The finding was the heart of the matter. Garbing the truth in words was just normal followup.

One indispensable truth Franklin had learned in public life was the importance of trusting the people. During the convention debates, Franklin had been the most consistent champion of the people. He wanted to assure the future success of the government by assuring the people of their privileges and rights. "We should not depress the virtue and public spirit of our common people," he argued. He opposed making ownership of property a leading prerequisite for participation in the new government. Though quite aware that some of his colleagues at the convention were possibly the wealthiest in the Colonies, Franklin cheerfully admitted that among the greatest scoundrels he had known were a disproportionate number of the wealthy. He wanted the Constitution to avoid any special catering to the rich as a lesson to the world and as an encouragement to immigration. Franklin was already considering it the manifest destiny of Americans to settle the continent. For that great task, many people would be needed.

If only we could somehow share Doctor Franklin's reflections as other delegates made their last minute comments before the vote! For him it was the end of a journey that had started long before. He could remember most of it in clear detail. As the oldest delegate, he had seen the matter through from the beginning. His years spanned nearly the whole of the eighteenth century. Perhaps for a moment his thoughts wandered even farther back than the scope of his own life, back to another September 17th in another century, when a ship set sail from Plymouth, England with one hundred passengers, and a special cargo of ideals, customs, and faiths for transplanting in the rich soil of a new continent. Among the passengers were *William Brewster* and *William Bradford*, Englishmen, who established and kept alive the first colonies in Franklin's home state of Massachusetts.

The ship was the *Mayflower*, and those aboard were English, the same as Franklin, the same as most of the delegates at the Federal Convention. Their ancestors had walked the medieval streets of London with *Geoffrey Chaucer*. Their ancestors had signed the *Magna Charta*. Somehow from those ancestors they had inherited a need to resist repressions and to find a soil in which only seeds of freedom would flourish.

Perhaps Doctor Franklin entertained such thoughts that morning in Philadelphia. The other delegates as well. Certainly they would have been appropriate. A vast undertaking in the name and instinct of liberty lasting nearly two centuries was achieving one of its milestones.

The members of the delegations began signing the execution form prepared by Morris. The signing took place following the geographic order of the colonies, north to south. New Hampshire to Georgia.

WHITHER THE SUN?

While the signatures were being affixed, Franklin was seen to stand, though he found it difficult. His colleagues in turn wrote their names, some bold, some light, on the Document:

> DONE in Convention by the Unanimous Consent of the States present the Seventeenth Day of September in the Year of our Lord one thousand seven hundred and Eighty seven and of the Independence of the United States of America the Twelfth *In witness* whereof We have hereunto subscribed our names.

Franklin pointed at the chair normally occupied by George Washington. Not everyone listened, though many did, when the old man spoke reflectively, to himself as much as the others. He was simply voicing a thought, possibly addressed to the future more than the delegates of the Federal Convention who were finishing their summer labors.

Franklin was staring at the back of the President's chair on which an artist had painted a sun. The presence of a painted sun on the chair has never been explained. Possibly the chair had originally been made for one of the Masonic Lodges in Pennsylvania, perhaps even Benjamin Franklin's Lodge. Or a chair painter with artistic impulses simply decided he needed to paint a sun and the chair was a convenient place. Public history has few details concerning the private history of George Washington's chair and the sun on it, but it was there for Benjamin Franklin to discover and see as a sort of revelation, a promissory note for the future of America.

At that moment it was eleven years, one month, and thirteen days since his participation in another signing, that of the Declaration of Independence.

On that occasion he had warned prophetically with a typical Franklin quip, "We must all hang together or assuredly we shall all hang separately." In 1776 the chance of hanging at the end of strong British hemp as convicted traitors may have seemed stronger than the prospects of becoming free and unfettered with royal shackles.

But Franklin in 1776 and later had possessed the courage to be an optimist. A year after the Federal Convention, with his own death no longer distant, he wrote to *Louis Le Veillard* in Paris:

> The world is growing wiser and wiser: and as by degrees men are convinced of the folly of wars for religion, for domination, or for commerce, they will be happier and happier.

In his letter and in his hopes for the Constitution, Franklin relied on the future. He would not have changed his words to Le Veillard in all probability even had he known that his friend would be guillotined during the hysterias that so tragically followed the French Revolution. The French struggle for the "Rights of Man" in their Revolution may have been an European godchild of the American experience, but France was less fortunate in the aftermath of its struggle. France did not have Washington, or Madison, or Hamilton, or Franklin. Once France had possessed Benjamin Franklin and tried hard to keep him, but in the end the old philosopher went home to America and to the final great endeavor of his life—the fruition of a dream.

The octogenerian had accepted the difficult responsibility of hope, man's ideal condiment for seasoning the future. With hope there was always a chance of finding a sunny road. Without it, there was paralysis. *Doctor Franklin, lifelong optimist and facer of facts, had learned that with sufficient effort most dreams could be persuaded to bear fruit.*

Looking at the sun on the back of Washington's chair, Franklin noted that artists had difficulty indicating whether a sun was rising or setting. *"I have often and often, in the course of the session,"* he began, *"and the vicissitudes of my hopes and fears as to its issue, looked at that behind the President without being able to tell whether it was rising or setting; but now, at length, I have the happiness to know that it is a rising, and not a setting sun."*

It was the perfect comment, an eminently proper birth-of-a-nation benediction. James Madison and others carefully wrote it down. Despite his age and weakness, Doctor Franklin was still a man who could be trusted to find direct, simple words that gave extra insight, significance, and wit to a memorable event.

The work of the Federal Convention was completed with Franklin's prediction of a rising sun. The Constitution was approved and ready for ratification by the states. Approval was not unanimous, but nearly so. Without Franklin, the general guess was that the margin of victory would have been reduced, and the chances for ratification correspondingly reduced.

In his diary for Monday, 17th, George Washington prosaically noted:

> Met in Convention, when the Constitution received the unanimous vote of 11 States and Colonel Hamiliton's from New York and was subscribed to by every member present except Governor Randolph and Colonel Mason from Virginia, and Mr. Gerry from Massachusetts.

Business done, the delegates, according to Washington "adjourned to the City Tavern" where they dined and "took a cordial leave of each other." Thus is a document completed to guide a nation through childhood to the maturity of two hundred years.

It had been Doctor Franklin's day. His speech set the necessary tone of conciliation and compromise. His last words were both a valedictory to the past and an official christening of the future. For better or worse, the Constitution was stitched together, baby clothes for a new nation. Would its rules be sufficiently simple and flexible to let the infant grow without smothering, and yet sufficiently consistent and strong to impress the world with the sincerity and viability of the continuing experiment on the western continent?

The delegates had done their best to make it such an instrument, flexible and yet strong, strong and yet flexible. When Benjamin Franklin signed, it was the fourth major document of America's brief history in which he had played a role. He had also signed the Declaration of Independence, the Treaty with France, and the final Treaty of Peace with Great Britain. Only Franklin had participated in all these events.

Yet ironically, for all his participation in matters of rare historical import, what the Doctor really wanted to do, what he had wanted to do for more than forty years, was to concentrate his time not on temporal political problems, but on studying and trying to resolve the eternal puzzles of nature and the universe. Fate through his countrymen asked him to join in winning and building a nation. He did, but *nation building* was a pastime forced on him by circumstances. Politics was a curious game for men to play when they weren't preoccupied with really interesting matters such as the nature of the Gulf Stream, or why birds migrate, or electrical phenomena. *They* brought questions demanding *all* the wit and ingenuity a searcher could muster. Science was where Benjamin Franklin's deepest impulses had always turned from boyhood, as if science were the official North Pole of his spirit and he was magnetized to seek that direction in accord with nature's laws.

Magnetism? Now there was another mystery. Exactly why did. . .

With science for a North Pole, other directions might influence, but they could never completely rule. The magnetized spirit would turn back again with every new question. And in the natural world, for a man with clear vision or with good spectacles of his own design, there was always an infinity of questions.

1976

Dear Doctor Franklin, Sir,

We imagine it would be difficult, perhaps impossible to surprise you. Anyone who lives eighty-four active years must find his capacity for astonishment gradually reduced, and the world was very much with you from the first steps you took in Boston.

Still we do have information you might at least find curious, as well as pleasing and amusing. Our information concerns your reputation as a scientist. You made it clear often that you wanted science to be the main part of your life, but were habitually distracted.

The fact is that the science you appropriated time occasionally to do has earned you recognition as the most important American scientist of the eighteenth century and one of the most important in the world. A good way to learn about that is to visit New York, Mr. Alexander Hamilton's hometown.

New York is radically altered now, and much larger than Philadelphia. Your town is still in business at the same old place, but it is no longer considered the queen city of the new world or the Athens of America. Of course, it no longer has you and your friends except in statues and libraries. It's difficult to have a convincing Athens without a Socrates, or a Philadelphia without a Franklin.

If a centennial stop in New York is possible, you should visit the Hall of Fame. You'll have no trouble finding the place in the Bronx. Just take the Major Deegan Expressway and drive a little way past Yankee Stadium. Ask anyone. (Except a cabdriver, of course. Some might take you by way of Jersey City.)

The Hall of Fame is an immense granite colonnade on the New York University Campus near the Harlem River. It is dedicated to the accomplishments of great Americans. A Citizens' Committee of one hundred elects new members. Between 1900 and 1955, nineteen scientists were elected to the Hall of Fame. You received ninety-four votes. Robert Fulton and Wilbur Wright, those closest in the voting, received eighty-six votes each.

If you couldn't find the leisure for science in your day, Americans in this later day are determined to honor you for the science you worked in with precious little leisure at all. Your modern countrymen, indeed, are inclined to think of you as the founder of American Science. Does that surprise you?

We Are, &c.,
YOURS, THE PEOPLE

II. Home is the Traveller

SCIENTIST AT SEA AGAIN

Two summers before the summer of the Federal Convention, Benjamin Franklin was at sea. And having the time of his life. He was on his way home to Philadelphia. His responsibilities in France had been turned over to Thomas Jefferson, and for the first time in many years he felt young and eager for the new revelations of each succeeding day. He was only a few months short of his eightieth birthday, but that wasn't too young to start a new career: Science. In truth, of course, he was just resuming an old career he had been forced to postpone.

With his public career presumably behind him at last, Doctor Franklin thought he could concentrate exclusively on the various fields of science that stirred his interest. There were few that didn't.

During the return voyage, political and diplomatic concerns outlived, he could observe, and record, and speculate, and write to his heart's content. The second day out, assisted by fellow passenger Jonathan Williams, he began recording the air and water tempera-

17

ture. His old curiosity about the Atlantic and the phenomenal Gulf Stream effect was back with full, youthful impact.

His mind was teeming with ideas, and they flowed from his pen. During August, 1785, as the winds slowly worked the ship across the Atlantic, Franklin began a letter to his scientist friend *Jan Ingenhousz* dealing in basic ways with a basic problem: *On the Causes and Cure of Smoky Chimneys.* The sea voyage supplied time as well to put down the details of another Franklin Stove, which he had invented and used in London before the Revolution. Among his most important August writings were his maritime observations with the accumulated sea lore of a man who had been running back and forth across the Atlantic for six decades. Written as a letter to *Julien-David Le Roy*, a friend in Paris, the observations showed how observant Franklin had been during those decades. He had useful suggestions concerning more practical rigging, diets of sailors, managing the preparation and digestion of sea food, ship handling in emergencies, swimming anchors for use in gales, luggage lists for passengers, etc. He even included an aside condemning the use of the seas for ignominious traffic in slaves, which was, he wrote, "clearly the means of augmenting the mass of human misery."

His letter, which is almost thirty-eight printed pages in *John Bigelow's* 1888 edition of the Works, also contained valuable notes on the use of water-tight compartments to increase shipboard security, and his conclusions concerning the Gulf Stream.

The year before in a letter to *St. John de Crevecoeur*, Franklin had discussed a Chinese custom which inexcusably had not been introduced into European vessels: water-tight compartments. "If a leak should happen in one apartment, that only would be affected by it, and the others would be free; so that the ship would not be so subject as others to founder and sink at sea."

He returned to this subject in his letter to Le Roy, and concluded his comments this way:

> We have not imitated this practice. Some little disadvantage it might occasion in the stowage, is perhaps one reason, though that I think might be more than compensated by an abatement in the insurance that would be reasonable, and by a higher price taken of passengers, who would rather prefer going in such a vessel. But our seafaring people are brave, despise danger, and reject such precautions of safety, being cowards only in one sense, that of *fearing* to be *thought afraid*.

His maritime observations throughout show the range and imagination of Franklin the scientist, aided and abetted by the grace, wit, and directness of Franklin the writer.

He suggested a new design for sails and a new rigging (Figure 4) which would offer less resistance to the air, and described experiments that could prove whether or not his plan for smaller and more numerous sails would reduce resistance. To avoid breaking anchor rope cables, a developing possibility in Figures 5 and 6, he recommended not straining the rope with a 90° bend as in Figure 7, but instead using a large pully wheel, which would bend the rope "gradually to the round of the wheel," and prevent the loss of many anchors. Figure 8 shows how water rushes in swiftly at first through a bottom leak, but slows later as the water levels inside and outside come closer together. Franklin was arguing that crews and passengers often were in too great a haste to abandon a ship that would stay afloat. They "might have remained on board in safety, without hazarding themselves in an open boat on the wide ocean."

He wrote of the islanders in the Pacific whom he called "the most expert boat-sailors in the world" venturing great distances in their *proas*. He wondered if Europeans couldn't learn from the islanders and others how to improve their own mastery of the sea. On and on, he continued giving a scientist's lifetime summation of observations while voyaging, from the design of a swimming anchor to the cooking of dry peas at sea. (*"If your dry peas boil hard, a two-pound iron shot put with them into the pot will, by the motion of the ship, grind them as fine as mustard."*)

Realizing what he is doing, he interjects at one point that "the garrulity of an old man has got hold of me, and, as I may never have another occasion of writing on this subject, I think I may as well now, once and for all, empty my nautical budget."

His nautical purse was encyclopedic. He had thought even about the planking of a ship and believed laying planks crosswise might provide greater strength (Figure 23). Figure 25 is an idea suggesting individual water troughs for fowls carried alive on shipboard to be used as food. Figures 26 and 27 are soup containers designed so that "when the ship should make a sudden heel, the soup would not in a body flow over one side, and fall into people's laps and scald them, as is sometimes the case."

An Appendix contained a discussion of the Gulf Stream, tables of temperatures and other observations made at sea, and details of one more experiment to settle a point of curiosity.

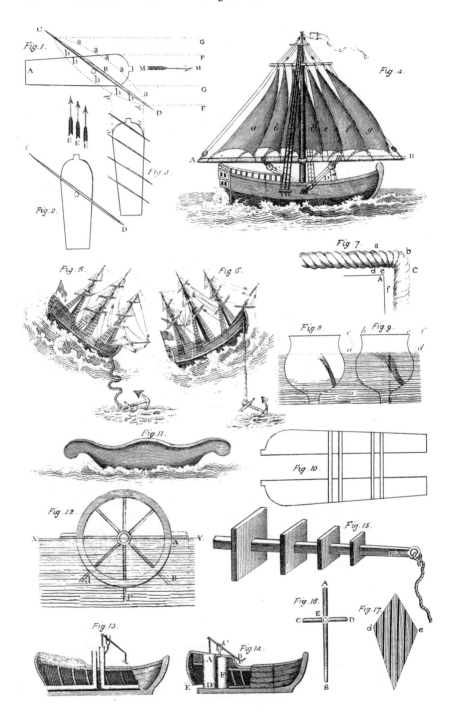

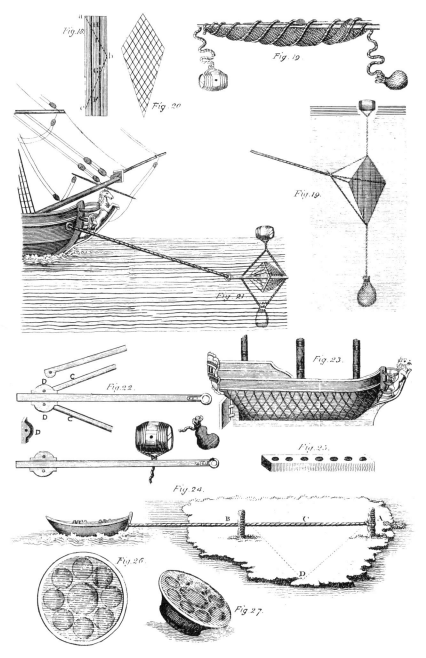

Reproduced from the William Duane Edition of The Works of Benjamin Franklin, Philadelphia, *1809, illustrating the maritime observations written to Julien-David Le Roy, August 1785.*

> On the 14th of August . . . the weather being perfectly calm, an empty
> bottle, corked very tight, was sent down twenty fathoms, and it was
> drawn up still empty. It was then sent down again thirty-five fathoms,
> when the weight of the water having forced in the cork, it was drawn
> up full; the water it contained was immediately tried by the thermom-
> eter, and found to be 70, which was six degrees colder than at the sur-
> face.

So the voyage went. Long hours of writing on scientific subjects
unrelated to political intrigue, a relief after the years in France.
Experiments, weather and celestial observations, reflection on his
favorite scientific subjects.

The voyage began with pain, and warning from the physicians
that he could never make so perilous a journey in his condition. He
made it, worked as hard as ever, and enjoyed himself thoroughly.

THE HOUSE THAT FRANKLIN BUILT

The scientist's entry in his journal for September 14, 1785 was
not scientific, but it was eminently human and historically memorable for Americans.

> With the flood in the morning came a light breeze, which brought us
> above Gloucester Point, in full view of dear Philadelphia! when we
> again cast anchor to wait for the health officer, who, having made his
> visit and finding no sickness, gave us leave to land. My son-in-law
> came with a boat for us; we landed at Market Street wharf, where we
> were received by a crowd of people with huzzas, and accompanied with
> acclamations quite to my door. Found my family well. God be praised
> and thanked for all his mercies.

It was Market Street, Philadelphia, where Doctor Franklin was
set ashore, returned from France in triumph. It was that same
Market Street where a boy of seventeen named Ben Franklin had
first landed in Philadelphia after running away from Boston. And
it was in his house on Market Street that an old man with young
thoughts reestablished residence and began planning his future.
It was supposed to be exclusively scientific, but political matters
inevitably intervened. He was, after all, Benjamin Franklin, and
there were various trifles requiring attention, including the preparation of a Constitution, as well as public offices to accept. The
General Assembly by a vote of 75 to 2 (he was one of the 2)
elected him *President of Pennsylvania*. Franklin accepted. In matters of public duty, he found that the habits of a lifetime could not
be set aside.

Nevertheless, in Philadelphia there was more time than he had enjoyed in France for science, invention, and philosophical meditation.

There was also the challenge and the fun of getting his Market Street house comfortable and functional for a scientist with more than 4,000 books, as well as the family of *his daughter Sarah Bache, her husband Richard*, and their six children.

The eighty year old Franklin applied himself to remaking his house as he did everything, with enthusiasm. He wrote to his sister *Jane Mecom* in Boston about his scheme:

(September 21, 1786)

I had begun to build two good houses next the street, instead of three old ones which I pulled down, but my neighbour disputing my bounds, I have been obliged to postpone till that dispute is settled by law. In the meantime, the workmen and materials being ready, I have ordered an addition to the house I live in, it being too small for our growing family. There are a good many hands employed, and I hope to see it covered in before winter. I propose to have in it a long room for my library and instruments, with two good bedchambers and two garrets. The library is to be even with the floor of my best old chamber; and the story under it will for the present be employed only to hold wood, but may be made into rooms hereafter. This addition is on the side next the river. I hardly know how to justify building a library at an age that will so soon oblige me to quit it; but we are apt to forget that we are grown old, and building is an amusement.

He was building a laboratory and a home suitable for an octogenerian with work to do and a lot of books. Predictably the library became the most fantastic room in the house, and in the 1780's must have been among the most remarkable rooms in America. Certainly it housed one of the largest and most comprehensive libraries, especially in the sciences, to be found outside Europe. In addition to books, the library became home port for the working models of Franklin's old and new inventions, and during the last three years of his life, the library was the summit of the universe for him. There at last with the books, the inventions, and the writing table that put him in touch with learned men in every part of the world, Doctor Franklin was truly at home.

A scientist, or any man, can be known or judged substantially by his work. The habitation he prepares for himself is also strongly indicative of his style, inclinations, and habits of thought. Doctor Franklin we can see clearly in both work and house.

A revealing account of the house and its master was given by a fellow scientist who visited Doctor Franklin during the Constitution summer. He was *Manasseh Cutler*, Massachusetts clergyman and scientist. One evening during the convention he was taken to meet Doctor Franklin. No urging was needed. Cutler went eagerly. As a member of the *American Philosophical Society*, which Franklin had founded and still actively served as President, Cutler perhaps would have placed Franklin's name first as the living American most worth meeting.

The conversation that Manasseh Cutler and Benjamin Franklin conducted that evening supported the argument that Franklin's deepest interests were remote from politics and public affairs. His true passions were natural history and science.

Later Cutler would write of their initial meeting:

> There was no curiosity in Philadelphia which I felt so anxious to see as this great man, who has been the wonder of Europe as well as the glory of America . . . I felt as if I was going to be introduced to the presence of an European Monarch. But how were my ideas changed, when I saw a short, fat, trunched old man, in a plain Quaker dress, bald pate, and short white locks, sitting without his hat under the tree, and as Mr. Gerry introduced me, rose from his chair, took me by the hand, expressed his joy to see me, welcomed me to the city.

Cutler was especially welcome to Doctor Franklin because of his scientific credentials. In addition to astronomical and meteorological observations, Cutler had also done useful work in botany. In those respects, he was very much Franklin's sort, and worthy of seeing a special gift Franklin had recently received.

TWO-HEADED CURIOSITY

"What do you think of it?" the guest was asked.

Manasseh Cutler readily agreed that a two-headed snake preserved in a bottle was fully qualified for classification as another curiosity. Franklin was impatient to discuss the phenomenon and speculated about the problems a two-headed creature would have while traveling if one head chose a particular direction while the other head preferred another. The political men accompanying Cutler thought they recognized political implications. They believed Franklin was concerned about the problems for America if the men at the convention could not decide on a common direction. But there was also the possibility that Franklin was simply thinking as objectively as possible about a two-headed snake.

The men sat in the garden where *Sarah Bache* served tea.

Franklin and Cutler continued to discuss scientific subjects while the other men talked politics. After tea, Franklin took his guests on a tour of the house, with particular attention reserved for the library, which Cutler described as "the largest, and by far the best, private library in America."

The books were impressive for their quality and numbers, but the most interesting items in the library were the many devices showing Doctor Franklin's inventive genius for making his and other lives more comfortable. There was the unique Franklin machine designed to show the circulation of human blood and his famous rolling press for copying letters. Plus many others. Manasseh Cutler described several.

> ... his long, artificial arm and hand for taking down and putting up books on high shelves; and his great armchair, with rockers, and a large fan placed over it, with which he fans himself, keeps off the flies, etc., while he sits reading, with only a small motion of the foot; and many other curiosities and inventions, all his own but of lesser note. Over his mantel he has a prodigious number of medals, busts, and casts in wax or plaster of Paris which are the effigies of the most noted characters in Europe.

As a botanist, Cutler was especially fascinated by the folio Franklin produced of *Linnaeus's Systema Vegetabilium*. The Swedish genius who gave the world systematized classification had been dead nine years and yet had been born in 1707, a year later than Franklin. Considering the folio and discussing botany, Franklin told Cutler he "lamented that he did not in early life attend to this science."

The younger man had the impression that Doctor Franklin intended forthwith to make up for that neglect in all the sciences. Franklin impressed Cutler with the breadth and variety of his knowledge in natural philosophy. The Doctor's alertness, sharp memory, and mental liveliness added to the impression, as well as his characteristic humor.

> His manners are perfectly easy, and everything about him seems to diffuse an unrestrained freedom and happiness. He has an incessant vein of humor, accompanied with an uncommon vivacity, which seems as natural and involuntary as his breathing.

Cutler stayed until ten P.M. and was asked to return. He left excited, certain he had visited one of the greatest men America or the world would manage to produce. Enfeebled by gout and age,

Franklin physically was not the tireless worker he had been; but a scientific discussion with a kindred spirit could still stir the juices. *Carl Van Doren,* one of Franklin's biographers, described him as a "harmonious multitude." If Franklin was a multitude, science was the majority party, and that was the side of Franklin, Cutler had been privileged to see.

In America and Europe during the eighteenth century, there were few vocations or avocations that in some way had not occupied the occasional attention of Doctor Franklin. The vocations of saint or gigolo were possible exceptions, but suspicion whispers that even those may simply have been cases of well covered tracks.

As a scientist visiting a scientist, Manasseh Cutler was given a rare chance to glimpse what the Doctor himself clearly considered the real Franklin, a man who would serve his country because it was a man's duty to serve, but whose particular pleasure in life was solving the mystery of a two-headed snake, or any other natural mysteries that ventured along.

Cutler's visit was near the end of Franklin's long life, and he encountered a vitality and a zest for matters of science that amazed him. It was as if Franklin by a special act of will had managed to retain, together with the businessman and statesman, all the expectant attitudes of the questioning and curious youth he had been more than six decades earlier in Boston and Philadelphia.

Remembering ones youth was not remarkable. But to have it intact in substantial portion at the age of 82 certainly could not be considered ordinary.

1976

Dear Doctor Franklin, Sir,

Ninety-four good American citizens and true voted to include Benjamin Franklin among the American scientists in the national Hall of Fame.

In case you wryly speculate that the ninety-four citizens might have been voting for the signer of the Declaration of Independence rather than the scientist, consider how seriously your work as a scientist was taken by other scientists.

Your original contributions in electricity are still considered top level achievements that earn you a niche beside and equal to those of more orthodox scientists (those who didn't sign the great documents that launched America on its merry way).

One outstanding American scientist of modern times, Robert Millikan made a list of the most influential scientists of the eighteenth and nineteenth centuries. It wasn't an American list, but a world list. The list contained eleven names, including Darwin, Pasteur, Maxwell, and Faraday. Your name headed the list.

The only other American included by Millikan was J. Willard Gibbs, the mathematical physicist, who the same as yourself won the distinguished Copley Medal from the Royal Society of London for original scientific research.

The National Academy of Sciences, a lineal descendant of your scientific organizing efforts in the eighteenth century, for its Washington Building approved a bronze display of eighteen internationally known scientists. Among the eighteen—Doctor Franklin.

Such recognition is yours by right of science and for no other reason. Congratulations, Sir, but don't worry. If you can make the centennial, we promise not to waste your time travelling around to see bronze statues of Benjamin Franklin. "Where's the library?" you might ask, bored after the first statue. We'll take you to the library you started in Philadelphia. Yes, it is still in service. You can read there in many books the respect earned by your science.

We Are, &c.,
YOURS, THE PEOPLE

III. The Making of an American Scientist

COMING OF THE FATHER

The Indians were first, and it was their wisdom to adapt themselves to the land, to obey the rules of the land, and in their time, by their ways, the land was not changed. Other men came, voyaging great distances to reach a new world, and it was their wisdom to adapt the land to themselves, to change the land that it might be richer than before, to do what had not been done before, and the land was changed in their time. Such men were pioneers. One among them was a tall Englishman who directed his steps to Boston in Massachusetts where he made candles and soap that others might see the light and be clean. His name was Josiah Franklin, and on the bodies of two wives, Josiah sired seventeen children. The fifteenth was called Ben for Benjamin, and all the legends of his early life show that he was future-minded from the start. He was always more of a "Be" than a "Ben." And in his time he changed the name of the land and the history of the world.

"The Child is Father of the Man," wrote the poet *Wordsworth*. He has a point there. To understand the man grown it is useful to look at the child growing. A man of distinction in any field does

29

not suddenly appear upon the stage, full-grown from the brow of the Junior Chamber of Commerce, to perform his given or selected role in the drama of his times. Often the performance first begins to fit credible measurements when we leave temporarily the later volumes of his biography and go to the earliest ones.

In the case of Franklin, thanks to his own versatile pen and the reports of his contemporaries, we know in detail about his childhood and youth. We know too about the ideas, books, people, and forces that gave shape to the mind and character of the man he became.

Benjamin Franklin was born in Boston on January 6, 1706 (Old Style). The English calendar, rather than the modernized *Gregorian calendar*, was used then in England and throughout the growing colonial empire. The Calendar Act of 1750 was passed to adopt the more efficient Gregorian calendar for Great Britain and the Colonies. This was done by calmly adding eleven days. When the change officially occurred in 1752, the day following September 2nd became September 14th, and the beginning of the year was changed from March 25th to January 1st. Other dates, such as those of births, were correspondingly altered to the Gregorian. Thus in one wheeze by Parliament, Benjamin Franklin retroactively was declared to have been born on January 17, 1706 (New Style) and in the first month of the year rather than the tenth. It was Parliament's first but not last interference in the life of Benjamin Franklin. Less rational moves by Parliament were destined to complicate Franklin's life frequently until he helped declare his and his country's independence and got away with it.

His father was *Josiah Franklin*, Whig, emigrant from Oxfordshire, England, and a successful candle and soap maker. Those who look for the prankish—prophetic gestures of destiny can note the coincidental touch of wit in the fact that the father of the man who did much to lighten and enlighten the world was a maker of candles. In his *Autobiography*, Franklin wrote that his father's business was that of "Tallow Chandler and Soap-Boiler."

Josiah Franklin had immigrated to New England in 1683 with his wife Ann and three children. *Ann Franklin* in the Colonies died giving birth to her seventh child. Josiah soon married again, *Abiah Folger* of Nantucket whose mother had originally come to America as an indentured servant. Thus Benjamin Franklin's maternal grandmother was one of the "bound-out girls" who served their periods of voluntary servitude, married, and added their progeny to the roster of those available for the subduing of a continent.

Benjamin was the eighth of Abiah Folger Franklin's ten children and his father's last son. The Franklin family record casts doubt on the popular and recurrent superstition that the first children in a family tend to be the healthiest and the brightest. *Elbert Hubbard* during one of his "Little Journeys," reflecting on the Franklins, wrote: "Science has explained many things, but it has not yet told why it sometimes happens that when seventeen eggs are hatched, the brood will consist of sixteen barnyard fowls and one eagle."

When such situations develop, it must be difficult on the fowls as well as the eagle.

If he had bothered to consider the subject, young Benjamin no doubt would have found a clever way to suggest that theories about the superiority of early children were the flagrant inventions of an international fraternity of the firstborn to justify the foolish law of primogeniture. Whatever the truth concerning biological inheritance in large families, the record shows that Benjamin had big brother problems from an early age and that he conspicuously failed to develop reverence on the subject.

There was, of course, one obvious benefit from being the fifteenth child in a family that was not rich. Benjamin had to recognize the necessity of looking after himself early and to master the practical arts of self-reliance.

Many decades later in the Codicil to his Will, Benjamin Franklin seeking to dispose compassionately of his not inconsiderable fortune, added this paragraph which sounds much like an echo from eighty years earlier:

> It has been an opinion, that he who receives an estate from his ancestors, is under some obligation to transmit the same to posterity. This obligation lies not on me, who never inherited a shilling from any ancestor or relation. I shall, however, if it is not diminished by some accident before my death, leave a considerable estate among my descendants and relations. The above observation is made merely as some apology to my family, for my making bequests that do not appear to have any immediate relation to their advantage.

Doctor Franklin presumably was referring to his generous donations of books, scientific equipment, and funds to schools, scientific societies, and other groups that could assist the progress of young people.

In addition to big brother problems, young Benjamin in Boston also had a pious father to satisfy. What about the father? If the child is father of the man, the influence of the father of the child must also be considered. Franklin describes his father in the *Autobiography*:

> I think you may like to know something of his person and character. He had an excellent constitution of body, was of middle stature, but well set and very strong. He was ingenious, could draw prettily, was skill'd a little in music and had a clear pleasing voice, so that when he play'd Psalm tunes on his violin and sung withal as he sometimes did in an evening after the business of the day was over, it was extremely agreeable to hear. He had a mechanical genius too, and on occasion was very handy in the use of other tradesmen's tools.

Many parts of the picture start echoes going: The taste and gift for music, the mechanical aptitude, the variety of interests and talents. But the father, who sounds amiable, even charming in this portrait, was also old-fashioned, strict, and a conscientious, orthodox member of Old South Church. This meant that he was convinced Bible reading and prayer were therapeutic exercises for a growing child, whatever the child's rebellious impulses. An environment of insistent piety and a practical boy's at once cynical and amused reaction to it reached a noteworthy juncture the day young Ben was helping his father pack a barrel of beef in the cellar. The boy told his father that he had thought of a good way to avoid repeated sayings of grace at the crowded dining table above.

"What's that?" questioned Josiah Franklin suspiciously. Ben explained: Why not say grace right then and ask a collective blessing once and for all on the entire barrel of beef. Get it done at once. It would save those listening to grace the trouble of many individual prayers, and would be an all around time-saver and efficiency move. Josiah may have known intimations right then that his intention for Benjamin to be his "tithe" to the church and to grow up as a minister was going to have stormy seas to cross.

A TRADESMAN'S SON

In addition to a rigorous fidelity to the teachings of the church, the father believed that hard work and temperate living are the keys to human contentment. His children were taught to be contemptuous of luxury. Later in life Benjamin overcame this particular instruction somewhat during his sybaritic years in Paris, but not entirely. The seeds of his father's household reappeared in the maxims of *Poor Richard's Almanack*. The Almanacs were published to make a profit, but there is ample evidence that the author agreed at least philosophically and morally with the contents, even though he didn't always scrupulously practice what they preached.

Early to bed and early to rise,
Makes a man healthy, wealthy, and wise.

God helps them that help themselves.

Little strokes fell great oaks.

Never leave that till tomorrow which you can do today.

Time has established Poor Richard's proverbs as clichés in good standing for the English speaking countries. They have been criticized for their dogmatic simplicity and their unabashed stress of materialistic values. But simplicity is an essential characteristic with any sententious bit of good advice. You have to know precisely what it means before you can accurately ignore it. More will need to be said concerning Poor Richard subsequently. He represented one aspect of the adult Franklin and had an affect on the nature and direction of Franklin's science.

Remembering Poor Richard's maxims in the context of Franklin's childhood, they almost seem to be intact offshoots from Josiah Franklin's mind rather than the inventions of a free-thinking, puckish, tongue-in-cheek leader of revolutions, both scientific and political.

Josiah Franklin was representative of the English tradesmen who departed England for the greater opportunities and potential liberty of the new world. In England, the privileges of the gentry could never be modified or invaded by a common tradesman. The Colonies offered the prospect of a land where an ambitious man might with hard work earn rewards for himself and his family. In Boston, Josiah valued his trade, the standing it brought him, and the security it promised. To his sons he preached the philosophy of freedom, whose benefits could be obtained and enjoyed by any man who was conscientious in a trade. Subsequent history proved that though it may not always have seemed so, Benjamin Franklin was paying attention to his father's words and example.

Pride was a quality of many exclusive trade groups in the eighteenth century. And in the Americas a view was slowly forming that this pride need not bend the knee to hereditary privilege. The precept that if a man would look after his trade, his trade would look after him was part of the atmosphere in the Franklin house at the corner of Union and Hanover Streets. They had moved there in 1712, when Benjamin was six, from the house on Milk

Street where he was born. Growing up in such an atmosphere might have had the effect of turning the boy against trade. That it did not was a tribute to the sagacity of Josiah Franklin's teaching, which must have been stern enough to pain but loving enough to endure.

Martin Luther held that great and learned men achieve distinction despite their parents. An impressive list of names undoubtedly could be compiled proving this, but there is doubt that Benjamin Franklin's should be included. It is true that his father wanted him to be a minister and failing that a tallow-chandler, with each ambition proving too mild by half for Benjamin's growing curiosity and appetite. But the father's influence on his son was conspicuous in many ways, from a life-long commitment to hard work, thrift, and indifference to luxuries to a love of conversation and fraternal exchange of ideas.

The *Autobiography*:

> At his table he lik'd to have as often as he could, some sensible friend or neighbour, to converse with, and always took care to start some ingenious or useful topic for discourse, which might tend to improve the minds of his children. By this means he turn'd our attention to what was good, just, and prudent in the conduct of life; and little or no notice was ever taken of what related to the victuals on the table . . . so that I was bro't up in such perfect inattention to those matters as to be quite indifferent what kind of food was set before me; and so unobservant of it, that to this day, if I am ask'd I can scarce tell, a few hours after dinner, what I din'd upon. This has been a convenience to me in travelling, where my companions have been sometimes very unhappy for want of a suitable gratification of their more delicate because better instructed tastes and appetites.

Franklin's claim to indifference concerning victuals may be more indicative of what he thought his attitude should be than what it was. As an adult, his writings contain many references to food, including complete recipes His enthusiasm for certain foods in both quantity and quality was no secret, but the comment in the *Autobiography* suggests that the mind given its initial training by Josiah Franklin couldn't wholeheartedly approve the gusto of the appetite. Franklin the man employed table cutlery with enthusiasm, but Josiah Franklin's little boy Ben must have lectured him frequently about the sin of excess, and of granting the animal function of eating equality with conversation, one of the arts of reason.

SCHOLAR DAYS IN BOSTON

Since it was Josiah's intention for Benjamin to be trained in the service of the church, something the other Franklin children had not received was thought appropriate for Benjamin: Education.

My early readiness in learning to read (which must have been very early, as I do not remember when I could not read) and the opinion of all his friends that I should certainly make a good scholar, encourag'd him in this purpose of his.

At the age of eight, Benjamin was entered in the grammar school. Boston in the early eighteenth century maintained a system of free grammar schools that began preparing students for *Harvard College*, which had been serving the Colonies continuously since 1639 when Puritan minister *John Harvard* willed the institution half his estate and his 260 books. When Benjamin Franklin was growing up, another collegiate possibility was developing in the adjacent state at New Haven, Connecticut. On October 16, 1701, the General Court of the Colony issued a charter "for the founding, suitably endowing and ordering a Collegiate School within his Majesty's Colony of Connecticut." Not long after Benjamin Franklin began grammar school in Boston, the Connecticut school received a gift of one thousand books from London, plus more books as well as funds from a former Bostonian named *Elihu Yale*. So they named the school *Yale*.

Free grammar schools and colleges of quality meant that it was no longer necessary to cross the Atlantic and explore England for an education. Respectable scholarship in natural philosophy as well as theology and the classics could be accomplished by staying home. As it turned out, Harvard and Yale were out of reach for Benjamin Franklin at that time, and his scholarship would have to be done staying literally at home. No matter. He would eventually have both Harvard and Yale Degreees without investing a second of time or a single pence. After the world fame of his electrical experiments and recognition by the Royal Society, Benjamin Franklin was awarded an honorary Master of Arts Degree in July 1753 by Harvard, and a similar degree from Yale in September 1753.

As a boy in Boston, though, his grammar school career was short-lived.

I continu'd however at the Grammar School not quite one year, tho' in that time I had risen gradually from the middle of the class of that year to be the head of it, and farther was remov'd into the next class above it, in order to go with that into the third at the end of the year. But my father in the meantime, from a view of the expense of a college education which, having so large a family, he could not well afford, and the mean living many so educated were afterwards able to obtain, reasons that he gave to his friends in my hearing, altered his first intention, took me from the Grammar School, and sent me to a school for writing and arithmetic kept by a then famous man, Mr. Geo. Brownell, very successful in his profession generally, and that by mild encouraging methods. Under him I acquired fair writing pretty soon, but I fail'd in the arithmetic, and made no progress in it.

The boy who failed arithmetic would become a man who wrote very learnedly about mathematics as the language of natural philosophy. And the boy who received less than a year of grammar school would remember that year with gratitude for more than seven decades.

In his Will of July 17th, 1788, Doctor Franklin included this bequest:

I was born in Boston, New England, and owe my first instructions in literature to the free grammar schools established there. I therefore give one hundred pounds sterling ... to the managers or directors of the free schools in my native town of Boston, to be by them, or the person or persons, who shall have the superintendence and management of the said schools, put out to interest, and so continued at interest for ever; which interest annually shall be laid out in silver medals, and given as honorary rewards annually by the directors of the said free schools, for the encouragement of scholarship.

Doctor Franklin in a codicil to his will expressed a "wish to be useful even after my death, if possible, in forming and advancing other young men, that may be serviceable to their country in both these towns." With that prelude he left substantial sums to Boston and Philadelphia for the purpose of making loans to young married artisans in need of funds to start their businesses. He remembered the loans he had received to open his printing business in Philadelphia. He may also have remembered his father's house and the realization there that an education could be acquired as readily by a tradesman as by a student at Harvard. Especially, it should be added, if the youth involved happened to be a native American genius named Benjamin Franklin.

The boy's career at Geo. Brownell's school was also brief. And at the age of ten it was decided that his formal schooling was complete though it totaled less than two years. Still it exceeded the schooling of his brothers and of most Bostonians at the time.

At the age of ten, following in the footsteps of his brothers, John, Peter, and Josiah, he entered the family business and applied himself half-heartedly to cutting wicks, filling molds, attending shop, going errands, etc. "I dislik'd the trade," wrote Franklin later, "and had a strong inclination for the sea, but my father declar'd against it."

APPRENTICE IN A SHOP OF LETTERS

One of his brothers, Josiah, had developed such a distaste for the family business he ran away to sea. Josiah senior wanted to protect his youngest son from such a move; and fate, good luck, or his own instincts finally helped Benjamin's father find *the ideal "university" for his book-absorbing and why-asking son: A print shop.* Benjamin was apprenticed to his brother James, who had come home from England with equipment and experience as a printer.

> In 1717 my brother James return'd from England with a press and letters to set up his business in Boston. I lik'd it much better than that of my father, but still had a hankering for the sea. To prevent the apprehended effect of such an inclination, my father was impatient to have me bound to my brother. I stood out some time, but at last was persuaded and signed the indentures, when I was yet but twelve years old. I was to serve as an apprentice till I was twenty-one years of age, only I was to be allow'd journeyman's wages during the last year.

James was only twenty-one when Benjamin became his apprentice. The difference in years may not have been sufficient to give James the necessary authority over his younger brother, and the situation wasn't helped by the fact that Benjamin's was a rebellious spirit. Ben had horizons in his eyes and on the mind, while James, back from his London period, had stay-at-home impulses. Relations between the brothers were seldom cosy and were sometimes stormy, but the apprenticeship served a vital purpose for Benjamin Franklin's development. It taught him printing, his first profession, and the ultimate source of financing for his scientific studies and other activities. At his brother's print shop, Benjamin was able to begin indulging in earnest his unlimited zest for learning that would never slow or stop throughout his life. His "bookish inclination" could be nourished in the print shop. The boy proceeded voraciously to read everything he helped set and print as well as books borrowed from all who could and would supply useful volumes. Josiah Franklin had done remarkably well for his son, and without knowing it, for his country. He had taught Benjamin the virtue of work, the opportunity of trade, and he had maneuvered him into his natural niche in the world. Many richer fathers with more strings to pull have done much worse for their sons.

The print shop also gave Benjamin his first significant chance to use and develop a skill that the circumstances of his age and the needs of his country would require him to use more than any other, his ability to write clear, entertaining, informative prose with a satirical bite to it when needed. Franklin's brilliance as a writer would in time serve his genius as a scientist to give the world highly readable scientific writings. But in his brother's shop, Benjamin's talent had to seek another direction.

On August 7, 1721, James Franklin introduced the fourth newspaper in the English Colonies, the *New-England Courant*. It was in this newspaper that Benjamin Franklin successfully began his career in journalism that would continue for almost seventy years.

But because of the situation between the brothers and Benjamin's age, he had to write and submit his articles secretly. Using the penname of *Silence Dogood*, the sixteen year old youth wrote a series of fourteen letters on a range of moral and satirical subjects. Silence Dogood was pleased to report herself the grieving widow of a minister and that it was her wish to communicate important matters to the readers of the *Courant*. Franklin penned the articles in a disguised hand and deposited them under the door of the print shop at night.

James Franklin would find the articles the next morning, enjoy them, and then share them with others who visited the shop. Working at his job, Benjamin could listen as the articles were discussed and delight in the fact that "in their different guesses at the author none were named but men of some character among us for learning and ingenuity."

Silence Dogood's miscellaneous fortnightly epistles do not, without straining, give evidence of Franklin's later scientific writings, but they do show cleverness, originality, and more amused good sense than is normally expected, or received, from teenagers:

> And since it is observed, that the generality of people, nowadays, are unwilling either to commend or dispraise what they read, until they

are in some measure informed who or what the author of it is, whether
he be poor or rich, old or young, a scholar or a leather apron man, etc.,
and give their opinion of the performance, according to the knowledge
which they have of the author's circumstances, it may not be amiss to
begin with a short account of my past life and present condition, that
the reader may not be at a loss to judge whether or no my lucubrations
are worth his reading.

Silence Dogood continues in the next paragraph to announce
with a certain insouciance that she had been born on shipboard
between London and New England and that her father, poor man,
had been washed overboard by a "merciless wave" while rejoicing
at her birth. A diligent reading of Silence Dogood and other Franklin creations proves that so-called "black comedy" was not exclusively a twentieth century invention. The eighteenth century had
it in full flower.

In another letter, Silence Dogood reports on a dream, which
reads as if it might have been initiated by Josiah Franklin and
then translated freely by Benjamin. Silence in her report was
greatly critical of the college education which insisted on measur-
ing a person's intellectual achievements by his success with the
Latin classics. Franklin was then of college age, and typically disposed to criticize whatever he could about a world he was not invited to enter. He also made a point too about the inbreeding college approach to education that seemed to discourage new ideas
and to close intellectual doors instead of opening them. Perhaps
Franklin as a youth did not fully realize that encouraging new
ideas and throwing all doors wide open would be the dominant
theme of eighteenth century science, when suddenly the "old way"
of doing things had to prove that it was the "right way" against
any competition that applied. Franklin grown would be one of the
leading encouragers and door openers. If he did not guess that aspect of his future as a boy, his thoughts, when Silence Dogood
whimsically expressed them, were moving in that direction. If
learning inevitably became a competition between traditional pos-
tures and practical, scientific truth, Benjamin Franklin, apprentice, was certain on which side he belonged.

In the temple of learning, Silence Dogood's dream showed that:

Every beetle-skull seemed well satisfied with his own portion of learning, though perhaps he was even just as ignorant as ever. And now the
time of their departure being come, they marched out of doors to make
room for another company, who waited for entrance. And I, having
seen, all that was to be seen, quitted the hall likewise, and went to

make my observations on those who were just gone out before me. Some I perceived took to merchandising, others to traveling, some to one thing, some to another, and some to nothing; and many of them henceforth, for want of patrimony, lived as poor as church mice, being unable to dig, and ashamed to beg, and to live by their wits it was impossible . . . I reflected in my mind on the extreme folly of those parents, who blind to their children's dullness, and insensible to the solidity of their skulls, because they think their purses can afford it, will needs send them to the Temple of Learning.

"And back they come," added Silence, "after abundance of trouble and charge as great blockheads as ever."

The sketch was an undisguised portrait of Harvard College, but it would be an error to diagnose it as an example of youthful anti-intellectualism. Franklin may have been envious, at least privately, of the popular acceptance of such graduates, "masters of the obvious and the familiar," as educated. His own persistent reading was already building him a broad foundation of knowledge that would grow with the years. It was the education he was acquiring on his own that led Franklin to criticize the classics curricula of the academies and colleges. It was time for new ideas and opened doors, and the clock was moving. The world and the human race were aging fast, already it was 1722 and soon would be 1723. Andiamo!

BOOKS AND THE BOY

The boy's reading was moving quickly and broadly into science and philosophy. The first quarter of the eighteenth century was a time of ferment and beginnings. Isaac Newton was still alive, and the great science that gave mankind a new way of looking at the universe and the world was a liberating force, awake and urgent. The eighteenth was destined to be the first great century of scientific exploration and advance, building on the work of the seventeenth century's isolated practitioners, *Galileo, Descartes, Newton*. And Benjamin Franklin had the luck to be born near the beginning of the first century of modern science. Such thoughts would not have bothered the boy as he read in the print shop, read on the streets of Boston, read in the libraries of friends, read at home. His job was to keep reading. Figure out what this "empiricism" thing is. Determine what that fellow *John Locke* is driving at. Grasp the implications of Newton's Laws. What made them laws? Why were they laws? Who said so? What did it all mean? Keep reading! Keep thinking!

Matthew Adams "an ingenious tradesman" who frequented the shop proved to have "a pretty collection of books" which Benjamin was welcome to explore and use, if he wished. He wished. Other sources were sought and exploited with equal zeal. He began to acquire books of his own and found them the most consoling of possessions.

Owning the book, having it near, meant that anytime, day or night, it could be turned to for answers and advice. The boy learned that by purchasing a book and keeping it close he had a trustworthy friend for life. There was soon "a pretty collection of books" identified as the property of Benjamin Franklin, residence at Union Street, Boston.

The excitement of science had entered his reading to stay. Then he discovered the *Spectator* papers of *Joseph Addison* and *Richard Steele*. Their literary virility and wit appealed to him, and they helped to polish the vigorous but congenial writing style he mastered. But the Spectators were chiefly for amusement and guides to style. Solider matters held him securely. He studied arithmetic, navigation, logic.

The *Autobiography*:

> And now it was that being on some occasion made asham'd of my ignorance in figures, which I had twice failed in learning when at school, I took Cocker's Book of Arithmetick, and went thro' the whole by myself with great ease. I also read Seller's and Sturmy's Books of Navigation, and became acquainted with the little Geometry they contain, but never proceeded far in that science. And I read about this time Locke on Human Understanding and the Art of Thinking by Messrs. du Port Royal.

Logic: or the Art of Thinking was a book that began giving Benjamin the tool of reasoning that he would apply carefully in his life as well as his scientific work. Many important decisions were approached by the routes prescribed in this basic text which Franklin found ready to hand in his brother's shop. Written by *Antoine Arnauld* and *Pierre Nicole* of the Jansenist Community at Port Royal, the book was mental caviar for young Franklin. He adopted the method permanently. As an apostle of work, Franklin was led naturally to "le grand Arnauld" one of the giants of intellectual effort in the seventeenth century. Arnauld's kinship to Franklin was clear in the reply he gave his collaborator Nicole who complained of being tired: "Tired! When you have all eternity to rest in." It was the sort of answer Franklin must have given himself more than once during his eighty-four years.

Logic supplied a method that was practical, manageable, and realistic. It was compatible with the teachings of Josiah Franklin. It served Franklin's own innate suspicion that there was something basically futile about counting chickens before their hatching. Yet there was a strong and profound dreamer side to the youth, or he would have troubled less with books and their confusion of ideas. The dreamer wanted to know the mysterious why of things, and he wanted to believe in the ultimate betterment of reality. But the logical Franklin wanted to manage every dream as effectively, efficiently, and reasonably as possible. He was in short on his way to becoming that special sort of eccentric who sometimes can manage to open new doors: the practical dreamer.

There was nothing escapist about his reading at that time. He wasn't trying to flee the occasional boredom of his job, the tyranny of his brother, or the limited horizons of Boston. His motive was much simpler, the classic one. He read and studied to find out, and thereby know. Of course, the more he knew, the more he would need to know. So there was no time to dally.

In the writings of John Locke, he discovered empiricism, which suited him as a philosophy for science and government. John Locke had died barely fifteen months before Franklin was born. The seventeenth century philosopher was credited by the eighteenth century scientist with having more influence on him than any other thinker.

In Locke's treatises on government, the sovereignty of the people and their right to govern themselves in accordance with the

◈ —— ◈

JOURNEY OF THE UNALTERABLE SALTS
The salt of tartar, or salt of wormwood, frequently prescribed for cutting, opening, and cleansing, is nothing more than the salt of lye procured by evaporation. Mrs. Stevens's medicine for the stone and gravel, the secret of which was lately purchased at a great price by the Parliament, has for its principal ingredient salt, which Boerhaave calls the most universal remedy. . . . It is highly probable, as your doctor says, that medicines are much altered in passing between the stomach and bladder; but such salts seem well fitted in their nature to pass with the least alteration of almost anything we know; and, if they will not dissolve gravel and stone, yet I am half persuaded that a moderate use of them may go a great way towards preventing these disorders, as they assist a weaker digestion in the stomach, and powerfully dissolve crudities such as those which I have frequently experienced. As to honey and molasses, I did not mention them merely as openers and looseners, but also from conjecture that, as they are heavier in themselves than our common drink, they might when dissolved in our bodies increase the gravity of our fluids . . .
(To Josiah and Abiah Franklin, September 6, 1744)

principles of democracy, toleration, and public liberty were adopted as axioms by Benjamin Franklin; and he worked with others to translate Locke's axioms into first a revolution, and finally a new country.

In his *Second Treatise on Government*, Locke held that rulers are in power conditionally, not absolutely, and that the responsibility of governing, being a moral trust, must be fulfilled or the people have a right to set aside the rulers. Such ideas were like large stones dropped from a great height into still waters, setting off infinite waves. Locke's views are an interlinear presence in both the *Declaration of Independence* and the *Constitution*. Benjamin Franklin helped see to it.

Locke's views on scientific education also influenced Franklin. This was evident in later years when Franklin was founding schools and writing treatises on education. Locke's position, which became Franklin's, was that ideas had to be allowed to inspire minds and awaken them. Overstressing and overusing authority and custom, he held, could smother imagination and initiative. By extension, excessive worship of what has been done could stifle the ability to do. Two words that seem to summarize this attitude toward education and the stimulation of thought are "fresh air." Let winds blow through the smoky corridors and wake the sleepers. As Benjamin Franklin came awake in Boston, he recognized John Locke as one of the men preparing the way for something grand to happen in the world. He couldn't foresee the great awakening of mankind in the eighteenth century, or his own vital part in it; but a sense of things ahead came to him when he indulged in mental calisthenics with the philosopher as his guide.

Benjamin carefully read the *Essay Concerning Human Understanding*, in which Locke wrote that knowledge begins with the *idea*. The idea is indispensable and must be given freedom to find its own natural port. This means raising anchor and shoving off from the arid shores of preconceptions and fixed, unquestioned principles. Conceptions and principles have to be questioned constantly. They must be subject to free examination and new proof at all times. Relying on and surrendering to an unexamined authority could imprison truth—could in effect burn it at the stake.

Locke believed ideas depend upon "experience" gained by experimentation through the senses or by reflection. He emphasized the ability of the mind to examine ideas and expand them, but held that "no man's knowledge here can go beyond his experience."

Locke believed strongly in the use of scientific observation to determine the foundations of knowledge and such tools as mathematics to establish precise relationships and definitions.

Together with Francis Bacon, Isaac Newton, and a few other European philosophers of the seventeenth century, Locke began establishing the parameters of the scientific method. His influence on the scientists and philosophers of the eighteenth century, including Benjamin Franklin, was significant.

Locke favored the empirical methods of experiment and experience to determine natural facts and answer scientific questions. Metaphysical doubts, however, established mental roadblocks. Most, but never all questions could be answered by man proceeding empirically, he decided. The mists of mysticism began closing in when he wrote that there is forever a "most powerful and most knowing Being, in which, as the origin of all, must be contained all the perfections that can ever after exist."

This religious endpoint to Locke's argument was sufficiently vague and unorthodox to support Benjamin's rapidly growing doubt concerning his father's austere church. Locke's stress in religion as well as politics was the importance of tolerating different points of view. This fed Benjamin's feeling that outward form mat-

◦⊰┨ —— ┠⊱◦

FROM THE PENNSYLVANIA GAZETTE
ADVERTISEMENT—Good Rhode Island Cheese, and Codfish, sold by the Printer hereof.
(March 15, 1733)

ADVERTISEMENT—There is to be sold a very likely Negro woman aged about thirty years who has lived in this city, from her childhood, and can wash and iron very well, cook victuals, sew, spin on the linen wheel, milk cows, and do all sorts of housework very well. She has a boy of about two years old, which is to go with her. The price as reasonable as you can agree. And also another very likely boy aged about six years, who is son of the abovesaid woman. He will be sold with his mother, or by himself, as the buyer pleases. Enquire of the Printer.
(May 3, 1733)

Yesterday a marriage was consummated between Charles Read, Esq.; one of the Trustees of the Loan-Office of this Province, and the Relict of Mr. Joseph Harwood, Gent. A Lady of Considerable Fortune.
(October 18, 1733)

ADVERTISEMENT—Saturday next will be published, for 1733: The Second Edition of POOR RICHARD: AN ALMANACK containing the lunations, eclipses, planets motions and aspects, weather, sun and moon's rising and setting, high-water &c. besides many pleasant and witty verses, jests and sayings . . . A few of the first that were printed had the months of September and October transpos'd; but that fault is now rectified.
(January 11, 1733)

tered little in religious matters and encouraged his development as a deist (i.e. nature proves the existence of God but little more is known or can be known about the matter). Deism was the religious extension of rationalism and the common religious preference of freethinkers and scientists. Franklin, on his own, thought his way to that position from reading John Locke and seventeenth century sceptics and deists such as *Anthony Ashley Cooper* and *Anthony Collins*.

Such studies left Franklin basically religious, but on his personal terms. He decided that Sunday could be more constructively used as a day for study rather than churchgoing. Later in Philadelphia when he was persuaded to attend an occasional service, he usually found that the reading he lost by attending would have been more valuable than the meager contents of the sermon. Raised a Presbyterian, Franklin eventually decided that church's purpose was simply to make more Presbyterians rather than good citizens. In good Lockean terms, he came to view all churches with calm tolerance as variations on an identical theme; and there was little point in choosing among them.

THE BENIGN QUEERNESS

Franklin's deism, which he shared with Voltaire, Rousseau, and a young man whom he may profoundly have influenced, *Thomas Jefferson*, agreed with Locke's conclusion that man's interpretations of nature inevitably fall short of complete understanding and final knowledge. There was a Force out there who would always play it close to the vest and would never show his hole card.

This Lockean "uncertainty principle" supported by Franklin was in disrepute among rational scientists in the nineteenth century and part of the twentieth. The arrogance of science was that eventually all could be explained fully. But as physicists began probing the atom and the stars in the twentieth century, science came full circle to the "uncertainties" predicted by John Locke and echoed by Benjamin Franklin. In our era, *J. B. S. Haldane*, has written, "My own suspicion is that the universe is not only queerer than we suppose, but queerer than we can suppose."

Benjamin Franklin, whether youth or man, refused to be perturbed about any queerness in the universe. "God" was a word to cover that sort of thing, and Franklin was an optimist about the essential goodness of the total scheme. The principles of creativity freely operating would not have gone to so much trouble with the universe to make a mess, and the always logical natural laws couldn't produce a mess if they tried. Nature was profuse but fundamentally neat. *If nature seemed wasteful or uneconomical, man's way of observing was at fault.*

Benjamin's studies persuaded him that the world could be managed and life could be lived by consistently applying logic and rational rules. Of course, the rules regularly had to be revised to keep up with the advancing state of knowledge, though basic principles remained constant. With these reflections the uncharted musings of a scientist were beginning to stir. The apprentice knew that old opinions had to be challenged to find the truth. By then he also recognized the danger warned about in the letter of dedication to Locke's *Essay on Human Understanding*: "New opinions are always suspected, and usually opposed, without any other reason but because they are not already common."

If Franklin did not know, he would learn when the reaction came to his findings about electricity. He would learn during the years before the Revolution, when his pacifist logic was often denounced by the extreme emotions of bitter men in America and Britain, unable to hear reason because of noise from their own rage.

Locke wrote that most men "put passion in the place of reason" or they concentrate exclusively on merely one small part of the available evidence. Look further, he seemed to be saying, have the courage to question what previously may have been deemed unquestionable.

Young Franklin was a receptive audience for these instructions. Such books as Locke's invited him to do what he felt an insatiable urge to do anyway, question and learn.

> While I was intent on improving my language, I met with an English grammar (I think it was Greenwood's) at the end of which there were two little sketches of the arts of rhetoric and logic, the latter finishing with a specimen of a dispute in the Socratic method. And soon after I procur'd Xenophon's Memorable Things of Socrates, wherein there are many instances of the same method. I was charm'd with it, adopted it, dropt my abrupt contradiction and positive argumentation, and put on the humble enquirer and doubter... I took delight in it, practis'd it continually and grew very artful and expert in drawing people even of superior knowledge into concessions the consequences of which they did not foresee, entangling them in difficulties out of which they could not extricate themselves, and so obtaining victories that neither myself nor my cause always deserved.

Incorrigible young scamp! He would use variations of this method to make himself a delightful old scamp. But let us be fair, he normally used his skill in this method for the cause of scientific truth and political freedom, and he became esteemed in Europe and America as one of the most persuasive conversationalists, both speaker and listener, of his century.

He conversed on technical subjects with the supreme thinkers of the era, and on lesser topics with politicians, kings, queens, courtiers, and flirtatious ladies. When Thomas Jefferson joined his old friend in France in 1784 he noted with delight that Franklin had the French so well "trained" "it may truly be said that they were more under his influence than he under theirs."

Whether it was from his books, or from the effort to survive the criticisms and cuffs of his brother James, or from the practical lessons experience could teach a good student, *Franklin learned to dispute without disagreeing, to argue without angering, to convince without humiliating.*

What more did Benjamin Franklin learn during his first seventeen years in Boston? He obtained an example in good-humored perseverance and learned certain precepts as well as the habits of endurance from his father. He mastered the printing trade. He began the reading that a lifetime could not see finished. He became his own professor and started his education from life and nature as well as books, a process that also could not be finished in a lifetime. He learned to communicate with people, to learn from them by means of careful questions. He learned to amuse and instruct them with his writing. From John Locke and the Jansenist logicians he obtained the technique of reason and the weapon of common sense. He learned the importance of thinking for himself, of not accepting too much or too readily on faith, but of testing, probing, checking, questioning. He learned to follow the spoor of truth wherever it seemed to lead, even if it led to trouble. He learned to think and to work, and he knew something about the tools he might need to do his work. The child was prepared to become the father of the man, America's eighteenth century scientist. Not bad, actually, for a seventeen year old kid. If you doubt it, try reading John Locke's *Essay Concerning Human Understanding* sometime and see what it gets you. At the age of sixteen, Benjamin Franklin read Locke and understood. It was clearly inevitable that he would go far. And that he would carry quite a few things with him, mostly in his head.

1976

Dear Doctor Franklin, Sir,

You were only seventeen when the time came for you to enact symbolically the full chronicle of America in the eighteenth century. What you did was run away from home.

There's nothing new in that, of course. Hundreds did it in your day, many for the same reason as yours, to escape indentured servitude under an unpleasant employer and be free. Hundreds of thousands are runaways in America now. Most of them, unfortunately, just run for the sake of running, going nowhere in particular.

But you made running away respectable by running *to* something, probably to a great deal more than you knew. The parallel with the Colonies is plain. The American Colonies, unable or unwilling to wear the yoke of England with any comfort, ran away and called it a Revolution. The philosopher John Locke, whom you admired, held that the necessity of liberty sometimes made revolution an obligation as well as a right. Applied domestically, Locke's argument would seem to justify a lad disappearing like smoke for the sake of personal liberty.

You learned from John Locke, and the country learned from you the occasional necessity of running.

The country is still running. Sometimes we find it difficult to tell whether the country is now running toward something or away from something. It started out running toward "life, liberty, and the pursuit of happiness." Those were the words you and John Adams approved in that bit of writing Thomas Jefferson pieced together in June 1776. There are those who argue the country is now just running, nowhere in particular, having strayed somewhat from the "lif., lib., & purs. of hap." route.

Sir, if we could talk it over, consider the meaning and implications of running away, maybe we could study our map and find the route again. Since you were an expert on the subject, we could benefit from your views. Tell us again why you ran away from Boston and why America ran away from England.

That should help us remember what made America run in the beginning, and give us a fresh "Ready, Set, Go!" for the next two hundred years.

We Are, &c.,
YOURS, THE PEOPLE

IV. Philadelphia, Here I Come

NEW CITIZEN FOR ATHENS ON THE SCHUYLKILL

Wherever Benjamin Franklin decided to make his home, erect his business, and invest his life's energies was inevitably going to be a city where a great number of things would be tried and where many of them would be accomplished. It would be a city that could never again relax into a sleepy stodginess or be complacent about its problems. It would have to be hospitable to new ideas or drown under the deluge. The city would also have to accept the honor of becoming the cradle of American science, and it would have to assume the responsibility of reigning culturally and politically as America's leading city throughout the eighteenth century.

Philadelphia in 1723 was a growing community, but its ambitions were not so grandiose. Most Philadelphians were content to swim and fish in the Schuylkill River, carry on with business, and watch the ships come in from mother England across the sea. Some though wanted to call the community America's Athens, and a few citizens were already striving to earn the comparison. A new recruit for such efforts would soon arrive in town with awesome talents and vitality for the task. Benjamin Franklin was about to happen to Philadelphia.

The city had been founded in 1683 by *William Penn* to serve as the official capital for his Quaker state of Pennsylvania. He intended it to be a city of "brotherly love" and to serve as a refuge for his fellow Quakers and others fleeing persecution.

In that respect Benjamin Franklin qualified. Benjamin arrived in the city when Philadelphia was in its fortieth year, and he was fleeing the persecution, both real and imagined, of his brother James. In James' defense it might be observed that some individuals find it difficult to suffer geniuses gladly, especially when they are younger brothers.

Franklin was a town boy with a profession that required the facilities of a town and a growing population. His personal need was for a community that had the courage to grow, with his ready assistance, into a city. In the first quarter of the eighteenth century, many young men were leaving towns behind and venturing out into the American wilderness. They cleared fields, planted crops, raised families, and began observing in themselves some of the symptoms of liberty.

The wilderness way was not for Benjamin Franklin. He needed the people, the excitement, the challenge, and the opportunity of a town, a town sufficiently daring to become a city. Another essential criterion was that it must be alive, sophisticated, ambitious for itself and willing to tolerate ambition. Not a second Boston.

Reading furiously in Boston, Franklin's pilgrimage through all the books he could find brought him to this by John Locke: "Nature never makes excellent things for mean or no uses."

That described the waiting opportunity of the Colonies. Franklin could see it. The new world was ready to bestow an infinite bounty. It was waiting for those who would work and who would open their eyes to see the opportunity. The opportunity was not just in the wilderness land waiting to be developed. It was in the air, assuming the form of ideas, available to be seized by those who would notice and act.

"Dost thou love life?" Poor Richard demanded, "Then do not squander time, for that is the stuff life is made of."

Young Franklin more acutely than most others heard the ideas and sensed the opportunity of a green new world waiting to be used. Yet it may have been something more immediately domestic that sent him south from Boston: too much older brothering. That has been a considerable force in the settling of America as well as other frontiers. It sent *Owen Wister's* fictional Virginian and many of his real-life counterparts to the American West. "Always with us one son has been apt to run away," said the Virginian, "and I was the one this time. I had too much older brothering to suit me."

In 1723, at the age of seventeen, older brothering and the inquisitiveness of youth, placed Benjamin Franklin's name on the list of runaways. He was a child of the new world self-trained in logic, and it seemed eminently logical that he should leave a place of discontent and seek a better.

He had no funds to escape the tyranny of James. But he showed his seriousness by making a critical sacrifice. "I sold some of my books to raise a little money," he wrote. Then he went by ship to New York. *Books made Boston too narrow a place for the youth, and books financed his exit.* It was all somehow a symbolic and appropriate runaway for Benjamin Franklin.

Eventually Franklin would succeed in making his own name and that of his country internationally esteemed in science. He did so by having the courage to reject the false answers of the past and to concentrate on the truth that could be established only one brief step at a time. It was true, then, as it is true now, that a man who has it in him to accomplish imaginatively creative science must also have the strength to turn away from all the safety and familiarity of the past. He must, in brief, have the nerve and purpose to run away from home, whether it is across the street or across the world, or only in his own mind. He has to be willingly independent of the safe and familiar. Franklin qualified.

Writing in the *Autobiography* at a distance of nearly half a century, Franklin stressed the big brother problem in his case, admitting that he had perhaps been "too saucy and provoking." But if the trigger had not been James Franklin, it would have been something or someone else. Or it would simply have been youth's need and lust to wander. It wasn't that Boston was too small for Benjamin Franklin. It was that the world was enticingly larger. And the boy had to widen his acquaintance to absorb as much as he could reach.

New York was his first stop. The runaway's initial plan was to remain there. He applied at *William Bradford's shop.* No openings. But Bradford suggested that *Andrew Bradford,* his son, might give Franklin employment in Philadelphia, to replace a dead foreman, *Aquila Rose.* So prodded by destiny, it was on to Philadelphia.

Does fate arrange these coincidences deliberately? Aquila Rose contributed to American history by his death, though he might have complained with justice that "Franklin could have found some other way to reach town than at my expense." But history doesn't listen to complaints and is blithely casual about rights.

THREE PENNY BREAD AND A FUTURE WIFE

Benjamin Franklin arrived at Philadelphia in October 1723, and he wrote of it much later with the instincts of a mature genius shaping a legend:

> I have been the more particular in this description of my journey, and shall be so of my first entry into that city, that you may in your mind compare such unlikely beginnings with the figure I have since made there. I was in my working dress, my best clothes being to come round by sea. I was dirty from my journey; my pockets were stuff'd out with shirts and stockings; I knew no soul, nor where to look for lodging. I was fatigu'd with travelling, rowing and want of rest. I was very hungry, and my whole stock of cash consisted of a Dutch dollar and about a shilling in copper. The latter I gave the people of the boat for my passage, who at first refus'd it on account of my rowing, but I insisted on their taking it, a man being sometimes more generous when he has but a little money than when he has plenty, perhaps through fear of being thought to have but little.
>
> Then I walk'd up the street, gazing about, till near the Market House I met a boy with bread. I had made many a meal on bread, and inquiring where he got it, I went immediately to the baker's he directed me to in second street. . . I bade him give me three penny worth of any sort. He gave me accordingly three great puffy rolls. I was surpriz'd at the quantity, but took it, and having no room in my pockets, walk'd off, with a roll under each arm, and eating the other. Thus I went up Market Street as far as fourth street, passing by the door of Mr. Read, my future wife's father, when she standing at the door saw me, and thought I made as I certainly did a most awkward ridiculous appearance.

Less than an hour in town and Benjamin Franklin had managed surprising quantities of bread and the vague promise of romance. How accurate is this picture of the Hero's arrival? Why surely it is as accurate as a man's memory and inclinations writing of a matter forty-eight years later. The temptation is to accept it all, including his future wife standing in the doorway. How much was fact and how much fancy there is no particular need to know. Let it be fact. The point is that Benjamin Franklin had arrived in Philadelphia, and was the right man in the right place at the right time if that ancient formula has ever been fulfilled.

The same as the youth, Philadelphia too could be said in 1723 to be not far removed from adolescence. On the outskirts of the community, the American wilderness began and stretched on for more thousands of miles than most of the residents then imagined. Philadelphia might be called an Athens of America, but for the time being that was more future fancy than present fact.

The city had grown swiftly during its first decades thanks to the Penns and their open door policy toward the persecuted, harassed runaways of the world. There was ample room for one more, especially a Boston boy with freedom in his step and a twinkle in his eye. The freedom would still be present even when the boy had become a very old man crippled by gout. And the twinkle held its place despite a century of troubles. Something rare in his character enabled Benjamin Franklin to resist occasional opportunities to be miserable. Even in the darkest hours he managed to keep his equanimity and sense of humor.

In that respect perhaps Franklin was something like his chosen city, which has enjoyed the reputation historically of seldom finding adequate reasons to become upset. Through social and political storms, Philadelphia has offered a genial facade of placidity. Philadelphia has kept its head when most others were losing theirs, not because it lacked all the facts, but because it went back a very long way and had learned that most new problems are variations of old ones. And as Poor Richard noted in the *Almanac* of 1733: "God helps them that help themselves."

When Benjamin Franklin arrived in Philadelphia there were nearly 7,000 inhabitants. It had an incomplete, unsettled, under construction look, and thus to clever eyes, opportunity was manifest. A lad who wants to work and get on in the world does not, if he is wise, seek a comfortable, finished sort of place where all the work has been done. He heads for Philadelphia in 1723, or the most likely substitute on the nearest frontier in his own time. When all the frontiers are gone, he does as Franklin would have. He makes his own.

The streets were unpaved in Philadelphia that year. Indians, with whom the Penns humanely established treaties instead of killing them and appropriating their land in the holy name of progress, wandered about freely. Wild animals, including wolves and bears, were uninvited guests on occasion inside the confines of the town. Philadelphians at that time went to sleep with soothing wolfish howls from nearby hills.

The right place? Looking back, it would be difficult to think of a better place than Philadelphia for Benjamin Franklin that particular year. He could have studied in other places, done his experiments, written his papers. But Philadelphia allowed all of those and cherished them and provided friends of like interests with whom to share and challenge truth.

The right time? The eighteenth century was approaching the end of its first quarter, and picking up speed for the coming sprints. Scientific knowledge lay ahead of the willing worker like a bottomless cornucopia from which only a meager part had been removed, or like a lush orchard where only a few pickers had started the harvest.

The right man? He arrived as a boy with a Dutch dollar, and made himself an outstanding Philadelphian, trusted, admired, and successful, while little more than a boy. Within a quarter of a century, he would be a leading citizen of the community and on the verge of retiring from business to become a full-time scientist, though circumstances would require him instead to become a full-time revolutionist.

The man, the time, the place rendezvoused so ideally, there seems in retrospect a plot among the Muses, or Clio, the Muse of History, showing off for her sisters, saying, "Look at this, girls, I'm sending Ben Franklin to Philadelphia and you can bet your lucky stars something will come of that!"

His first day in town he learned that bread was inexpensive and he saw the girl he would later marry, following Poor Richard's advice perhaps that a single man is incomplete, resembling half a pair of scissors, or the more philosophical observation that "there are three faithful friends: an old wife, an old dog, and ready money."

But before reinforcing his initial impression on Deborah Read, he first had to see the new town and to get some sleep. The first he managed by walking the streets. For the second, he followed a group into a Quaker Meeting House on Market Street and had a pleasant nap there until the meeting broke. Then a young Quaker advised him to *try the Crooked Billet on Water Street for respectable lodgings.*

"But Friend, avoid the Sign of the Three Mariners," warned the Quaker of a place nearby, "it entertains strangers, but it is not a reputable house."

Benjamin Franklin had not come to Philadelphia for bawdy games, frivolous scandal, or self-indulgence. He sought work, freedom to think and study, and a chance to develop as a vegetarian philosopher. Vegetarianism was an experiment in health and frugality he had begun in Boston. Only the vegetarianism would prove an insurmountable difficulty, because of an eventual and formidable affection for beef pies as prepared by Deborah Read.

So a choice between the Three Mariners and the Crooked Billet for his first night in Philadelphia was easily made, and the Quaker approvingly walked him to the door of the Crooked Billet. There Franklin dined, slept soundly without hearing the nearby wolves, and rose next morning to tidy himself and call on Andrew Bradford for employment.

The position vacated at the demise of Aquila Rose had been filled, but Bradford promptly recommended Franklin to *Samuel Keimer*, another printer hoping to establish himself in Philadelphia. Keimer gave Benjamin Franklin his first job in Philadelphia and found him permanent lodgings in the home of John Read, Deborah's father. The Muse of History was sparing no pains, apparently, for Franklin's comfort and convenience. Wise Muse. He had important work to do and would benefit from a minimum of distractions, unless he chose them himself.

> My chest and clothes being come by this time, I made rather a more respectable appearance in the eyes of Miss Read, than I had done when she first happen'd to see me eating my roll in the street. I began now to have some acquaintance among the young people of the town, that were lovers of reading with whom I spent my evenings very pleasantly and gaining money by my industry and frugality.

A PHILOSOPHER'S HOMETOWN

Franklin would live many adult years in London and Paris representing the American Colonies, but from 1723 until his death, Philadelphia was either the place he lived or the place where he expected to return. The intellectual climate of England attracted him during the years he spent there representing the Colonies; and before the divisions with Great Britain became permanent, he considered staying. Scientist friends such as *Joseph Priestley* and *Peter Collinson* made England an attractive place to live and do his research. The temptation was made stronger by his high reputation and position in the Royal Academy of London, the outstanding scientific organization in the world. But family and politics were powerful forces drawing him always back to America and Philadelphia. Later during the years of Revolution when he served his country in France, he considered remaining in France where he was admired and loved more than anywhere else on earth including his own country. To the French he came to epitomize the rights and progress of man intellectually and politically. But in the end he left France and returned to Philadelphia. That was the place of his beginning. The roots of his spirit were permanently planted there. Philadelphia became his home as a youth, and he found through the decades that he could always go home again to Philadelphia. He always did.

Viewed from a distance of two centuries Franklin's choice of his city seems to be an event of inspired serendipity, and the relationship between the two one of perfect symbiosis. They got along beautifully together, and the conclusion has to be that the city and the boy were luckier that day in October 1723 than either could know at the time.

Did American institutions happen to be born in Philadelphia because Benjamin Franklin decided to be a printer there? A case could be made. But a case could also be made that it was certainly in part to the credit of Philadelphia that Franklin was loved for his gifts, tolerated for his crotchets, and complacently allowed his minor scandals and eccentricities. Other cities such as Boston, being less broad-minded, could have clipped the young man's wings and suffocated his spirit. Even so, Benjamin Franklin would have proved remarkable. But Philadelphia cheerfully accepted Benjamin Franklin as he was, sought no special amendments or compromises of his normal character, and let him have the freedom to be fully himself and run at his best speed. That was the city's gift, and he repaid by building the most important printing establishment in America, serving as postmaster, founding colleges, hospitals, libraries, scientific societies, organizing America's first insurance company, and countless other enterprises. Among his gifts to the city were life, liberty, and the greatest pursuit of civic happiness that has ever taken place. Franklin made Philadelphia one of the healthiest, best educated, and even the most fireproof city in the world of the eighteenth century. And if Franklin had done none of these things, it would still have been a beneficial relationship simply because Franklin the scientist chose to fly his kite in the vicinity. Philadelphia perhaps never quite became another Athens in the classic sense. Nature seldom allows exact repetition of such miracles. But Philadelphia, with Benjamin Franklin on the job, came close perhaps in the sense that Shelley meant: "Let there be light! said Liberty, And like sunrise from the sea, Athens arose!"

There was a remarkably long arising in Philadelphia during the eighteenth century, and it hardly seems a coincidence that much of it took place after 1723. Franklin would have 67 more years of adult life, and in those years Philadelphia would join Boston and other cities in leading a rare experiment in revolution and political democracy. Perhaps the times helped shape men such as Franklin who in turn certainly shaped the times. The question about priority in connection with the chicken and the egg, the revolutionist and the revolution, or the man and his times cannot be answered convincingly and needs asking only for whimsical speculation. In the case of Franklin and Philadelphia, the facts bear out that the community had shown promise through a number of distinguished sons from William Penn to *James Logan*; but scientific, cultural, and political achievements before Franklin were not extraordinary. The facts also indicate that during the Franklin years, beginning in the 1730's, the town seemed to accelerate remarkably in all these directions. In the instance of Franklin and Philadelphia, it was a spiritual marriage between man and metropolis. The man was given rein to romp freely, and he did so to the benefit and abiding glory of the other half of the union. William Blake's verse about men and mountains can be amended to, " Great things are done when men and cities meet," if the man is Franklin and the city a country village named Philadelphia with an appetite for grandeur.

Franklin's scientific and social contributions didn't show themselves with dramatic suddenness. The Muse of History had no need for hurry. There would be nearly seven decades together, with interludes of separation, for the philosopher and Philadelphia, the name of the first meaning "love of knowledge" and the name of the second meaning "brotherly love." The common word was "love."

The first years, however, were Franklin's for getting settled, getting acquainted, and getting on. He knew almost at once that the city could use a printer with his skills and education. His competition, Bradford and Keimer were untalented in the printing and publication arts, while he, thanks to the cuffs of Brother James, was both a good makeup man and pressman, as well as facile arranger of clever words.

> These two printers I found poorly qualified for their business. Bradford had not been bred to it, and was very illiterate; and Keimer tho' something of a scholar, was a mere compositor, knowing nothing of presswork.

Guided by the principles of "Industry and Frugality," the boy worked and bided his time, agreeable with the present and optimistic about the future. A letter to his brother-in-law *Captain Holmes* explaining his reasons for leaving Boston came to the attention of *Sir William Keith, Governor of the Province,* who decided Franklin was a "young man of promising parts." The Governor urged him to set up his own business, and to obtain the necessary funds from his father in Boston.

STOOP, STOOP!

Thus in May 1724 he was back in Boston earlier than he had expected after an absence of little more than seven months. Dressed in a "genteel new suit from head to foot, a watch, and my pockets lin'd with near five pounds sterling in silver," he went to his brother James' print shop. James looked him over and turned to his work again without a word. The rest of the family was glad to see the prosperous prodigal, however, though his father eventually refused business funds on the grounds of his excessive youth. Josiah Franklin instead offered a goodly portion of valuable advice.

> He gave his consent to my returning again to Philadelphia, advis'd me to behave respectfully to the people there, endeavour to obtain the general esteem, and avoid lampooning and libelling to which he thought I had too much inclination; telling me, that by steady industry and a prudent parsimony, I might save enough by the time I was one and twenty to set me up, and that if I came near the matter he would help me out with the rest.

During that Boston visit, Franklin made a courtesy call on the redoubtable minister of the Second Congregational Church, *Cotton Mather.* For all his Christian orthodoxy, Mather was a simpatico spirit, being a friend of science and a bold defender of smallpox inoculation at a time when the majority still viewed such medical activities with superstitious fear. Franklin wrote amusingly of the visit and the advice received in the minister's house. Seventeen twenty-four was a good year for advice in Boston, but a poor one for financial investment in a teenager's business prospects.

> He received me in his library and, on my taking leave, showed me a shorter way out of the house through a narrow passage, which was

crossed by a beam overhead. We were still talking as I withdrew, he accompanying me behind, when he said hastily: "Stoop, stoop!" I did not understand him, till I felt my head hit against the beam. He was a man that never missed any occasion of giving instruction, and upon this he said to me: "You are young, and have the world before you; stoop as you go through it, and you will miss many hard bumps."

It was a practical suggestion, but probably superfluous for the clever young man who was rapidly mastering not only the prudent art of ducking, but many other arts and sciences as well, both the familiar and arcane, for getting along with people and making his way in the world.

With his parents' blessing, back he went to Philadelphia. There he practiced his trade, amused himself by employing the Socratic Method with great skill to confuse and confound his employer Keimer.

An inept businessman and a poor printer, Keimer made an excellent eccentric with an avocation of founding new religious movements. He had a wife "somewhere in England" he admitted. Behind him in England there was also a record of imprisonment for debt and publishing seditious materials. Franklin had little respect for Keimer's ability as either printer or journalist, but he was intrigued by the man's vigorously independent and unpredictable mannerisms. For one thing, Keimer "wore his beard at full length, because somewhere in the Mosaic Law it is said, *'thou shalt not mar the corners of thy beard.'*" (*Leviticus* 19:27).

In addition to Keimer and work, Franklin was also swiftly making friends who had interests paralleling his own.

My chief acquaintances at this time were, Charles Osborne, Joseph Watson, and James Ralph; all lovers of reading.

Together they discussed philosophy, writings, readings, and in general behaved as a quartet of young intellectuals is expected to behave, all their activities embroidered through with grand ideas, grand words, and grand dreams. Later that year, one of the friends, Ralph, for the sake of poetry, would abandon his wife and child and accompany Franklin to London. "I think I never knew a prettier talker," wrote Franklin of Ralph. In the *Autobiography*, he noted that Watson "died in my arms a few years after, much lamented, being the best of our set." The range of their youthful speculations is shown by Franklin's comment about Osborne who also died young in the West Indies.

He and I had made a serious agreement that the one who happen'd first to die, should if possible make a friendly visit to the other, and acquaint him how he found things in that separate state. But he never fulfill'd his promise.

The summer of 1724 in Philadelphia included more for Benjamin Franklin than study, intellectual friends, and the amiable peculiarities of Samuel Keimer. It was his first summer with Deborah Read.

I had made some courtship during this time to Miss Read. I had a great respect and affection for her, and had some reason to believe she had the same for me: but as I was about to take a long voyage, and we were both very young, only a little above 18, it was thought most prudent by her mother to prevent our going too far at present, as a marriage if it was to take place would be more convenient after my return, when I should be as I expected set up in my business. Perhaps too she thought my expectations not so wellfounded as I imagined them to be.

Mrs. Read's caution may have directly affected scientific and political history. If impetuous nature had been allowed to take its course and Franklin had married at eighteen, would he have been able to spend a year and a half in London? London at that time was probably the most brilliant city in the world with *Isaac Newton* for science and *Jonathan Swift* for letters and charming young ladies for Benjamin Franklin. Married young and raising a family, would Franklin have found time for the study and thought that prepared him for his experiments and for his decades of American leadership, politically, culturally, and scientifically? Perhaps. But logic offers generous odds against it.

THE WATER AMERICAN AND AN INTERLUDE OF LONDON

He made the "long voyage" to England aboard the *London Hope*. But hope, not for the first time, made a poor breakfast. The plan had been for Franklin to go to London with letters of credit from Governor Keith, who had offered to provide funds for a new business when Josiah Franklin refused. But the governor proved more inclined to promise than to practice. Letters of credit were not aboard the *London Hope* or anywhere else, and Franklin was on his way to England with no prospects whatever.

"What shall we think of a governor's playing such pitiful tricks, and imposing so grossly on a poor ignorant boy! It was a habit he had acquired. He wish'd to please every body; and having little to give, he gave expectations." Thus Franklin wrote of the incident much later.

But if the governor had betrayed the boy, he had not betrayed mankind. It was an excellent time for Franklin to find himself foot loose and extremely fancy free in cosmopolitan London. He had a marketable trade and was in no danger of starving wherever there were presses to run and type to set. He found work immediately in the shop of *Samuel Palmer*, publisher of *The Grub Street Journal.* At that time, *Grub Street*, as *Dr. Johnson* noted was "much inhabited by writers of small histories, dictionaries, and temporary poems." *Daniel Defoe* was one of the geniuses of Grub Street, and it was a colorful neighborhood of ha'penny tales and hack journalism. In 1830 Grub Street would be renamed Milton Street and something useful, a place where writers could go to be bad, would have left the world. In 1724 it was thriving, and so was the rest of London. Franklin had been unable to attend Harvard College, but he attended a greater university for more than a year: The City of London.

The print shops of London were a college in themselves. In the rest of Europe printing was strictly controlled by government censors. There were also regulations in England against irreligious and "improper" publications, but the regulations were only fitfully enforced. According to *Bernard Fay*, one of Franklin's biographers, "even at the respectable Palmer's, Franklin worked on books which would have led their author and printer to the stake anywhere else in the world."

The following year, 1725, Franklin transferred to the large print shop of *John Watts* in Wild Court. At Watts, the youth was known with amused respect by the other printers as the "Water American" because of Franklin's unprofessional refusal to drink strong beer. Franklin argued that there was more strength for the money in plain bread.

Living temperately with regard to spirits was in accordance with Franklin's commitment to reason. His fellow pressman at Watts thought strong beer was essential to give him strength for work. The "Water American" argued that the bodily strength afforded by beer could only be in proportion to the grain or flour of the barley dissolved in the water of which it was made; that there was more flour in a penny-worth of bread, and therefore if he would eat that with a pint of water, it would give him more strength than a quart of beer." Such technically indisputable sermonettes no doubt inspired his fellow pressmen to wish piously at times that the Lord would preserve them from scientific and logical teetotalers.

But the pressmen saw that the "Water American" was a good worker, eager to do his share and more. He was skillful and helpful. And it wasn't long until Franklin was "on a fair footing with them, and soon acquir'd considerable influence."

London, however, was much more than a place to work for the Water American. It was sufficiently far from the critical eyes of Boston and Philadelphia for a vigorous sowing of youthful wild oats, and the record strongly hints that few young men on their lonesome and their own amid the anonymity of a great city have ever sowed more diligently and merrily than the energetic Franklin. "Foolish intrigues with low women" were easily managed by a young man so inclined, and such intrigues had the virtue of not requiring one to engage in the costly indiscretions of strong beer and gambling. All we know of those years is what Franklin, the world renowned statesman, was willing to recall later with judicious selectivity. But he recalled enough to indicate that he threw himself into the revelry and riot of London with typical Franklin thoroughness. *James Parton*, one of his early biographers, wrote with combined regret and prudish pride that, "Franklin, with all his great understanding and good heart, was not able long to preserve that unconceivably precious treasure of man and woman, as precious to man as to woman, sexual integrity. But we are permitted to infer that at eighteen he was still virtuous." Franklin turned nineteen, however, during his stay in London.

It was in London that he wrote and published his first work, an essay entitled *"A Dissertation on Liberty and Necessity, Pleasure and Pain."* The epigraph to the essay was from *John Dryden*: "Whatever is, is in its Causes just, Since all Things are by fate, but purblind Man, Sees but a part o' th' Chain, the nearest Link. . ."

The basic argument of the piece was that an all-wise God makes the world as he wishes. Thus there are no natural virtues or vices, men do what they must in accordance with their nature, and they should therefore never be blamed for their actions, which being dictated by necessity eliminate all concerns about right and wrong. On the whole, it was a clumsy bit of metaphysics, though perhaps creditable for a busy nineteen year old trying to establish a plausible philosophical base for behaving as he pleased. "So convenient a thing it is to be a *reasonable creature*," wrote the Autobiographer decades later, "since it enables one to find or make a reason for every thing one has a mind to do." His 1725 dissertation showed his impulse, if not yet developed skill, to push an argument to its polar limits.

The essay, which he later humorously but emphatically denounced as an "erratum," was dedicated to James Ralph and printed by the author for limited distribution. Later in life Franklin reputedly burned all copies but one. Today four copies are known to exist, and if a fifth should appear from some long neglected trunk in England, its value to Franklin collectors would make it an awesome "Pleasure" with no pain whatsoever.

Metaphysics and London vagaries were, of course, not the full extent of his activities. He was a student carrying a multitude of courses. Time was also found for roaming, new acquaintances, coffee house conversation sessions that filled the universe with words, and much more thought and study. The young man may not yet have known what he was preparing for, but he continued to prepare.

> While I lodg'd in Little Britain I made an acquaintance with one Wilcox a bookseller, whose shop was at the next door. He had an immense collection of second-hand books. Circulating libraries were not then in use; but we agreed that on certain reasonable terms which I have now forgotten, I might take, read and return any of his books. This I esteem'd a great advantage, and I made as much use of it as I could.

During the London visit, there was also a chance for one of the interesting might-have-beens of history, a meeting between Science of the seventeenth century and the Science-to-be of the eighteenth. But, alas, it wasn't managed. Clio missed an opportunity.

> Lyons (a surgeon who sought the author of the Dissertation) too introduc'd me, to Dr. Pemberton, at Batson's Coffee House, who promis'd to give me an opportunity some time or other of seeing Sir Isaac Newton, of which I was extremely desirous; but this never happened.

Franklin and Newton didn't meet, not then, and Newton would be dead two years later, with Franklin back at Philadelphia. But they did meet in a sense, as immortals, in a curious way that will be explained later.

There were other men of science in London and the youth was communicating with them. The scientist in Benjamin Franklin was eager to appear and beginning to do so.

Among others, he met and corresponded with *Sir Hans Sloane,* then Secretary, and after Newton, President of the Royal Society. Sloane was also President of the Royal College of Physicians and a scientist of note in several fields. In 1754 Sloane's scientific and technical literature collections would be left to Great Britain and form the nucleus of the *British Museum*, one of mankind's indispensable reservoirs of the past.

Among the earliest surviving letters written by Franklin was this addressed to Sloane on June 2, 1725:

> Sir: Having lately been in the northern parts of America, I have brought from thence a purse made of the stone asbestos, a piece of the stone, and a piece of wood, the pithy part of which is of the same nature, and called by the inhabitants salamander cotton. As you are noted to be a lover of curiosities, I have informed you of these; and if you have any inclination to purchase them, or see 'em, let me know your pleasure by a line directed for me at the Golden Fan in Little Britain, and I will wait upon you with them.

Sir Hugh promptly did as instructed. He visited Franklin and invited the American to see his collection at Bloomsbury Square. The specimens from America were purchased and paid for "handsomely." The asbestos purse, now in the British Museum, became one of England's mementoes of Benjamin Franklin. Sloane did not forget the name Franklin, and years later he would have excellent reason to justify the remembering. Though still a boy, Franklin had presence and an alert intelligence that showed promise.

In spite of all these activities, the time eventually came when London seemed to have given him everything it could for the time being. Perhaps Benjamin Franklin simply became homesick. He had experienced a bit of the world, he had dissipated with maximum educational effect (to the point of waning interest in dissipation), and his mind had engaged successfully in sinewy exercises for the great mental wrestling matches ahead.

After an extended period of such strenuous business, young men not unusually decide that they would be willing to go home if a way were provided. Benjamin Franklin began to feel the same:

> I was grown tired of London, remember'd with pleasure the happy months I had spent in Pennsylvania, and wish'd again to see it.

Perhaps he remembered as well a particular girl named Deborah Read to whom he found time to send one letter during his months in England. True, he had been exceptionally busy. And absence serves as often to make the heart indifferent as to grow fonder, especially for youths in stimulating new cities.

A Quaker merchant from Philadelphia, *Mr. Denham*, helped at that point by offering Franklin his fare home and the position of clerk in his Philadelphia store. It seemed an excellent opportunity to return home and to enter a promising new career other than printing. Franklin agreed.

The timing of Mr. Denham's offer was historically apropos. It it had been delayed slightly, Franklin might have remained permanently in England as a swimming instructor. He seriously considered an English Swimming School as a way "to get a good deal of money," after an English gentleman asked him to teach his two sons the skill.

Looking back, the Autobiographer would see fit to summarize his initial London interlude with more emphasis on study than on "giddiness and inconstancy," charges he would later bring against himself in connection with the neglected Deborah Read.

> Thus I spent about 18 months in London. Most part of the time, I work'd hard at my business, and spent but little upon myself except in seeing plays and in books. My friend Ralph had kept me poor. He owed me about 27 pounds; which I was now never likely to receive; a great sum out of my small earnings. I lov'd him notwithstanding, for he had many amiable qualities. I had improved my knowledge, however, tho' I had by no means improv'd my fortune. But I had pick'd up some very ingenious acquaintance whose conversation was of great advantage to me, and I had read considerably.

Many Americans after him would visit Europe and return with considerably less. He had very much "improved his fortune," of course. Franklin's true fortune was his eager curiosity and busy mind. With those, probably no day passed throughout his life without improvements. He constantly added to his fortune by constantly learning. His voyage home at the age of twenty was an excellent example of that remarkable process in action. From Gravesend to Philadelphia, the Atlantic was just one more vast university and the *Berkshire* another schoolroom for Benjamin Franklin. *The Water American was passing up his chance to teach swimming to the upperclass of England.*

ERRATA IN THE FIRST EDITION
They have printed all my electrical papers in England, and sent me a few copies, of which I design to send you one per next post, after having corrected a few errata.

(To Jared Eliot, December 10, 1751)

1976

Dear Doctor Franklin, Sir,

When you come to the centennial party, perhaps you can help us answer an important question. You're the one to ask, since you posed the question.

Are we paying too much for our whistle?

Remember? You wrote the story of the whistle, one of your best known, first for a nephew, then for the amusement of Madame Brillon in Paris. You were always kind to nephews and the ladies of Paris. In the tale, you recount buying a whistle with holiday coppers at the age of seven, and then being told by brothers, sisters, cousins, half the Colony of Massachusetts, that you "had given four times as much for it as it was worth."

> As I grew up, came into the world, and observed the actions of men, I thought I met with many, very many, *who gave too much for the whistle.* When I saw any one too ambitious of court favor, sacrificing his time in attendance on levees, his repose, his liberty, his virtue, and perhaps his friends to attain it, I have said to myself, *This man gave too much for his whistle.*

Today your fellow Americans have many whistles and a wide range of prices. Chances are that many are paying way too much. Some whistles, of course, must be worth more than others. But often it almost seems that we are paying least for the whistles that make the nicest sounds, peace and love and human well-being, and most for the whistles that can sound terrifying and raucous, war, ruthlessness, power, and greed.

What about the price of our whistles, Sir. Could you spare us your view? It would help.

> We Are, &c.,
> YOURS, THE PEOPLE

V. Aquatic Sciences

DOCTOR FRANKLIN, SWIMMER

When a man achieves outstanding distinction as a scientist, it becomes interesting, certainly, and instructive, possibly, to consider his first efforts to be "scientific," especially when the efforts are concentrated in an area completely unrelated to the work for which he becomes celebrated. The parallels are often curious and revealing.

In Franklin's case, we know, from the *Autobiography* as well as correspondence, the subject that intitially inspired his inventiveness, methodical thought, and careful analysis: Swimming.

Swimming had been his favorite sport as a child, and when Franklin was interested in a particular matter, he had to analyze and understand it thoroughly, even if it was simply the routine achievement of mobility in water. He also had to attempt improvements. As a boy he did his swimming in Boston Harbor a few blocks from Milk Street, and very early he was devising "little machines" to extend his enjoyment. One effort with wooden swimming fins of his own design didn't turn out especially well, but the next experiment did. He found a pragmatic way to combine the pleasures of flying a kite and swimming. "I found," he wrote, "that lying on my back and holding the kite's stick in my hands I was drawn along the surface of the water in a very agreeable manner."

Who knows, when the time came for his greatest experiment, perhaps the idea for the world's most famous kite in history came from a recollection of lying in the warm water of Boston Harbor and staring lazily up at a placidly sailing kite overhead. If the child is father of the man, the kites of childhood may be lineal ancestors of adult kites.

Young Benjamin Franklin Being Towed by His Kite

Reproduced from The Works of Benjamin Franklin, *published by William Duane, Philadelphia, 1809. The picture also appeared on the title-page of the 1806 edition of Franklin's works published by J. Johnson & Co., London. . . . Being desirous of amusing myself with my kite and enjoying at the same time the pleasure of swimming, I returned; and, loosing from the stake the string with the little stick which was fastened to it, went again into the water . . .*

During his apprentice and study years in Boston, the zeal he lavished on science and philosophy, he also applied to a scientific mastery of swimming. In a French swimming manual by *Thevenot*, he found thirty-nine chapters with a medley of complicated strokes, each of which he practised to perfection.

Clearly, this fondness for swimming carried over from childhood to youth and beyond. During his first visit to England, the evidence is that Franklin impressed the English considerably more with his swimming prowess than with his "Dissertation on Liberty et al."

The *Autobiography:*

> At Watts's Printinghouse I contracted an acquaintance with an ingenious young man, one Wygate ... I taught him, and a friend of his, to swim, at twice going into the river, and they soon became good swimmers. They introduc'd me to some gentlemen from the country who went to Chelsea by water to see the College and Don Saltero's Curiosities. In our return, at the request of the company, whose curiosity Wygate had excited, I stripped and leapt into the river, and swam from near Chelsea to Blackfriars, performing on the way many feats of activity both upon and under water, that surpriz'd and pleas'd those to whom they were novelties. I had from a child been ever delighted with this exercise, had studied and practis'd all Thevenot's motions and positions, added some of my own, aiming at the graceful and easy, as well as the useful.

His companions were impressed and persuaded that the Water American was aptly nicknamed. Near the end of Franklin's stay in London, he was called by a political leader, *Sir William Wyndham,* who had heard about the Chelsea-Blackfriars swim, and asked to teach the politician's two sons the art of swimming, for a handsome fee. It was too late to take the assignment, but Franklin speculated that earlier he might have used such an invitation to make his fortune by opening a swimming school. "It struck me so strongly," he wrote, "that had the overture been sooner made me, probably I should not so soon have returned to America." But Mr. Denham had already given him ten pounds for passage to America aboard the *Berkshire* in July.

MIND OVER WATER

His interest in swimming was with him through his life. It was a sport that lent itself peculiarly to experiment and speculation. Perhaps his first experiments were in connection with the sport, and he obviously enjoyed writing letters on the subject, that were typically charming, ebullient, and technical.

> *To Oliver Neale:* I cannot be of opinion with you that it is too late in life for you to learn to swim. The river near the bottom of your garden affords a most convenient place for the purpose.

To help Neale gain confidence in the power of the water to support him, Franklin suggested walking down the sloping shore until the water was breast deep, facing the shore, and throwing an egg into the water between himself and the beach. Diving for the egg would quickly teach the tendency of the water to "buoy you up against your inclination."

He agreed it was mentally difficult to trust the water, and that in troubled situations, it would be hard to remember to remain confident.

> The surprise may put all out of your mind. For though we value ourselves on being reasonable knowing creatures, reason and knowledge seem on such occasions to be of little use to us; and the brutes to whom we allow scarce a glimmering of either, appear to have the advantage of us.

In other words, some people think too much, especially about consequences, to keep their heads in deep water. So Franklin proceeded to list various things a person should memorize to keep from drowning as a result of emotional ignorance and panic. One point was that the trunk of the human body because of hollowness is lighter than water and some part will stay afloat until the lungs fill with water. Another point: If a person unfamiliar with swimming falls accidentally into the water, he should avoid struggling, should let the body assume the floating or suspended position, and he "might continue long safe from drowning till perhaps help would come."

Franklin went on to express his preference for "schools . . . where an opportunity was afforded for acquiring so advantageous an art, which once learned is never forgotten."

It is believed historically accurate that Oliver Neale did *not* drown in the river at the bottom of his garden.

In a letter to *Barbeu Dubourg*, Franklin busy with his usual multitude of other matters, wrote on the same topic of being "apprehensive that I shall not be able to find leisure for making all the disquisitions and experiments which would be desirable on this subject."

Insufficient leisure was a chronic complaint for Franklin in connection with most of his experiments. But leisure or not, he found or took the time for an amazing number of diverse studies, allowing his curiosity to go anywhere and feeling that one journey was as exciting and worthwhile as another. In his letters to Neale and

Dubourg, he wrote about swimming as seriously and thoroughly as he wrote about electricity on the Gulf Stream.

Obviously, he used the letters both as a chance to instruct, share information, and to think through his quill. For Dubourg's benefit, he discussed the specific gravity of the human body and the fact that a fat person with small bones floats easier than others. He examined the good points and the bad ones of his childhood inventions to facilitate swimming. And he told what to do in the case of a cramp: "The method of driving it away is to give to the parts affected a sudden vigorous and violent shock." He warned about the "imprudence which may prove fatal" of leaping into cold spring water while hot. He described in detail his boyhood experiment with a kite for the Frenchman's edification.

> Having then engaged another boy to carry my clothes round the pond, to a place which I pointed out to him on the other side, I began to cross the pond with my kite, which carried me quite over without the least fatigue, and with the greatest pleasure imaginable ... I have never since that time practised this singular mode of swimming though I think it not impossible to cross in this manner from Dover to Calais. The packet-boat, however, is still preferable.

In addition to the techniques of swimming, the swimming scientist had also paid attention to the numerous benefits of the art.

> The exercise of swimming is one of the most healthy and agreeable in the world. After having swam for an hour or two in the evening, one sleeps coolly the whole night; even during the most ardent heat of summer. Perhaps the pores being cleansed, the insensible perspiration increases and occasions this coolness. It is certain that much swimming is the means of stopping a diarrhea, and even of producing a constipation. With respect to those who do not know how to swim, or who are affected with a diarrhea at a season which does not permit them to use that exercise, a warm bath, by cleansing and purifying the skin, is found very salutary, and often effects a radical cure. I speak from my own experience, frequently repeated, and that of others to whom I have recommended this.

Franklin's thoroughness with any subject that lent itself to logical dissection was a key part of his success as an accurate observer. When he noted that swimming was effective therapy against diarrhea, he did so, we can be confident, only after checking the matter, repeatedly.

Many of his swimming tips, in fact, are excellent, quite useful in achieving greater water safety, and certainly show much more than superficial reflection on the subject. Franklin may have been dozens of men simultaneously, but one of them was a scientist, and he couldn't avoid being "scientific" when there was the slightest opportunity.

Because of his mind's scope, it seems unlikely that he would have been content to remain nothing more than the proprietor of a swimming school if he had accepted Sir William Wyndham's offer. A task so unchallenging could not have held Benjamin Franklin long.

Once *Thomas Carlyle* took *Milburn*, a blind preacher, to the position in Chelsea where Franklin undressed, jumped in the Thames, and swam to Blackfriars Bridge. The story has it that Carlyle said, "He might have stayed here and become a *swimming* teacher, but God had other work for him."

Whatever that work was to be, on July 21, 1726, Benjamin Franklin, aboard the *Berkshire*, started home to do it. In time, his work would return him to England again, and then again; but during that summer of his twentieth year, his destination was Philadelphia and much more.

1976

Dear Doctor Franklin, Sir,

Thanks in part to the technological forces you and your scientific colleagues set in motion, today when we want to travel from the Former Colonies to England, we fly. And complete the journey in a few hours. Before the flight though, we have to buy a ticket, quarrel with traffic to reach the airport, endure the hassle of baggage checking, seat assignments, and waiting for the bright-eyed stewardesses to let us enter our streamlined bullet. Inside we are strapped in place, human cargo ready for transport, so we won't bounce in case of mishap. Then, in a matter of hours, plus another hassle getting into London, we could reach 7 Craven Street in the Strand where you lodged with Mrs. Stevenson. All accomplished in one hectic day.

Contrast with your crossings of the Atlantic, Sir. For the 1726 voyage from London to Philadelphia, you were aboard the *Berkshire* July 21st to October 11th, over seven weeks. You spent some of the time during those weeks devising a careful Plan for the conduct of your future life. As you noted later you kept to it "quite thro' to old age."

In 1757 when you went to England as agent for the Pennsylvania Assembly, the voyage from June 20 to July 17 was almost four weeks. You used the time constructively again to organize Poor Richard's "The Way to Wealth" containing the most popular of the maxims from the Almanacs.

Furthermore, during each of your Atlantic voyages, you always used those weeks of "enforced" leisure in typical Franklin fashion, with scientific observations of sky, sea, ship, and sun—with writing, reading, corresponding. Nothing comparable occurs today.

Such things were done at sea routinely during the days of sail. Thomas Babington Macaulay, the historian born in 1800, for instance, during a three month voyage to India devised a scheme of education for the country and when he arrived made English rather than Persian the official language.

Your voyages too gave you time to think, plan, and work without the hectic pressures of the shore. Today's amazing flights, Sir, which you essentially predicted, never afford much useful leisure. In the main they provide speed plus uncomfortable jet lag.

We have to wonder if your sailing ships weren't a blessing. Modern technology moves us fast, but deprives us of "The Way to Wealth," or at least sea-leisure to compile one. The evidence is that you enjoyed your voyages immensely and used them to enormous benefit. What availeth speed?

We Are, &c.,
YOURS, THE PEOPLE

WHERE ONCE THE ELEPHANTS ROAMED
I return you many thanks for the box of elephants' tusks and grinders. They are extremely curious on many accounts; no living elephants having been seen in any part of America by any of the Europeans settled there, or remembered in any tradition of the Indians . . . It is remarkable, that elephants now inhabit naturally only hot countries where there is no winter, and yet these remains are found in a winter country; and it is no uncommon thing to find elephants' tusks in Siberia, in great quantities, when their rivers overflow, and wash away the earth, though Siberia is still more a wintry country than that on the Ohio; which looks as if the earth had anciently been in another position, and the climates differently placed from what they are at present.
(To George Grogan, August 5, 1767)

VI. "Rational Creature"

A SURFEIT OF FLOUR IN THE PUDDING

Benjamin Franklin was no longer a boy. Of course, he never would "grow up" in the stuffy, unadventurous sense that phrase normally conveys. His humor, wit, readiness for adventure, hospitality for new ways and new ideas . . . some of the attributes associated with youth, despite exceptions . . . were to stay with him for life. But it was an exuberant young man, not a boy, who started home for Philadelphia in the summer of 1726 aboard the *Berkshire*.

London had been good for him, wild oats and all. Sheer vitality made it inevitable that there would be further wild oats for sowing and more peccadilloes for atonement; but they would be handled with discretion. Franklin was returning with a purpose: to establish himself; and a dedication: to accomplish useful work.

During the voyage he began writing meticulously in his journal, making a record of all the phenomena encountered during an ocean voyage. It was the beginning of a practice that would con-

75

tinue through many decades and subsequent voyages. In those journals would be found the concentrated essence of Franklin thought, intriguing scientific speculations, and some of the crispest writing in the English language.

Homeward bound, the philosopher entered these journal observations:

> ... I believe it is impossible for a man, though he has all the cunning of a devil, to live and die a villain, and yet conceal it so well as to carry the name of an honest fellow to his grave with him, but some one, by some accident or other, shall discover him. Truth and sincerity have a certain distinguishing native lustre about them which cannot be perfectly counterfeited; they are like fire and flame, that cannot be painted.

> ... I will venture to lay it down for an infallible rule, that if two persons equal in judgment play (checkers) for a considerable sum, he that loves money most shall lose; his anxiety for the success of the game confounds him. Courage is almost as requisite for the good conduct of this game as in a real battle; for if the player imagines himself opposed by one that is much his superior in skill, his mind is so intent on the defensive part that an advantage passes unobserved.

> ... I have sometimes observed that we are apt to fancy the person that cannot speak intelligibly to us, proportionately stupid in understanding, and when we speak two or three words of English to a foreigner, it is louder than ordinary, as if we thought him deaf and that he had lost the use of his ears as well as his tongue.

The twenty year old obviously was thinking and keeping his eyes open wide. Everything went into the journal in lavish detail. There was plenty of time. When he became interested in something, the curious habits of dolphins for instance, a light didn't flash on demanding that seatbelts be fastened preparatory to landing.

There are dozens of instances through the journal that the appetite of the young man for natural data and technical knowledge was insatiable. All the sea creatures that came close enough to observe were diligently studied and notes were made. He corrected a misconception, fostered by painters, that dolphins were crooked and deformed. Obviously the painters had not seen what was "in reality as beautiful as any fish that swims."

To cool off on calm days, Franklin would dive into the Atlantic and apply various strokes of Thevenot's or his own devising as he swam about the ship. One such swim was prevented by a shark moving "around the ship at some distance, in a slow, majestic manner." The shark was accompanied by a retinue of pilot fish. "Two of these diminutive pilots keep just before his nose, and he seems to govern himself in his motions by their direction."

More amiable and just as interesting as the shark was gulfweed.

> *Wednesday, September* 28: . . . the wind is come about westerly again, but we must bear it with patience. This afternoon we took up several branches of gulf-weed (with which the sea is spread all over, from the Western Isles to the coast of America); but one of these branches had something peculiar in it. In common with the rest, it had a leaf about three quarters of an inch long, indented like a saw, and a small yellow berry filled with nothing but wind; besides which it bore a fruit of the animal kind, very surprising to see . . . upon this one branch of the weed there were near forty of these vegetable animals; the smallest of them, near the end, containing a substance somewhat like an oyster, but the larger were visibly animated, opening their shells every moment, and thrusting out a set of unformed claws, not unlike those of a crab; but the inner part was still a kind of soft jelly. Observing the weed more narrowly, I spied a very small crab crawling among it, about as big as the head of a ten-penny nail, and of a yellowish colour, like the weed itself. This gave me some reason to think that he was a native of the branch; that he had not long since been in the same condition with the rest of those little embryos that appeared in the shells, this being the method of their generation; and that, consequently, all the rest of this odd kind of fruit might be crabs in due time. To strengthen my conjecture I have resolved to keep the weed in salt water, renewing it every day till we come on shore, by this experiment to see whether any more crabs will be produced or not in this manner.

Silkworms, butterflies, and other insects underwent startling metamorphoses in the course of their development. Why not tiny crabs living parasitically on seaweed. The following day, the weed was beginning to wither, and most of the embryos were dead; but there was one tiny new crab, convincing Franklin his theory was correct. But he kept checking. Truth was shy and needed careful coaxing.

There was sufficient time for natural phenomena, and he didn't waste it. On Friday, the 30th of September, Franklin went sleepless in order to watch an eclipse of the moon. It was too grand an event to miss for a little sleep.

> I sat up last night to observe an eclipse of the moon, which the calendar calculated for London informed us would happen at five o'clock in the morning, September 30. It began with us about eleven last night, and continued till near two this morning, darkening her body about six digits, or one half; the middle of it being about half an hour after twelve, by which we may discover that we are in a meridian of about

four hours and half from London, or 67½ degrees of longitude, and consequently have not much above one hundred leagues to run. . . We have had abundance of dolphins about us these three or four days; but we have not taken any more than one, they being shy of the bait. I took in some more gulf-weed to-day with the boat-hook, with shells upon it like that before mentioned, and three living perfect crabs, each less than the nail of my little finger. One of them had something particularly observable, to wit, a thin piece of the white shell which I before noticed as their covering while they remained in the condition of embryos, sticking close to his natural shell upon his back. This sufficiently confirms me in my opinion of the manner of their generation. I have put this remarkable crab with a piece of the gulf-weed, shells, &c., into a glass phial filled with salt water, (for want of spirits of wine) in hopes to preserve the curiosity till I come on shore. The wind is South-West.

Reading the journal of that voyage now, it is impossible not to be struck by the careful reasoning, the caution, the boundless curiosity of Franklin's approach to the natural world. He wanted to know whatever was around him to know, not superficially but in the finest detail. It was a catholic curiosity, ranging from the tiny creatures on weeds of the ocean to solar events. *His approach, even then, was conspicuously scientific. Prove all things. Deduce from the evidence. Attempt reasonable conclusions. Verify the conclusions.*

And being Benjamin Franklin, he also found time to learn about his twenty-one fellow passengers and to make friends with many. Into the journal went memorable details: "This morning our steward was brought to the gears and whipped, for making an extravagant use of flour in the puddings, and for several other misdemeanors."

One of the passengers was found guilty of cheating at cards. His punishment, determined by the other passengers, was to be displayed to the ship's company for three hours and to be fined two bottles of brandy. Until the man agreed to pay the fine, he was ostracized by the others. But when he gave in, he was reaccepted into the society of the ship. In this incident, Franklin immediately saw a lesson.

Man is a sociable being, and it is, for aught I know, one of the worst of punishments to be excluded from society. I have read abundance of fine things on the subject of solitude, and I know 'tis a common boast in the mouths of those that affect to be thought wise, that they are never less alone than when alone. I acknowledge solitude an agreeable refreshment to a busy mind; but were these thinking people obliged to be always alone, I am apt to think they would quickly find their very being insupportable. . . I think it was Plato, used to say that he had rather be the veriest stupid block in nature than the possessor of all knowledge without some intelligent being to communicate it to.

His journal of the voyage was not the work of a shallow man or a trifler. Reading, observing nature, conversing and gaming with the others occupied his hours; but he must have given considerable time each day to the journal. In the *Autobiography* he mentioned another matter that concerned him during the summer, and that too was put down.

For the incidents of the voyage, I refer you to my journal, where you will find them all minutely related. Perhaps the most important part of that journal is the *Plan* to be found in it which I formed at sea, for regulating my future conduct in life. It is the more remarkable, as being form'd when I was so young, and yet being pretty faithfully adhered to quite thro' to old age.

There is a strong suggestion in this that Benjamin Franklin during the voyage had made a separate voyage of discovery through himself, what is called soul-searching, and had decided that the future would be better than the past, what is called turning-over-a-new-leaf. Considering what he would accomplish during the decades after landing at Philadelphia, his planning must have been thorough and to the point. Something, at any rate, worked.

The landing came at 10 P.M. on October 11th. A Philadelphia pleasure boat took Franklin and three other passengers, the rest having gone ashore at Chester, Pennsylvania, from the *Berkshire* which had been stilled by a failing wind off Redbank. It ended with the voyagers "heartily congratulating each other upon our having happily completed so tedious and dangerous a voyage. Thank God!"

FINE PRINTING TO ORDER

The new life initially had its troubles. Philadelphia was not as he had left it. He found, as he wrote, "sundry alterations." One of them was especially unpleasant and distressing. Deborah Read, at the urging of family and friends and in the absence of assurances from Franklin, had married a potter named Rogers.

With him however she was never happy, and soon parted from him, refusing to cohabit with him, or bear his name it being now said that he had another wife. He was a worthless fellow tho' an excellent workman which was the temptation to her friends. He got into debt, and ran away in 1727 or 28. Went to the West Indies, and died there.

So much for "one Rogers, a potter." There was other trouble for Franklin and soon. He went to work in Mr. Denham's store as pre-arranged, but in the second month of 1727, both Franklin and Denham became seriously ill. It was pleurisy in Franklin's case, and he nearly died. His friend and patron Denham did succumb to his disease. When he had finally recovered, Franklin ended his merchant career and returned to his first profession, printing. Keimer gave him the management of his print shop, which was badly run and in a state of great confusion. The job called for Franklin to train beginners and to put a backward "Printing House in Order." This he did cheerfully, applying his do-it-yourself ingenuity in the process.

> Our printing-house often wanted sorts (individual letter fonts of type), and there was no letter founder in America. I had seen types cast at James's in London, but without much attention to the manner: however I now contriv'd a mold, made use of the letters we had, as puncheons, struck the matrices in lead, and thus supply'd in a pretty tolerable way all deficiencies. I also engrav'd several things on occasion. I made the ink, I was warehouseman, and everything, in short quite a factotum.

He was not pleased to leave the respectability of merchantdom to work again for the irresponsible Keimer, but circumstances made that practical. So he did his best in compliance with four resolutions, perhaps established in harmony with the Plan he had made at sea aboard the *Berkshire*.

"I have never fixed a regular design as to life," he wrote, "by which means it has been a confused variety of different scenes. I am now entering upon a new one; let me therefore make some resolutions, and form some scheme of action, that henceforth I may live in all respects like a rational creature."

1. Economy: It is necessary for me to be extremely frugal for some time, till I have paid what I owe.
2. Perseverance: To apply myself industriously to whatever business I take in hand, and not to divert my mind from my business by any foolish project of growing suddenly rich; for industry and patience are the surest means of plenty.
3. Goodwill: I resolve to speak ill of no man whatever not even in a matter of truth, but rather by some means excuse the faults I hear charged upon others, and, upon proper occasions, speak all the good I know of everybody.

4. Loyalty: To endeavor to speak truth in every instance: to give nobody expectations that are not likely to be answered, but aim at sincerity in every word and action; the most amiable excellence in a rational being.

The same as most touchstones for living, these were imperfectly executed, but they were sincerely meant. During this period of his early twenties, Franklin was reassessing some of his youthful views and changing them when they couldn't stand up to the tests which travel, sickness, study, and growth had suggested to him. His freethinking deism, for instance, which had allowed if not encouraged cruelty to Deborah Read, his brother James, and others, no longer suited him.

> Revelation had indeed no weight with me, as such; but I entertained an opinion that, though certain actions might not be bad because they were forbidden by it, or good because it commanded them, yet probably these actions might be forbidden because they were bad for us, or commanded because they were beneficial to us.

In 1728 he was thinking of such matters. That year he wrote the principles of his faith in the "Articles of Belief and Acts of Religion" paper. He kept the paper with him, and a copy was found in his pocket when he died. The Articles established his personal commitment to the "one supreme, most perfect Being, Author and Father of the Gods themselves." The document impaled the sort of revelry he had enjoyed in London (and would again) as pleasure that was not innocent and thus to be avoided. The document was also used by Franklin to drop all pretext of taking public worship services seriously. He held to the deist position of aloofness from religious cliques and sects, with their narrow tendency to preach churchgoing rather than humanity. Observing the natural universe as a revealed proof of the great Author, he made certain assumptions concerning the Author's attitude:

> I conceive for many Reasons, that he is a *good Being*; and as I should be happy to have so wise, good, and powerful a Being my Friend, let me consider in what manner I shall make myself most acceptable to him.

> Next to the praise due, to his Wisdom, I believe he is pleased and delights in the Happiness of those he has created; and since without Virtue Man can have no Happiness in this world, I firmly believe he delights to see me Virtuous, because he is pleas'd when he sees me Happy.

And since he has created many Things, which seem purely design'd for the Delight of Man, I believe he is not offended, when he sees his Children solace themselves in any manner of pleasant exercises and Innocent Delights; and I think no Pleasure innocent, that is to Man hurtful.

These were demanding precepts inasmuch as Philadelphia girls had not in a spirit of cooperation with his conversion and vows seen fit to stop being attractive. Furthermore, practical Franklin himself for all his new interest in behaving virtuously and soberly, even to the point of writing a personal if not quite sober epitaph, had not ceased to be attractive to women. But of course virtue would have less moral value if it were easy.

The following epitaph was written by Dr. Franklin for himself, when he was only *twenty three years of age,* as appears by the original (with various corrections) found among his papers, and from which this is a faithful copy.

[*Epitaph written* 1728.]

The Body

of

BENJAMIN FRANKLIN,

Printer,

(Like the cover of an old book,

Its contents torn out,

And stript of its lettering and gilding)

Lies here, food for worms.

But the work shall not be lost,

For it will (as he believed) appear once more,

In a new, and more elegant edition,

Revised and corrected

by

THE AUTHOR.

———

END OF MEMOIRS.

———

Benjamin Franklin's Epitaph reproduced from the authorized edition of the "Memoirs of the Life and Writings of Benjamin Franklin," William Temple Franklin Edition, Printed by T. S. Manning, Philadelphia, 1818.

They were extremely active and productive years for Benjamin Franklin as we shall see later in his founding of the Junto, important in the history of American science, as well as founding the Philadelphia Library, and other civic betterment projects. Such activities in time would establish Franklin as the leading citizen of Philadelphia. Some might try hard to win the title, but Franklin kept it by trying harder still.

His personal qualities made him popular and admired wherever he went. This was proved among strangers when he accompanied Keimer to Burlington, New Jersey where Franklin built the first copperplate press in America for the purpose of printing paper currency to replace earlier New Jersey money that had been too easy to counterfeit. Printing from copper plates is still a preferred method for truly fine printing, just as it was in Benjamin Franklin's day. At Burlington, Franklin was sought after by members of the currency committee and other friends he quickly made. Keimer, on the other hand, was not entertained much at all, probably because he was not entertaining. "My mind having been much more improv'd by reading than Keimer's, I suppose it was for that reason my conversation seem'd to be more valu'd," wrote Franklin in the *Autobiography*.

Even while the Burlington job was being done, Franklin and another Keimer employee, *Hugh Meredith*, whom he had trained, befriended, and had prevailed on "to abstain long from dramdrinking," were secretly waiting for the arrival of printing equipment and types from England. *Simon Meredith*, Hugh's father, impressed with Franklin's ability, had agreed to finance the two young men in their own business. The Merediths supplied the capital, and Franklin put up his skill for an equal share of stock and profits. It was just the sort of opportunity he had hoped would come along, the chance to work in his own place, using *all* his skills and powers of invention to some greater purpose than keeping Keimer from failure.

The big event came early in 1728. With the dramatic significance of starting his own business, his other concerns, religious and moral, begin to seem motivated in part by a determined effort to be successful. Franklin knew his abilities, and he wanted to use them. He didn't want to be distracted or encumbered by wasteful activities. For himself he was convinced finally that immorality in its various guises was among the most impractical of human enterprises. A prudent elderly hand scratched through these words in the manuscript of the *Autobiography*, but a younger man obviously had lived them sufficiently to suspect their truth: " ... some foolish intrigues with low women excepted, which from the expense were rather more prejudicial to me than to them."

Benjamin Franklin would never fully manage to abandon intrigues of many types and with many types, but assuming the duties of his own business and with ever widening prospects, he had to set aside the idea that there was no such thing as right or wrong, and that everything was permitted. Even if true, the doctrine was not very useful; and it could be harmful.

It wasn't long after Franklin's return to Philadelphia following the currency project in Burlington that the expected printing equipment arrived from London. They settled matters with Keimer, rented a house (today the site is 139 Market Street) for *"The New Printing-Office,"* and arranged to share the space and the rent with *Thomas Godfrey* and his family. Godfrey was a glazier by profession and one of America's first scientists by inclination. He had taught himself mathematics and astronomy and was noted for an intuitive brilliance in scientific matters. He was, in fact, inclined to neglect business for the sake of mathematics. " He knew little out of his way," wrote Franklin, "and was not a pleasing companion, as like most great mathematicians I have met with, he expected unusual precision in everything said, or was forever denying or distinguishing upon trifles, to the disturbance of all conversation."

When Mrs. Godfrey unsuccessfully tried matchmaking with Franklin as the target, they had a disagreement which led to the departure of the Godfreys and Franklin living, more contentedly, in the house alone. That development brought new thoughts, however, that did not leave the house a lonely one for very long. But first there was the shop to open and to make succeed.

> We had scarce opened our letters and put our press in order, before George House, an acquaintance of mine, brought a countryman to us; whom he had met in the street enquiring for a printer. All our cash was now expended in the variety of particulars we had been obliged to procure and this countryman's five shillings being our first fruits, and coming so seasonably, gave me more pleasure than any crown I have since earn'd.

He had his business at last and promptly began giving it virtually all his energy. The partnership with Meredith was dissolved on July 14, 1730. Simon Meredith had eventually been unable to provide all the funds required for the new business and to meet the demands of a particularly insistent creditor. The younger Meredith, who had resumed drinking, then decided that as a farmer he should never have left the country for Philadelphia and the hazards of a difficult new business. He made Franklin an offer, the entire business if his father was repaid the first hundred pounds he advanced, payment of Meredith's personal debts, plus thirty pounds and a new saddle. Franklin agreed, obtaining the necessary financial backing in the venture equally from two other friends who had volunteered separately to help.

Perhaps Meredith found the saddle to his liking. He moved to Carolina and from there sent Franklin the sort of letters he delighted to receive, a detailed account of the "country, the climate, soil, husbandry, &c." The reform was not permanent. Later Meredith returned to Philadelphia where he depended on and received Franklin's frequent assistance.

THE PRINTER TAKES A WIFE

With the business entirely his and with many debts to pay, Franklin worked harder than ever.

> In order to secure my credit and character as a tradesman, I took care not only to be in *reality* industrious and frugal, but to avoid all *appearances* of the contrary. I dressed plainly; I was seen at no places of idle diversion; I never went out a-fishing or shooting; a book, indeed, sometimes debauch'd me from my work; but that was seldom, snug, and gave no scandal: and to show that I was not above my business, I sometimes brought home the paper I purchas'd at the stores, thro' the streets on a wheelbarrow.

Finally it was 1730. He was making some progress and managing to see above the weeds of debt. Progress was also evident in Philadelphia. Houses that had been empty when he arrived were inhabited, and new houses were going up in open spaces. With more people and more business, in July of 1730, he opened a stationer's shop. He hired the son of Aquila Rose as an apprentice, and *Thomas Whitmarsh*, a compositor from England, joined him briefly as a journeyman printer. In 1732, using equipment supplied by Franklin, Whitmarsh became the founder of *The South-Carolina Gazette* in Charleston.

On September 1, 1730, an event of personal significance occurred. Benjamin Franklin described the event and those preceding it with his customary felicity and succinctness:

A friendly correspondence as neighbors and old acquaintances, had continued between me and Mrs. Read's family, who all had a regard for me from the time of my first lodging in their house. I was often invited there and consulted in their affairs, wherein I sometimes was of service. I pity'd poor Miss Read's unfortunate situation, who was generally dejected, seldom cheerful, and avoided company. I consider'd my giddiness and inconstancy when in London as in a great degree the cause of her unhappiness; tho' the mother was good enough to think the fault more her own than mine, as she had prevented our ‚marrying before I went thither, and persuaded the other match in my absence. Our mutual affection was revived, but there were now great objections to our union. . . We ventured however, over all these difficulties, and I took her to wife Sept. 1, 1730. None of the inconveniences happened that we had apprehended, she prov'd a good and faithful helpmate, assisted me much by attending the shop, we throve together, and have ever mutually endeavour'd to make each other happy. Thus I corrected that great *Erratum* as well as I could.

The marriage took place in accordance with the common law, no ceremony having occurred or official record made. That was necessary for safety's sake. *John Rogers*, the man Deborah Read married, had been reported dead, or previously married and with a living wife, but neither possibility was confirmed. If Rogers reappeared, the Franklins with a recorded marriage on the books could be charged with bigamy and given thirty-nine lashes on their bare backs and imprisoned for life.

A common law union was perhaps not entirely discreet by the standards of the time but it was certainly the better part of valor. And the marriage worked splendidly. Franklin enjoyed his wife's cooking, and she gave him two children in addition to his first son, William. Furthermore, she tended the business competently, when Franklin was occupied with experiments, &c.

In connection with William, since the *Autobiography* was written to him, Franklin did not mention in the description of his marriage arrangement with Deborah Read that one of his early gifts to the bride was a child named William, mother unknown to the general public or to subsequent history. Franklin's son was accepted without protest by Deborah Read and raised as one of her own. The boy's unorthodox beginning did not hinder his subsequent development and activities, including the office of assistant to his father in the famous kite experiment. Perhaps the most serious criticism that historians have found to make of William Franklin was that he became a politician—Governor of New Jersey. The identity of William's mother is still a matter of historical guesswork. One recurrent guess is that Deborah was his natural mother and that the child hastened her common law marriage with the father. Or equally possible, Deborah's own complicated marital situation may have made her tolerant of a new husband's suddenly manifest and highly tangible past.

Whatever the truth, the matter caused no scandal for the Franklins. They were superior to it. They took no time to feed or hear the petty mischief of gossip. Instead they went blithely about their business, and Philadelphia proved big enough for the Franklins, ignoring what mattered very little in the light of what mattered enormously.

With a business growing into health and with the biological amenities of life suitably and affectionately resolved, Franklin increasingly could focus his attention on the natural universe and the larger needs of society. As Carl Van Doren put it, "The most unreasonable of Franklin's impulses had now been quieted by this most reasonable of marriages, and he was free to turn his whole mind and will to work."

John T. Morse, Jr., a nineteenth century biographer, summarized: "At the time of his marriage . . . he is upon the verge of development; a new period of his life is about to begin; what had been dangerous and evil in his ways disappears; the breadth, originality, and practical character of his mind are about to show themselves. He has settled to a steady occupation; he is industrious and thrifty; he has gathered much information, and may be regarded as a well-educated man; he writes a plain, forcible style; he has enterprise and shrewdness in matters of business, and good sense in all matters—that is the chief point, his sound sense has got its full growth and vigor, and of sound sense no man ever had more."

On January 6, 1731 (old style), by the calendar of the time, Benjamin Franklin was twenty-five. If he bothered that day with a personal summing up, he could have been pleased with carrying out a remarkable program since arriving back in Philadelphia at the age of twenty.

He had built a business that showed promise of expanding without devouring every minute of his time as it had earlier done. He had abandoned, or at least moderated profligacy. Taken a wife. Begun successfully running a newspaper, *The Pennsylvania Gazette* (on October 3, 1729), after Keimer failed with it. He had founded the Junto and seen to its success. Had made himself one of the most effective writers in America. Later that year he would implement an idea already taking shape, a library for Philadelphia. The following year he would print and distribute the first in a long series of *Poor Richard's Almanacks*. Further he had kept up his studies and had begun correspondence on a variety of subjects. They would be increasingly scientific.

The year before he had become the official printer for the state of Pennsylvania using the simple competitive measure of reprinting an address by the Governor and distributing it free to the members of the Assembly who had the address already from the then official printer, Andrew Bradford. Franklin's superior quality won him the assignment in 1730.

He had already made his plans to become one of the leading book publishers in the Colonies. Ahead for the Franklin press were such milestones as one of the first classics, M. T. Cicero's *Cato Major or His Discourse of Old-Age*, translated and published by Americans, James Logan and Benjamin Franklin respectively. That would appear in 1744, be considered an excellent example of printing and bookmaking, and in time become a valuable collector's item.

That same year Franklin would publish the first novel, *Samuel Richardson's Pamela*, to appear in America with an American imprint. In addition, a wide range of other works, theological, political, social, would emerge from Franklin's shop. He had the equipment, the intelligence, and the will to be much more than a printer. He could become the first disseminator of knowledge, art, and culture throughout the Colonies. He was ready to try. Further details of these matters and the results of his efforts will appear subsequently.

Knowing what had already been done, Franklin in 1731 would have had strong feelings about what could be done and what lay ahead. He was always a realist and within the natural framework of his realism, customarily an optimist. He believed instinctively that the universe, and his own position in it, were designed to turn out well. He wasn't a *Samuel Mickle*.

There are croakers in every country always boding its ruin. Such a one then lived in Philadelphia, a person of note, an elderly man, with a wise look, and a very grave manner of speaking. His name was Samuel Mickle. This gentleman, a stranger to me, stopped one day at my door, and asked me if I was the young man who had lately opened a new printing house: being answer'd in the affirmative; he said he was sorry for me, because it was an expensive undertaking and the expense would be lost; for Philadelphia was a sinking place . . . and he gave me such a detail of misfortunes, now existing or that were soon to exist, that he left me half-melancholy.

Samuel Mickle, certain Philadelphia was going bankrupt, delayed buying a house he wanted while he waited for the crash, and eventually Franklin could record that Mickle had bought the house at last, paying five times what he would have paid when "he first began his croaking."

An optimistic summing up at the start of 1731 would have been appropriate. The years 1730-31 seem historically to mark a sort of demarcation between Franklin the striver, of the first quarter century, and Franklin the successful man of many affairs. After 1731 there was never any doubt about his importance in America and his growing importance in the world.

Part of the summing up inevitably would cover the unique experiments in personal morality that he had undertaken quite methodically during the last phase of his "reform" period. "It was about this time," he wrote, "that I conceiv'd the bold and arduous project of arriving at moral perfection."

SCIENTIFIC VIRTUE

Like the little girl with the curl in the middle of her forehead, Franklin didn't simply want to be good, he wanted to be very, very good. He wanted in fact to "live without committing any fault at any time."

At first he ran into the same quicksands that have swallowed others who aspired to do only right, while avoiding all wrong. When he was taking care of one fault, another was hurrying to the back and stealthily crawling through the window.

Unlike most others, he didn't simply forget about it and hope that competing faults would considerately cancel each other out. He attacked the challenge of virtue with the zeal and methods of science. He contrived a Method—a scientific method of virtue. First he listed the virtues, thirteen of them, and a brief definition or statement of intent.

The objective was to make a habit of each virtue. And since it was obviously naive and futile to try mastering all at once, he would take them up one at a time in the order established after careful reflection. Next was needed some way of grading his progress.

These names of *virtues,* with their precepts, were;

1. TEMPERANCE.—Eat not to dulness: drink not to elevation.

2. SILENCE.—Speak not but what may benefit others or yourself: avoid trifling conversation.

3. ORDER.—Let all your things have their places: let each part of your business have its time.

4. RESOLUTION.—Resolve to perform what you ought: perform without fail what you resolve.

5. FRUGALITY.—Make no expense but to do good to others or yourself: i.e. waste nothing.

6. INDUSTRY.—Lose no time: be always employed in something useful: cut off all unnecessary actions.

7. SINCERITY.—Use no hurtful deceit: think innocently and justly: and, if you speak, speak accordingly.

8. JUSTICE.—Wrong none by doing injuries, or omitting the benefits that are your duty.

9. MODERATION.—Avoid extremes: forbear resenting injuries so much as you think they deserve.

10. CLEANLINESS. — Tolerate no uncleanliness in body, clothes, or habitation.

11. TRANQUILLITY.—Be not disturbed at trifles, nor all accidents common or unavoidable.

12. CHASTITY.—Rarely use venery, but for health or offspring; never to dulness or weakness, or the injury of your own or another's peace or reputation.

13. HUMILITY.—Imitate *Jesus* and *Socrates.*

By giving each virtue a week's concentrated attention and doing his utmost to serve it every day, he could make a circuit of the virtues every thirteen weeks, which meant four complete circuits in a year. When a fault occurred in connection with any of the virtuous thirteen, a dot was made under the appropriate day against the transgressed virtue. The goal was to continue making the circuit until, with some consistency, no dots appeared on the weekly record.

There are amazing aspects to this astonishing scheme of virtue, and somehow it appears at once charming, practical, and preposterous. Others before and after Franklin have attempted variations on the theme by actively organizing programs of morality, but Franklin's was uniquely thorough, relentlessly methodical, and

TEMPERANCE.

Eat not to dulness: drink not to elevation.

	Sun.	M.	T.	W.	Th.	F.	S.
Tem.							
Sil.	*	*		*		*	
Ord.	*	*	*		*	*	*
Res.		*			*		
Fru.		*				*	
Ind.			*				
Sinc.							
Jus.							
Mod.							
Clea.							
Tran.							
Chas.							
Hum.							

Reproduced from the first authorized edition of the "Memoirs of the Life and Writings of Benjamin Franklin," 1818.

even *scientific*. If it is possible to make a science out of virtue, Franklin did it; and being Franklin, he made it serve a useful purpose in his own life. For some it has been a temptation to interpret the whole matter as an elderly man's jest for the benefit of suggestible youth. The project of codifying virtue proves a considerable challenge of credibility to the cynical. But it was no jest. Franklin not only took his program seriously, he kept it active for years; and eventually he could report:

> After a while I went thro' one course only in a year, and afterwards only one in several years, till at length I omitted them entirely, being employ'd in voyages and business abroad with a multiplicity of affairs, that interfered, but I always carried my little book with me.

He not only established the system, he carried it out exhaustively, and it worked for him. There was a trio of Franklin astonishments. Add also that the system has been tried with varying degrees of success by many individuals during subsequent generations. Franklin's method did not make virtue triumphant through all the ages of man. He would have been greatly surprised if it had. But it did provide a practical, easy-to-follow technique with which people could give virtue a trial run to see how much it hurts. Or helps.

EDUCATING A PRESIDENT

Since the methodical use of his time was the number one problem for Franklin, he gave "Order" special attention with a twenty-four hour page in his record book. Franklin's orderly use of time scheme has benefitted others in organizing the hours of their days to get the maximum utility from them, *Harry Truman* for one.

In *Merle Miller's* book *Plain Speaking*, Truman is quoted as saying to *Judge Albert A. Ridge*, concerning the *Autobiography*: "Al, you'll find a good deal in there about how to make use of every minute of your day and a lot of horse sense about people."

HOW TO ENJOY LONG LIVES & HEALTHY BODIES
Eat and drink such an exact quantity as the constitution of thy body allows of, in reference to the services of the mind.
They that study much, ought not to eat so much as those that work hard, their digestion being not so good.
The exact quantity and quality, being found out, is to be kept to constantly. Excess in all other things whatever, as well as in meat and drink, is also to be avoided.
Youth, age, and sick, require a different quantity.
And so do those of contrary complexions; for that which is too much for a phlegmatick man, is not sufficient for a cholerick.
The measure of food ought to be (as much as possibly may be) exactly proportionable to the quality and condition of the stomach, because the stomach digests it.
That quantity that is sufficient, the stomach can perfectly concoct and digest, and it sufficeth the due nourishment of the body.
A greater quantity of some things may be eaten than of others, some being of lighter digestion than others.
The difficulty lies, in finding out an exact measure; but eat for necessity, not pleasure, for lust knows not where necessity ends.
Wouldst thou enjoy a long life, a healthy body, and a vigorous mind, and be acquainted also with the wonderful works of God, labour in the first place to bring thy appetite into subjection to reason.

To author Miller, the former President added, "There's always, almost always plenty of time. There are always twenty-four hours in a day if you make use of them. I think I mentioned that that's one of the lessons I learned from reading old Benjamin Franklin's *Autobiography*. He gives you some very good hints on how to make the best use of your time."

Franklin, like Harry Truman and many other busy men, had too many things to do, too many irons in too many fires, *not* to organize his time pretty much as he did, and to make a habit of the scheme. "Tho' I never arrived at the perfection I had been so ambitious of obtaining," he wrote, "but fell far short of it, yet I was by the endeavour a better and a happier man than I otherwise should have been, if I had not attempted it."

At the suggestion of a Quaker friend, what began as a list of twelve virtues was expanded to thirteen with the addition of Humility. The friend "kindly inform'd me that I was generally thought proud." To overcome this fault, Franklin made it a rule never to contradict and instead used diplomatic language, modest phrases, and a consistently tolerant, pacifying manner. This was basically the Socratic method with all the fangs removed. Franklin could never remove wit from his spoken and written discourse, however, and many went away thinking themselves gently treated, but reflecting on Franklin's words, realized that they had been adriotly "gummed" to death. For all his efforts at humility, Franklin learned that fangs were not needed to make an incisive point. But he was sincere in the effort, and it served his purpose.

> I soon found the advantage of this change in my manners. The conversations I engag'd in went on more pleasantly. The modest way in which I propos'd my opinions, procur'd them a readier reception and less contradiction; I had less mortification when I was found to be in the wrong, and I more easily prevail'd with others to give up their mistakes and join with me when I happen'd to be in the right. And this mode, which I at first put on, with some violence to natural inclination, became at length so easy and so habitual to me, that perhaps for these fifty years past no one has ever heard a dogmatical expression escape me.

This was the adult's reemphasis of the identical method espoused by the student Franklin in Boston some eight years earlier. As a boy he had recognized the practicality of establishing a "habit of expressing myself in terms of modest diffidence." By twenty-five it was a fixed mode that would make Franklin one of the most persuasive writers and conversationalists of his century. Jefferson would say that he valued an evening's conversation with Franklin more than the rest of the week in Paris.

The fact that Benjamin Franklin became America's first diplomat and among the most effective in its history was the result of a carefully thought out, personal policy. It was not an accident of temperament and character.

The young businessman with nascent impulses to be much more . . . everything he could be . . . may have convinced himself that he should pursue his chosen virtues for their own sake; but the practical side of his nature wasn't taking a nap. Each of those virtues would help him do more and be more. Each was a practical bit of luggage for a man with a long journey to make. That was why he took the trouble, why he went after them so tenaciously and furiously. They were needed, and Benjamin Franklin knew what he was doing, from virtue one through virtue twelve. As for thirteen. . .

The Quaker may have pinpointed the most elusive of the virtues for Franklin when he suggested Humility. We can't see Franklin clearly through the eyes of his contemporaries when he was in his early twenties. Physically we can see him, a man of middle height, about 5 feet 10 inches, a round face with a high forehead, calm eyes, and a suggestion of humor at the thin lips that seem always on the verge of a large smile. He is thinner than he would be in later years, but already there is an indication of a propensity in the direction of girth. Deborah Franklin's cookstove can be trusted to supply the rotundity needed for a man of renowned sagacity, scientific distinction, and large affairs. But we are not entirely certain about the attitude of his fellow Philadelphians, what they thought about Benjamin Franklin. We can surmise much from the fact that they followed his lead in a number of civic matters. From the surmise, we leap to a conjecture that even his contemporaries realized that Benjamin Franklin at twenty-five was not one of the ordinaries and that he had far less than most men to be modest about. Humility, imitating that of Jesus and Socrates, needed to be on the list, of course; but like Order and Frugality, it was not among the natural virtues for Benjamin Franklin. Silence he could maintain until there was something appropriate to say; but if funds were needed to help a friend or to finance an experiment, then spend today and make it up tomorrow was often his practice rather than his rule. Tranquillity and Moderation were the characteristics from day to day of a philosopher with *faith in tomorrow's sunrise.* But with a multitude of lives to lead, how could a perfect Order be achieved and maintained? Resolution, Industry, Justice were amply on deposit waiting for withdrawals, but Humility? Ah, well. He could manage the appearance of it. The reality was harder to reach.

> In reality there is perhaps no one of our natural passions so hard to subdue as *Pride.* Disguise it, struggle with it, beat it down, stifle it, mortify it as much as one pleases, it is still alive, and will every now and then peep out and show itself. You will see it perhaps often in this history. For even if I could conceive that I had completely overcome it, I should probably be *proud* of my *humility.*

That was Franklin in 1731, with virtue scientifically organized for a practical man to use, with some of the work already begun that would affirm his value to the world, and much more of it ahead than the most deft of crystal balls could anticipate. With the business and bed side of life provided for, he could begin looking around at the world again. Twenty-six years later an artist would be born in London who would write: "If the doors of perception were cleansed everything would appear to man as it is, infinite. For man has closed himself up till he sees all things thro' narrow chinks of his cavern." Franklin was always too large for such cramped confines, whether of work, religion, politics, or science.

Franklin, as he anticipated so many others, was anticipating *William Blake's* "Marriage of Heaven and Hell." His own doors of perception had been kept clear, but he had lacked the leisure to walk through them as far and as often as he wished. That was a condition he had to remedy in the future, and by 1731 he had made a good beginning. The *apprentice* was ready to emerge as the *toolmaker.*

WHERE COMPLAINING IS A CRIME
Grievances cannot be redressed unless they are known; and they cannot be known but through complaints and petitions. If these are deemed affronts, and the messengers punished as offenders, who will henceforth send petitions? And who will deliver them? It has been thought a dangerous thing in any state to stop up the vent of griefs. Wise governments have therefore generally received petitions with some indulgence, even when but slightly founded. Those who think themselves injured by their rulers are sometimes, by a mild and prudent answer, convinced of their error. But where complaining is a crime, hope becomes despair.

(To Thomas Cushing, September 15, 1774)

1976

Dear Doctor Franklin, Sir,

If you give your bifocals a bicentennial workout in our neighborhood, one thing you are certain to notice is how incredibly helpless some of us are.

It astonishes us that you could be a master of so many fields at once. Today a man might be an editor, a publisher, a copywriter, a printer, a pressman, a typographer, a purchasing agent, or *one* of the other functionaries necessary to put out a newspaper. He would be *one* of them, rarely more than one, and virtually never *all* of them. The trade unions, among others, would frown furiously on multiple functions.

You were all of those people, and more. You were everything on your newspaper, including no doubt, from time to time, the deliverer. You were skillful in all these functions without thinking anything special about it. You apparently took it for granted in the eighteenth century that men should be proficient in many arts and skills, from growing food and making soap to writing books and studying the stars.

In your day if something broke down, you fixed it. We call the expert, the specialist, the repairman, and wait, and wait, and wait for his availability and willingness. We don't wait as long for his bill, however, and *it* is normally impressive, just as a dragon or a whale is impressive.

Specialization may be an inevitable result of industrial progress and large populations, but it makes us vulnerable in comparison with you and your friends. Versatile with your mind and your hands, you could reach out and firmly grasp many handles of the world at once.

We can operate a light switch. But fewer and fewer of us can fix the light if it doesn't answer the switch. The expensive and often cranky specialist has to be called. At the same time we lose the satisfaction and freedom of doing for ourselves. Self-reliance was a necessity of life in the Colonies and a stout asset in the war with Britain. Specialization and self-reliance are not comfortable allies.

Sacrificing self-reliance in favor of specialization is a contemporary way of things and fact of life. The sheer complexity of modern living probably makes it inevitable and necessary, but we look back nostalgically and wonder.

We Are, &c.,
YOURS, THE PEOPLE

VII. Gazette Galley Proofs

EDITOR AT THE TYPE CASE OF POWER

Go through Benjamin Franklin's life from beginning to end. Read every letter. Study the *Autobiography*, the *Pennsylvania Gazette* during Franklin's years, the Silence Dogood letters in the *New-England Courant*, the Busy-Body letters in the *American Weekly Mercury*, the thousands of pages of published Franklin writings. Work through the biographies, noting the anecdotes, the ever-repeated, ever-delightful Franklin stories. Follow the young man to London for a swim in the Thames. Follow a middle-aged man to London for a long and futile struggle to prevent a war. Follow an old man to France for the support needed to give a small weed of a nation its chance to sprout into a tree of human liberty. Exhaust the exhausting record. And if anywhere in that record you find a single paragraph, sentence, or footnote indicating that Benjamin Franklin had any ambitions to acquire personal power in order to manipulate and use other men, then go back and check those particular lines again. You have misread them.

Franklin's instincts were those of an educator. He spent his life trying to instruct his fellow man, not for the sake of power but for the sake of reason. He was too interested in acquiring knowledge to think of it as a personal weapon for carving out a Franklin Kingdom in the world. It would have been easy to do, much easier than the solitary business of writing and the frustrations of experimental science. If he had wanted power, he could have taken it. It was lying ready-to-hand, Benjamin Franklin's hand, through the middle years of the eighteenth century. He didn't take it because he didn't want it or need it. Power took too much of a man's time. It insisted on attention. It tyrannized the tyrant as much as his subjects. The power available in the eighteenth century was probably surprised that Benjamin Franklin showed no interest in it. Power was accustomed to being sought, courted, and fought over. But that Franklin fellow was endlessly puttering around with something entirely unrelated. Queer duck!

On May 9, 1731, the queer duck was reading history in his library, and he wrote down a number of "Observations" he could still write in 1976 without changes, including these:

> That few in public affairs act from a mere view of the good of their country, whatever they may pretend; and tho' their actings bring real good to their country, yet men primarily consider'd that their own and their country's interest was united, and did not act from a Principle of Benevolence.
>
> That fewer still in public affairs act with a view to the good of mankind.
>
> There seems to me at present to be great occasion for raising an united Party for Virtue, by forming the virtuous and good men of all nations into a regular body, to be govern'd by suitable good and wise rules.

Queer duck! Not a word about power as we normally think of it. If there is any power involved, it is that inherent in good and wise rules, it is the power of goodness. Was the man daft? Such ideas were alien in a world dedicated to the gospel of "Blessed are the Powerseekers for they shall make the Kingdom their own, a brief while."

Could it have been simply that Franklin, exclusively interested in knowledge, didn't trouble to remember that most men are indifferent and a few are ruthlessly ambitious?

What he was doing was pointing out the possibilities if men would take the small trouble needed to be good and wise. They simply had to wake up, to cease being indifferent. Then something could be done. Wise men and good together then could see to it.

Franklin was indulging in the age old dream of every true scientist. If men could only be reasonable, if they could only be superior to the squalid pettiness, if they could only lift their eyes and their minds from selfish, meager backyard concerns, if they could only join with the virtuous and good men of all nations.

If they could only.

Two hundred and eighteen years later in 1948, Franklin's colleague in science, *Albert Einstein* wrote essentially the identical message:

> We are here to take counsel with each other. We must build spiritual and scientific bridges linking the nations of the world. We must overcome the horrible obstacles of national frontiers... We must revolutionize our thinking, revolutionize our actions, and must have the courage to revolutionize relations among the nations of the world. Clichés of yesterday will no longer do today, and will, no doubt, be hopelessly out of date tomorrow. To bring this home to men all over the world is the most important and most fateful social function intellectuals have ever had to shoulder.

Franklin and Einstein were issuing the same basic plea for the same reasons. Instead of getting on with the beautiful work crying to be done, men foolishly let themselves be drawn into power games that can lead only to regrets, waste, and perhaps despair. "All of us who are concerned for peace and the triumph of reason and justice must today be keenly aware how small an influence reason and honest good-will exert upon events in the political field," wrote Einstein in 1950.

"Reason represents things to us, not only as they are at present, but as they are in their whole nature, and tendency," published Franklin in the *Pennsylvania Gazette*, No. 363, November 20, 1735, "passion only regards them in their former light; when this governs us, we are regardless of the future, and we are only affected with the present."

Two centuries before Einstein and the maniacal antics of the twentieth century, Franklin believed hopefully in the great achievements ahead of man through his scientific discoveries. Even in the twentieth century, his optimism would probably remain intact concerning the contributions of science. He would simply point out much as he did in 1731 that the principle of benevolence has still not been given a place in the affairs of men and that good and wise rules reigning over virtuous and good men represent a development clearly needed more even in the twentieth than in the eighteenth century. He would be disappointed that human nature has not enormously improved, but probably not astonished. Being a practical man, his conclusion would be that there is more work to do. *Get on with it.* Scientific discoveries are a better way to get on than most.

In the *Pennsylvania Gazette*, No. 409, October 14, 1736:

> The world but a few ages since, was in a very poor condition, as to trade and navigation, nor indeed, were they much better in other matters of useful knowledge. It was a green-headed time, every useful improvement was hid from them, they had neither looked into heaven, nor earth, into the sea, nor land, as has been done since. They had philosophy without experiments, mathematics without instruments, geometry without scale, astronomy without demonstration... They went to sea, without compass, and sailed without the needle. They viewed the stars, without telescopes, and measured latitudes without observation. Learning had no printing-press, writing no paper, and paper no ink... They were clothed without manufacture, and their richest robes were the skins of the most formidable monsters; they carried on trade without books, and correspondence without posts; their merchants kept no accounts, their shopkeepers no cash books, they had surgery without anatomy, and physicians without the *materia medica*, they gave emetics without ipecacuanha, drew blisters without cantharides, and cured agues without the bark.

The Publisher of the *Gazette* noted how little had been known concerning the geography of the planet. Men inhabited tiny portions of the surface and knew nothing of the territories or the creatures beyond their own. America was unknown except to the aborigines living there, and the same was true of many other inhabited but isolated portions of the earth. Gad, could it be true, even "Coffee and tea, (those modern blessings of mankind) had never been heard of." The list of the unknown was long and the Publisher did not try to exhaust it. He wanted to reach his conclusion.

> In these narrow circumstances stood the world's knowledge at the beginning of the 15th century, when men of genius began to look abroad, and about them. Now, as it was wonderful to see a world so full of people, and people so capable. of improving, yet so stupid, and so blind, so ignorant, and so perfectly unimproved; it was wonderful to see, with what a general alacrity they took the alarm, almost all together; preparing themselves as it were on a sudden, by a general inspiration, to spread knowledge through the earth, and to search into every thing, that it was impossible* to uncover.

(*The Publisher obviously intended "possible" but was typographically betrayed and frustrated as he could be and probably would be today.) Pages for the *Pennsylvania Gazette* were set letter by letter, word by word, and line by line from a type case. But when there were many lines to set, what wonder if the eyes sometimes became blurred staring at a sheet of handwritten copy and if the fingers plucked too many or the wrong letters from the case. Typos with their lecherous animosity then and now have been occupational offspring of the incredible printing business. William Blake in "A Memorable Fancy" visited Hell and saw how knowledge was transmitted from generation to generation, and lo, there too, the work was done with a "Printing-house." In the case of the Publisher of the *Gazette*, since he was a printer of much experience and with sufficient knowledge of the sorts to make them and of type to arrange them, perhaps his article on "Discoveries" was not written in advance. Reflect and you may see B. Franklin, Publisher, busy at the type case. His fingers move swiftly when an idea comes and the words take shape. The fingers move automatically. They know where to go, having been there thousands of times before. Reflect and you may see the Publisher pause. Yes, the fingers pause as well. Awaiting another signal. Under such circumstances, what wonder if a word is wrong. The thought comes, the signal goes to the fingers, they hurry to the type. The thought changes, but perhaps just for the moment there are too many signals, and the fingers, already busy with the next thought, neglect to make the change. But who can blame them. There they go again, swifter than the pecking heads of birds, diving in and out, composing the thoughts of B. Franklin, Publisher, or borrowing from other men thoughts the Publisher wanted to share with his readers.

> How surprising is it to look back, so little a way behind us, and see, that even in less than two hundred years, all this (now so self-wise) part of the world did not so much as know, whether there was any such place, as a Russia, a China, a Guinea, a Greenland, or a North Cape? That as to America, it was never supposed, there was any such place, neither had the world, though they stood upon the shoulders of four thousand years experience, the least thought, so much as that there was any land that way!

THE "FOOLISHNESS" OF TRUTH

Have we held that he was not interested in power? Consider the busy hands obeying the head to put words in the form. Then the words could be fixed to paper that would last a thousand years or at least until it was used to line the dresser drawers of Philadelphia? Not interested in power, when for years and years drawers might open and show the fading but still legible words of Benjamin Franklin? Not interested in power, yet he started a newspaper and financed others in an era when newspapers were usually the only voices from the outside world able to cry in the wilderness? Not interested in power when his canny Yankee shrewdness must have let him know as early as the Silence Dogood days at the *New-England Courant* that there was no power in the long run greater than the power of the Press? Consider the truth of that power as Benjamin Franklin's busy hands and head finish another article for the *Gazette.*

> As they were ignorant of places, so of things also; so vast are the improvements of science, that all our knowledge of mathematics, of nature, of the brightest part of human wisdom, had their admission among us within these two last centuries.
>
> What was the world then, before? And to what were the heads and hands of mankind applied? The rich had no commerce, the poor no employment; war and the sword was the great field of honor, the stage of preferment, and you have scarce a man eminent in the world, for any thing before that time, but for a furious outrageous falling upon his fellow-creatures, like Nimrod, and his successors of modern memory.
>
> The world is now daily encreasing in experimental knowledge; and let no man flatter the age, with pretending we have arrived to a perfection of discoveries.
>
> *What's now discovered, only serves to show,*
> *That nothing's known to what is yet to know.*

"We're ready to close the page, Ben; your piece is all we need to go to press."

"Then take it, lad, and see you keep the ink strong. If anyone is listening, I want them to hear this. Making a living keeps most men too busy to do anything good or bad that would be interesting on a tombstone. Science could change that. Science may free men to live in ways that give more interesting work to epitaph writers. I think it will in time. I think it will."

"What *is* science, Ben? You keep talking about it. Is science what you're up to when you're forever and always fussing with a rock or a root or a whatchacallit?"

"You mean when I'm trying to unlock nature slightly and remove a tiny fact, what Mrs. Franklin calls 'Foolishness! But don't let me stop you.' That's it, lad, science. Or if you'd like something fancier. Science is reason used to find the truth and make it work for man."

"Is that what this article is about, Ben?"

"This piece, lad, is about the future. Go to press."

In all probability, Franklin himself was part of the press team. After he selected the letters he wanted from the typecase and arranged them on the composing stick, he would lock them in position on his handpress with care and skill. Then Franklin and his printer's devil would take their places as puller and beater. The beater would apply black ink to the type with leather ink pouches. The puller would position the paper above the type, and when all was ready, pull the handle. The words, arranged a letter at a time by the Printer-Publisher or his journeyman, would then appear, firm and sharp, on the paper. The sheet was ready to be set aside and another taken up and another and another. Efficient pullers and beaters were supposed to be able to average about 240 sheets an hour, and Benjamin Franklin was among the best and most efficient in the world, as he had proved during his period of work in the great shops of London. He made himself at home many places and in many professions, but certainly one of his principal homes to the end of his days was a printshop.

Thus on an Autumn day in 1736 the *Gazette* went to press, and Benjamin Franklin once more lectured the citizens of the Colonies. They were reasonably attentive, because his was among the best edited, and unquestionably it was the best written newspaper in America, with the widest range of subjects, anything in fact that interested Benjamin Franklin, which given time enough, meant nearly everything.

He was not interested in power, political or social, as the word is normally meant. Power was a much pettier ambition than knowledge. He was quite aware of the power of the press, and he used it with more skill than anyone before him. But his purpose was educational. The contents of the *Gazette* were proof. He considered his newspaper "another means of communicating instruction, and in that view frequently reprinted in it extracts from the *Spectator* and other moral writers, and sometimes publish'd little pieces of my own."

Those little pieces made various issues of the *Gazette* documents for museums. They served to inform Franklin's contemporaries about the advancements and concerns of the world beyond their local neighborhoods. They prepared men for new knowledge and made them part of the great age of discovery that Franklin believed they had entered at their births and that would go on and on, because nothing could stop the advance of science or man's urge for knowledge. He wanted his newspaper to be a vehicle in the service of that advance, even if sometimes printing the truth landed him in hot water, whether of superstition, political or theological orthodoxies, or the sensitive corns of tradition. He would do his best and trust to the "common virtue and good sense of the people of this and the neighbouring provinces." As for hot water, he was an expert swimmer.

Fairly early in his tenure as Publisher of the *Pennsylvania Gazette*, Franklin printed a "standing apology." It appeared in the issue of June 10, 1731 and contained matter of note for those interested either in keeping the press free or selectively muzzling it for the sake of . . . well, something or other.

> Being frequently censured and condemned by different persons for printing things which they say ought not to be printed, I have sometimes thought it might be necessary to make a standing apology for myself, and publish it once a year, to be read upon all occasions of that nature . . .
>
> I request all who are angry with me on the account of printing things they don't like, calmly to consider these following particulars:
> . . . That the opinions of men are almost as various as their faces: an observation general enough to become a common proverb: *So many men so many minds.*
>
> . . . Printers (Publishers) are educated in the belief that when men differ in opinion both sides ought to have the advantage of being heard by the public; and that when truth and error have fair play, the former is always an over-match for the latter . . .
>
> . . . That if all printers were determined not to print anything till they were sure it would offend nobody, there would be very little printed.
>
> . . . That if they sometimes print vicious or silly things not worth reading, it may not be because they approve such things themselves, but because the people are so viciously and corruptly educated that good things are not encouraged. I have known a very numerous impression of Robin Hood's Songs go off in this province at 2s. per book, in less than a twelvemonth; when a small quantity of David's Psalms (an excellent version) have lain upon my hands above twice the time.

The Publisher went on in this vein at length, obviously having suffered much and given grave thought to the matter. He closed with a parable concerning a well-meaning man, his son, and their ass which they were taking to market. When the man rode alone, other travellers criticized him for making his son walk. When both rode, they were accused of making the poor ass suffer. When both walked, leading the ass, they were ridiculed as fools for walking when they had a healthy beast to ride. "My son," said the man at last, "it grieves me much that we cannot please all these people. Let me throw the ass over the next bridge, and be no further troubled with him."

If that was the man's solution, it was not the solution of the Publisher of the *Pennsylvania Gazette*.

Had the old man been seen acting this last resolution, he would probably have been called a fool for troubling himself about the different opinions of all that were pleased to find fault with him. Therefore, though I have a temper almost as complying as his, I intend not to imitate him in this last particular. I consider the variety of humours among men, and despair of pleasing everybody; yet I shall not therefore leave off printing. I shall continue my business. I shall not burn my press and melt my letters.

EQUATIONS FOR A RATIONAL CREATURE

He would use those letters to instruct his readers concerning the official language of science, as in the *Pennsylvania Gazette*, No. 360, October 30, 1735, "On the Usefulness of the Mathematics."

Mathematics originally signifies any kind of discipline or learning, but now it is taken for that science, which teaches or contemplates whatever is capable of being numbered or measured. That part of the mathematics which relates to numbers only, is called *arithmetic*; and that which is concerned about measure in general, whether length, breadth, motion, force, &c. is called *geometry*.

Arithmetic he labels essential from the merchant to the shopkeeper since "the assistance of numbers" is indispensable to business. Furthermore, it is the *"primum mobile* (or first mover)" for all worldly affairs, touching every man.

As to the usefulness of geometry, it is as certain, that no curious art, or mechanic work, can either be invented, improved, or performed, without its assisting principles. It is owing to this, that astronomers are put into a way of making their observations ... It is by the assistance of this science, that geographers present to our view at once, the magnitude and form of the whole earth, the vast extent of the seas, the divisions of empires, kingdoms, and provinces. It is by help of geometry, the ingenious mariner is instructed how to guide a ship through the vast ocean, from one part of the earth to another, the nearest and safest way, and in the shortest time.

Listening to the enthusiastic Publisher, one begins to wish one had paid greater attention and advanced somewhat further than parallel lines never meeting and the square of the hypotenuse equalling... whatever it is. Then we remember in the *Autobiography* a frank admission was made concerning efforts at the School for Writing and Arithmetic kept by Mr. Geo. Brownell: "I fail'd in the Arithmetic, and made no progress in it." So the Publisher of the treatise on the usefulness of mathematics had his trouble too, and yet in time he would be compared with such scientists as Newton. Listen further.

Mathematical demonstrations, are a logic of as much or more use, than that commonly learned at schools, serving to a just formation of the mind, enlarging its capacity, and strengthening it so, as to render the same capable of exact reasoning, and discerning truth from falsehood in all occurrences, even subjects not mathematical. For which reason it is said, the Egyptians, Persians, and Lacedemonians, seldom elected any new kings, but such as had some knowledge in the mathematics, imagining those who had not, men of imperfect judgments, and unfit to rule and govern.

Here is expert Public Relations for mathematics. *Francis Bacon* tried to help in "Of Studies" but he forced mathematics to compete with other disciplines of the mind. "Histories make men wise; poets, witty; the mathematics, subtile; natural philosophy, deep ... so, if a man's wit be wandering, let him study the mathematics; for in demonstrations, if his wit be called away never so little, he must begin again."

The *Pennsylvania Gazette* does not scatter its shots. When the subject is mathematics, it does not distract from the point with history, poetry, and philosophy. It deals with mathematics. And those with the thought in mind of getting a book somewhere and mastering a few axioms are not likely to be discouraged by the Publisher's praise. Enthusiasm, as Poor Richard probably said, is often contagious.

Though Plato's censure, that those who did not understand the 117th proposition of the 13th book of Euclid's Elements, ought not to be ranked amongst rational creatures, was unreasonable and unjust; yet to give a man the character of universal learning, who is destitute of a competent knowledge in the mathematics, is no less so. . . . Philosophers do generally affirm, that human knowledge to be most excellent, which is conversant amongst the most excellent things. What science then can there be, more noble, more excellent, more useful for men, more admirably high and demonstrative, than this of the mathematics. I shall conclude with what Plato says, *lib.* 7. of his Republic, with regard to the excellence and usefulness of geometry, being to this purpose: "Dear Friend. . . . You see then that mathematics are necessary, because by the exactness of the method, we get a habit of using our minds to the best advantage: and it is remarkable, that all men being capable by nature to reason and understand the sciences; the less acute, by studying this, though useless to them in every other respect, will gain this advantage, that their minds will be improved in reasoning aright; for no study employs it more, nor makes it susceptible of attention so much; and these who we find have a mind worth cultivating, ought to apply themselves to this study.

Franklin had applied himself and whatever his mature regrets concerning the weakness of his mathematics, the evidence from his electrical writings and other scientific papers is that he would have satisfied even Plato's stern Euclidean requirement for acceptance as a rational creature. Franklin was indisputably "rational," and his devotion to mathematics was not simply feigned to produce newspaper copy. Mathematics was the most accurate way of defining order, and exactly three weeks after the mathematics piece, Franklin would tell his readers in the November 20th *Gazette* that "all true happiness, as all that is truly beautiful, can only result from order."

The views he shared in the *Gazette* were typically presented in simple, reasonable words. They echo in the mind, and like a refutation of Euclid, cause parallel lines to meet in the seventeenth and twentieth centuries. *Bertrand Russell* in the twentieth century was struck by the supreme beauty, cold and austere like that of sculpture, that he found in mathematics, which "takes us into the region of absolute necessity, to which not only the actual world, but every possible world, must conform." In the seventeenth century, *Sir Thomas Browne*, born exactly 101 years before Franklin, became in his writing, science, and philosophy a partial Benjamin Franklin. Before the age of thirty, he wrote, "All things begin in order, so shall they end, and so shall they begin again; according to the ordainer of order and mystical mathematics of the city of heaven."

Franklin would have fought the temptation to put it quite so fancifully; yet he probably would have agreed. His newspaper piece about mathematics had been published when he was a few months shy of his thirtieth birthday.

Years later, writing to his close friend, the British scientist Joseph Priestley, Franklin introduced a new kind of "mathematics" which he called *Prudential Algebra*. Priestley wanted Franklin's advice about taking a position he had been offered as a librarian for the *Earl of Shelburne*, and Franklin answered on September 19, 1772:

> Dear Sir: In the affair of so much importance to you wherein you ask my advice, I cannot, for want of sufficient premises, advise you *what* to determine, but if you please I will tell you *how*. When these difficult cases occur, they are difficult chiefly because while we have them under consideration, all the reasons *pro* and *con* are not present in the mind at the same time; but sometimes one set present themselves, and at other times another, the first being out of sight. Hence the various purposes or inclinations that alternately prevail, and the uncertainty that perplexes us. To get over this, my way is to divide half a sheet of paper by a line into two columns; writing over the one *Pro*, and over the other *Con*. Then during three or four days' consideration I put down under the different heads short hints of the different motives that at different times occur to me, *for* or *against* the measure. When I have thus got them all together in one view, I endeavour to estimate their respective weights; and where I find two (one on each side) that seem equal, I strike them both out. If I find a reason *pro* equal to some two reasons *con*, I strike out the three . . . thus proceeding I find at length where the balance lies; and if after a day or two of farther consideration, nothing new that is of importance occurs on either side, I come to a determination accordingly. And though the weight of reasons cannot be taken with the precision of algebraic quantities, yet when each is thus considered separately and comparatively, and the whole lies before me, I think I can judge better, and am less likely to make a rash step; and in fact I have found great advantage from this kind of equation, in what may be called *moral* or *prudential algebra*.

If understanding prudential algebra were a criterion for gauging a rational creature, curiosity rises whether or not Plato would qualify. Franklin's method of reaching a decision is eminently logical and reasonable. It is practical and orderly. And it is exactly the sort of regulating scheme for living that could make a dark romantic such as *D. H. Lawrence* begin slavering at the mention of Franklin. "I am a moral animal," wrote Lawrence, "But I am not a moral machine. I don't work with a little set of handles or levers . . . I'm really not just an automatic piano with a moral Benjamin getting tunes out of me."

Those like Lawrence would have fits rather than practice such methodical exercises as prudential algebra. But Priestley after laughing perhaps at the incredible thoroughness of his friend might very well have done some "Pro"ing and "Con"ing in his mind even if he didn't write it all out. When a really tough decision came along, he probably did write it out, just as Franklin recommended.

Prudential algebra, of course, makes excellent sense. It is a rational aid in decisionmaking. Some may not like doing things in such a calculated way, but it makes good sense. Practically everything Benjamin Franklin bothered to say or write made good sense. He tried hard to make it so, not because he wanted to turn men into moral machines or lock them in neat enclaves of order, but because men had important assignments in the world calling for their maximum, undistracted powers. If rational aids were available, such as basic systems to reduce the dilemmas of decisionmaking, men would be silly and perverse to refuse them.

These were among the messages delivered to Philadelphians and subscribers throughout the Colonies by the *Pennsylvania Gazette*. Naturally, the man who was writing the pieces was also addressing them to himself. He needed the rational aids as much or more than anyone, since he had as many or more tasks to accomplish. The twentieth century commentator *Elmer Davis* wrote during one of the shadowy eras of this century:

> The Scottish scientist J. B. S. Haldane once said that the people who can make a positive contribution to human progress are few; that most of us have to be satisfied with merely staving off the inroads of chaos. That is a hard enough job—especially in these times, when those inroads are more threatening than they have been for a long time past. But if we can stave them off, and keep the field clear for the creative intelligence, we can feel that we have done our part toward helping the human race get ahead.

WALKING ABOUT WHILE YOUR BED COOLS
For when the body is uneasy, the mind will be disturbed by it, and disagreeable ideas of various kinds will in sleep be the natural consequences . . . When you are awakened by this uneasiness, and find you cannot easily sleep again, get out of bed, beat up and turn your pillow, shake the bed-clothes well, with at least twenty shakes, then throw the bed open and leave it to cool; in the meanwhile, continuing undrest, walk about your chamber till your skin has had time to discharge its load . . . Those who do not love trouble, and can afford to have two beds, will find great luxury in rising, when they wake in a hot bed, and going into the cool one.
The Art of Procuring Pleasant Dreams, *Inscribed to Miss Shipley, 1786*

That was exactly what Benjamin Franklin was trying to do with his newspaper, his prudential algebra, etc., keep the field cleared of brambles, weeds, and stones enough to make it through the Winter. That was why he did his pieces on science for the *Gazette*, so the people would know as much as he, and they could all move ahead together. That was why he believed in democracy, for all its faults, and trusted the people, for all their weaknesses. He became, ironically, a great man proclaiming the greatness of all men. To stand tall among giants means more than superior stature among Lilliputians.

E. M. Forster in *Two Cheers for Democracy* praised Franklin without naming him: "The people I admire most are those who are sensitive and want to create something or discover something, and do not see life in terms of power, and such people get more of a chance under a democracy than elsewhere... Democracy has another merit. It allows criticism, and if there is not public criticism there are bound to be hushed-up scandals. That is why I believe in the Press, despite all its lies and vulgarity, and why I believe in Parliament. Parliament is often sneered at because it is a Talking Shop. I believe in it *because* it is a talking shop ... so Two cheers for Democracy: one because it admits variety and two because it permits criticism. Two cheers are quite enough: there is no occasion to give three."

Franklin gave two, three, infinite cheers for democracy, and when it needed criticizing, he kidded its pants off. He used reason, humor, wit, and enthusiasm, plus solid information, to instruct and improve his fellow citizens. He lined up the facts as attractively as he could and let other men convince themselves that Ben Franklin must have something there. It was a benevolent use of *Ignatius Loyola's* technique for maneuvering other men to get where you want to go: "Follow the other person's road to your own destination." In the end the Church served by Loyola decided to call him a Saint. The country served by Benjamin Franklin decided to call him a Founding Father. Some called him the first American. Oth-

FREEDOM OF THE RESPONSIBLE PRESS
The conductor of a newspaper should, methinks, consider himself as in some degree the guardian of his country's reputation, and refuse to insert such writings as may hurt it. If people will print their abuses of one another, let them do it in little pamphlets, and distribute them where they think proper. It is absurd to trouble all the world with them; and unjust to subscribers in distant places, to stuff their paper with matters so unprofitable and disagreeable.
(To Francis Hopkinson, December 24, 1782)

ers such as John Adams and D. H. Lawrence (odd duo) could agree he was a "first" but they weren't so sure what. Franklin would gladly have published all sides in the *Gazette* and let the public decide, trusting to their sense, good will, and collective wisdom, at least that portion of the public reading the *Gazette*. They were among the best informed public in the eighteenth century because the Publisher was interested in knowledge rather than power. Elbert Hubbard, who was interested in power as well as knowledge, wrote of him, "In point of all-round development, Franklin must stand as the foremost American. The one intent of his mind was to purify his own spirit, to develop his intellect on every side, and make his body the servant of his soul. His passion was to acquire knowledge, and the desire of his heart was to communicate it."

"Too long for a tombstone," Franklin would have been likely to say, "too brief for an eulogy, too vague for science, but, Sir, thank you."

In his first issue of the *Pennsylvania Gazette*, October 2, 1729, Benjamin Franklin spoke to his readers and asked their help. It wasn't simply a pro forma request. He meant it. Franklin was one of the first sincere believers in the possibilities of teamwork to get things done. All his efforts to organize scientific clubs and various participatory groups were clearly aimed in that direction. He believed that a group of good men was likely to progress faster and go farther than one man alone. Even if the main work was done by a few, the others were needed to add their approval, spirit of collaboration, and group permission. That was important. If a teacher took the trouble to instruct his neighbors in how to think, he wanted them to use their new skill for the benefit of the public as well as themselves. Cooperative effort, he considered the key to any public enterprise, even though many would be capable of contributing only their numerical presence. "We must hang together," he would say, and finish with a quip on a later cooperative occasion of some importance. Cooperative effort was needed in a revolution if only to put the enemy to the trouble of using more than one rope. Cooperative effort was needed in science because every step needed to be explained and discussed with knowledgeable colleagues. The new "author of a gazette" had such matters in mind when he wrote his first editorial:

There are many who have long desired to see a good newspaper in Pennsylvania; and we hope those gentlemen who are able will contribute towards making this such. We ask assistance, because we are fully sensible that to publish a good newspaper is not so easy an undertaking as many people imagine it to be. The author of a gazette (in the opinion of the learned) ought to be qualified with an extensive acquaintance with languages, a great easiness and command of writing and relating things clearly and intelligibly, and in few words; he should be able to speak of war both by land and sea; be well acquainted with geography, with the history of the time, with the several interests of princes and states, the secrets of courts, and the manners and customs of all nations. Men thus accomplished are very rare in this remote part of the world; and it would be well if the writer of these papers could make up among his friends what is wanting in himself. Upon the whole, we may assure the public that as far as the encouragement we meet with will enable us, no care and pains shall be omitted that may make the *Pennsylvania* Gazette as agreeable and useful an entertainment as the nature of the thing will allow.

Franklin knew something that modern editors on occasion forget, that a newspaper is only as good as its readers. He knew also that culture, knowledge, and progress are almost impossible to impose on a people. They must first want them, and in that can be inspired by a teacher who is also author of a gazette. They must seek them, and accept them. In reaching that point, an agreeable and useful gazette can help to show them the available ways. Franklin would entertain his readers inevitably. Humor followed him like a puppy waiting for permission to bark. But he would also talk to them about a thousand serious subjects, from mathematics to virtue, and then no doubt after brief reflection stand at the type case and compose a piece to the effect that "mathematics is virtue."

One conclusion in retrospect seems clearly dictated by the historical facts: In the archives of American science, issues of the *Pennsylvania Gazette* beginning October 2, 1729 should be present. They shared knowledge, and they helped to foster a spirit of hospitality toward science and invention that never quite left America after finding a haven in the print shop of a gazette's author.

THE GREAT BEGETTER
Remember that money is of the prolific, generating nature. Money can beget money, and its offspring can beget more, and so on. Five shillings turned is six, turned again it is seven and three-pence, and so on till it becomes an hundred pounds. The more there is of it, the more it produces every turning, so that the profits rise quicker and quicker. He that kills a breeding sow destroys all her offspring to the thousandth generation.
(Advice to a Young Tradesman from An Old Tradesman)

1976

Dear Doctor Franklin, Sir,

You'll be interested, of course, in the state of our sciences, what your age called "natural philosophy." Some things may impress you technologically, though many of our marvels you predicted accurately just by squinting a bit at the future.

The shove forward given to science by you and your colleagues in the eighteenth century still has effect. In fact, science has been so successful, sometimes it scares us because it proves just as effective at blowing things up as building them.

That's the dark side, you would insist, and ask for the bright side. There's one of those too. The electricity you studied and expanded into a science has been domesticated and put to work performing hundreds of vital jobs for mankind. Electricity does so many things for us, we take about ninety per cent of them for granted. Seen through your bifocals, perhaps we could learn to appreciate them better.

You were confident science would serve man beneficently. It does. But it has reached the point where misused it could also destroy man. During recent years the world has become so complex and dangerous, at times we lose faith in ourselves, in science, and even in the country you took time to invent along with the Franklin Stove, the glass harmonica, and the lightning rod.

During the bicentennial and later, hopefully you could suggest ways to renew and strengthen lost faith. The right words will come to you. They did during those fateful summers of '76 and '87. Do you still have that rare ability for cutting through falsehoods to the central truth?

A good-humored Franklin truth might show us what we've lost and help us get it back again.

We Are, &c.,

YOURS, THE PEOPLE

VIII. Toolmaker

TWO WAYS OF SCIENCE

Donald Culross Peattie called Franklin our "Ben-of-all-trades" and a multiple genius. Considering Franklin's range of interests you could well call him "America's first conglomerate." These descriptions are apt. He had the gifts and the energy to be many men, and living before our modern age of almost compulsory specialization, he could indulge his impulse to go ahead. That is, if he could find the time.

Franklin worked hard to organize his life, his emotions, and even the individual hours of his day for this purpose. Perhaps when he began his virtue grading system and his "Scheme of Employment for the Twenty-four Hours of a Natural Day," he was not fully aware of all the reasons. He knew only that there was a great deal he could accomplish in twenty-four hours, including study, business, experiments, family, public service, writing, and all the rest; and he was by instinct predisposed to be frugal with time. Josiah Franklin's instructions at Milk Street and later at Union Street in Boston had their permanent consequences. Virtue number 6, Industry, may have been more important to him in practical terms than any of the others. "Lose no time. Be always employ'd in something useful. Cut off all unnecessary actions."

The scope of his accomplishments proves his success in this respect. It was all right with Franklin if others wanted to try his virtue grading system for their own benefit. He made it available to serve those who could use it. But the young man who put the system together was not thinking about its practicality for others. He needed it himself in order to squeeze more lives than one into the available day.

Two of those lives involved science, though Franklin might have resisted the word. One of his scientific directions, he called natural philosophy, the other for want of a better word, toolmaking. Each direction was with him from childhood. He was an observer of the natural world and fascinated by the mysteries there at every turn. What strange impulse in nature operated to persuade a caterpillar to transform itself into a butterfly? The seasons and their regular cycle could be attributed to the sun, but what made the sun so rigidly obedient? The slow fall of soap bubbles? Lightning? All were fascinating and all were mysteries. He wanted to observe them with care and note down everything. Everything! Then perhaps all the notes could be added together and one of nature's secrets be revealed. That would be something to cherish. The migratory instincts of birds, the hibernation customs of many animals, fireflies, the common human cold? Mysteries all, waiting to be observed. That was natural philosophy, noting the infinity of facts in the universe and using them for philosophical conclusions. For instance, was God the sum of all things, did metaphysical mathematics push the facts to that conclusion? It could not be rejected or assumed. In the eighteenth century, a practical man couldn't wait for revelation, he investigated.

The other direction, toolmaking, derived from the fact that the American Colonies, though proud and civilized British communities, were on the edge of a vast wilderness. The edge of every town was a frontier. On a frontier, practical men couldn't devote all their attention to the cold phosphorescence of fireflies. Focus was needed badly on things that would sustain and improve life and hopefully make it easier. Americans might be printers, lawyers, writers, planters, doctors, merchants, etc., but many of them also had to be frontiersmen. British philosophers might offer grand ideas of liberty and the rights of free individuals. It was the job of

American frontiersmen to turn ideas into working realities. There were many ways to be a frontiersman, and only one of them required wearing deerskin garments and shoving off into the wilderness to find the headwaters of a river or found a settlement. Benjamin Franklin's was one of the better ways to be a frontiersman. Go to a small place and invest your labor, intelligence, and enthusiasm in helping it grow. That meant if you had any scientific ability, to observe nature and learn from the process, or if you possessed fertile skills as an inventor, frontier responsibilities required using them as practically as possible. Pure science might be more fun, but the immediate task was taming a wilderness, and breaking it to the saddle.

Franklin's genius lay in both natural philosophy and toolmaking. In some ways his basic science has been taken less seriously than it might have been simply because he was such an effective inventor. Later historians of science, trapped by preconceptions, have had difficulty conceiving that a person might be equally adroit in theoretical science (the so-called pure variety) *and* gadgeteering. Inventions were needed in the American Colonies to solve problems, so Franklin invented. What should he have done, suppressed ideas when they came to him as they did like summer swallows, and stammered aghast that a scientist couldn't diminish himself by inventing? The notion would have amused, as would *Kenneth Clark's* denigration of gifted inventors as not true scientists in his book *Civilisation*:

> Science had achieved great triumphs in the nineteenth century, but nearly all of them had been related to practical or technological advance. For example, Edison, whose inventions did as much as any to add to our material convenience, wasn't what we would call a scientist at all, but a supreme "do-it-yourself" man—the successor of Benjamin Franklin. But from the time of Einstein, Niels Bohr and the Cavendish Laboratory, science no longer existed to serve human needs, but in its own right.

Clark's assessment is historically correct. "Scientist" has not been stamped traditionally on the library or identification cards of inventors. Edison who noted that everything comes to him who hustles while he waits could have cared less. Calling it science or not wouldn't have made the light bulb burn one iota brighter or one day sooner.

Professor Clark should have done a little more research, however, on Benjamin Franklin. He was Edison's predecessor, of course, but he was also Einstein's. He was the exception, the scientist who happened to be an inventor, the inventor who happened to be a scientist. All came from the same busy head that tried to be always employed in something useful.

It is quite true that Ben-of-all-trades was a confirmed and inevitable do-it-yourselfer. When sorts were needed in the printshop, he contrived the molds and produced them. Who else? *Franklin had the realistic suspicion that if he didn't do it himself, it wouldn't be done.* In that he was Josiah Franklin's son and committed to practicality. Yet it would be conspicuously inaccurate to assume that he was not "scientific" because he sought useful applications for his science when they were available. His curiosity was incurably wide-ranging, leaping from the weather to the Gulf Stream to fossils to the solar system to infinity. Not all of what he learned and studied could be made useful and put to work, but when something could, he felt an obligation to bring it about.

His country of frontiers needed all the practical help available. Furthermore, in the pursuit of historical accuracy, it is logical to recall that Franklin lived in a century when modern science was struggling with its diapers. A full-scale assault on the closely guarded secrets of nature was just beginning, with Franklin as one of the conspicuous attackers. The management of the human environment and the command of matter for the benefit of man were ideas taking shape much more than existing realities. Science was on the move in the eighteenth century, but most of the great breakthroughs were still ahead when Franklin began his adult experiments aboard the ship carrying him home from London in 1726 and continued them later in Philadelphia.

Before science could begin achieving rapidly, observers such as Franklin had to lay the groundwork and establish hospitality for the work and speculations of science.

HEAT RIDDLES

There were other experiments, of course, but the first Philadelphia experiment for which records exist was Franklin's effort to settle his curiosity concerning the effect of heat from sunlight on different colored materials. The details are in his September 20, 1761 letter to *Polly Stevenson*, the daughter of his London landlady, who had asked him for the sake of her education to correspond with her exclusively on subjects concerned with natural philosophy. Nothing pleased Doctor Franklin more. He could think on paper concerning his favorite subjects and at the same time help in the cultivation of a young mind. History owes a benediction to Polly Stevenson for addressing a rather strange request to Doctor Franklin. Some of his speculations might otherwise have been lost.

In the 1761 letter, Franklin described an experiment he had conducted, probably about 1729.

> My experiment was this. I took a number of little square pieces of broadcloth from a tailor's pattern card, of various colours. There were black, deep blue, lighter blue, green, purple, red, yellow, white, and other colours, or shades of colours. I laid them all out upon the snow in a bright sunshiny morning. In a few hours (I cannot now be exact as to the time) the black, being warmed most by the sun, was sunk so low as to be below the stroke of the sun's rays; the dark blue almost as low, the lighter blue not quite as much as the dark, the other colours less as they were lighter; and the quite white remained on the surface of the snow, not having entered it at all.

It was a simple experiment, but cleverly devised, and carried out with empirical care. The point was made that the sunlight penetrated heavily colored materials more intensely than the others. Franklin wasn't content to stop there. What he had learned was interesting, could it be used?

> What signifies philosophy that does not apply to some use? May we not learn from hence that black clothes are not so fit to wear in a hot sunny climate or season as white ones; because in such clothes the body is more heated by the sun when we walk abroad and are at the same time heated by the exercise, which double heat is apt to bring on putrid dangerous fevers? That soldiers and seamen, who must march and labour in the sun, should in the East or West Indies have an uniform of white? That summer hats, for men or women, should be white, as repelling that heat which gives headaches to many, and to some the fatal stroke that the French call the *coup de soleil?* ... That fruit-walls, being blacked, may receive so much heat from the sun in the daytime as to continue warm in some degree through the night, and thereby preserve the fruit from frosts or forward its growth?—with sundry other particulars of less or greater importance that will occur from time to time to attentive minds?

In another letter to Polly Stevenson, Franklin answered her questions about insects, pointing out amid a flood of data that "superficial minds are apt to despise those who make that part of the creation their study, as mere triflers; but certainly the world has been much obliged to them." The good Doctor ranged from silkworms to honeybees and even wickedly inserted a veiled technical reference that a sheltered English girl of the eighteenth century may not have understood, but probably did: "The usefulness of the cantharides, or Spanish flies, in medicine is known to all, and thousands owe their lives to that knowledge." His conclusion to Polly Stevenson sounds almost prophetic of Walter Reed and the battle against yellowjack as well as dozens of other skirmishes in the unending war between certain insects and man: "A thorough acquaintance with the nature of these little creatures may also enable mankind to prevent the increase of such as are noxious, or secure us against the mischiefs they occasion."

The practical wisdom of his speculations about insects and his experiment with sunlight and colors anticipated later science by many decades. The leap from the experimental and theoretical to the practical was characteristic of Franklin's approach to science. He delighted in the "impractical" stages. There was the pleasure of *pursuing truth for its own sake.* But duty obligated later stages whenever possible. "What signifies philosophy. . ."

In 1758, during his first mission to England as the agent of the Pennsylvania Assembly, Franklin the public man struggled to obtain colonial rights from a sluggish Crown and a constipated Parliament, but in May of that year, Franklin the scientist went to Cambridge University for a rare period of fun, working with Professor of Chemistry *John Hadley* on the phenomenon of evaporation. The research was basic. Experimenting with ether, they recorded temperatures of twenty-five degrees below freezing through evaporation. Covering a mercury thermometer with a cloth soaked in alcohol and swinging the thermometer in air to induce evaporation caused the temperature to drop to zero. Franklin tried and achieved the -25° temperature. The two men were then in a position to begin reaching fundamental conclusions about the phenomenon of heat in liquid evaporation. It was basic science. And it was one case in many of Franklin sharing with a fellow scientist as well as the other way around. The previous year one of his correspondents, *Professor Simpson* of Glasgow, had reported "the curious experiments of a physician of his acquaintance" who had induced lower temperatures in a thermometer by dipping it in wine and accelerating evaporation. Doctor Franklin happened to have wine available, and he had immediately experimented with the phenomenon, reporting on it at length to *Doctor Lining* in South Carolina, in his letter of April 14, 1757. After instigating the interlude of pure science with Professor Hadley, Franklin reported again to Doctor Lining on June 17, 1758, and quickly began making leaps from observed phenomena to practical possibilities.

The wetting was then repeated by a feather that had been dipped into ether, when the mercury sunk still lower. We continued this operation, one of us wetting the ball, and another of the company blowing on it with the bellows, to quicken the evaporation, the mercury sinking all the time... The ice continued increasing till we ended the experiment, when it appeared near a quarter of an inch thick all over the ball, with a number of small spicula, pointing outwards. From this experiment one may see the possibility of freezing a man to death on a warm summer's day, if he were to stand in a passage through which the wind blew briskly, and to be wet frequently with ether, a spirit that is more inflammable than brandy or common spirits of wine. It is but within these few years, that the European philosophers seem to have known this power in nature, of cooling bodies by evaporation. But in the east they have long been acquainted with it. A friend tells me, there is a passage in Bernier's Travels through Hindustan, written near one hundred years ago, that mentions it as a practice (in travelling over dry deserts in that hot climate) to carry water in flasks wrapped in wet woolen cloths, and hung on the shady side of the camel, or carriage, but in the free air; whereby as the cloths gradually grow drier, the water contained in the flasks is made cool.

Questions began pouring from Doctor Franklin's pen. Didn't perspiration when evaporated from the surface of the skin cool the body and thus make it possible to work under the hot sun? Were Negroes better able to bear the sun's heat than whites because of "a quicker evaporation of the perspirable matter from their skins and lungs?" "Would not the earth grow much hotter under the summer-sun if a constant evaporation from its surface, greater as the sun shines stronger, did not, by tending to cool it, balance, in some degree the warmer effects of the sun's rays?" "Is it not owing to the constant evaporation from the surface of every leaf, that trees, though shone on by the sun, are always, even the leaves themselves, cool to our sense?" He reflected on the accelerated evaporation that produced cooling when we fan ourselves. And he even paused to remember a hot Philadelphia Sunday in June, 1750 when human blood must have been close to the boiling point without nature's therapy of evaporation:

... when the thermometer was up at 100 in the shade, I sat in my chamber without exercise, only reading or writing, with no other clothes on than a shirt, and a pair of long linen drawers, the windows all open, and a brisk wind blowing through the house, the sweat ran off the backs of my hands, and my shirt was often so wet, as to induce

me to call for dry ones to put on; in this situation, one might have expected that the natural heat of the body 96, added to the heat of the
air 100, should jointly have created or produced a much greater degree
of heat in the body; but the fact was, that my body never grew so hot
as the air that surrounded it, or the inanimate bodies immersed in the
same air. For I remember well, that the desk, when I laid my arm
upon it; a chair, when I sat down in it; and a dry shirt out of the
drawer, when I put it on, all felt exceeding warm to me.

He went on in this vein, testifying to the absorption of heat in
the process of evaporation and trying to draw forth all the ramifi-
cations, item by item, as if pulling on an invisible line to ease
another ship of knowledge into port. Doctor Franklin continued
on and on, walking around and around the subject, pecking at it,
sniffing at it, squinting at it close and farther away, drawing analogies, speculating, and thinking constantly, observing constantly,
seeking the facts, struggling to determine the sense and significance of it. And at the end, as we expected all along, a use:

To these queries of imagination, I will only add one practical observation; that wherever it is thought proper to give ease, in cases of painful
inflammation in the flesh (as from burnings, or the like) by cooling
the part; linen cloths, wet with spirit, and applied to the part in-
flamed, will produce the coolness required, better than if wet with
water, and will continue it longer. For water, though cold when first
applied, will soon acquire warmth from the flesh, as it does not evapo-
rate fast enough; but the cloths wet with spirit, will continue cold as
long as any spirit is left to keep up the evaporation.

This one from hundreds of Franklin experiments carried out in
comparable detail and reported to one or more of his numerous
scientific correspondents is useful for noting his curiosity in action
and where it tended to lead him. First there would be a natural
matter to check out, either witnessed by himself or submitted by
one of the correspondents. The challenge would be to establish the
facts: 1) *What happens?* 2) *Why does it happen?* So the matter
would be carried further. More information would be sought
through experimental variations that tested the original facts and
perhaps supplied fresh ones. Then, experimental facts established
as well as possible for the moment, comments and queries would
start as the reflective Franklin mind took charge. If there was
some practical, immediate way the new data could help people,
then by all means, it had to be distributed widely as quickly as it
could be done. If there was some future application that a bit fur-

ther effort, a touch of inventiveness, an additional fact could help bring about, then Franklin would try to outline the best way to proceed. He would share all his findings, ideas, theories, schemes for further experiments with other scientists in an unhesitating spirit of total generosity. If nature's truths were secrets, it was only because men hadn't managed to learn them. Once a secret was deciphered it belonged to all men. Indeed, the quest for the secret belonged to all men. A scientist's job was opening the vault, not guarding it.

Franklin's correspondence indicates that he was among the world's first internationalists in science. The search for truth was an enterprise for humanity, not simply for individuals or their nations.

His scientific correspondence was remarkably detailed, informative, and bubbling with effervescence like warm mineral waters. Ideas, notions, and reasoned guesses filled the pages in his small, tight, economical handwriting. Each was an ambassador from the kingdom of knowledge seeking further development, broader experiment, utility. In these letters, the do-it-yourself inventor is at best simply one of the multiple Benjamin Franklins present. He is surrounded by the scientist, the philosopher, the humanist, the moralist, the practical man, the historian. This is not to minimize the importance of the do-it-yourself inventor, but necessary to be true to what Benjamin Franklin was in his totality. He was always more "colors" than one. He wasn't just the honest, reliable brown of a tinkerer, inventor, toolmaker. He was gifted in brown matters, yes, but at the same time he was red, orange, yellow, green, blue, indigo, and violet as well as the shades between, a uniquely full spectrum of human possibilities.

Still, he was a toolmaker and proud to claim the title, not merely for himself, but for the entire race of man.

WORD DOCTOR VERSUS TOOL DOCTOR

Doctor Franklin represented the Colonies in London during many of the heyday years of his distinguished contemporary, *Doctor Samuel Johnson*, dictionary-maker. As a man of consequence, Franklin was sought out by *James Boswell*, who made it a point to know everyone of consequence in case their lives should touch that of Samuel Johnson and thus be needed in the *Life*.

If Franklin and Johnson had approached one another, sparks likely would have flashed from the lexicographer and laughter from the electrician. Franklin would have been amused that Johnson could never appreciate or approve the irreverant attitude of the Plantations, as he called the Colonies, toward the Crown. In the case of Franklin, that especially irreverent representative of those Plantations, Johnson would decide eventually that he was a "master of mischief," and Johnson may have had Franklin in mind when he stated that he was quite willing "to love all mankind except an American."

Doctor Franklin is mentioned in the second volume of Boswell's indispensable *Life of Johnson*. During a conversation with Johnson, Boswell remarked: *"I think Dr. Franklin's definition of Man a good one—'A toolmaking animal.' "*

Johnson may have been out of sorts (the printer's equivalent Franklin had manufactured many years earlier in Philadelphia). Or he may have been enviously competing with his renowned competitor for the "great man of his time" title. In that year of 1778 many Englishmen as well as Frenchmen, Americans, Italians, and knowledgeable individuals of all nations might quickly have selected Franklin as *the* leading person of the eighteenth century. Or perhaps Johnson's intolerance of the Plantations was showing, since his answer seems barely to the point, though it usually was: "But many a man never made a tool; and suppose a man without arms, he could not make a tool."

Doctor Franklin may have been seeking a definition for himself when he spoke of man as a tookmaker. His toolmaking skills appeared in childhood and never left him. As a child working with his father in Boston, Franklin had watched the men around him at their jobs:

> It has ever since been a pleasure to me to see good workmen handle their tools; and it has been useful to me, having learned so much by it, as to be able to do little jobs myself in my house, when a workman could not readily be got; and to construct little machines for experiments while the intention of making the experiment was fresh and warm in my mind.

This capacity to construct little machines would be less important today, but it was critical for a scientist of the eighteenth century who wanted to keep busy. He lacked the casual luxury of extracting a supplies catalog from the shelf and ordering all the "little machines" needed from scientific supply houses.

One of the many scientific works that Franklin took up in Boston as a boy feeling his way toward knowledge was *Boyle's Lec-*

tures, written by *Robert Boyle*, the seventeenth century British physicist and chemist, who made his name survive by attaching it to a "Law". Everyone remembers that Boyle had a Law, even if they don't exactly remember what it is. Not everyone remembers that he spent the year 1641 in Florence, Italy studying the "paradoxes of the great star-gazer" Galileo, and that he came home to England resolved to devote his life to research in the sciences. Boyle became a leading member of the "Invisible College," a small group that met in London, usually at Gresham College, to discuss their various experiments in natural philosophy, or the "new philosophy" of science. Later the "Invisible College" would become the "Royal Society of London" which will deserve special attention later because of its important and extensive connections with Benjamin Franklin, who was made a member following his electrical experiments, and then four times chosen a member of the Royal Society Council (in 1760, 1765, 1766, 1772).

Robert Boyle in 1680 was offered the presidency of the Royal Society but declined because of an opposition to taking oaths. Boyle's Law (that the volume of a gas is inversely proportional to its pressure) and his other contributions to science were the result of scientific investigation and experimentation, following Francis Bacon's seventeenth century scheme for progress in natural knowledge.

The book of lectures by Boyle that Franklin studied was a gallimaufry of science and theology, at once fascinating, useful, and foolish, rather like a recipe book compiled by a mad monk, a farmer's wife, and one of the most brilliant scientists of his age. The suggestions that caught young Franklin's attention would have been those insisting nature's ways and laws could be learned by watching carefully and by using simple tools available at the workbench or in the kitchen. The message was clear as the summer sky, sharp as the breeze off Boston Harbor. It was possible to learn about nature and do useful work in science without going through the curriculum at Harvard. All he, Ben Franklin, needed was his eyes and his head and the patience to add the facts up properly.

Years later as a member of the Royal Society of London, Franklin would possess an honorary degree from Harvard and other universities. One of his many services in London during those years would be to purchase and send scientific instruments to Harvard.

There was irony in the fact of that service. The instruments were the best and most delicate manufactured in Europe. Yet the great experiments that earned Franklin his scientific standing had largely been made with "little machines" of his own devising and ordinary items that could be found ready to hand in the typical colonial house.

In his own work, he followed, either through necessity or choice, the instructions of Robert Boyle to use simple tools and then to proceed cautiously and logically in seeking natural truth.

Franklin's adaptation was to study a phenomenon as patiently as he could. He sought to understand it fully before moving on to the next puzzle. His approach was essentially the classic scientific method honed to the essentials for the specific needs of the American Colonies. There would be long and fruitful periods of science for Doctor Franklin that would seem to have no purpose other than knowledge, and he would enjoy them immensely; but the toolmaker could never indulge himself exclusively in that direction. The quest for knowledge was a magnificent use of human time, but the scientist, the same as other men, had his duties around the house.

"A better, less cumbersome way of turning the meat roaster, Ben, that would be useful, if it's something useful you're looking to do." Did Deborah Franklin, busy with her bread-making, say something of the sort in hurried passing when she noticed her resident toolmaker looking around in his sly way? If she said it, she may not have expected that anything could or would be done. But she may have known her husband well enough to realize that with Ben Franklin, the "nothing can be done" judgment should never be prematurely made.

What Franklin did was to review the problem, consider the natural energies, and proceed to cut a hole in the kitchen wall for a small windmill which very efficiently did the needed task, to the best of the wind's ability.

"What about when there's no wind, Ben?"

It was a good question. The answer had to wait awhile, too hundred years or so, until other energies could be harnessed to do man's work. Doctor Franklin would be striving for future answers and better ways to turn the roast when he went out to discuss truth with the lightning. He knew, though Deborah and the neighbors might not, that sort of research was the scientist's way of investing in the future. There were more immediate problems that couldn't wait for answers, such as the problem of fire and a safe, practical way of supplying household heat "in these northern colonies" where "the inhabitants keep fires to sit by, generally *seven months* of the year; that is, from the beginning of *October* to the end of *April*; and in some winters near *eight months*, by taking in part of *September* and *May*."

FIRE ALERT IN PHILADELPHIA

Franklin lived in the area concerned, and he made himself an expert on the subject of fire. As a man who despised waste, his interest was inevitable; since there was no greater source of waste than uncontrolled fire. Calmly he declared a personal war on fire which could destroy a house in minutes, a community in an hour, or even devastate a great city with vicious efficiency as flames were picked up and carried by the wind. There was still talk of the great 1666 fire in London and men alive who had seen it or heard of it first hand. London had suffered devastation. Fire fighting equipment had consisted of poles with iron hooks for pulling down burning structures, axes, ladders, and primitive hand-operated water projectors, all futile against the wind and the flames that lasted nearly four days.

Franklin didn't want to see even a miniature reenactment of that event in Philadelphia; and to help guard against the threat of fire, a busy man made himself busier. First he took the lead by dramatizing the subject. In the guise of an elderly citizen, he wrote a letter to the editor of the *Gazette*, himself, concerning practical ways to protect houses from fire, with heaviest stress on prevention. Then working though his Junto Club, Franklin brought about the formation of the *Union Fire Company* in 1736, the first in Philadelphia. Members of the Company were volunteers, trained in fire-fighting, who obliged themslves by their Articles of Agreement to keep their equipment and themselves ready for emergencies. The purpose of the Company was "the more ready Extinguishing of Fires, and mutual Assistance in Removing and Securing of Goods when in Danger." Mutual assistance was the cornerstone of virtually every Franklin civic project, and with Franklin as the guiding spirit, it usually worked. Philadelphia's fire companies for long periods made it a paragon among cities with regard to security from fires.

But warning neighbors about precautions and establishing a Company of fire-fighters was just the initial phase of Franklin's struggle. In his newspaper he had cautioned Philadelphia that "an ounce of prevention is worth a pound of cure" and he had even told them how to carry coals from one floor to another (in a closed warming pan). Otherwise. . .

> ...Scraps of fire may fall into the chinks and make no appearance
> until midnight, when your stairs being in flames, you may be forced
> (as I once was) to leap out of your windows and hazard your necks to
> avoid being over-roasted.

Many years later, Franklin would organize the first insurance
company in the Colonies, again with fire as the number one ad-
versary. The company was another mutual assistance undertaking,
with a full name of formidable dimensions: *"Philadelphia Contributionship for the Insurance of Houses from Loss by Fire."* The
idea of fire insurance had been initiated in London by an eccentric
doctor named *Nicholas Barbon*, but it took Franklin to make it
function. Late in life, at the age of 82, Franklin wrote: "I have
always believed that one man of tolerable abilities may work great
changes and accomplish great affairs among mankind, if he first
forms a good plan... and makes the execution of the same plan
his sole study and business." He tirelessly labored to make certain
that when it was his plan and he was the man of tolerable abilities,
the results supported his argument. They nearly always did.

The organization meeting for the insurance company was held
at a tavern on September 7, 1751, and Benjamin Franklin's name
was at the top of the directors list. The first meeting went well,
and subsequent meetings were held at various taverns, the Sign of
the George, Widow Pratt's, Ben Davis's Golden Fleece, etc. In
1752 the Contributionship was in operation and writing insurance.
Policies 19 and 20 were written on two Franklin houses, on July
4, 1752. According to Franklin, *the mutual insurance plan* was one
"whereby every man might help another, without any disservice
to himself."

With the Contributionship successfully launched (remarkably
so, since the company Franklin founded would still be going strong
in the twentieth century), and after starting a fire company as
well as trying to educate the public, Franklin had done all he could
in a public way, short of travelling from door to door to lecture
parents on prevention and persuade children not to play with fire.
He attempted both in the pages of the *Gazette*.

THE FRANKLIN STOVE

There was something more he could do of great value in a private way. He could apply his scientific skills and invent a new,
safer fireplace. Certainly the fireplaces commonly used at that
time needed improvement badly. Heat from logs in the traditional

fireplaces was for the most part lost up the chimney. European stoves, the few in use throughout the Colonies, kept reheating stale air without recirculation.

Those were the challenges when Franklin began working on a new fireplace, about 1739 or 1740. By 1742 it was perfected, and soon offered for sale by Franklin's friend, *Robert Grace*. It wasn't a business arrangement in Franklin's case. He wanted the fireplaces available to the public because they would warm houses more efficiently, save fuel, and protect against fires. Those who think of Franklin as a businessman whose various enterprises for all their public value ultimately rewarded him with ample private profits should consider the *Pennsylvanian Fireplace* as he named it, or the *Franklin Stove* as others and history have named it.

Franklin invented the fireplace. He wrote the sales pamphlet that publicized it and helped assure widespread use. But he consistently *refused any personal profits from the enterprise.*

The *Autobiography*:

> In order of time I should have mentioned before, that having invented an open stove, for the better warming of rooms and at the same time saving fuel, as the fresh air admitted was warmed in entering, I made a present of the model to Mr. Robert Grace, one of my early friends, who having an iron furnace, found the casting of the plates for these stoves a profitable thing, as they were growing in demand. To promote that demand I wrote and published a pamphlet entitled, *An Account of the New-Invented PENNSYLVANIA FIRE PLACES: Wherein their Construction and manner of Operation is particularly explained; their Advantages above every other Method of warming Rooms demonstrated; and all Objections that have been raised against the Use of them answered and obviated.* &c. This pamphlet had a good effect. Govr. Thomas was so pleas'd with the construction of this stove, as describ'd in it that he offer'd to give me a patent for the sole vending of them for a term of years; but I declin'd it from a principle which has ever weigh'd with me on such occasions, viz. *That as we enjoy great advantages from the inventions of others, we should be glad of an opportunity to serve others by any invention of ours, and this we should do freely and generously.*

Franklin could have used the stove to make a fortune. He didn't use it to make anything for himself except satisfaction. His stove warmed the houses of America more safely and effectively than before. Of course, the value of such satisfaction should not be underestimated. Franklin had something better than a fortune as his payment for the stove. He had the knowledge that it was his work, and that it did what he hoped, assured better ventilation and greater fuel efficiency. The time of his work on the stove also happened to be the time he was trying to establish the *American Philosophical Society*. His pamphlet was presented through the Society and brought it valuable publicity as it was getting started. Franklin's stove showed the Colonies the kind of practical, useful work that scientists could accomplish if they added social consciences to technical genius. If a particular bit of scientific work served a specific human need, Doctor Franklin was always gratified.

The pamphlet he wrote on the subject is informative and fun to read. If the test of literary genius is the ability to be fascinating about stoves, as a biographer wrote of Franklin, then the toolmaker qualified.

The second paragraph, read in the final quarter of the twentieth century, promptly and inevitably strikes home. You've hit a nerve, Doctor.

> Wood, our common fuel, which within these 100 years might be had at every man's door, must now be fetch'd near 100 miles to some towns, and makes a very considerable article in the expense of families.

Forty-four years later making his last voyage home from France, a weary and ailing old man stirred himself to put down his latest scientific speculations in a series of fascinating papers. One of them, "On the Causes and Cure of Smoky Chimneys," included this additional palpable hit at twentieth century nerve endings:

> Much more of the prosperity of a winter country depends on the plenty and cheapness of fuel, than is generally imagined. In travelling I have observed, that in those parts where the inhabitants can have neither wood, nor coal, nor turf, but at excessive prices, the working people live in miserable hovels, are ragged, and have nothing comfortable about them. But when fuel is cheap (or where they have the art of managing it to advantage) they are well furnished with necessaries, and have decent habitations.

His 1744 pamphlet again:

> As therefore so much of the comfort and convenience of our lives, for so great a part of the year, depends on the article of *fire*; since fuel is become so expensive, and (as the country is more clear'd and settled) will of course grow scarcer and dearer; any new proposal for saving the wood, and for lessening the charge and augmenting the benefit of fire, by some particular method of making and managing it, may at least be thought worth consideration.

Two hundred years do make a difference. In Franklin's age, his invention was greeted with enthusiasm, the governor of the state almost urged him to let the stove make him wealthy, and the people bought the stove in large numbers from Robert Grace, starting at the Philadelphia Post Office where he initially sold them. In these later days, the reaction to methods of saving fuel usually start not with the question whether it will work, but whether it is convenient and will make a profit. If so, and if it saves something worth saving, such as fuel, fine; but the convenience and the profit come first. Poor Richard would have found a proverb to make us squirm.

The Franklin stove, manufactured from cast-iron, was designed to sit inside the existing fireplace and to collaborate efficiently with the "Properties of Air and Fire" which Franklin troubled to explain technically before covering the fourteen advantages of the new fireplace. Reading the advantages, one has the feeling there are fourteen because Franklin decided that was enough, but that he could have gone on for another fourteen. Franklin's verbosity separates him from modern advertising men with their *multum in parvo* strictures, but he had an advertising instinct and the selling patter when his product was a good one and he believed in it.

After a warmup lecture on the behavior of heated and cold air, Franklin suggested a number of experiments his readers could try at home to convince themselves that heated air fills more space than cold air. The experiments are simple, but carefully thought through and give proof of Franklin's gift for small details. This is a useful trait for a scientist, though not all scientists have possessed it. The fact that counts most is sometimes the smallest fact, unobserved until someone leans close and frowns, "What have we here?" The essential truth often conceals itself among the minutia.

Franklin in his paper on the fireplace leaned close; but he knew what he had, and did not need to frown. He was in one of his favorite roles as teacher. He wanted to share everything he knew about heating a house, which was considerable, and to emphasize the real advantages of the new invention. Part of the process was to let his readers participate a bit in the "science" involved. He suggested one experiment involving a Florence flask upturned in water and heat used to force some of the water out because of expanded air. An alternate was to heat a bladder that had been partially filled with air and then tightly closed. "As the air within heats, you will perceive it to swell and fill the bladder."

With this property of air established, he then began making his background points about heated air and smoke leaving through the chimney if a proper circulation is in effect, with heavier outside air coming in to replace the lighter, heated air. Circulation was a must.

> Fire (i.e. common fire) throws out light, heat, and smoke (or fume.) The two first move in right lines, and with great swiftness, the latter is but just separated from the fuel, and then moves only as it is carried by the stream of rarefied air: and without a continual accession and recession of air, to carry off the smoky fumes, they would remain crowded about the fire, and stifle it.

Forty years later in his letter to Dr. Ingenhausz on "Smoky Chimneys," he went over these same matters more thoroughly with many additional details about what to do and what not to do. It was clear that Franklin knew chimneys, probably better than any other living individual, because he took them seriously and had studied them carefully. They might seem trivial. They were just the opposite, affecting the lives and comfort of human beings almost everywhere except the tropics. He had a typical suggestion for Ingenhausz, physician to the Emperor at Vienna:

> For many years past, I have rarely met with a case of a smoky chimney, which has not been solvable on these principles, and cured by these remedies, where people have been willing to apply them; which is indeed not always the case; for many have prejudices in favor of the nostrums of pretending chimney-doctors and fumists, and some have conceits and fancies of their own, which they rather choose to try, than to lengthen a funnel, alter the size of an opening, or admit air into a room, however necessary; for some are as much afraid of fresh air as persons in the hydrophobia are of fresh water. I myself had formerly this prejudice, this *aerophobia*, as I now account it, and dreading the supposed dangerous effects of cool air, I considered it as an enemy, and closed with extreme care every crevice in the rooms I inhabited. Experience has convinced me of my error. I now look upon fresh air as a friend: I even sleep with an open window. I am persuaded that no common air from without is so unwholesome as the air within a close room that has been often breathed and not changed.

AN END TO BEING "SCORCHED BEFORE & FROZE BEHIND"

More than a generation earlier, promoting his stove, he was concerned with the same subject; and his first concern was to point out the disadvantages of the competition, the German stove, the

Holland iron stove, and old-fashioned chimneys that might draw properly but tended to turn an abode into a dangerous maelstrom of drafts by pulling outside air furiously in through every crack.

"The Spaniards have a proverbial saying," wrote Benjamin Franklin, "If the wind blows on you through a hole, Make your will, and take care of your soul."

Then with the insight of a marketing master fully aware that women would be the final decisionmakers when it came to warming their houses, he inserted a dire warning specifically for the women:

> Women particularly, from this cause, as they sit much in the house, get colds in the head, rheum and defluctions, which fall into their jaws and gums, and have destroyed early many a fine set of teeth in these northern colonies.

This one sentence may have sold two thousand stoves. Destroyed teeth would be bad enough, though poor teeth seemed to happen in spite of drafts during the eighteenth century, but the word *"defluctions"* would have proved especially troublesome, and would have made women of all ages shudder and instruct their husbands that Ben Franklin's stove was what they most wanted in the world, and they would never ever ask for anything again, but they had to have the stove, &c.

"Defluction" was not good enough for Merriam-Webster's Third Unabridged, but it made the *Oxford English Dictionary.* "Defluction, bad form of Defluxion." "Defluxion" has many meanings associated with the idea of flowing or falling, including "a running at the nose or eyes," catarrh, *and* a falling out of the hair. The sentence above from Franklin's pamphlet is quoted in the OED to illustrate "defluction."

The perils of catarrh, women could have lived with, but falling hair? Benjamin Franklin not only knew how to invent stoves, he also knew how to sell them. As every advertiser learns, sometimes to his despair, you have to have a product capable of fulfilling a reasonable portion of the claims made for it. Franklin had no qualms on that score. The stove had proved itself in service long before his pamphlet was compiled. In that respect he chose not to anticipate the practices of twentieth century advertising, when promotional materials praising the benefits of a new product are frequently completed while the new product is still struggling on the drawing board.

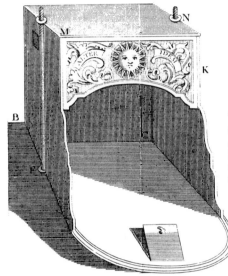

The Franklin Stove Alter Idem *translates as "another exactly similar." See the Illustration Section for a reproduction (from an early edition of Franklin's works) of the stove and all its component parts.*

Easy to follow instructions for installation followed. Modern authors of "assembly" and "use" instructions would do well to study the technical writings of Benjamin Franklin on such matters as the stove. Methodically and simply he spells out everything so that it can be followed without reading instruction thirty-seven for the seventy-third time, making no sense of it, bursting into tears, falling on the knees in anxious prayer, and then closing the eyes, and inserting rod Z into grommet J with an agony of uncertainty. There is none of that with Franklin. His instructions are instructions, not obstacle courses.

GENTLEMEN, IS IT A SHOE?

. . . This prudence of not attempting to give reasons before one is sure of facts, I learned from one of your sex, who, as Selden tells us, being in company with some gentlemen that were viewing and considering something which they call'd a Chinese Shoe, and disputing earnestly about the manner of wearing it, and how it could possibly be put on; put in her word, and said modestly, Gentlemen, are you sure it is a shoe? Should not that be settled first?

(To Mary Stevenson, September 13, 1760)

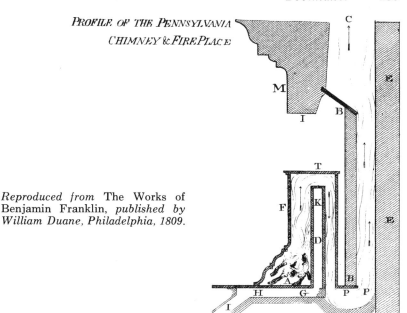

Its operation may be conceived by observing the plate entitled, Profile of the Chimney and Fire Place.

M The mantle-piece, or breast of the chimney.
C The funnel.
B The false back and closing.
E True back of the chimney.
T Top of the fireplace.
F The front of it.
A The place where the fire is made.
D The air-box.
K The hole in the side-plate, through which the warmed air is discharged out of the air-box into the room.
H The hollow filled with fresh air, entering at the passage I, and ascending into the air-box through the air-hole in the bottom plate near.
G The partition in the hollow to keep the air and smoke apart.
P The passage under the false back and part of the hearth for the smoke.

How does it work? Flame and smoke rise from the fire at A, strike T. The smoke passes down the back of the air-box, warming it in passage, and then out the chimney. The air-box is a key feature. It "means the air in the room is continually changed, and kept, at the same time, sweet and warm."

Franklin tried to anticipate every possible problem, and may have come close to succeeding. If a room was used for considerable tobacco smoking, for instance, he suggested a small, shuttered hole in the ceiling through to the funnel of the chimney. When the hole was opened, smoke would quickly egress. Best results could be had by burning dry hickory or ash, woods that burn with a clear flame and are "less apt to foul the smoke-passages with soot."

By the time Franklin reaches the fourteen advantages for his stove, the reader is thoroughly convinced that the inventor knows enormously more about the subject than he does. He is drummed into admiring submission by the neatly marshaled battalion of supportive facts. The advantages are rather an afterthought to fortify a decision already made. "Yes, Mr. Franklin, I'll take one. Don't bother to wrap it."

Unlike common fireplaces, notes Franklin, with the new one, the whole room is equally warmed, and people need not crowd close. "If you sit near the fire, you have not that cold draught of uncomfortable air nipping your back and heels, as when before common fires, by which many catch cold, being scorched before, and, as it were, froze behind." The stove efficiently uses heat instead of letting it escape up the chimney. Since less heat is lost *"much less wood* will serve you, which is a considerable advantage where wood is dear." "This fire-place cures most smoky chimneys, and thereby preserves both the eyes and furniture." Because of the superior burning qualities, fouling of chimneys is prevented. Chimneys are much less likely to catch fire. If one does, the fire is easily stifled. "And lastly, the fire is so secured at night, that not one spark can fly out into the room to do damage."

THE SWEETNESS OF IRON

If the potential purchaser is not convinced, Franklin is ready with "Objections answered" including an erstwhile complaint concerning the "offensive smell of iron stoves."

> This smell, however, never proceeded from the iron itself, which, in its nature, whether hot or cold, is one of the sweetest of metals, but from the general uncleanly manner of using those stoves. If they are kept clean, they are as sweet as an ironing-box, which, though ever so hot, never offends the smell of the nicest lady: but it is common to let them be greased, by setting candlesticks on them, or otherwise; to rub greasy hands on them; and above all, to spit upon them, to try how hot they are, which is an inconsiderate filthy unmannerly custom.

Franklin is at some pains to prove that iron when hot cannot be held responsible for any unpleasant odors in the vicinity. He describes the absence of such smells in the vicinity of furnaces, the benefits of mineral waters containing iron, and an experiment conducted by *Dr. Desaguliers* in which a small bird was exposed to air that had been passed through hot iron. The bird thrived. But a bird quickly died when its air passed through hot brass. Franklin concludes the subject by insisting that "iron is always sweet and every way taken is wholesome and friendly to the human body—except in weapons."

The objection that "warmed rooms make people tender, and apt to catch cold" is countered by several years experience with the stove and warm rooms.

> By the use of such rooms, people are rendered *less liable* to take cold, and, indeed, *actually hardened.* If sitting warm in a room made one subject to take cold on going out, lying warm in bed, should by a parity of reason, produce the same effect when we rise. Yet we find we can leap out of the warmest bed naked, in the coldest morning, without any such danger; and in the same manner out of warm clothes into a cold bed.

Finally, there is a significant *public advantage* that must result from the use of the fireplaces. The fireplace, being economical of fuel, would allow new wood to be grown as fast as it is consumed; and "our posterity may warm themselves at a moderate rate, without being obliged to fetch their fuel over the Atlantic; as if, pit-coal should not be here discovered (which is an uncertainty) they must necessarily do."

A number of Franklin's assumptions would be set aside by later developments, but his prescience is still impressive, as the super-tankers cross and recross the Atlantic carrying fuel to the energy voracious Americans. "We leave it to the *political arithmetician*," wrote Franklin, "to compute how much money will be saved by a country, by its spending two-thirds less of fuel."

His remarkably thorough treatise on the stove ends with meticulously detailed "Directions to the Bricklayer" concerning the chimney, the air passage, positioning of the stove, etc.

Having gone to such lengths of study and work to design a stove, he didn't want to be defeated at the end by poor workman-

THE HUMILITY OF GENIUS
I am glad my little paper on the Aurora Borealis *pleased. If it should occasion further inquiry, and so produce a better hypothesis, it will not be wholly useless.*
(To Joseph Priestley, February 8, 1780)

ship. Every function that many men and departments serve in a modern company, Franklin himself did in connection with the fireplace. He designed it, saw to its manufacture, trial use, market research on the competition, writing the advertising and the instruction manual, troubleshooting, supervising installation, and including a practical method for persuading the chimney to draw when the first fire was made. Users were even amiably advised that people tended initially to keep their rooms too warm, and the designer - inventor - manufacturer - advertiser - bricklayer - publicist - engineer provided a tip for keeping rooms comfortable: Let the plates be "no hotter than that one may just bear the hand on them."

Franklin did virtually everything in connection with his stove except make a profit on it, and that exception was by choice. Others made plenty of profit. Franklin's objective was simply to achieve the best possible stove and assure its best possible use, even if that required him to inform the residents of the Colonies as well as posterity that on some occasions, at least, he was disposed to sleep nude in a warm bed.

Not surprisingly, the fireplace was not a perfect heating device. As with other inventions, flaws appeared in the course of widespread use. Predictably, some failed to follow the inventor's careful instructions. And copiers of the stove, trying to make improvements, sometimes made it worse. According to Franklin, this occurred in the hands of European workmen "who did not, it seems, well comprehend the principles of that machine, it was much disfigured in their imitations of it."

The original Franklin Stove had its critics in the eighteenth century because of performance difficulties, due in part to design and in part to the neglect of manufacturers and users to heed Benjamin Franklin's advice. Historians in the twentieth century have also been critical of the claims made for the Franklin Stove.

Historian Samuel Edgerton, Jr. has written that the original Franklin Stove had largely ceased to be used by the time of the Revolution because of functional failures. Professor Edgerton noted that iron fireplaces were sold in Philadelphia, 1785-1830, and that they were called Franklin Stoves though they had only superficial resemblance to Franklin's original.

Because of his enthusiasm and writings on the subject over several decades, it is natural that the name "Franklin Stove" would attach itself generically to the iron fireplaces of the eighteenth and early nineteenth centuries. If some of these stoves had no specific connection with Franklin, all could be considered, at least in purpose, derivative from his original.

EARTHBOUND WITH WINGS

In an introduction to the *Autobiography, Woodrow Wilson* once described Doctor Franklin as "half peasant, half man of the world." The historian with a Presidency in his future was fairly close to the mark, and he could very well have been thinking of the Franklin inventions, especially the Franklin Stove, when he noted these aspects of Franklin's character.

The stove exemplifies Franklin's earthbound practicality, and at the same time his citizen of the world curiosity and liberality. It shows his concern with and wish to alleviate immediate needs, a peasant commitment. The pamphlet he wrote to help sales, however, displays a wide-ranging interest in peripheral matters that had no reference to immediate needs.

The word "Yankee" might be substituted for "peasant," but in the sense Wilson meant, the words are almost synonymous. Eighteenth century American Yankee-Peasants, whether they lived in towns as did Franklin, in villages, or on farms with tree stumps littering the fields, were essentially men of the earth, not men of the world. Franklin's difference and fate were to be both.

He worked for the future by dedicating himself to the present. He lived near the ground, was nourished by it, and derived his strength from contact with the earth like Antaeus in classical mythology. He adhered to the established verities and values, because they were solid rocks a man could stand on when a storm arose. He was encouraged by his circumstances to develop a generous measure of wit and cunning. He might be viewed as a country innocent by careless thinkers, but the ignorant rube cliché was a calculated invention to help him run miles faster and farther than the typical babe in the woods city slicker. In a horse trade, whether dealing with stallions or nations, it is usually smart to bet on peasant shrewdness, realism, stubbornness, and caution. Yankee peasants outfought and outlasted European aristocrats during the American Revolution.

The eighteenth century American peasant developed endurance and strength, earth qualities, because there was no better way to survive. It was centuries before Social Security, the Welfare State, and Unemployment Compensation. It was an era of brother help brother and neighbor help neighbor, but chiefly it was an age in which personal responsibility in the main meant looking after one-self.

Franklin built and tried out his stove himself. That was the first step, the practical move of an American peasant. It was only later that he tried actively to make the advantages of the stove available throughout the Colonies. Then he had it manufactured for commercial sale and wrote his pamphlet. The stove warmed his house and the houses of his friends effectively. The man of the earth could be content with that; but the man of the world wanted the installation of a Franklin Stove in every house in America.

Benjamin Franklin throughout his life was by birth and choice a city slicker. Boston, Philadelphia, London, Paris were or became cities by eighteenth century standards, though the first two were simply large towns by modern standards. While duty and necessity made him travel much, and often in hard places, Franklin never showed any pioneer impulse to get very far away from home cooking and a comfortable bed for the night. He felt no urge to become a "noble savage" à la Rousseau.

But there was a homespun, peasant, Quaker simplicity to the man. Perhaps it was partially a facade, conveniently invented as an expression of the philosopher's strategy. Yet it wasn't all facade. There was always a Yankee peasant behind the sophisticate who later would flirt with the ladies of Paris, play chess with them in their baths, and amuse them with his Bagatelles. Achievements in science, philosophy, and diplomacy would make Benjamin Franklin a man of the world. But birth, background, instincts, inclinations, and the good sense that never left him, kept Franklin a man of the earth with the peasant wisdom to plan and assemble a stove that would do the job, as well as other useful tools for himself and his neighbors.

True, he may have chosen to make himself the most sophisticated peasant that ever lived. It added electricity to life and made it more amusing. It was this combination of the earthy and the worldly that established Franklin as *le grand homme* of Paris and one of the most admired men of his century. The combination meant self-reliance yet superiority to the narrowness that sometimes afflicts men with limited horizons.

There was no limitation to the toolmaker's horizons. His mind was never content to stay put in the comfortable and familiar. And where his mind led, his feet followed. Scientists, the brave ones, often have a *professional urge to keep moving on.* Franklin moved often.

His Yankee peasant character went along for the journey. Peasants long ago mastered the arts of survival by realizing that if you lack the funds to buy your way into heaven, you have to arrive there by wit and stubbornness. There was such a reservoir of undefeatable peasant will and instinct in Benjamin Franklin, even while sipping Madeira with the Queen of France.

The peasant toolmaker figured out ways to make a better stove. The internationalist applied the heavy artillery of salesmanship and reason to make the stove famous and put it to work warming houses around the world.

Was Woodrow Wilson perhaps consciously, or unconsciously, thinking of Franklin's fireplace pamphlet with its list of fourteen advantages, when he offered his Fourteen Points as the basis for the Versailles Peace Treaty in 1919? It makes an intriguing historical "perhaps." Woodrow Wilson may have been trying to sell the war-troubled nations of Europe another Franklin Stove, complete with fourteen excellent advantages. "Open covenants of peace, openly arrived at, after which there shall be no private international understandings of any kind ... Absolute freedom of navigation upon the seas ... A general association of nations must be formed." It was a "stove" conceived in boldness and innocence. It was audacious and naive, yet it gave the world a *gift of hope.*

But the men of the world were unable to buy his peasant American formula for peace. It was too simple, too remote from traditional intrigue and ways of doing business. Too bad. Wilson it can be said wasn't a good salesman. He offered his fourteen advantages, and they were beautiful, but in the end he couldn't sell them even to his own countrymen. Too bad. Wilson had a pretty good "Franklin Stove" to offer the world. It might have worked better if men of the world had contained more of earthbound reason in their compositions.

Wilson was right about Doctor Franklin, who uniquely combined the man of the earth and the man of the world. Both qualities were needed to make a revolution and win it, to earn the love of both peasants and aristocrats and hold it, to build a stove and sell it. Both qualities were actively involved in most of the major undertakings in Franklin's life. He was always the peasant toolmaker united with the man-of-the-universe scientist. Down to earth matters received total attention for the sake of human welfare and comfort. After all, the stove had to work properly and warm the house effectively before the natural philosopher could find the comfort and leisure to satisfy his curiosity with out-of-this-world speculations. The chimney had to draw suitably, or the scientist might return from a speculative journey out-of-this-world to find his house on fire. The peasant realist in Franklin knew the importance of dealing with first things first and applying an ounce of prevention to avoid the pound of cure.

Then with tranquil mind he could rush off to join his fellows at the Junto and discuss with easy and undisturbed pleasure why the flame of a candle tends upwards, or "which is least criminal, a *bad* action joined with a *good* intention, or a *good* action joined with a *bad* intention."

Perhaps discussions at the Junto led Franklin in 1731 to include among his reflections in the *Autobiography*, the note about it being an "occasion for raising an united Party for Virtue, by forming the virtuous and good men of all nations into a regular body, to be govern'd by suitable good and wise rules, which good and wise men may probably be more unanimous in their obedience to, than common people are to common laws."

Was Woodrow Wilson conscious of those lines when he conceived the *League of Nations*, that hopeful dream from which the world too soon awoke? If the tree of evolution for the present *United Nations* were traced to its roots, might not one of them be found in Franklin's notes for May 9, 1731 when he meditated on virtuous and good men.

What is the relevance of the "grand perhaps" in history? Let us call a special meeting of the Junto and discuss it thoroughly.

ASCENDING VERSUS DESCENDING HONORS
. . . among the Chinese, the most ancient, and from long experience the wisest of nations, honor does not descend, but ascends. If a man from his learning, his wisdom, or his valor, is promoted by the emperor to the rank of Mandarin, his parents are immediately entitled to all the same ceremonies of respect from the people that are established as due to the Mandarin himself; on the supposition that it must have been owing to the education, instruction, and good example afforded him by his parents, that he was rendered capable of serving the public. This ascending honor is therefore useful to the state, as it encourages parents to give their children a good and virtuous education. But the descending honor, to a posterity who could have no share in obtaining it, is not only groundless and absurd, but often hurtful to that posterity, since it is apt to make them proud, disdaining to be employed in useful arts, and thence falling into poverty, and all the meannesses, servility, and wretchedness attending it; which is the present case with much of what is called the noblesse in Europe.
(To Mrs. Sarah Bache, January 26, 1784)

1976

Dear Doctor Franklin, Sir,

Many of your observations in electricity, medicine, etc., are still accepted as perfectly good science. You were correct about the common cold and what to do about it. You were remarkably on target when you hypothecated positive and negative electricity and when your speculations brought you at least to the microcosmic borders of the electron.

Some of your shrewd scientific "guesses" still have our contemporary wise ones scratching their chins in wonder. How could old Ben Franklin have been so smart, they fret, without modern microscopes, telescopes, and computers. Perhaps the rich, rare wine of freedom had something to do with it?

Governments, foundations, boards of trustees, committees, accountants, status investigators, etc., were never checking on you and your science. All directions were open and you could eagerly take any one of them. If you journeyed a distance in one direction and found it not to your or truth's liking, you could cheerfully return to the starting point and choose another. No watchdog committee would begin howling at the fiscal moon.

Science costs too much money these days for many to enjoy the luxury of freedom. When an institute or a foundation or a federal agency decides to spend a million dollars to find out why children like gumdrops; it feels a responsibility, not so much to science as to its money; and it is constantly looking over your shoulder when you are inflicting gumdrops on babies and studying their reactions.

Perhaps all this watchfulness by the custodians of the moneybags inhibits science and scientists. Perhaps it sours the wine of freedom.

Sir, what, if anything, should we do about this?

We Are, &c.,

YOURS, THE PEOPLE

IX. A Club of Ingenious Acquaintance

Woodrow Wilson at the 1919 Peace Conference talked the leaders of Europe into forming a "general association of nations" they would call a League, but he didn't talk them into doing much of anything to make it work. Benjamin Franklin had better luck with the Junto, his association of Philadelphians who assembled every Friday evening, not for poker, revelry, or a prayer meeting, but to discuss serious topics seriously for general self-betterment and the progress of knowledge.

Franklin's "luck," in fact, viewed retrospectively, was rather amazing, considering the usual fate of such enthusiastically begun organizations for intellectual talkfests. By the fourth or fifth meetings, it is usually noticed that fewer and fewer members are showing up. Two just happened to have dates on the meeting night, another was kept late at the office, and a fourth had to stay home with his sick turtle. Then the motion is made, seconded, and approved that meetings not be held during the month of August because that is an outdoors month and in the northern hemisphere, one should take advantage. So that particular club disappears from the face of the earch, and if the organizers are slow to learn, they may try again in the Fall with a new name and a revised roster of members. Such has been the customary fate of clubs organized to talk (poker, revelry, and prayer meetings are different matters with different organizational results depending on the funds, the energy, and the piety of the members).

Franklin's Junto lasted for decades, received more applications for membership than could be accommodated, became the forerunner of the American Philosophical Society, and achieved a place of importance in the history of American science. It can be assumed that the enthusiasm, commitment, and leadership of the founder and organizer had much to do with this success.

Even if it hurts Doctor Franklin's intellectual standing in the ivory tower set, it should be admitted in the interests of historical accuracy that he was an incurable social creature, a joiner, and a booster. He seriously believed it possible that *when intelligent men met together intelligent results were possible.* The Junto was an outgrowth of this belief, and since he was only twenty-one when the Junto was founded, he clearly had the conviction from his early years.

Throughout his years in Philadelphia, Citizen Franklin made himself available for community projects with indefatigable energies left over from business, experiments, writing, and study. He was one of those human clocks that seemed never quite to run down and need rewinding. The tasks themselves, when mentally rewarding and emotionally satisfying, served to recharge his energy cells.

Unlike some of his scientific friends, such as *Henry Cavendish* in England, Franklin could never hide himself away from the world. He needed fresh air too much for comfortable work in a cloister or an ivory tower. Each shut out too much of importance, and thus smothered rather than expanded.

Franklin was most contented in a group of kindred spirits. A glass of Madeira, an intimate conversation about science or philosophical ideas, and private leisure at a later time to recollect and write out his conclusions in tranquillity were essential ingredients in his formula of happiness. Happiness springs from the mind, he argued in the *Gazette* for November 20, 1735, with such factors as health of body merely circumstances establishing an environment for mental happiness. One of the discussion questions to be considered by the Junto at a Friday meeting was: "Wherein consists the happiness of a rational creature?" The wish rises that one could have been present that evening to listen. Of course, the wish also rises that one could have been present any evening to see Franklin in one of his milieus, and to hear him speak. He talked slowly, we are told, thoughtfully, disinclined to hurry either thoughts or tongue. That evening the "happiness" discussion would have ranged from the Greeks and Romans to John Locke. Inevitably, someone, *Joseph Brientnal* perhaps, would have quoted *Alexander Pope's* lines from "An Essay on Criticism."

> A little learning is a dang'rous thing;
> Drink deep, or taste not the Pierian spring:
> There shallow draughts intoxicate the brain,
> And drinking largely sobers us again.

They might have considered Pope's own brilliant and tormented career as the *enfant terrible* of British poetry in discussing their weekly question. Master of Greek and Latin in childhood, claimed to have written his "An Essay on Criticism" at the age of twelve though it was published in 1711 when he was twenty-three, his health ruined by excessive study at the age of seventeen. Pope's knowledge was great indisputably, but being physically deformed, *could the man really be happy?*

"I doubt he is unhappy," someone might have said, perhaps Franklin, "Fame is what he seems to want, and he receives it."

Franklin that evening would have presented as his view the thought that knowledge does not make men unhappy, but knowledge without the ability to share it. He could have pointed out that the Junto was formed specifically to guard against that frustration. The members of the Junto could become men of great knowledge and preserve themselves from moral melancholy and mental torpor by sharing their knowledge weekly at the club.

Franklin founded the Junto in 1727. By a coincidence that baffles the word into silence, 1727 was the year that Sir Isaac Newton died in England. It is hard to ignore the sense of an official baton passing from the seventeenth to the eighteenth centuries, and from one continent to another. The Junto was to be more than just a group of young Philadelphians, *"The Leather Apron Club,"* as they were condescendingly nicknamed by the rich Philadelphia merchants at the *"Every Night Club."* The Junto because of its

membership and commitment to learning as well as its endurance
and results can accurately be seen as a true ancestor of modern
American science. Franklin described the Junto's beginning in the
Autobiography:

> I should have mention'd before, that in the Autumn of the preceding
> year I had form'd most of my ingenious acquaintance into a club for
> mutual improvement, which we call'd the Junto. We met on Friday
> evenings. The rules I drew up requir'd that every member in his turn
> produce one or more queries on any point of morals, politics, or nat-
> ural philosophy, to be discuss'd by the company, and once in three
> months produce and read an essay of his own writing on any subject
> he pleased. Our debates were to be under the direction of a President,
> and to be conducted in the sincere spirit of inquiry after truth, with-
> out fondness for dispute, or desire of victory; and to prevent warmth
> all expressions of positiveness in opinion, or of direct contradiction,
> were after some time made contraband and prohibited under small
> pecuniary penalities.

The name of the group which literally meant "a body of men
combined for a common purpose" had been considerably used in
English history before the eighteenth century (e.g. the Cabinet
Council of Charles I, the Rump Parliament led by Cromwell). But
the Philadelphia club perhaps found its name in a 1708 suggestion by William Penn: "You should form a small junto, and
meet for that and other publick ends."

The need for the organization came from the wish of Franklin
and his friends to meet regularly in an organized way for the purpose of talking truth rather than simply local politics or the mistresses of the Hanoverian Georges in London. The year the Junto
was organized *George I* died and handed on the British crown to
George II. Would the new George be any better than the old
George? Not conspicuously, though in tears he did protest his dying Queen's urging that he should marry again. "No, no," insisted
the King of England, "I shall keep mistresses," and was faithful
to the promise. Ahead in a few decades would be another George,
George III, fated to have world-changing influence on the history
of the American plantations.

However fascinating the hijinks of royalty, the Junto had higher
commitments than gossip; and it would also be faithful to its initial promises.

Oddly, it was the Mathers of Boston with their concerns about
preparing properly for eternity who provided inspiration for the
organizational makeup of the Junto.

QUERIES

During his youthful orgy of reading, a book that made an abiding impression on Franklin was Cotton Mather's *Essays to do Good*. Mather's objective was to save souls, and one of the best ways to accomplish that result was listening to Cotton Mather and doing good in accordance with his careful suggestions. In Boston, Cotton Mather organized neighborhood benefit societies, which began their meetings by reading and thinking about a series of questions Mather prepared for the purpose. Franklin used these questions as a guide when he prepared a similar set for the Junto.

Increase Mather, father of Cotton Mather and also a Congregational minister, as well as an influential president of Harvard, founded America's first scientific society in Boston about 1683. As a Bostonian, Franklin would have been familiar with this achievement by the second of the three distinguished Boston Mathers, and he had admired the Mathers' strong stand in favor of smallpox inoculation. His interest in science must have been stimulated in part through the emphasis given to it by the Mathers. Both Cotton and Increase Mather published many books on scientific subjects. The fact that their names have come to be associated with religious fanaticism and witchcraft has more to do with the sloppiness of history than its thoroughness. Cotton Mather apparently did believe in the existence of witches, but it is doubtful that he was actively involved in the Salem trials and persecutions of 1692. It should also be clear that his championing of science helped to stimulate Franklin in that direction.

The scientific society started by Increase Mather had the ambitious goal of "adding to the store of natural history." But it lacked, apparently, a member with the commitment of Benjamin Franklin, and like most such organizations, quickly disappeared having done little more than enter its name in the chronicles of America as the first scientific society here. Increase Mather did not die until 1723, the year Franklin left for Philadelphia. The boy growing up could have seen and heard him often.

Late in life at seventy-nine, Franklin wrote from France on May 12, 1784 to *Samuel Mather*, Cotton Mather's son, who was one year younger than Franklin.

> When I was a boy, I met with a book entitled *Essays to do Good*, which I think was written by your father. It had been so little regarded by a former possessor that several leaves of it were torn out;
> but the remainder gave me such a turn of thinking as to have an in-

fluence on my conduct through life; for I have always set a greater value on the character of a *doer of good* than on any other kind of reputation; and if I have been, as you seem to think, a useful citizen, the public owes the advantage of it to that book.

Probably the ideas triggered in Franklin's own mind were the chief benefits he derived from Mather's book. The two men were not alike except in a common affinity for natural philosophy and science. Franklin's concerns were chiefly with this world, Mather's with the next. Mather's questions for his neighborhood societies in some cases paralleled Franklin's, but they diverged at Mather's obsession with divinity ("Can any further methods be devised that ignorance and wickedness may be chased from our people in general, and that household piety in particular may flourish among them?") and Franklin's involvement with humanity ("Have you lately observed any encroachment on the just liberties of the people?).

Cotton Mather affected the format of the Junto. His book, neighborhood societies, and personal support of science were influences, as was perhaps the short-lived scientific society of Increase Mather. Other sources, however, can be assumed to have enjoyed influence as well. As a student of John Locke's *Essay on Human Understanding*, Franklin would have known the work came from informal discussions held by the philosopher with his friends. Another influential tributary leading to the Junto were the coffee and conversation clubs Franklin enjoyed during his months in London. Then too, as a boy the Spectator essays of Addison and Steele had delighted him, and he had tried to imitate their style. The idea of the Junto where members could drink wine and discuss philosophy might have come to him through the Spectator Club and its famous members, Sir Roger de Coverley, Will Honeycomb, and the rest. At night, or before work in the mornings, during his apprentice years in Boston, he found the time for such writing exercises and reading. As he encountered and absorbed the world's great ideas through books, the hope some day of being able to discuss those ideas with his peers must have come to him. That would have been Franklin's unspoken dream "on Sundays, when I contrived to be in the Printing House alone, evading as much as I could the common attendance on public worship, which my father used to exact of me when I was under his care: and which indeed I still thought a duty; tho' I could not, as it seemed to me, afford the time to practise it."

The Junto like the Spectator Club of Sir Roger remedied that condition of solitude too often imposed on those who prefer learning to playing. At the Junto he could have it all, play, pleasure, companionship, conviviality, in a continuous atmosphere of civilized learning.

Clearly the Junto filled both a social and intellectual vacuum for the young men who joined it. It is equally clear that it was designed by and for Benjamin Franklin. He was the Great Architect, creating the Junto in his own image. His example and leadership persuaded his friends it was in their interest to follow. The club probably would have been less successful if it had been exclusively an intellectual debating society. It was more. In the beginning, they met at a tavern. Later when they were securely established, they had a rented room for their meetings. But in both places there was always a traditional pause between discussion questions for members and guests to refill their wine glasses. "Mutual improvement" they were convinced had nothing to do with stuffiness or total abstinence from life's available pleasures, including wine. And with Benjamin Franklin as a guiding spirit, we can be quite certain that laughter was not absent from the meetings. "If we may believe our logicians," noted *The Spectator*, Number 494, "man is distinguished from all other creatures by the faculty of laughter." Each month during the warm half of the year, the Junto met outdoors for sport and exercise. Annually they held a dinner when questions were kept to a minimum and celebration to a maximum.

New members, however, had to make a serious commitment in the presence of the others, designed to convince them that sin and song were not regular activities of the Junto.

Any person to be qualified, to stand up, and lay his hand on his breast, and be asked these questions, viz.
1. Have you any particular disrespect to any present members?—*Answer.* I have not.
2. Do you sincerely declare, that you love mankind in general; of what profession or religion soever?—*Answer.* I do.
3. Do you think any person ought to be harmed in his body, name, or goods, for mere speculative opinions, or his external way of worship?—*Answer.* No.

> 4. Do you love truth for truth's sake, and will you endeavor impartially to find and receive it yourself and communicate it to others?—*Answer.* Yes.

The members of the Junto intended to help each other regularly in other aspects of life such as business and society as well as the club. They would be continually available to one another for discussion, advice, and aid in anyway required. This was more than rhetoric. Apparently the members of the Junto sincerely worked at fellowship, and in this too the fine Boston and Philadelphia hand of Benjamin Franklin can be glimpsed. In addition to Franklin, other members of the Junto distinguished themselves in their work and careers. The support received from the Junto shouldn't be dismissed as a factor. Franklin in his *Autobiography* makes the Junto sound like a cooperative and cheerful group achieving in eighteenth century Philadelphia something of the objective that Addison alluded to in *The Spectator*, No. 72, when he wrote about the *Everlasting Club*.

> The *Everlasting Club* consists of an hundred members who divided the whole twenty four hours among them in such a manner, that the Club sits day and night from one end of the year to another; no party presuming to rise till they are relieved by those who are in course to succeed them. By this means a member of the *Everlasting Club* never wants Company; for tho' he is not upon duty himself, he is sure to find some who are; so that if he be disposed to take a whet, a nooning, an evening's draught, or a bottle after midnight, he goes to the Club, and finds a knot of friends to his mind.

The Junto imitated the *Everlasting Club*, however, chiefly in the fidelity of its members to one another. Metaphysics and Madeira *before* midnight were more their speed than serious bottles after. Since all the members were employed by day, they probably were home sound asleep, oblivious of the wolves on nearby hills, well before dawn ninety-nine nights in a hundred.

In some particulars the Junto paralleled Masonic Lodges, the private clubs of London, and fraternal organizations generally. But it differed from those in the strength of its commitment to scientific discussions, study, and acquisition of knowledge. The topics it considered were often similar to those on the agenda of the Royal Society of London. This was no accident. Franklin, in

London, had been fascinated by the Royal Society and its traditions.

Franklin set the tone and the direction of Junto discussions with the twenty-four questions he had adopted as the queries which members were expected to think about and arrive prepared to discuss at the Friday meetings. The questions provide an interesting X-ray view of Benjamin Franklin's mind at the age of 25 or 26.

QUERIES FOR THE JUNTO
Previous question, to be answered at every meeting.

HAVE you read over these queries this morning, in order to consider what you might have to offer the Junto touching any one of them? viz.

1. Have you met with anything, in the author you last read, remarkable, or suitable to be communicated to the Junto? particularly in history, morality, poetry, physic, travels, mechanic arts, or other parts of knowledge.
2. What new story have you lately heard agreeable for telling in conversation?
3. Hath any citizen in your knowledge failed in his business lately, and what have you heard of the cause?
4. Have you lately heard of any citizen's thriving well, and by what means?
5. Have you lately heard how any present rich man, here or elsewhere, got his estate?
6. Do you know of any fellow-citizen, who has lately done a worthy action, deserving praise and imitation? or who has lately committed an error, proper for us to be warned against and avoid?
7. What unhappy effects of intemperance have you lately observed or heard? of imprudence? of passion? or of any other vice or folly?
8. What happy effects of temperance? of prudence? of moderation? or of any other virtue?
9. Have you or any of your acquaintance been lately sick or wounded? If so, what remedies were used, and what were their effects?

10. Who do you know that are shortly going voyages or journeys, if one should have occasion to send by them?

11. Do you think of anything at present, in which the Junto may be serviceable to *mankind*? to their country, to their friends, or to themselves?

12. Hath any deserving stranger arrived in town since last meeting, that you heard of? and what have you heard or observed of his character or merits? and whether think you, it lies in the power of the Junto to oblige him, or encourage him as he deserves?

13. Do you know of any deserving young beginner lately set up, whom it lies in the power of the Junto any way to encourage?

14. Have you lately observed any defect in the laws of your *country*, of which it would be proper to move the legislature for an amendment? or do you know of any beneficial law that is wanting?

15. Have you lately observed any encroachment on the just liberties of the people?

16. Hath anybody attacked your reputation lately? and what can the Junto do towards securing it?

17. Is there any man whose friendship you want, and which the Junto, or any of them, can procure for you?

18. Have you lately heard any member's character attacked, and how have you defended it?

19. Hath any man injured you, from whom it is in the power of the Junto to procure redress?

20. In what manner can the Junto, or any of them, assist you in any of your honorable designs?

21. Have you any weighty affair in hand, in which you think the advice of the Junto may be of service?

22. What benefits have you lately received from any man not present?

23. Is there any difficulty in matters of opinion, of justice, and injustice, which you would gladly have discussed at this time?

24. Do you see anything amiss in the present customs or proceedings of the Junto, which might be amended?

These rules inescapably emphasize Franklin's public inclinations and his civic commitment. He could not live in a community without doing everything possible to improve it. The Junto in part was an expression of this impulse. He wanted his friends available to talk about what he wanted to talk about, but he also wanted all of them *together to serve the public good.*

It was a spirited discussion at the Junto concerning paper currency and its need in an economy trying to grow that led to Franklin's paper on *The Nature and Necessity of a Paper-Currency* (1729) in which he noted the opposition of rich landowners and other wealthy men to paper currency because of the dangers of depreciating all currency, but he insisted that "those who are lovers of trade, and delight to see manufactures encouraged, will be for having a large addition to our currency."

The large addition came, and when it did, Benjamin Franklin printed it. Eventually he had most of the government printing contracts, allowing cynics to point out that there was profitable method in his civic zeal. Such criticisms occurred during Franklin's own time and later, that his public service was calculated self-interest. The criticisms are not convincing, or rather they are simply inadequate. He always went to considerably more trouble than self-interest would have required, in the sense of business profit or public position. Of course, self-interest in the sense of satisfaction, acquired knowledge, and personal pleasure was involved in everything he did, as it must be with the actions of everyone, even a saint or a devil. Franklin, being neither, was somewhere between serving his own interest with a civic zeal that must have been sincere because it was *consistent and intense.*

The Junto became part of all his activities by choice. That was one of its functions. There he could read his new papers, describe his experiments, try out his ideas, and listen to the ready, healthy criticism. It was a Franklin organization, but not a Franklin rubber stamp. If so it would have been useless to him. But in the *Autobiography* Franklin observes that it continued almost forty years and "was the best school of Philosophy, Morals and Politics that then existed in the Province, for our queries which were read the week preceding their discussion put us on reading with attention upon the several subjects, that we might speak more to the purpose: and here too we acquired better habits of conversation, every thing being studied in our rules which might prevent our disgusting each other. From hence the long continuance of the club . . . "

The success of the first Junto brought eventual need for either enlargement of the original group from twelve members or *formation of new Juntos.* Franklin and the majority opted for the latter

—more clubs throughout Philadelphia that would imitate the Junto to encourage intellectual activities, scientific, literary, and moral discussions, among other young men. More clubs with names such as the Vine, the Union, the Band, were formed by members of the original Junto, following the same Rules, using the same practice of starting meetings with a reading of the twenty-four queries "distinctly at each meeting; a pause between each, while one might fill and drink a glass of wine." Then an essay would be read by one of the members, and a discussion held on questions ranging from the philosophically cosmic such as "What is wisdom?" to the technically specific, "Whence comes the dew that stands on the outside of a tankard that has cold water in it in the summertime?"

At the start, the Junto probably was not as ambitious as history might tempt us to think. The young men who joined Benjamin Franklin were no doubt intrigued about why dew formed on a tankard of cold water or the "difference between knowledge and prudence?" But they were young, wine was provided, and Query Number Two must inevitably have distracted meetings with laughter and delays at the expense of Query Number Eight and others many Friday nights. Since there was no better or more enthusiastic storyteller than Benjamin Franklin, he no doubt added Number Two simply so he would have a ready-made and attentive audience for his latest kneeslapper every week.

But the Junto has to be judged historically for its effects, and those are impressive. The club obviously helped Franklin develop his own scientific gifts by providing him an audience, a lecture platform, and when needed, associates. Other members of the club became public champions of science and helped establish the climate of encouragement that new knowledge, especially in the sciences, enjoyed in Philadelphia and eventually other parts of the Colonies during the eighteenth century.

Because the Junto was Franklin's personal vehicle, it had to play a role in the scientific areas of his own influence. Thus it was that the American Philosophical Society, which Franklin would formally move to organize in 1743, has counted its actual beginning from 1727 when the Junto was founded. Franklin linked the two.

The first members, without making individual contributions, are rightfully remembered today as part of America's scientific youth.

The first members were Joseph Brientnal, a Copier of Deeds for the Scriveners; a good-natur'd friendly middle-ag'd man, a great lover of poetry, reading all he could meet with, and writing some that was tolerable; very ingenious in many little nicknackeries, and of sensible conversation. Thomas Godfrey, a self-taught mathematician, great in his way, and afterwards inventor of what is now call'd Hadley's Quadrant . . . Nicholas Scull, a surveyor, afterwards Surveyor-General, who lov'd books, and sometimes made a few verses. William Parsons, bred a shoemaker, but loving reading, had acquir'd a considerable share of mathematics, which he first studied with a view to astrology that he afterwards laughed at. He also became Surveyor-General. William Maugridge, a joiner, a most exquisite mechanic and a solid sensible man. Hugh Meredith, Stephen Potts, and George Webb, I have characteris'd before. Robert Grace, a young gentleman of some fortune, generous, lively and witty, a lover of punning and of his friends. And William Coleman, then a merchant's clerk, about my age, who had the coolest clearest head, the best heart, and the exactest morals, of almost any man I ever met with.

As an extension of its founder, the Junto came to be highly respected and influential in Philadelphia. Franklin writing later in life and looking back at himself as a young man in his early twenties thought that his own industry, by giving the public an impression of almost constant hard work, was chiefly responsible. *Patrick Baird*, a surgeon from Scotland, secretary to Governor Keith, and a member of the Every Night Club, was reported as saying of Franklin that he "is superior to any thing I ever saw of the kind: I see him still at work when I go home from Club; and he is at work again before his neighbours are out of bed."

Thus the "Leather Apron" Junto, benefitting from its organizer's "nose to the grindstone" obsession, came to be viewed much like a wide-awake Junior Chamber of Commerce with a willingness to pitch in, soil its hands, and do the necessary. The reputation of the Junto and the support it gave Franklin were a potent combination when Franklin sought wider public backing in various undertakings such as founding the Union Fire Company, the Pennsylvania Hospital, the Academy of Philadelphia (later the University of Pennsylvania), the Library Company, and the 1747 Association for the defense of Pennsylvania.

PLAIN TRUTH STARTS SOMETHING

The Association organized following Franklin's publication in November, 1747 of a pamphlet entitled *Plain Truth* by "A Tradesman, of Philadelphia." The pamphlet warned Pennsylvanians, and other colonials, that they might have to defend themselves against attacks by French and Spanish privateers during the War of the Austrian Succession, or King George's War. King George II (the one who preferred mistresses to remarrying and thus being disloyal to his dead queen) was ready to fight for *Maria Theresa* to hold her Hapsburg estates, but showed no willingness to do anything about defending Pennsylvania. Franklin warned that it was an unfortunate English trait to close the stable door after the steed has been stolen.

> When it is too late, they are sensible of their imprudence; after great fires, they provide buckets and engines: after a pestilence, they think of keeping clean their streets and common sewers: and when a town has been sacked by their enemies, they provide for its defence, &c.

The essay was a vigorous one and brought results, including the Association Franklin recommended; and his own reputation was established as that of a man to call on in a time of public need or danger. *Plain Truth*, inspired by need and danger, informed the public that "UNION would make us strong, and even formidable." Following the appearance of *Plain Truth*, public attention and public tasks were virtually always clamorous for his time. His missions to England and France can be judged as direct growths therefrom. In France, by another of the coincidences of history, the daughter of Maria Theresa, *Marie Antoinette*, received and recognized Doctor Franklin at the Court of Versailles and perhaps listened to him talk about the exciting new experiments in science taking place at Lavoisier's laboratory in France and his own work in electricity long interrupted by the peculiar necessities of politics. It probably did not occur to the Queen—or the scientist— that her mother's war was partially responsible for his presence in France, and even for the Revolution then occurring. Franklin's paper and the Association that came from it showed the Colonies they could look after themselves against foreign invaders, if they had the will. It was a small step to the corollary conclusion that they could defend themselves even if the invaders were fellow Englishmen. A precedent was set that another *George of England* would find expensive and immensely troublesome, as an empire was shaken and changed forever.

The Junto backed Franklin in this matter as in others, and some members were active participants in persuading Pennsylvanians that Franklin was correct and deserved to be followed.

The year of the Association and his conspicuous public efforts directly affected his future. It was also one of the most productive scientific years of his life. That year, 1747, was when his electrical experiments began to intensify and move toward a climax. It was in March of 1747 that he first began writing to *Peter Collinson*, his friend and scientific correspondent in London, that he and his fellow experimenters were beginning to observe "some particular phenomena that we look upon to be new."

Ironically, at a time when he was entering an avenue of science that he could travel on productively and preferably full-time for the rest of his life, his performance of an unrelated public duty ordained a different future for him. It would not be a future without science; but it would not be what he wanted, *a future exclusively with science.*

In a letter on November 27, 1755, to *William Shipley*, Secretary of the Society for the Encouragement of Arts, Manufactures, and Commerce, Franklin gratefully accepted the offered position of a corresponding member, and then mentioned the frustration that the French War and other public affairs had put before him in his continuing effort to promote "useful knowledge in America." The new corresponding member promised however that "if I live to see our present disturbances over in this part of the world, I shall apply myself to it with fresh spirit."

In the same letter Franklin included what could be viewed as a restatement of his conviciton that a prime function of the Junto was to *preserve, share, and communicate knowledge.*

> As yet, the quantity of human knowledge bears no proportion to the quality of human ignorance. The improvements made within these 2000 years, considerable as they are, would have been much more so if the ancients had possessed one or two arts now in common use. I mean those of copperplate-and letter-printing. Whatever is now exactly delineated and described by those can scarcely (from the multitude of copies) be lost to posterity. And the knowledge of small matters being preserved, gives the hint and is sometimes the occasion of great discoveries, perhaps ages after.

Franklin was writing about the vital contributions of his own profession. But the interlinear message stresses the importance of scientists talking to scientists, and of disseminating ideas as broadly as possible instead of sitting on them like cold eggs in darkness, hoping that eventually something interesting and useful may hatch. Franklin had no fondness for either cold eggs or darkness. He preferred coffee-houses, taverns, or the Junto meeting room where he could sip Madeira and struggle with other men over the great puzzles of life, or even the not so great puzzles if the exercise was amusing and the mind was kept from laziness and sloth. "He that riseth late must trot all day," commented Poor Richard in 1742, "and shall scarce overtake his business at night."

What is to be said of such a man as Benjamin Franklin in his young and middle years, who rose early, trotted all day, and though old business was overtaken, saw ahead of him much new and urgent business that meant even earlier rising on the day ahead?

What can be said? Say simply that in spite of pulls in other directions he was a man who from youth on had the wisdom to be happy. Franklin chose to like other men, and they liked him. He chose to make laughter his greeting, and he was greeted by laughter.

One of the questions Franklin offered for discussion at a Junto session was, "Is any man wise at all times and in all things?" He scribbled his own answer: "No, but some are more frequently wise than others."

Another question: "What is wisdom?" Franklin's answer: "The knowledge of what is best for us on all occasions, and the best way of obtaining it."

If happiness, based on a reasoned acceptance of the universe as it is, qualifies as wisdom; then Franklin was apparently wise most of the time. Even when he was in pain, his humor was never very far away or long absent and always quickly returned.

An English scholar *F. L. Lucas* in *The Art of Living* wrote graciously, and I believe accurately of Benjamin Franklin that while "leaving his lasting imprint on the Western Hemisphere... unlike most great men, and many successful men, he had also succeeded in being happy." Lucas added:

> Johnson would not have repeated a single week of his own life, not though an angel offered; but Franklin would, he said, have been willing to run through his again—wishing, if possible, to have an author's privilege of amending certain *errata*; yet ready for a repetition, even were that denied.... to have got so much zest from a life of over eighty years is perhaps still more remarkable than for a tallow-chandler's son to have disarmed the lightning, and checkmated a king.

The Junto was one of the chief places Franklin's happiness

found both source and outlet. He obtained vast and continuing enjoyment from the questions and the preparations for their discussion, whether a particular Friday evening took a serious or a frivolous turn. The Junto was a multi-purpose organization for a multi-purpose man. It was *simultaneously his wine palace, game room, and Institute of Advanced Study.* The Junto provided a place where Franklin, his colleagues, and others when they had something to say could go to be heard. It was also a place where they could go to listen.

Historically, the significance of the Junto, aside from its importance in the career of Benjamin Franklin, lies in the forum it provided for new ideas and new science. Researchers with particular "bees in their bonnets" received conscientious and alert hearings from the Junto.

When the Junto became respectable, it made American science respectable. And through the persistent good offices of its founder, in effect, it accelerated the development of American science.

1976

Dear Doctor Franklin, Sir,

There seems no doubt that you managed the spectacular feat of enjoying work as much as play. Each was a vital part of life's wonder, and you refused to waste either. It would benefit us if we could master your secret.

The fact is that few of your fellow Americans these days think of their "work" as pleasure. "Pleasure" virtually by definition has come to mean *something other* than the work we do to pay our way in the world. Yet most of us spend the bulk of our time working. Where's the reason?

A man of calculations such as Poor Richard (or yourself) could easily solve the equation: If mostly what we do is work, and work is not pleasure, then in the main, life is not pleasure.

That's it, sir. Whatever our work is, we leave it occasionally to have "fun." We slide down mountains on pieces of wood, watch young men fight over an inflated bladder, or try to hit balls with peculiar clubs of one sort or another. We exhaust ourselves, get sunburn and indigestion, sprain an ankle, and then reluctantly go back to work, where we are at least reasonably safe, if bored and miserable.

We make a frantic ordeal out of "having fun," and often that turns out miserably too. What in the world are you going to do with us?

Your way was different . . . and better. You played games and indulged in pleasant "frolics," chess, Madeira, good conversation, the ladies, and enjoyed yourself immensely. But you seemed to make a point of enjoying your work even more. You certainly derived a special satisfaction from the long hours at the print shop as you worked on clever compositions to help people think and laugh. You even used the word "amusements" to describe your scientific labors. Those burned the oils of midnight, violating your own clever advice about "daylight saving" and working when the sun works. You loved every laborious midnight.

You simply recognized the bad logic in making work a drudgery. "Work and play are expressions of life; we should cherish one as much as the other." That was in effect the credo you practised, and effectively preached by example. "Fun and work" went as well together as "fun and games." Work itself, you seemed to insist, can be a wonderful sort of "play," and always a pleasure.

That wisdom somehow has slipped away from us. We become anxious to finish boring duties so we can have some "fun." Can you help us start our third century realizing that life is to enjoy —whether work or play? Can you help us recover from the madness of pretending there is "fun" in "killing time?"

We Are, &c.,
YOURS, THE PEOPLE

A FORTUNE SUFFICIENT FOR BENJAMIN
. . . I think Miss Betsey a very agreeable, sweet-tempered, good girl, who has had a housewifely education, and will make, to a good husband, a very good wife . . . The family is a respectable one, but whether there be any fortune I know not; and as you do not inquire about this particular, I suppose you think with me, that where every thing else desirable is to be met with, that is not very material. If she does not bring a fortune, she will help to make one. Industry, frugality, and prudent economy in a wife, are to a tradesman, in their effects, a fortune; and a fortune sufficient for Benjamin, if his expectations are reasonable.
(To Mrs. Jane Mecom, May 21, 1757)

X. Games of a Scientist

LEISURE FOR STUDIES AND AMUSEMENTS

On September 29, 1748, Franklin wrote to fellow scientist *Cadwallader Colden:*

> I too am taking the proper measures for obtaining leisure to enjoy life and my friends, more than heretofore, having put my printing-house under the care of my partner, David Hall, absolutely left off bookselling, and removed to a more quiet part of town.

Franklin was confident about *David Hall,* a thirty year old journeyman printer, born in Edinburgh, who had been sent to Philadelphia at Franklin's request by *William Strahan,* the London publisher. Franklin had heard about Hall's wish to relocate in the Americas through a competing bookseller and relative by marriage, *Jimmy Read.* Hall proved to be a godsend.

The original plan was to establish Hall in a West Indies shop, but Franklin kept him in Philadelphia, where he became Franklin's foreman, and in 1748, his partner.

With the "very able, industrious, and honest" Hall as a partner qualified and willing to take off his hands "all care of the printing-office," Franklin could do what in essence he had been struggling toward throughout his business career. He could quit work (business) in order to go to work (science), at the age of 42.

His partnership agreement with Hall assured Franklin half the profits from the business. That would average 467 pounds a year for the eighteen years of the partnership. Supplemented by income from his other properties and his political offices, Franklin's total annual income would be substantial by the standards of the time. The quiet part of town he picked was at Race and Second Streets, not far from the Delaware River, at what was then near the edge of Philadelphia.

> When I disengag'd myself as above mentioned from private business, I flatter'd myself that by the sufficient tho' moderate fortune I had acquir'd, I had secur'd leisure during the rest of my life, for philosophical studies and amusements.

By philosophical studies, we know that he meant his electrical studies specifically and science, especially physics, in general. Franklin chose his words with some care usually, and the word "amusements," if accepted as a precise entry in the *Autobiography*, is an interesting one.

What were the amusements of Benjamin Franklin?

The answer is obvious in part. *Work was clearly one of his chief amusements.* He made it almost a rule of life to enjoy doing what he did, with the result that he invariably did what he enjoyed. Science was one of his dominant amusements. The whole arrangement with David Hall clearly was made with science as the intended result, and Benjamin Franklin's greater amusement as one of the dividends.

Conversation with friends over glasses of Madeira, temperately taken of course, was a major Franklin diversion. He implied as much in his letter to Colden: "to enjoy life and my friends."

Books and study were unmitigated delights for Franklin from boyhood. His *Autobiography*, letters, casual essays emphasize the joys of learning too consistently to be even moderately a pose. Years earlier in 1733 when the pressures of business gave him time for self-indulgence, Franklin dissipated wantonly by taking up the study of languages.

I soon made myself so much a master of the French as to be able to read the books with ease. I then undertook the Italian. An acquaintance who was also learning it, us'd often to tempt me to play chess with him. Finding this took up too much of the time I had to spare for study, I at length refus'd to play any more, unless on this condition, that the victor in every game, should have a right to impose a task, either in parts of the grammar to be got by heart, or in translation, &c. which tasks the vanquish'd was to perform upon honour before our next meeting. As we play'd pretty equally we thus beat one another into that language. I afterwards with a little painstaking acquir'd as much of the Spanish as to read their books also.

Painstaking study of Spanish thus makes the official list of Franklin leisure amusements. But what of the unofficial list? What games did the great man play? Did he doodle and if so, what sort did he make? When he wasn't preoccupied with improving himself or the world, what did he do to amuse himself for an hour or a day simply to while away the time? How does such a scientist fill his leisure between experiments and talk and correspondence and business and politics and language lessons?

The questions are relevant to an understanding of Doctor Franklin or any other person. A man can only be partially and imperfectly known through his work and the results of it, even when that work is a central part of his life. Every life is inevitably more than work, if only through the inescapable biological facts of existence. Each person eats, for instance, or else, and what he chooses to eat can disclose as much or more about him than what he said to reporters on emerging from Number Ten Downing Street. Is he indifferent to food, throwing it down whether apricots or pickles, with an attitude of "it's all the same to me." Or does he dine with leisurely devotion, fletcherizing* his food, and never forgetting that man is what he eats?

To complete the portrait of an individual, he has to be caught unawares. Indeed, so far as respectability allows, he must be ob-

---

*John D. Rockefeller was a dedicated Fletcherite. William James, Harvard philosopher, fletcherized his food for three months, but then gave up the practice with the simple objection that "it nearly killed me." Horace Fletcher started it and published a series of popular books such as *Fletcherism: What it is, or, How I Became Young at Sixty.* "Nature will castigate those who don't masticate," warned the Fletcherites, and the cornerstone of their system was to chew each bite before swallowing thirty to seventy times. All food had to be chewed, even soup, until it was sufficiently liquefied and could in effect "swallow itself."

served *en deshabille*. It is, in fact, less titillation than insight to learn the color of a person's pajamas, if any. A genuinely thorough biographer to the extent possible must follow his subject everywhere as Boswell did Johnson, not only listening to what is said, but noting the expressions, and when the subject drops a scrap of paper, retrieving it and checking the contents. The pencil scratches a man makes instead of sleeping during a dull sermon or a boring meeting can be a revealing part of the record.

In Franklin's case, since he was a lifelong man of letters, his amusements are always present and fully accounted for. They show as conspicuously as anything else, even more conspicuously than his closeted strategy sessions with military and political associates, both American and French, during the Revolution. Many secret conversations were held, secret plots made, and secret agreements arrived at, with absolutely no tape recordings available for historical auditing.

A TONIC BATH WITHOUT WATER

But his secret scribbles we have. Like the other materials, including private letters and reports to his friends, they were published in his own time and later. *Franklin must have known his letters would be published.* He wrote, probably even doodled for publication. In addition to the rest, Franklin was a writer from his youth when he practised imitating *The Spectator* and was encouraged to think "I might possibly in time come to be a tolerable English writer, of which I was extremely ambitious." This impulse to put everything on paper either in the *Autobiography* or a letter makes it convenient to see Franklin completely, work, amusements, et al., including Franklin *deshabille*. Doctor Franklin had nothing to hide from posterity, just as *Winston Churchill*, an Englishman it is easy to think of as another Franklin because of the range of his achievements, when unexpectedly visited by *Franklin Roosevelt* and caught naked after a bath at the White House, commented with the aplomb of genius, "The Prime Minister of Great Britain has nothing to hide from the President of the United States." Being interviewed while undressed by a U.S. President may not have been a normal amusement for the Prime Minister, but it provides a dramatic reminder of a healthy amusement which Doctor Franklin described in detail for *Barbeu Dubourg* in a letter from London, July 28, 1760. Much is revealed in the letter, but no mention is made of pajamas or their color.

... I greatly approve the epithet which you give, in your letter of the 8th of June, to the new method of treating the smallpox, which you call the *tonic* or bracing method; I will take occasion, from it, to mention a practice to which I have accustomed myself. You know the cold bath has long been in vogue here as a tonic; but the shock of the cold water has always appeared to me, generally speaking, as too violent, and I have found it much more agreeable to my constitution to bathe in another element, I mean cold air. With this view I rise almost every morning, and sit in my chamber without any clothes whatever, half an hour or an hour, according to the season, either reading or writing. This practice is not in the least painful, but, on the contrary, agreeable; and if I return to bed afterwards, before I dress myself, as sometimes happens, I make a supplement to my night's rest of one or two hours of the most pleasing sleep that can be imagined. I find no ill consequences whatever resulting from it, and that at least it does not injure my health, if it does not in fact contribute much to its preservation. I shall therefore call it for the future a *bracing* or *tonic* bath.

Barbeu Dubourg, the great ladies of Paris, the acquaintance with whom Franklin studied Italian in 1733, and his friends everywhere knew the particular game Franklin was wont to play under any and all circumstances: *Chess.*

There is evidence that he was a true chess addict, enough so to suspect often that he should drop the game. 1733 was the occasion of one such decision. As a young man, chess took too much time away from study, but he resolved the problem with the penalty arrangement that helped him accelerate learning Italian.

He continued to play chess. The correspondence is sprinkled with mentions of the game from Philadelphia to London to Paris. And it continued to be an amusement that was not completely harmless. "If an amusement is totally harmless it is not an amusement." Poor Richard may have intended to say that in the Almanac of 1759, which never appeared because Richard Saunders collaborator was occupied in England with business of the Colonies.

In 1780, at Franklin's house in Passy, overlooking Paris and the Seine, his formidable and recurrent enemy "Gout" named "Chess" as a particular villain causing his physical ills. One of the pieces (bagatelles) Franklin wrote and printed on the press he had installed at Passy ... for his amusement ... was titled: "Dialogue Between the Gout and M. Franklin."

It was his reply to a verse sent him by *Madame Brillon de Jouy,* a lady friend, chess partner, protégé, correspondent (she sent him 103 letters, he sent her 29), and who knows for sure what. Franklin played considerable chess with the gentlewomen of Paris, including one game in Madame Brillon's bathroom while she was soaking in the tub. The reality is less risqué than it sounds, since the bathtubs then used in France were sabot or shoe-shaped affairs with wooden coverings at the top through which the chaste head of the bather could comfortably emerge. The correspondence of the principals does not indicate who won the game.

Madame Brillon's poem to Franklin was called "Le Sage et la Goutte," and accused the Sage of immoderation, playing chess when he should go for a stroll, overeating, and giving excesssive attention to the ladies.

Franklin, though his enemy was at him, replied in good humor, admitting that most of the charges were unfortunately not false.

> Franklin: Eh! oh! eh! What have I done to merit these cruel sufferings?
>
> Gout: Many things; you have ate and drank too freely, and too much indulged those legs of yours in their indolence. . . . what is your practice after dinner? Walking in the beautiful gardens of those friends with whom you háve dined would be the choice of men of sense; yours is to be fixed down to chess, where you are found engaged for two or three hours! This is your perpetual recreation, which is the least eligible of any for a sedentary man, because, instead of accelerating the motion of the fluids, the rigid attention it requires helps to retard the circulation and obstruct internal secretions. Wrapt in the speculations of this wretched game, you destroy your constitution.

The Gout reminded Doctor Franklin that wherever he might be in Paris he would find lovely gardens and walks as well as beautiful women for "agreeable and instructive conversation: all which you might enjoy by frequenting the walks. But these are rejected for this abominable game of chess. Fie, then, Mr. Franklin!"

At the end, with the enemy punishing him worse than before for his own good, the victim capitulates, but is not believed.

> Franklin: Oh! oh! For Heaven's sake leave me! and I promise faithfully never more to play at chess, but to take exercise daily, and live temperately.
>
> Gout: I know you too well. You promise fair; but, after a few months of good health, you will return to your old habits; your fine promises will be forgotten like the forms of the last year's clouds.

Madam Gout, who called herself Franklin's physician, was sceptical of promises and certain she would have to return. On both scores, she was correct. Franklin played chess still, and he had the gout still.

MADAM GOUT'S "ABOMINABLE GAME OF CHESS"

What made chess a compelling amusement? For one thing, the antiquity of the game impressed Franklin. "... It has, for numberless ages, been the amusement of all the civilized nations of Asia, the Persians, the Indians, and the Chinese."

Since the game was sufficiently interesting in itself, monetary gain was not a consideration, decided Franklin. "Those, therefore, who have leisure for such diversions, cannot find one that is more innocent."

Would Doctor Franklin's favorite game prove to be a lighthearted and profitless frolic? Not for a minute. He considered the matter in his delightful essay, "Morals of Chess," printed on his press at Passy in 1779.

> The game of chess is not merely an idle amusement. Several very valuable qualities of the mind, useful in the course of human life, are to be acquired or strengthened by it, so as to become habits, ready on all occasions. For life is a kind of chess, in which we have points to gain, and competitors or adversaries to contend with, and in which there is a vast variety of good and ill events, that are, in some degree, the effects of prudence or the want of it.

So by playing at chess we gain in foresight, circumspection, caution. Foresight "looks a little into futurity, considers the consequences that may attend an action." Circumspection "surveys the whole chessboard, or scene of action." We learn Caution "not to make our moves too hastily."

Franklin, the reasoned optimist, also finds support for his philosophy in chess.

> We learn by chess the habit of *not being discouraged by present bad appearances in the state of our affairs,* the habit of *hoping for a favorable change,* and that of *persevering in the search of resources.* The game is so full of events, there is such a variety of turns in it, the fortune of it is so subject to sudden vicissitudes, and one so frequently, after long contemplation, discovers the means of extricating one's self from a supposed insurmountable difficulty, that one is encouraged to continue the contest to the last, in hope of victory by our own skill, or at least of giving a stalemate, by the negligence of our adversary.

Sport for sport's sake clearly was not a very convincing argument with Doctor Franklin. Only chess was sufficiently instructive and therefore suitably exciting to keep him up all night or entice him into a lady's chamber for the purpose of finishing a game and perhaps capturing her queen. He called chess the "beneficial amusement" and preferred it to others "which are not attended with the same advantages."

Chess was too important to treat casually or with disregard for the rules. False moves were absolutely to be avoided. Courtesy was to be scrupulous.

> If your adversary is long in playing, you ought not to hurry him, or to express any uneasiness at his delay. You should not sing, nor whistle, nor look at your watch, nor take up a book to read, nor make a tapping with your feet on the floor, or with your fingers on the table, nor do anything that may disturb his attention. For all these things displease; and they do not show your skill in playing, but your craftiness or your rudeness.

As for spectators, they should "observe the most perfect silence."

On Christmas, 1781, Franklin wrote a self-evaluation in which he referred to his method of playing chess: "You know that I never give up a game before it is finished, always hoping to win, or at least to get a move, and when I have a good game, I guard against presumption."

Obviously this "beneficial amusement" was considerably more than a "bagatelle" to Franklin. The game symbolized his attitude to life and within the confines of the ordered moves indicated his method in both science and politics. If an experiment failed, he tried another way. If a Valley Forge or a devastating defeat came in a Revolution, he waited for another chance. *His rule was: "Never give up a game before it is finished."*

THE EYES OF OUR RUIN
It has been computed by some political arithmetician, that if every man and woman would work for four hours each day on something useful, that labor would produce sufficient to procure all the necessaries and comforts of life, want and misery would be banished out of the world, and the rest of the twenty-four hours might be leisure and pleasure . . . Almost all the parts of our bodies require some expense. The feet demand shoes; the legs, stockings; the rest of the body, clothing; and the belly, a good deal of victuals. Our eyes, though exceedingly useful, ask, when reasonable, only the cheap assistance of spectacles, which could not much impair our finances. But THE EYES OF OTHER PEOPLE are the eyes that ruin us. If all but myself were blind, I should want neither fine clothes, fine houses, nor fine furniture.
(To Benjamin Vaughan, July 26, 1784)

Where did chess end and life begin? Perhaps they were often the same. Thomas Jefferson recorded the occasion in France when Franklin mated the king of the *Duchesse de Bourbon,* and took it from the board. The lady protested that in France the king was never captured. "We do not take kings," she said. Franklin, representing a country that was in the process not of taking but of discarding a king, told the Duchesse de Bourbon that *"the king" was always taken in America.* In another decade, France would begin imitating Franklin and chess by taking a king. Plump Louis XVI would be removed to make France leaner. Franklin could have told them that was only a beginning. Immediately there would be another game to start, another game to finish.

THE MOST MAGICALLY MAGIC OF ANY MAGIC SQUARE

So much for Franklin's beneficial amusement. He had another which occupied him during special periods of compulsory boredom: devising magic squares and circles. It was a strange hobby for one who could remember having "failed" arithmetic at the age of nine, but he obviously had contrived to master the subject later on his own.

In 1736 he became clerk of the General Assembly of Pennsylvania. The job was not among the most demanding or intriguing. He was required to attend all sessions of the Assembly, keep his mouth shut, and spend his time listening to politicians talk.

> I was at length tired with sitting there to hear debates in which as clerk I could take no part, and which were often so unentertaining, that I was induc'd to amuse myself with making magic squares, or circles, or anything to avoid weariness.

Years later visiting at the home of James Logan, the distinguished Pennsylvanian, one time secretary to the founder William Penn, a long time contributor to the arts and sciences of the Colonies, and a patron of Franklin until his death in 1751, Franklin saw a copy of *Bernard Frénicle's* 1693 posthumous work, *Divers Ouvrages de Mathématique par Messieurs de l'Académie des Sciences,* an elaborate treatment of magic squares.

Franklin was surprised to learn that reputable mathematicians had studied the field and that scholarly works such as Frénicle's were available. James Logan, whose opinions Franklin valued, took the squares seriously, calling them an example of ingenuity and dexterity in the management of numbers.

Reporting later on his "arithmetical curiosities" to Peter Collinson in London, Franklin had decided to agree that such exercises might not be as useless as he had supposed:

"...if it produces by practice an habitual readiness and exactness in mathematical disquisitions, which readiness may on many occasions be of real use."

Franklin was also impressed to learn that magic squares had a very long history, having been used widely as magic charms and amulets in ancient China, India, and other places. Magic squares came to Europe early, with documents on the subject dating back at least to 1300. A Greek mathematician named *Emanuel Moschopoulus*, living in Constantinople, prepared a work about that time. Franklin told James Logan of his own dalliance in the medium.

I then confessed to him that in my younger days, having once some leisure which I still think I might have employed more usefully, I had amused myself in making these kind of magic squares, and at length had acquired such a knack at it that I could fill the cells of any magic square, of reasonable size, with a series of numbers as fast as I could write them, disposed in such a manner as that the sums of every row, horizontal, perpendicular, or diagonal, should be equal; but not being satisfied with these, which I looked on as common and easy things, I had imposed on myself more difficult tasks, and succeeded in making other magic squares with a variety of properties, and much more curious.

At Logan's request, Franklin showed him subsequently one of his efforts in this line, a square of 8. He explained the details of the square in his letter to Collinson.

A CUNNING LOAN WTH A LONG LIFE
I send you herewith a bill for ten louis d'ors. I do not pretend to give you such a sum; I only lend it to you. When you shall return to your country with a good character, you cannot fail of getting into some business that will in time enable you to pay all your debts. In that case, when you meet with another honest man in similar distress, you must pay me by lending this sum to him; enjoining him to discharge the debt by a like operation, when he shall be able, and shall meet with such another opportunity. I hope it may thus go through many hands before it meets with a knave that will stop its progress. This is a trick of mine for doing a deal of good with a little money. I am not rich enough to afford much in good works, and so am obliged to be cunning and make the most of a little.
(To Benjamin Webb, April 22, 1784)

52	61	4	13	20	29	36	45
14	3	62	51	46	35	30	19
53	60	5	12	21	28	37	44
11	6	59	54	43	38	27	22
55	58	7	10	23	26	39	42
9	8	57	56	41	40	25	24
50	63	2	15	18	31	34	47
16	1	64	49	18	33	32	17

The properties are:

(1) That every straight row, horizontal or vertical, of 8 numbers added together makes 260, and half each row half 260.

(2) That the bent row of 8 numbers, ascending and descending diagonally, viz., from 16 ascending to 10, and from 23 descending to 17, and every one of its parallel bent rows of 8 numbers, make 260. Also the bent row from 52, descending to 54, and from 43 ascending to 45, and every one of its parallel bent rows of 8 numbers, make 260. Also the bent row from 45 to 43 descending to the left, and from 23 to 17 descending to the right, and every one of its parallel bent rows of 8 numbers, make 260. Also the bent row from 52 to 54 descending to the right, and from 10 to 16 descending to the left, and every one of its parallel bent rows of 8 numbers, make 260. Also the parallel bent rows next to the above-mentioned, which are shortened to 3 numbers ascending and 3 descending, etc., as from 53 to 4 ascending, and from 29 to 44 descending, make, with the 2 corner numbers, 260. Also the 2 numbers, 14, 61, ascending, and 36, 19, descending, with the lower 4 numbers situated like them, viz., 50, 1, descending, and 32, 47, ascending, make 260. And, lastly, the 4 corner numbers, with the 4 middle numbers, make 260.

So this magical square seems perfect in its kind. But these are not all its properties; there are five other curious ones which at some other time I will explain to you.

What the additional five properties may be, Doctor Franklin left Peter Collinson and us to guess or find. Or after a prodigious explanation, did he see a playful chance to add to the lunacy of mankind by dangling another curious five? Find them if you can.

James Logan, admired the square of 8, then showed Franklin another item from his collection, "an old arithmetical book in quarto, wrote, I think, by one Stifelius, which contained a square of 16." The square "if I forget not, it had only the common properties of making the same sum, viz., 2056, in every row, horizontal, vertical, and diagonal."

Even with such limitations, however, the square of 16 dimmed the luster of Franklin's square of 8. It immediately became a sort of mathematical chess game between Franklin and one Stifelius, long departed. Franklin that same night at home worked out his own square of 16.

200	217	232	249	8	25	40	57	72	89	104	121	136	153	168	181
58	39	26	7	250	231	218	199	186	167	154	135	122	103	90	71
198	219	230	251	6	27	38	59	70	91	102	123	134	155	166	187
60	37	28	5	252	229	220	197	188	165	156	133	124	101	92	69
201	216	233	248	9	24	41	56	73	88	105	120	137	152	169	184
55	42	23	10	247	234	215	202	183	170	151	138	119	106	87	74
203	214	235	246	11	22	43	54	75	86	107	118	139	150	171	182
53	44	21	12	245	236	213	204	181	172	149	140	117	108	85	76
205	212	237	244	13	20	45	52	77	84	109	116	141	148	173	180
51	46	19	14	243	238	241	206	179	174	147	142	115	110	83	78
207	210	239	242	15	18	47	50	79	82	111	114	143	146	175	178
49	48	17	16	241	240	209	208	177	176	145	144	113	112	81	80
196	221	228	253	4	29	36	61	68	93	100	125	132	157	164	189
62	35	30	3	254	227	222	195	190	163	158	131	126	99	94	67
194	223	226	255	2	31	34	63	66	95	98	127	130	159	162	191
64	33	32	1	256	225	224	193	192	161	160	129	128	97	96	65

Franklin's square of 16 went Stifelius's square several better as he had intended. It matched the ability to total 2056 on the rows and diagonals, plus this astonishing feature:

> . . . a four-square hole being cut in a piece of paper of such a size as to take in and show through it just 16 of the little squares, when laid on the greater square, the sum of the 16 numbers so appearing through the hole, wherever it was placed on the greater square, should likewise make 2056.

Franklin sent the new square to James Logan and received it back with compliments that he said were too extravagant to repeat. But Franklin was ready with a more subdued compliment of his own: "I make no question but you will readily allow this square of 16 to be the most magically magical of any magic square ever made by any magician."

Franklin ended his first letter to Collinson on the subject by mentioning another exercise, his magic circle, but did not enclose it because "at present I believe you have enough."

The circle being requested, he did send it later together with another list of properties. The device had been arranged with 8 concentric circles and 8 radial rows filled with numbers from 12 to 75. The numbers of each circle, or radial row, plus the 12 at the center equalled 360. A number of relationships ending in 180 or 360 were pointed out, and then this conclusion:

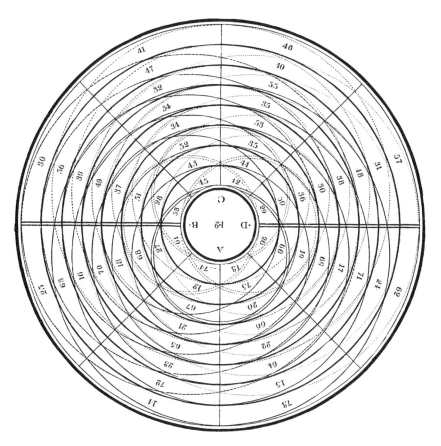

It may be observed that there is not one of the numbers but what belongs at least to two of the different circular spaces; some to three, some to four, some to five; and yet they are all so placed as never to break the required number 360, in any of the 28 circular spaces within the primitive circle. These interwoven circles make so perplexed an appearance that it is not easy for the eye to trace every circle of numbers one would examine, through all the maze of circles intersected by it; but if you fix one foot of the compasses in either of the centres, and extend the other to any number in the circle you would examine belonging to that centre, the moving foot will point the others out, by passing round over all the numbers of that circle successively.

In July and October, 1768, the *Gentleman's Magazine* in London published Doctor Franklin's magic squares and circle, commenting on their "Surprizing Properties of Numbers." How did he do it? Obviously he had discovered a relationship among numbers with regard to the magic squares of whatever size that allowed him to fill the squares as fast as he could write them. Not Doctor Franklin, or Isaac Newton, or a Professor of Mathematics at Harvard could simply pluck the numbers from the air and put them down without a system.

On July 2, 1768, Franklin wrote to one of the gentlemen at Harvard, *John Winthrop*:

> The magic square and circle, I am told, have occasioned a good deal of puzzling among the mathematicians here; but no one has desired me to show him my method of disposing the numbers. It seems they wish rather to investigate it themselves.

So he had a method. Theories of conspiracy having occurred between the bored and underworked clerk of the Pennsylvania Assembly and a journeyman devil passing through town need not be credenced. As for the method, Benjamin Franklin apparently worked it out for himself; which would likely have occasioned considerable wonder in the mind of schoolmaster Geo. Brownell who had the unique distinction of having "failed" Benjamin Franklin in arithmetic during Franklin's second—and last—year of school in Boston.

Because of the times involved between Franklin's casual experiments with numbers at the Assembly and publication some thirty years later, he obviously thought of them as unimportant trifles, a sort of mental solitaire. But when electricity and colonial politics made him famous, those casuals done for amusement became Doctor Franklin's Puzzles, and were no longer unimportant.

MISS POLLY BAKER, THE PROSECUTED MATRON

Chess and magic squares were his amusements. He called them that, but only chess was kept up most of his life. Magic squares seem to have been for the early period only, and not indulged in later. Perhaps chess was never successfully put aside because it was such a useful aid in *another of his life-long diversions, seeking and enjoying the company of women.* He never tired of their society, and that was true not only at nineteen when he was loose of foot and free of fancy in London, but also at seventy when he arrived in France under orders from the Continental Congress accompanied by two grandsons, *Benjamin Franklin Bache*, age seven, and *William Temple Franklin*, age sixteen, the illegitimate son of his illegitimate son.

William Temple, known as *Franklinet* by some of his grandfather's friends, carried on the tradition by having an affair with a married Frenchwoman, *Blanchette Caillot*, who called Franklinet her "Little Excellency" and became the mother of his child.

Three generations of illegitimacy did not disturb Benjamin Franklin, for whom the word was only a social formula of little consequence. As long as the babies were healthy and looked after, nature was satisfied and so was Doctor Franklin.

In a celebrated hoax, "The Speech of Miss Polly Baker," Franklin had assumed the guise of a woman as in the Silence Dogood articles. But Miss Polly was special. In the *General Advertiser* of London, April 15, 1747, her speech to a group of judges in Connecticut was first printed as if authentic. It was an authentic, tongue-in-cheek Franklin way of saying that procreation was splendid no matter how it happened.

Polly Baker's speech was to protest her fifth prosecution for having a bastard child. "I have brought five fine children into the world, at the risque of my life; I have maintain'd them well by my own industry, without burthening the Township, and would have done it better, if it had not been for the heavy charges and fines I have paid." *Polly went on to insist that she had always been ready to enter the honourable state of wedlock.* "I defy any one to say I ever refused an offer of that sort; on the contrary, I readily consented to the only proposal of marriage that ever was made me, which was when I was a virgin, but too easily confiding in the person's sincerity that made it, I unhappily lost my honour by trusting to his; for he got me with child, and then forsook me." Her betrayer, Polly reported, was then a respected magistrate. She concluded with a compelling appeal to her judges which induced one of them, the story noted, to marry her the following day.

> What must poor young women do, whom customs and nature forbid to solicit the men, and who cannot force themselves upon husbands, when the laws take no care to provide them any, and yet severely punish them if they do their duty without them; the duty of the first and great command of nature and nature's God, increase and multiply; a duty, from the steady performance of which nothing has been able to deter me, but for its sake I have hazarded the loss of the public esteem, and have frequently endured public disgrace and punishment: and therefore ought, in my humble opinion, instead of a whipping, to have a statue erected to my memory.

A later account of this gallant woman's saga noted that she had fifteen children by her husband and lived irreproachably.

Polly Baker, of course, is a totally unrepentant Benjamin Franklin. She eloquently voiced many of his personal views, including the practical and obvious fact that a new country needs people. In a letter to Deborah Franklin, the Doctor wrote that he loved to hear of everything "that tends to increase the number of good people." He had done his part, and if prosecuted might have been tied to a whipping post and given "twenty-one of the best."

The criticism could be and has been made that he was simply rationalizing his own peccadilloes. Naturally. Very naturally. Never, in fact, has immorality been more charmingly defended. To Franklin there was no immorality involved in behaving very naturally, and frequently during his long life indications are that he found suitable occasions for behaving so.

The 1740's when Franklin was beginning to consider the mysteries of electricity must have stimulated literary creativity in what could be called the Polly Baker genre. About the same time Franklin wrote his *Advice to a Young Man on the Choice of a Mistress*. It was in the form of a letter suggesting that marriage was the proper remedy for "the violent natural inclinations you mention" but that if such counsel would not be taken and "commerce with the sex inevitable, then I repeat my former advice, that in all your amours you should prefer old women to young ones." A multitude of reasons were offered for choosing an old rather than a young mistress, e.g., "their minds are better stored with observations, their conversation is more improving and more lastingly agreeable," and finally, "they are so grateful."

In France, the logic of rewriting the same piece to emphasize the advantages of an old lover must have occurred to Franklin. But in

Paris at seventy he had no intentions of allowing age to defeat him. On March 16, 1780, he wrote to his friend and cofounder of the Pennsylvania Hospital, fellow scientist, *Dr. Thomas Bond*:

> Shake the old ones by the hand for me, and give the young ones my blessing. For my own part, I do not find that I grow any older. Being arrived at seventy, and considering that by travelling farther in the same road I should probably be led to the grave, I stopped short, turned about, and walked back again; which having done these four years, you may now call me sixty-six. Advise those old friends of ours to follow my example; keep up your spirits, and that will keep up your bodies.

In Paris Franklin kept up his spirits by having chess and tête á têtes with Madame Brillon, asking Madame Helvétius to marry him despite her ten dogs and eighteen cats, and even flirting with Marie Antoinette.

The *London Chronicle* in July 1778 reported that Doctor Franklin had demonstrated an electrical experiment for the Queen in the Gardens of Versailles. When she asked if he did not fear the same fate as Prometheus who was chained to a rock and his liver was eaten by an eagle for stealing fire from heaven, Franklin answered that her eyes had stolen more fire than ever he had done, and through their beauty, done more mischief than all his experiments. If the event occurred, the daughter of Maria Theresa was not excessively offended. She did not have the Sage from Philadelphia beheaded.

Whatever happened in the bathroom of Madame Brillon or in the Gardens of Versailles, the ladies of Paris were delighted with Doctor Franklin and he with them. *Whether he was an old lover or a dear papa is academic historically.* He was in Paris, growing younger by personal fiat, and very much alive, with young Madame Brillon writing to him with tease on every word:

> Do you know, my dear papa, that people have criticized the sweet habit I have taken of sitting on your lap, and your habit of soliciting from me what I always refuse.

Franklin enjoyed the companionship, the conversation, and the chess of women. He enjoyed them because they were life, and he enjoyed life. Even when occasionally refused.

In a poignant paragraph Franklin once combined the two leading amusements of man, war and love, and taught a lesson in natural logic that the human race in general has never seemed willing to learn.

Men I find to be a sort of beings very badly constructed, as they are
generally more easily provoked than reconciled, more disposed to do
mischief to each other than to make reparation, much more easily deceived than undeceived, and having more pride and even pleasure in
killing than in begetting one another; for without a blush they assemble in great armies at noonday to destroy, and when they have
killed as many as they can they exaggerate the number to augment
the fancied glory; but they creep into corners and cover themselves
with the darkness of night when they mean to beget, as being ashamed
of a virtuous action.

It is patent throughout his life that Franklin derived contented
merriment from all his multitudinous activities, work, wenching,
wining, *ad infinitum*. It is also patent that he had *one continuing
amusement that never failed him, life itself*. There was his chief
amusement always, the hurly-burly of human existence. That was
true, because come what might, willy-nilly, Benjamin Franklin
always had the luck and good sense to enjoy being Benjamin
Franklin.

During the Paris years, he sent a description of himself to a
ladyfriend in England. There were ways for Americans to correspond with the English, even during wartime, and Franklin found
them. If they did not easily exist, he made them.

I know you wish you could see me; but as you can't, I will describe
myself to you. Figure me in your mind as jolly as formerly, and as
strong and hearty, only a few years older; being very plainly dress'd,
wearing my thin gray strait hair, that peeps out from under my only
coiffure, a fine fur cap, which comes down to my forehead almost to
my spectacles. Think how this must appear among the powder'd
heads of Paris.

The portrait is a good one. Perhaps the most descriptive word
is "*jolly*."

1976

Dear Doctor Franklin, Sir,

You often displayed a lively curiosity and imagination in the
healing arts/sciences. In fact your advice was frequently sought
on medical matters, and you gave it generously.

Since the beginning of human ailments, it may be that no one
ever gave better medical advice than you did when you said:
"Wouldst thou enjoy a long life, a healthy body, and a vigorous

mind, and be acquainted also with the wonderful works of God, labour in the first place to bring thy appetite into subjection to reason."

Like much wisdom, sir, that is easier said than done; but when it is done, enjoyment surely will follow.

You must in some instances have been anxious about the consequences of advising your "patients" on the subtleties of caring for their most critical possessions (themselves). In 1744 you advised Josiah and Abiah Franklin (dad and mom) on the use of salt plus oil of turpentine (*sapo philosophorum*) for the stomach's sake, but included a warning:

> I apprehend I am too busy in prescribing and meddling in the doctor's sphere, when any of you complain of ails in your letters . . . I hope you consider my advice, when I give any, only as a mark of my good will, and put no more of it in practice than happens to agree with what your doctor directs.

Some of your best friends were doctors, and it was natural for you to pay them tribute. But there was no need in your time or in this one to fear the reactions of doctors. If some could have accused you of meddling, modern medicine can hardly do the same. You meddled with electricity, and today's awesomely versatile hospitals are among the end results. Most of the remarkable accomplishments of our intricate medicine today, one way or another, are plugged into the nearest electrical outlet.

The results are, to use your favorite word, ingenious. You would be impressed . . . transplants of bodily parts from one person to another for instance. And our modern treatments of cancers. You may recall writing to your sister Jane in 1731 about cancer patients wearing "a kind of shell made of some wood, cut at a proper time, by some man of great skill" and deriving benefit. However, you were "not apt to be superstitiously fond of believing such things."

Consider the latest thing here. A type of cancer is attacked with treatments so powerful they destroy the cancer *and* the bone marrow of the patient, which is replaced with healthy bone marrow from a donor. Something, eh! Your electricity is involved, of course, in many different ways. Sir, you have our permission to "meddle" anytime.

We Are, &c.,
YOURS, THE PEOPLE

XI. Medicine Man

PATIENT, HEAL THYSELF

If Benjamin Franklin who speculated about every mystery that came his way and never lost his curiosity in the natural world had not bothered with man himself, the contradiction would have been strange. It did not occur.

The fact is that Franklin throughout his adult life was fundamentally a humanist. Much that he studied and most of the things that he did had direct human significance or application. His science was directed more often than not toward bettering the conditions and lives of mankind. Thus, inevitably he conducted studies and researches on various medical topics of concern to man.

Franklin lived eighty-four years in a century when people still attempted to heal themselves. Now there is the ritual of calling the doctor, making an appointment, and waiting . . . and waiting, to be taken finally by a crisply efficient nurse into a neat and sanitary cubicle (except for the discarded Bandaid in the corner). "Doctor will see you soon," promises *Ms. Crisply Efficient.* By "soon" she means "some time."

There were practising physicians in the eighteenth century, but they were impossible to call unless by happenstance they lived nearby and the patient possessed enough volume despite the pain to cry for "Help." Many would find the only available doctor too distant for a visit except during rare trips to market. Those naturally would be times when the former and future patient would feel just fine.

The eighteenth century had to be a time of home remedies and do-it-yourself medicine. Today the Mayo Clinic or a reasonable alternative is only hours away by automobile or plane, but in Franklin's time "heal thyself" was a way of life, hopefully, for patients as well as physicians.

"Cures" were determined by trial and error in that age of instinctive experiment. If Jeter fell in the pig trough and got the chills, Aunt Minnie might recommend rubbing him dry with wool flannel to spare him from the lung death. If it worked on Jeter, a new folk cure could be added to the established repertoire. When a reasonable preventive of the lung death, or chilblains, or gout was determined, it was widely shared. Thus a body of traditional folk medicine developed and gradually spread.

Since folk medicine was based on tried and proven treatments, much of it was reasonably effective. Trial and error might give continuing work to cemetery sculptors, but it was also a process of learning what would work and what wouldn't. The modern pharmacopoeia with its thousands of items had its beginning with American Indians, with observant housewives attacking family ails, or with sick soldiers ready to experiment with something different because there was nothing else to try. And sometimes, whatever it was, worked. If so, it probably still is working today.

The doctor in today's busy clinic eventually arrives. He is as brisk as Ms. Crisply Efficient, but with a larger "what have we here" smile. Don't be surprised if he tells you to soak your aching finger in hot water with a little Epsom Salts and to take so-and-so every four hours. Great grandmother would have made the same diagnosis, with a less fancy name of course. Instead of calling it "paronychia" and secretly indulging in self-congratulations for recalling those second semester Med School notes, she would have looked it over, decided it was "poisoned," and recommended soaking it in salts.

In the eighteenth century any person with a scientific bent sooner or later bent his science in the direction of human ails, their treatments and cures. Even if his science was normally studying sun and moon and the fine harmonies of stars, when an ache developed somewhere in the vicinity of his own person, it was natural for him to pay attention and begin wondering about pain, the human body, and "Why?" That is the way scientists are. Get their attention and they begin asking why.

Much earlier than the eighteenth century, Galileo, for instance, whom some credit with starting the modern era of science, was essentially a stargazer; but he also examined the human pulse in relation to the oscillations of the pendulum and as a young man studied medicine. In addition, he designed and constructed an early ancestor of the modern thermometer which doctors and nurses use to do battle with tongues, &c.

Benjamin Franklin was a scientist whose long life made it inevitable that he too would be frequently alerted and intrigued by medical subjects, if only to observe and explain to himself his own symptoms. It wasn't personal symptoms, however, but a need expressed by his brother John in Boston that led Franklin to devise *the first American catheter.* Much of Franklin's science was the result of a quick response to an immediate need. His brother, a tallow-chandler like Josiah Franklin, was sick. He could be helped in a specific way. Franklin didn't respond with the customary, pro forma advice to see a good doctor. He thought about it, and, not unusual for him, in the process happened to think of an answer. He wrote to his brother on December 8, 1752:

Reflecting yesterday on your desire to have a flexible catheter, a thought struck into my mind, how one might probably be made; and lest you should not readily conceive it by any description of mine, I went immediately to the silversmith's and gave directions for making one (sitting by till it was finished) that it might be ready for this post ... This machine may either be covered with small fine gut, first cleaned and soaked a night in a solution of alum and salt and water, then rubbed dry, which will preserve it longer from putrefaction; then wet again and drawn on and tied to the pipes at each end, where little hollows are made for the thread to bind in and the surface greased. Or perhaps it may be used without the gut, having only a little tallow rubbed over it, to smooth it and fill the joints. I think it is as flexible as would be expected in a thing of the kind, and I imagine will readily comply with the turns of the passage, yet has stiffness enough to be protruded; if not, the enclosed wire may be used to stiffen the hinder part of the pipe while the fore part is pushed forward, and as it proceeds the wire may be gradually withdrawn. The tube is of such a nature, that when you have occasion to withdraw it its diameter will lessen, whereby it will move more easily. It is a kind of screw and may be both withdrawn and introduced by turning. Experience is necessary for the right using of all new tools or instruments, and that will perhaps suggest some improvements to this instrument.

INOCULATION AND THE MATHERS OF BOSTON

Throughout his life, Franklin seemed to make a point of not fearing progress. Thirty years earlier in Boston, Franklin had been witness to a medical crisis and had taken an opposite stand, on a question of improvements, from that of another brother, James. In 1721 and 1722, a smallpox epidemic ravaged Boston, and James Franklin's newspaper, the *New-England Courant*, took a strong position against inoculation, a practice advocated with at least equal vigor by Cotton Mather. The irreverent young Benjamin who showed more inclination for book reading than for church going, was not a pious favorite of Cotton Mather's. Franklin, however, could admire the fiery preacher for his public zeal and his championing of new science, without accepting the all or nothing, heaven or perdition theology. Franklin saw the dramatic results obtained by *Cotton Mather*, his father *Increase Mather*, and their associates using the "new to America" science of inoculation. Despite superstitious public protests, they inoculated 286 against smallpox. Only six died. Of 5,759 people not inoculated in Boston, 844 died. The statistics seemed conclusive. Franklin's logic persuaded him the effectiveness of inoculation in preventing smallpox was established.

But his brother James, influenced by the Boston medical establishment and especially by *William Douglass* who had the only official medical degree in the Colonies, took a counter view. Boston physicians opposed inoculation because they could not understand it. It seemed nonsensical to men who lacked even the rudiments of microbiological knowledge to try preventing a disease by deliberately causing a mild form of it. In 1722 medical science and the minds of men were still a great distance from Pasteur, antibodies, and comprehension of the phenomena of immunity. Since the lives of patients have always been involved, medicine at bedside has tended to be conservative and to stick with treatments that are known not to kill, at least directly and conspicuously. In the long run, the human race probably should be relieved that its doctors have resisted the temptation to experiment promptly on patients with every new quackery or gimmickry that came along. The result, before today's automated and specialized medicine changed everything, was that dramatic progress in medical knowledge tended to come from nonphysicians such as Pasteur, or a passionate minister of Boston such as Cotton Mather.

Inoculation was unproven, illogical, new, and therefore dangerously suspect to the doctors of Boston. It wasn't new to the world. Inoculation was known and practised in the areas of the Middle East, particularly Turkey, for a considerable period before the wife of the English Ambassador in Constantinople, *Lady Mary Montagu*, became an enthusiast and reported the discovery to London early in the eighteenth century.

Cotton Mather had read of the experiments in England, and considered them promising. As a science enthusiast rather than a physician, he was far less inclined to doubt the possibility of new knowledge from any direction, even the mysterious Middle East, than Douglass and the cautious doctors.

The story of medical progress in the world in each of its various chapters, however, usually includes the name of one maverick physician who proved willing to buck tradition, the aghast denunciations of his colleagues, and the anger of the community, in order to try something he believed in. During the Boston smallpox epidemic, that physician was *Zabdiel Boylston*. Encouraged by Cotton Mather, Boylston inoculated two of his own sons and two of his slaves. That started the inoculation program which supplied convincing evidence that inoculation was worthy of conscientious medical respect and further use as well as study. Benjamin Franklin, never a traditionalist in scientific matters, accepted the inoculation evidence. Reason allowed nothing else.

But James Franklin, supporting the condemnatory professional humphings of Douglass and others, railled against the practice vehemently. Since separation of church and state was far from a reality in the Boston of Cotton Mather, the Mathers had influence high up. Very high up—if the whispers were believed that the Reverend Mather on occasion held conversations with angels. One of his celestial visitors reportedly had a man's features, wore no beard, sported wings, his brow encircled by a splendid tiara, and robed in shining white garments, while "about his loins was a belt not unlike the girdles of the peoples of the East."

All James Franklin could do to balance this account of majestic influence was to assert that his father Josiah was a pious man, and that he himself did frequent good works by scolding his younger brother Benjamin severely whenever he showed signs of slack. James could also have challenged the truth of Cotton Mather's angelic visitations, but who would have believed that Cotton Mather would lie, or even fib.

When James Franklin attacked the Mathers, despite the fact that he had the medical profession behind him, he was clearly storing up trouble in heaven, or the parsonage of Cotton Mather, the latter being considered quite close to the former. As inoculation showed signs of saving lives, and considering the nature of Cotton Mather's guests, it was predictable that public opinion would prove fickle once again and decide that there was nothing so terrible about inoculation after all. When that happened it became even more predictable that the publisher of the Courant would be legally chastised by the civic authorities when they were given the least excuse. James inevitably gave them one. On June 11, 1722, the *Courant* implied that the authorities were being very casual, even dilatory, about going after a pirate vessel lying not far offshore. The *Courant* reported that a ship was being prepared by the government of Massachusetts to attack the pirates and that it would sail "sometime this month, if wind and weather permit."

James and his newspaper obviously had made enemies. The bit of sarcasm in the article about getting around to the pirates hardly seems enough in itself to warrant the next step. But perhaps the article seemed to authorities the proverbial last straw. James Franklin landed in jail as crusading editors often have where there are powerful toes to step on.

ACTING EDITOR OF THE NEW-ENGLAND COURANT

Benjamin Franklin took over the running of the *Courant* during his brother's absence, and had, we can be certain, a fine time.

> During my brother's confinement, which I resented a good deal, notwithstanding our private differences, I had the management of the paper, and I made bold to give our rulers some rubs in it, which my brother took very kindly. While others began to consider me in an unfavourable light, as a young genius that had a turn for Libelling and Satire.

Benjamin Franklin had not agreed with the newspaper's anti-inoculation policy, which had seemed at times an anti-sense policy in the face of the evidence. But he disagreed even more with the practice of jailing an editor for speaking out. In the July 9, 1722 issue, the 8th letter of Silence Dogood appeared; and that estimable lady had words for the subject, words she had borrowed from the *London Journal* for February 4, 1720:

... in those wretched countries where a man cannot call his tongue his own, he can scarce call anything else his own. Whoever would overthrow the liberty of a nation, must begin by subduing the freeness of speech; a thing terrible to public traitors ... Guilt only dreads liberty of speech, which drags it out of its lurking holes, and exposes its deformity and horror to daylight.

"Freedom of speech is ever the symptom, as well as the effect of a good government," quoted the Widow Dogood, at the same time expressing the broadening and intensifying public opinions of the acting editor.

That period of oppression did not permanently improve relations between the near relations, James and Benjamin; but it did hasten Franklin's departure from Boston. The town was too rigid, too regimented, too fearful of the freedom of thought and speech. A new town might be no better, but at least it would be new. That in itself offered the chance of improvement.

Improvement was essentially the lifelong goal of Benjamin Franklin at all times in all things. It was the goal for his own life, his community, and his science. He was too much a realist to make perfection the goal. But improvement was always possible. If life could not achieve permanent cures, it could hope for and seek alleviation.

In his commitment to the idea of improvement, Franklin was attuned to the underlying philosophy of healing. Doctors inescapably deal exclusively with the arts and sciences of improvement. There are no permanent "cures" for the "facts of life."

When Franklin left Boston he took away with him the conviction that inoculation was an effective means of improving human life by protecting it from the pox, and he worked for its wider acceptance during much of his life. Personal tragedy years later added emphasis to this work. In 1736, Franklin's son, Francis Folger Franklin, age 4, was unable to be inoculated because of an intestinal disorder. The boy died, and his father wrote:

I long regretted bitterly and still regret that I had not given it (smallpox) to him by inoculation; this I mention for the sake of parents, who omit that operation on the supposition that they should never forgive themselves if a child died under it; my example showing that the regret may be the same either way, and that therefore the safer should be chosen.

More than twenty years later, in England, Franklin sponsored distribution of a pamphlet written by a London physician, *William Heberden,* pointing out the benefits of inoculation. Franklin saw to it that fifteen hundred copies were dispatched to Philadelphia for free distribution by Franklin's partner, David Hall. Franklin added a preface to the Heberden work stressing the good sense of inoculation. By that time, Franklin's importance helped make inoculation important and to encourage dissemination of a valuable medical aid.

THE OLDEST DISEASE IN THE WORLD

The first man probably caught it from the first woman, or vice versa. It was still going strong a million years later.

A medical area that typically attracted the attention of Franklin, the natural philosopher, was the most common one in the eighteenth century. It is still the most common: that wide range of ailments grouped together euphemistically under the single word *"cold."* Excuse me, please, while I grab another tissue and take care of this eternal, infernal, nasal drip.

An article concerning colds appeared in *The Pennsylvania Gazette* for November 30, 1732. The tone of the report suggests that Pennsylvania and neighboring areas were struck that autumn by an influenza epidemic or a virus attack. Considering the apparent immortality of such human tormentors, perhaps today we are conscripted into misery by the same virus strains, or their descendants, that afflicted Franklin's neighbors in 1732 and led him to write as follows:

> From all parts of this province, and even from Maryland, people complain of colds, which are become more general than can be remember'd in these parts before. Some ascribe this distemper to the sudden change of weather into hard frost, which we had about the middle of November; but others believe it contagious, and think 'tis communicated by infected air, after somewhat the same manner as the smallpox or pestilence.

This was one of the earliest references to the possibly contagious nature of colds. The article also included a descriptive quotation from an article on "General Coughs and Colds" written by *Thomas Molyneux,* whom Franklin identified as a noted physician of Ireland. The Molyneux reference indicated the wide reading that Franklin was doing in the sciences and the service he provided through the *Gazette* for the dissemination of such information in the Colonies. The Molyneux article had nothing of particular interest other than a colorful description of the disease's effects that needs no alterations after 243 years.

> Rheums of all kinds, such as violent coughs that chiefly affected in the night, great defluction of thin rheum at the nose and eyes, immoderate discharge of saliva by spitting, hoarseness in the voice, sore throats with some trouble in swallowing, wheasings, stuffings, and soreness in the breast, a dull heaviness and stoppage in the head.

Such a monster running loose in Benjamin Franklin's neighborhood naturally would have been noticed, thought about, studied, perhaps for decades, until something could be decided one way or another. One of the clear advantages of analyzing the cold is the fact that the researcher never runs out of subjects. If the cold under observation disappears in a week or two, no matter. Another will be along in due course and more quickly than desired.

Among those with whom Franklin exchanged views on the subject was *Benjamin Rush*, a Philadelphia physician who was one of Franklin's cosigners of both the Declaration of Independence and the Constitution. Rush, a prominent member of the Founding Fathers generation, shared with Franklin an opposition to the institution of slavery, and it was Rush who with *James Pemberton* founded the first anti-slavery society in America in 1774. A Professor of Medicine as well as a physician, Rush was one of those qualified to benefit from Franklin's speculations about the contagious nature of colds. In 1773 Franklin must have had a cold that made a pronounced impression on him. It was a troubled year that saw the Tea Act passed on May 10th with the Boston Tea Party taking place on December 16th. In his scientific studies that year, Franklin invested time in the common cold. Germs were unknown, but Franklin's speculations came almost as far as knowledge has progressed on the subject in more than two centuries. On July 14, 1773, Franklin wrote to Rush from London. He thanked Rush for his pamphlet against slavery and expressed the hope that "in time the endeavours of the friends to liberty and humanity will get the better of a practice that has so long disgraced our nation and religion."

Then science took over, and Franklin was deep into the matter of colds again. Were they caused by contagions? He thought so from his own observations of influenzas. And the subject allowed him again to insist on the advantages of fresh air.

I shall communicate your judicious remark, relating to the septic quality of the air transpired by patients in putrid diseases, to my friend Dr. Priestley. I hope that having discovered the benefit of fresh cool air applied to the sick, people will begin to suspect that possibly it may do no harm to the well.

He thought it likely that people catch cold from one another "when shut up together in close rooms, coaches, etc., and when sitting near and conversing so as to breathe in each other's transpiration." The main cause of colds, however, he thought might be "too full living with too little exercise."

Reading these commonplace, taken-for-granted observations today, there is strangeness in realizing that when Franklin and Dr. Rush corresponded, their views were new ideas. They represented scientific minds watching ordinary events and beginning the slow process of adding fact to fact. *Fact:* When a person with a cold spent time in the close vicinity of another person, soon both were likely to have colds. *Fact:* Close, stuffy rooms and coaches seemed to be environments where colds were aggravated or had their origin.

These relationships had to be established by logical minds noting effects and trying to pinpoint causes. It was precisely this sort of empirical thoroughness in observation that made Franklin an effective scientist. He saw what other people saw, but with a difference. He brought analytical procedures and instincts to bear, and he wouldn't stop until the facts could be added together for a logical conclusion. It was like attacking a tooth with the tongue until a berry seed could finally be worked loose. Doctor Franklin found it difficult to leave a challenge until all the berry seeds were free. Millions of people developed coughs and received only distress for compensation plus sssh's from their neighbors during the sermon. *When Franklin developed a cough, he began comparing that cough with all other coughs,* dissecting his immediate past for patterns, and never doubting a natural reason existed for the cough rather than a punishment from one of Cotton Mather's celestial visitors for unwitting indiscretions.

PANACEA FOR GIDDINESS IN THE HEAD
I am at present meditating a journey somewhere, perhaps to Bath or Bristol, as I begin to find a little giddiness in my head, a token that I want the exercise I have yearly been accustomed to.
(To Mrs. Deborah Franklin, August 5, 1767)

Natural explanations had to be questioned and analyzed until they were compatible with all the available facts. If there were contradictions, however insignificant, the explanations weren't satisfactory, such as the popular assumption in the eighteenth century, and by many in the twentieth century, that cold weather and dampness cause colds.

> Travelling in our severe winters, I have suffered cold sometimes to an extremity only short of freezing, but this did not make me *catch cold*. And for moisture, I have been in the river every evening two or three hours for a fortnight together, when one would suppose I might imbibe enough of it to *take cold* if humidity could give it; but no such effect ever followed. Boys never get cold by swimming. Nor are people at sea, or who live at Bermudas or St. Helena, small islands where the air must be ever moist from the dashing and breaking of waves against their rocks on all sides, more subject to cold than those who inhabit part of a continent where the air is driest. Dampness may indeed assist in producing putridity and those miasmata which infect us with the disorder we call a cold; but of itself can never by a little addition of moisture hurt a body filled with watery fluids from head to foot.

It was a fundamental part of Franklin's personal scientific method, his special way of looking at the world, that he would not accept on faith commonly held assumptions that were supported by no stronger evidence than old wives' tales. The question, *"does it make sense?"* had to be answered. And its corollary, *"where's the proof?"*

FEARLESS OF AIR AND WATER

The old wives' tale that "you'll catch your death" if you get your feet wet didn't seem rational to Franklin since the feet as parts of the human body were largely composed of water. Catching your death from exposure to the cold was equally suspect. Perhaps dampness and cold could be part of a process that led to "catching your death," but there was no evidence that they were directly capable of doing anything more than causing a temporary pain or unpleasantness.

Centuries later explorers and scientists in the Arctic and the Antarctic confirmed Franklin's argument that cold in itself didn't cause colds. They learned that men could survive at the South Pole *but their colds could not*. Science at last had found a certain cure for the cold, freeze it to death at the South Pole.

Franklin's congenital impulse to question previously unquestioned assumptions was at the heart of his pragmatic approach to the natural world, including the natural world of his own body. Freeing himself from unproven and often untrue "home truths" about the body was an essential aspect of liberty. If a king and a country could be fought for freedom of conscience and pocketbook, an even more vigorous war against ignorance was justified in connection with the human body, which was man's companion whereever he went from the water closet to the cathedral.

In his long paper on Smoky Chimneys, written at sea on August 28, 1785 during his last voyage home, Franklin wrote to Dr. Ingenhausz, "I find it of importance to the happiness of life, the being freed from vain terrors, especially of objects that we are every day exposed inevitably to meet with." His own body certainly was one such object, constantly met with, and fear was a poor collaborator in establishing happiness. In a world filled with ladders, it was bad logic to make walking under one a thing of terror. The same applied to many other traditional concerns of man that, looked at closely, turned out to be idle nonsense. Again to Ingenhausz:

> Moist air too, which formerly I thought pernicious, gives me now no apprehensions: for considering that no dampness of air applied to the outside of my skin can be equal to what is applied to and touches it within, my whole body being full of moisture, and finding that I can lie two hours in a bath twice a week, covered with water, which certainly is much damper than any air can be, and this for years together, without catching cold, or being in any other manner disordered by it, I no longer dread mere moisture, either in air or in sheets or shirts.

Likewise he would conclude that it wasn't dampness that made the air poisonous from "putrid marshes and stagnant pools" but rather the "volatile particles of corrupted animal matter mixed with that water, which renders such air pernicious to those who breathe it." The same reasoning applied to rooms where the "perspirable matter is breathed over and over again." The pernicious element was added to the air by the people present. It was a weak argument that "they caught the malady by *going out* of the room, when it was in fact by being in it."

Experience taught Doctor Franklin that fresh air was healthier in nearly all circumstances than stale air, and he listened to the experience despite the fact that medical opinion for centuries had traditionally counseled the opposite. Franklin was modest in his own scientific undertakings, and he avoided settling permanently in the vicinity of hypotheses and theories that had to be fortified and defended against attacks by new truth. He expected that his ideas would be challenged, and he invited the challenges. That was the only way to detect error and continue working toward truth. Whenever experience, observed facts, or logic pointed in a particular direction, Franklin took it seemingly without hesitation. A passion for truth kept him moving forward even at ages when men often turn conservative and become rigid in their views, resisting new theories, knowledge, and innovations in order to preserve a familiar but mistaken position.

Franklin made few, if any, such efforts. When the truth convinced him, he was ready to rejoice even if it meant that some of his own work would fall into history's rag bag. On August 13, 1752 he answered a letter from Dr. Perkins of Boston indicating the success of inoculation in Philadelphia against smallpox. (Only 4 out of some 800 had died). In the same letter he indicated the view he took of his "philosophical amusements" which by that time included most of the electrical work.

> Whatever I have wrote of that kind, are really, as they are entitled, but *Conjectures* and *Suppositions*; which ought always to give place, when careful observation militates against them. I own I have too strong a penchant to the building of hypotheses; they indulge my natural indolence: I wish I had more of your patience and accuracy in making observations, on which, alone, true philosophy can be founded. And, I assure you, nothing can be more obliging to me, than your kind communication of those you make, however they may disagree with my preconceived notions.

Whatever his penchants, Doctor Franklin was unusually careful in his experiments, checking and rechecking. "Natural indolence" should be more gifted in idleness and sloth.

THE DRY-BELLY-ACHE AND OTHER AGGRAVATIONS

In a letter to *Benjamin Vaughan* on July 31, 1786, Franklin reported on observations he had been making for nearly sixty years, starting as a boy in Boston. The question concerned lead poisoning, and began with "a complaint from North Carolina against New England rum, that it poisoned their people, giving them the dry-belly-ache, with a loss of the use of their limbs." The distilleries were found to use leaden still-heads and worms.

In the London printshop where he worked in 1724, Franklin learned of other workmen who had lost the use of their hands as a result of working with lead type and drying it before the fire after it had been cast. The man in charge, Mr. James, a letter-founder, thought illness might come as a result of the workmen neglecting to wash their hands properly after working with lead. "This appeared to have some reason in it," decided Franklin, but he believed that an effluvia from the metal might also be dangerous since he had felt pains in his own hands from handling type before the fire.

Later still in Derbyshire, England, visiting the furnaces for smelting lead ore, he learned that smoke from the furnaces was "pernicious to the neighboring grass and other vegetables." Lacking proof that eating such vegetables caused sickness, Franklin advocated that Vaughan and others should make an enquiry in the matter.

He noted that "moss would not grow" on those parts of roofs that had been painted with white lead, and he warned against using rain water that had fallen first on roofs covered with such leaded materials. Franklin knew of a case in England where the entire family had contracted dry-belly-ache, or *colica pictorum*, as a result of drinking rain water that had fallen from a leaded roof.

In Paris, with *Sir John Pringle*, Franklin had inquired at *La Charité*, a hospital noted for treating dry-belly-ache and found that nearly all patients there for treatment of the disease were employed in trades that some way or other required them to work with lead. The presence of stone-cutters and soldiers confused his theory at first. But with questioning, he learned the stone-cutters used lead to fix iron balustrades in stone, and the soldiers had been recently employed as laborers to grind colors.

He concluded:

> This, my dear friend, is all I can at present recollect on the subject. You will see by it, that the opinion of this mischievous effect from lead, is at least above sixty years old; and you will observe with concern how long a useful truth may be known and exist, before it is generally received and practised on.

Where matters of scientific observation were concerned, his mind never really seemed to close, even temporarily for repairs. It was open for business at virtually all hours, and though he accused himself of preconceived notions; he was much too ready to cast them aside for the notions to represent the sort of emotional investment normally associated with stern opinions. *He developed opinions on the basis of observations.* He stated them objectively, but not dogmatically; and in every statement, he seemed to be inviting his listener to have the goodness to point out errors quickly so they could both go on to more intriguing and exciting work.

ELECTRICAL MEDICINE

One of the most intriguing and exciting projects Franklin explored in the medical field was his bold use of electricity in paralytic cases. He reported details of the experiment to Dr. Pringle from his lodgings at Craven Street, London, on December 21, 1757. It might be argued that Franklin was reckless in using the unknown force of electricity with human patients. Reckless or not, the use of electrotherapy put him ahead of his time. He proceeded with care, and scientific knowledge of value was obtained.

> A number of paralytics were brought to me from different parts of Pennsylvania, and the neighboring provinces, to be electrised, which I did for them at their request. My method was, to place the patient first in a chair, on an electric stool, and draw a number of large strong sparks from all parts of the affected limb or side.

He charged two six-gallon glass jars, each with three square feet coated, and then sent the combined current of the two jars through the paralyzed limb or other part of the body. The shock was repeated three times a day.

The first positive result Franklin noticed was greater sense of warmth in the affected parts. Some patients reported feeling stronger and better able to move paralyzed members. A man had a lame hand, which in the beginning he could not lift at all, but by the fifth day he was able to raise it sufficiently, though slowly and feebly, to remove his hat.

Lasting results were disappointing, however. Improvement was noticed during the treatments, but when the patients became distressed by increasing shocks and stopped accepting them, they soon found themselves the same as before. "I never knew any advantage from electricity in palsies that was permanent," wrote Franklin. He was careful not to make any claims the observed facts did not justify.

> How far the apparent temporary advantage might arise from the exercise in the patients' journey, and coming daily to my house, or from the spirits given by the hope of success, enabling them to exert more strength in moving their limbs, I will not pretend to say.

Franklin suspected that electrotherapy could be a valuable medical tool, but he recognized the importance of combining further uses with the normal functions of medicine. "Perhaps some permanent advantage might have been obtained, if the electric shocks had been accompanied with proper medicine and regimen, under the direction of a skillful physician." He had done enough to believe many paralytic cases would respond to electrical treatment. That encouraged the hope it could become a respectable arm of orthodox medicine.

Franklin, summoned by public business, did not continue the medical applications of electricity very long. Perhaps he feared that without close study, he would be entering dangerous and unknown country. He was too careful a scientist to court the threat of being considered a quack. In a conversation with Benjamin Rush during his last years, Franklin observed that "quacks were the greatest liars in the world . . . except their patients."

Because of the magic of electricity and the gullibility of scientifically naive people, Franklin could have made himself a medical "wonder worker" easily comparable to *Friedrich Anton Mesmer*, if he had been so inclined. He was not. Franklin tried electrotherapy because he was asked to do so, and because it was a logical extension of his electrical experiments. But he did not continue since the results, though important, were not definitive.

THE FRIEDRICH ANTON MESMER CONTROVERSY

Franklin became involved in the Mesmer case when both men were prominent on the Paris scene. Mesmer was a Vienna physician whose public treatments using hypnotic induction had made him a famous healer for many, a notorious quack to others. Ailing people flocked to his treatments or "performances," and he attracted strong support from noblemen such as the *Marquis de Lafayette*, Franklin's friend, and equally strong opposition from a distinguished scientist such as *Lavoisier*, Franklin's friend.

Mesmer apparently put on a good show. His method involved a form of hypnotism based on a force he called *animal magnetism*, the earthly counterpart of the force that filled the universe, he said, from heavenly bodies. Controlled by Mesmer, animal magnetism allegedly could cure. He was an impressive man physically, and wearing a bright silk cloak, while carrying an iron rod with which he solemnly touched the patients, he no doubt was impressive and quite effective at inducing hypnotic states in the believers who had come to him. But praised by some enthusiastically while damned by others with equal enthusiasm, Mesmer was increasingly controversial. In 1784 the King appointed commissions to investigate the man and his treatments. The most important commission included members from the Faculty of Medicine, such as *Doctor Guillotin* whose name in time would become a bloody symbol because of the execution device which he advocated, for humane reasons, as a less cruel method of execution than the headsman's axe. Also on the commission were members of the Royal Academy of Sciences, such as Lavoisier, the chemist, and *Jean Bailly*, French astronomer who calculated an orbit for Halley's comet of 1759 and became the first Mayor of Paris following Bastille Day, July 14, 1789. The commission was touched by ironic fate, since both Lavoisier and Bailly would lose their lives on the guillotine during the terror days of the French Revolution. Another appointee from the Royal Academy was Doctor Franklin. There were nine members altogether including Franklin's longtime friend, physicist *Jean-Baptiste Le Roy*.

Bailly was named president of the commission, but there was no doubt that the true scientific celebrity of the group was Doctor Franklin; and some of the experiments conducted in the course of the investigation took place in Passy at Franklin's house. On one occasion, Franklin accompanied by Madame Brillon visited the clinic where Mesmer performed his treatments. Franklin's purpose was both scientific interest in Mesmer's work, and artistic curiosity about the fate of his own invention, the *glass harmonica*, which Mesmer used for background music in his medical act.

Franklin saw the *baquet* or bucket, filled with iron filings around which the patients circled, grasping iron bars that protruded through the wooden walls of the shallow container. Thus situated, the faithful or hopeful would wait with their afflictions for the great Mesmer or one of his disciples to appear, touch them with the potent iron rod, and rid them of their sickness, theoretically. Franklin was sceptical from the start. The whole "mesmeric" program seemed theater rather than medicine. But with modern foresight, Franklin did recognize the mental impact that such a show could have on those who went to Mesmer believing. When he heard from a man who wanted to know if Mesmer was genuine or a fraud, Franklin with that calm reason he brought to most problems came remarkably close to psychosomatic medicine in his reply.

There being so many disorders which cure themselves and such a disposition in mankind to deceive themselves and one another on these
occasions; and living long having given me frequent opportunities of
seeing certain remedies cry'd up as curing everything, and yet so soon
after totally laid aside as useless, I cannot but fear that the expectation of great advantage from the new method of treating diseases will
prove a delusion. That delusion may however in some cases be of use
while it lasts. There are in every great city a number of persons who
are never in health, because they are fond of medications and always
taking them, and hurt their constitutions. If these people can be persuaded to forbear their drugs in expectation of being cured by only the
physician's finger or an iron rod pointing at them, they may possibly
find good effects tho' they mistake the cause.

Mesmer and his associates *Ledru* or *Comus*, whether through
fear or humility, declined the honor of being examined by Franklin's commission, but his student and follower *Deslon* agreed to the
examination. Since gout and gall stones afflicted Doctor Franklin,
Deslon, seven patients, and the commission met at Passy where
experiments were made in Franklin's garden. Blindfolded and hyp-
notized patients were told that the trees in Franklin's garden were
electrified, and when one was sent on a walk through the garden,
he reacted radically to the presence of the trees. The demonstration in hypnosis was impressive. Deslon had learned his lessons
well, even though Mesmer had denounced his appearance before
the commission and implied that Deslon in reality did not know
the real secret of animal magnetism.

Franklin and the other commissioners observed. They also participated, and the discovery was made that by wearing the special
garments of the mesmerizer and duplicating his behavior, they
could achieve similar results with the sometimes nearly hysterical
patients.

The commission agreed that the effects were due to excitement,
hysteria, and the gullibility of the troubled and eager-to-believe
patients. Their report to the king, with Franklin's name appearing
at the top, said essentially that. A private report to the king from
the commission considered the relation of *mesmerism and the
erotic,* concluding that sexually suggestive individuals, especially
women were highly vulnerable potential victims of mesmerism.
Claude-Anne Lopez in her useful book about Franklin's Paris
days, *Mon Cher Papa,* wrote: "With great emphasis, and not a
little condescension, it made the point that women, having less
stable nerves than men, a more inflammable imagination, and a
greater tendency to copy one another, were the predestined vic-

tims of such a system. 'Touch them in one point, and you touch them everywhere,' it said. Hence the report concluded, the practice of magnetism should be condemned on moral as well as medical grounds." Subsequent history has supported the report but given Mesmer credit for contributing to the knowledge and development of hypnotism.

Franklin's own view of the report was that though some might think it would put an end to mesmerism, nevertheless "there is a wonderful deal of credulity in the world, and deceptions as absurd have supported themselves for ages."

He perhaps didn't reckon with his own stature and the fact that his name led the other names on a report that said Mesmer performed no miracles and did not cure. The commission report effectively put an end to mesmerism in Paris, and eventually Mesmer left Paris to try his fortunes in England and elsewhere. He lived on, dying obscurely at Meersburg, Switzerland on March 5, 1815. After history's visions, revisions, and re-revisions, Mesmer today is viewed as a mystic who genuinely believed in his animal magnetism—in other words, not a charlatan—but that his treatments were worthless, except for their temporary psychological impact on the susceptible, just as Franklin took for granted pretty much from the beginning.

Later in Philadelphia, Franklin quoted *Dr. John Pringle* to Benjamin Rush with the argument that "Ninety-two fevers out of every hundred cured themselves, four were cured by art, and four proved fatal." Applying this formula, Franklin did not personally condemn Mesmer, he simply reported what he considered the facts. In these matters, reactions generally prove extreme and out the window goes the "baby as well as the bathwater." For a considerable period the useful medical tool of hypnotism was viewed critically as something fraudulent and suspect. The fact that Mesmer and his associates were demonstrating the usefulness of suggestion in alleviating mental illness was also missed during the negative reaction, although Franklin came close to this recognition in his letter to the inquiring patient.

A theatrical use of electricity would have easily given Franklin a chance to out-mesmerize Mesmer, but he did not. That would have been a wanton betrayal of the integrity of science, and Franklin was never ambitious for the sort of power obviously coveted by Mesmer.

Franklin's contributions to the medical knowledge of his time were thoughtful and reasonable, achieved with step-by-step care.

He observed himself and others as they made their way through lifetimes of cyclical pain and health, and he shared any tentative conclusions that the facts did not dispute.

Sometimes though, his conclusions, based on himself were too difficult for others. His tonic bath of morning air, for instance, simply tended to result in others catching colds. His young medical friend *Pierre-Georges Cabinis* pointed out that only a man of Franklin's hardiness could endure the morning shock of cold air. That such regimens worked for him was plain. Another admirer of Franklin's, *Abbé Lefebvre de la Roche*, who like Cabinis was a habitué of Madame Helvétius's home near Franklin at Auteuil, wrote of Franklin that he could "work eight days running without any more rest than short naps in his armchair," De la Roche, and probably the others, noted with awe that Franklin, close to eighty, had swum the Seine to show one of his grandsons how easy it was to swim.

A VERY BENEFICENT DESIGN

During his early years in Philadelphia that same gusto had regularly been called on by those who needed help in getting a civic project off the drawing board and into the building stages. It wasn't Franklin's scientific ability but his salesmanship and energy that were needed for one of his major contributions to American medicine, the creation of the distinguished *Pennsylvania Hospital*

In 1751, his friend Dr. Thomas Bond (to whom years later Franklin reported his chronological "turnabout" at the age of seventy) came to him with the idea of the hospital which would serve the sick and insane of Pennsylvania as a *free institution.*

> Dr. Thomas Bond, a particular friend of mine, conceiv'd the idea of establishing a hospital in Philadelphia, for the reception and cure of sick persons, whether inhabitants of the province or strangers. A very beneficent design, which has been ascrib'd to me, but was originally his. He was zealous and active in endeavouring to procure subscriptions for it; but the proposal being a novelty in America, and at first not well understood, he met with small success. At length he came to me, with the compliment that he found there was no such thing as carrying a public spirited project through, without my being concern'd in it; "for, says he, I am often ask'd by those to whom I propose subscribing, have you consulted Franklin upon this business? and what does he think of it? And when I tell them that I have not (supposing it rather out of your line) they do not subscribe, but say they will consider it." I enquir'd into the nature, and probable utility of his scheme, and receiving from him a very satisfactory explanation, I not only subscrib'd to it myself, but engag'd heartily in the design of procuring

subscriptions from others. Previous however to the solicitation, I endeavoured to prepare the minds of the people by writing on the subject in the newspapers, which was my usual custom in such cases, but which he had omitted.

At the science of public persuasion Franklin was by then one of the world's masters. It is a title he still merits in comparison with practitioners on the *Madison Avenues of America*. Techniques he began can be found from Midtown Manhattan to the glib phrase-shops of Franklin's descendants in the advertising agencies of all the other hard-selling American cities.

Once this talent and the Franklin enthusiasm were focused on the hospital project, it was perhaps inevitable that Philadelphia would soon have the first hospital in America. Franklin skillfully persuaded legislators of the Assembly that they should agree to supply two thousand pounds of public money if the same amount could be obtained from individual subscribers. The legislators responded, and Franklin believed they did so because it was a way for them to "have the credit of being charitable without the expense" since they expected it would be impossible to raise such a sum by general subscription. Franklin immediately turned around, used the commitment of the legislators to persuade private contributors they could double the effect of their donations. He got the two thousand from the public, two thousand from the Assembly. Philadelphia had its hospital, and Franklin wrote of the affair, "I do not remember any of my political maneuvers the success of which gave me at the time more pleasure, or wherein, after thinking of it, I more easily excused myself for having made some use of cunning." It was a first and highly successful application of the modern "matching pledges" system.

For the cornerstone of the hospital building erected on Eighth Street, Franklin composed an appropriate inscription which reflects its author:

> In the year of CHRIST MDCCLV George the Second happily reigning (for he sought the happiness of his people), Philadelphia flourishing (for its inhabitants were public spirited), this building, by the bounty of the government, and of many private persons, was piously founded for the relief of the sick and miserable, may the God of Mercies bless the undertaking.

When the business of the Colonies took Franklin away from Philadelphia, he retained his interest in the hospital and made it a point to visit hospitals wherever he went in order to keep abreast of developments. One important reason was obtaining information worth reporting back to Philadelphia.

To his merchant friend and long time associate, *Hugh Roberts*, he wrote on February 26, 1761:

> I was glad to hear that the hospital is still supported. I write to the managers by this ship. In my journeys through England and Scotland I have visited several of the same kind, which I think were all in a good way. I send you by this ship sundry of their accounts and rules, which were given me. Possibly you may find a useful hint or two in some of them. I believe we shall be able to make a small collection here; but I cannot promise it will be very considerable.

Another reason for inspection tours of hospitals was to check the ventilation. *Franklin was the world's first authoritative fresh air fiend*, and his writings are liberally endowed with numerous references to his conviction that fresh air and health are intimately correlated and directly proportional. James Parton in his major 1864 biography of Franklin grandiosely labeled him "the first effective preacher of the blessed gospel of ventilation." Parton added: "He spoke, and the windows of hospitals were lowered; consumption ceased to gasp and fever to inhale poison." Another nineteenth century biographer, Sydney George Fisher in *The True Benjamin Franklin*, considers the claim difficult to support; but a careful reading of Franklin's writings on his stoves, chimneys, etc., does confirm his confidence in fresh air and his championing of ventilation. His agitation for open windows influenced his friends, who being in many cases important scientists, influenced others. For instance, when the Pennsylvania Fireplace was invented and written about by Franklin, scientist friend *Cadwallader Colden* sent a copy immediately to the European scientist *Gronovius*:

> I send with this a curious and new invention for warming a room with a small fire, and more effectually than can be done by a large fire, in the common method, and is free of the inconveniences which attend the Dutch and German stoves, because by this contrivance there is a continual supply of fresh warm air. It may be particularly useful to you and Dr. Linnaeus, by preserving your health while it keeps you warm at your studies. It is the invention of Mr. Benjamin Franklin, of Philadelphia, the printer of it, a very ingenious man.

In Gronovius reply he indicated that the pamphlet would be promptly translated into Dutch. Franklin's ideas on the matter of ventilation had a pronounced impact on those of his contemporaries with sufficient scientific intelligence to judge cause and effect without surrendering to tradition. Franklin's friend Sir John Pringle wrote about the swiftness with which air became polluted in crowded wards, emphasizing the difficulty of remedying the situation because of the problem of convincing nurses and patients that a supply of fresh air was essential. It was Franklin whose work with stoves and chimneys began establishing the modern technology of air circulation and air conditioning. He illustrated the potentially poisonous nature of human breath with a simple experiment, blowing into a mug, and showing that a light was swiftly put out by the atmosphere. If a flame couldn't survive, could man?

Franklin's reputation in the field became so great he was even consulted on the proper ventilation of Parliament. There is no evidence that he used the occasion to make a jest about political "hot air." Instead he made serious recommendations for removing "the personal atmosphere" surrounding each member.

Typically for a man with as many interests as there are directions for the wind to blow, he corresponded with Cadwallader Colden, Sir John Pringle, and many others on a regiment of medical topics. On August 15, 1745 he was informing Colden of his speculations concerning the human heart:

> I do not remember that any anatomist that has fallen in my way has assigned any other cause of the motion of the blood through its whole circle than the contractile force of the heart, by which that fluid is driven with violence into the arteries, and so continually propelled by repetitions of the same force till it arrives at the heart again. May we for our present purpose suppose another cause producing half the effect, and say that the ventricles of the heart, like syringes, *draw* when they dilate as well as force when they contract?

To illustrate his point, Franklin as usual had a simple, everyday sort of example. He noted the prickly feeling resulting from sitting or leaning too long against an arm or leg, etc., and the pulling of blood from veins to the constricted area. "If the blood was not drawn by the heart," he reasoned, "the compression of an artery would not empty a vein, and I conjecture that the pricking pain is occasioned by the sides of the small vessels being pressed together."

Such speculations are not sufficient, of course, for the modern textbooks of medical schools, but they were careful early guesses based on available experimental evidence. Because of Franklin's fame and popularity, his medical papers the same as his other

scientific papers were printed and circulated. They influenced researchers, medical practitioners, and they probably did open quite
a few windows. Doctor Franklin was one fresh air fiend who
achieved worldwide attention.

Whatever his observations, whatever the subject, he kept his eye
on the main goal, truth. In that same August 15th letter to Colden, he added:

> I am not without apprehension that this hypothesis is either not new,
> or, if it is new, not good for anything. It may, however, in this letter,
> with the enclosed paper on a kindred subject, serve to show the great
> confidence I place in your candor, since to you I so freely hazard my-
> self (*ultra crepidam*) in meddling with matters directly pertaining to
> your profession, and entirely out of the way of my own.

All of the scientific efforts he made were "out of the way of his
profession." But he made them, communicated the results, and
waited to see their effect. A personal result of his efforts was his
election to and long association with the medical societies of England and France. Since he was more intensely involved with other
researches, his contributions in the medical field are less than in
such fields as electricity; but the contributions are on the records.
If *they* are quaintly wrong today, history whispers that the future
may find *we* are quaintly wrong. The important thing is to do
what can be done and to contribute what can be contributed.
Franklin did, and the results still seem positive. For instance,
thanks to the good Doctor, you probably haven't suffered much
recently from the dry-belly-ache. Give thanks for large favors.

1976

Dear Doctor Franklin, Sir,

It makes for a pleasant evening—we are relax'd, and surround'd
by the solace of the "charming science." That was your description for music, which was near the top of your personal pleasure
list. You contributed to everything you enjoyed, and music was
no exception. The delicate "glass music" of the eighteenth century especially enjoyed the Franklin "touch."

So do we as we place a record featuring the artist Bruno Hoffmann on the electrized stereo and listen to Beethoven played
on your glass harmonica (with bows to you as the inventor).

This particular evening as the gently haunting sounds recall
your century and presence, a surprising newspaper advertisement contributes to the eighteenth century mood:

We are Proud to Announce the Striking of
THE OFFICIAL
PHILADELPHIA BICENTENNIAL MEDAL...
A Limited Edition in Solid 18-Karat Gold

Thus reads the headline, and we recall that you helped develop modern advertising techniques in the *Gazette*. Sponsored by the Philadelphia Bicentennial Agency, the advertised medal will feature Independence Hall and a "mighty American Eagle" on one face. The obverse face will display "an original Gasparro sculpture of Benjamin Franklin, the Patriarch of the Revolution and one of the most impressive men in history."

The glass harmonica shifts from Beethoven to Johann Gottlieb Naumann's *Duo in G Major*. A lute joins the rubbed glass in an ethereal conversation. And we start wondering just how peaceful that Bicentennial Medal can be with you on one face and a bald eagle on the other. We remember what you wrote to your daughter Sarah Bache in January 1784:

> For my own part, I wish the bald eagle had not been chosen as the representative of our country; he is a bird of bad moral character; he does not get his living honestly ... like those among men who live by sharping and robbing, he is generally poor, and often very lousy. Besides he is a rank coward; the little king-bird, not bigger that a sparrow, attacks him boldly and drives him out of the district.

Were you somewhat severe with the eagle? Could your preference for the noble turkey, " a true original native of America," have been an influence? The eagle on the medallion will carry an olive branch representing peace and freedom. Can you resist the temptation to shoo it away and demand a turkey? If you and the eagle live and let live peacefully together on the medal, perhaps our nation too can begin its third century in collective tranquillity.

The music of your glass harmonica is splendidly peaceful. Now it is Johann Tomaschek's *Fantasie in E Minor*. A gift of serenity. It encourages us to imagine a winning combination in 1976 to begin our third century: Benjamin Franklin for integrity—the old eagle for its symbolic meaning if not its habits—and the "charming science" on the glass harmonica. Thank you, Sir.

We Are, &c.,
YOURS, THE PEOPLE

BENJAMIN FRANKLIN

im Hauskleide .

This is one of many Franklin portraits based on C. N. Cochin's 1777 drawing. It shows a warmer, chubbier, less cynical Franklin than the usual adaptation from Cochin. The drawing was found by the author in a dusty mountain of old prints on New York City's "Book Row." No clues were given concerning the original source. It no doubt was the frontispiece or other illustration in one of the multitude of Franklin editions published throughout the world since the eighteenth century.

THE BIRTH-PLACE OF FRANKLIN,
WHICH STOOD IN MILK STREET, OPPOSITE THE OLD SOUTH CHURCH, BOSTON.

"Let lightning be captured & explained," said the
natural universe. So Benjamin Franklin, on January
6th, 1706 (old style), was born in this house on
Milk Street.
According to Bernard Faÿ in a 1929 biography, Franklin, *this drawing has*
been identified since the eighteenth century as showing the house where
Franklin was born. If true, the chimney on the right was the first to receive
attention from one who would become the world's leading authority on chim-
neys, a veritable scientist of chimneys, and much more.

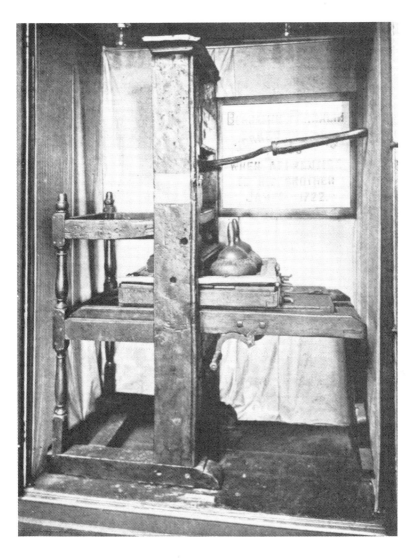

Eighteenth Century Printing Press
Used by Benjamin Franklin

With a knowing smile, printing apprentice Ben Franklin probably stood at this press to print his brother James' newspaper, The New-England Courant, *containing perhaps another letter from the mysterious, outspoken, and unidentified Mrs. Silence Dogood (alias Ben Franklin).*

Franklin Discovers Lightning and Electricity

Benjamin West was the painter of this allegorical study. Although born in Pennsylvania, West eventually settled in England where he became the "historical painter to the king" and succeeded Sir Joshua Reynolds as President of the Royal Academy. Despite hostilities between Britain and America, West and Franklin remained friends. On August 16, 1780, the war continuing, Franklin wrote to Mr. and Mrs. West from Passy to thank them for a family portrait and to say of their family, "I pray God to bless them all, particularly my godson, and grant them to live as long as I have done, and with as much health, who continue hearty as a buck, with a hand still steady, as they may see by this writing. I hope yet to embrace them once more in peace."

Deborah Read Franklin

She preferred home in Philadelphia to world roaming with Benjamin, but she sent him roast beef and mince pies when he was near enough to receive them. And when he was serving the Colonies in England, she sent him "goodys for my Pappy," including dried apples and other welcome delicacies. She was an amiable lady and lived sixty-six years (1708-1774). When she died, her husband had been gone ten years on his business in England. But they kept in touch.

213

Numb. XL.

THE
Pennſylvania *GAZETTE*.

Containing the freſheſt Advices Foreign and Domeſtick

From Thurſday, September 25. to Thurſday, October 2. 1729.

THE Pennſylvania Gazette being now to be carry'd on by other Hands, the Reader may expect ſome Account of the Method we deſign to proceed in.

Upon a View of Chambers's great Dictionaries, from whence were taken the Materials of the Univerſal Inſtructor in all Arts and Sciences, which uſually made the Firſt Part of this Paper, we find that beſides their containing many Things abſtruſe or inſignificant to us, it will probably be fifty Years before the Whole can be gone thro' in this Manner of Publication. There are likewiſe in thoſe Books continual References from Things under one Letter of the Alphabet to thoſe under another, which relate to the ſame Subject, and are neceſſary to explain and compleat it ; theſe taken in their Turn may perhaps be Ten Years diſtant ; and ſince it is likely that they who deſire to acquaint themſelves with any particular Art or Science, would gladly have the whole before them in a much leſs Time, we believe our Readers will not think ſuch a Method of communicating Knowledge to be a proper One.

However, tho' we do not intend to continue the Publication of thoſe Dictionaries in a regular Alphabetical Method, as has hitherto been done; yet as ſeveral Things exhibited from them in the Courſe of theſe Papers, have been entertaining to ſuch of the Curious, who never had and cannot have the Advantage of good Libraries ; and as there are many Things ſtill behind, which being in this Manner made generally known, may perhaps become of conſiderable Uſe, by giving ſuch Hints to the excellent natural Genius's of our Country, as may contribute either to the Improvement of our preſent Manufactures, or towards the Invention of new Ones ; we propoſe from Time to Time to communicate ſuch particular Parts as appear to be of the moſt general Conſequence.

As to the Religious Courtſhip, Part of which has been retal'd to the Publick in theſe Papers, the Reader may be inform'd, that the whole Book will probably in a little Time be printed and bound up by it ſelf ; and thoſe who approve of it, will doubtleſs be better pleas'd to have it entire, than in this broken interrupted Manner.

There are many who have long deſired to ſee a good News-Paper in Pennſylvania; and we hope thoſe Gentlemen who are able, will contribute towards the making This ſuch. We ask Aſſiſtance, becauſe we are fully ſenſible, that to publiſh a good News-Paper is not ſo eaſy an Undertaking as many People imagine it to be. The Author of a Gazette (in the Opinion of the Learned) ought to be qualified with an extenſive Acquaintance with Languages, a great Eaſineſs and Command of Writing and Relating Things cleanly and intelligibly, and in few Words ; he ſhould be able to ſpeak of War both by Land and Sea ; be well acquainted with Geography, with the Hiſtory of the Time, with the ſeveral Intereſts of Princes, and States, the Secrets of Courts, and the Manners and Cuſtoms of all Nations. Men thus accompliſh'd are very rare in this remote Part of the World; and it would be well if the Writer of theſe Papers could make up among his Friends what is wanting in himſelf.

Upon the Whole, we may aſſure the Publick, that as far at the Encouragement we meet with will enable us, no Care and Pains ſhall be omitted, that may make the Pennſylvania Gazette as agreeable and uſeful an Entertainment as the Nature of the Thing will allow.

The Following is the laſt Meſſage ſent by his Excellency Governour Burnet, to the Houſe of Repreſentatives in Boſton.

Gentlemen of the Houſe of Repreſentatives,

IT is not with ſo vain a Hope as to convince you, that I take the Trouble to anſwer your Meſſages, but, if poſſible, to open the Eyes of the deluded People whom you repreſent, and whom you are at ſo much Pains to keep in Ignorance of the true State of their Affairs. I need not go further for an undeniable Proof of this Endeavour to blind them, than your ordering the Letter of Meſſieurs Wilks and Belcher of the 7th of June laſt to your Speaker to be publiſhed. This Letter I ſaid (in Page 1 of your Votes) to incloſe a Copy of the Report of the Lords of the Committee of His Majeſty's Privy Council, with his Majeſty's Approbation and Order thereon in Council ; Yet theſe Gentlemen had at the ſame time the unparallell'd Preſumption to write to the Speaker in this Manner ; You'll obſerve by the Concluſion, when is propoſed to be the Conſequence of your not complying with His Majeſty's Inſtruction (the whole Matter to be laid

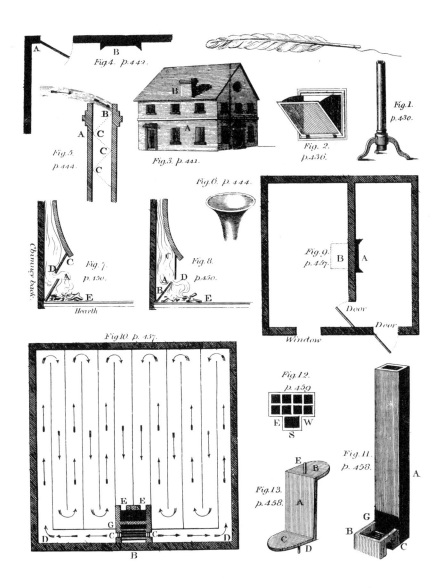

"On the Causes and Cure of Smoky Chimneys"

Drawings illustrating Franklin's long letter on chimneys, written "At Sea, August 28, 1785" to his scientist friend Jan Ingenhousz. Reproduced from The Works of Benjamin Franklin, *published by William Duane, Philadelphia, 1809. "What is it then which makes a smoky chimney, that is, a chimney which, instead of conveying up all the smoke, discharges a part of it into the room, offending the eyes and damaging the furniture?" Franklin asks the question, and then details nine causes with their remedies. Smoky chimneys have met their conqueror. "In general, smoke is a very tractable thing, easily governed and directed when one knows the principles..."*

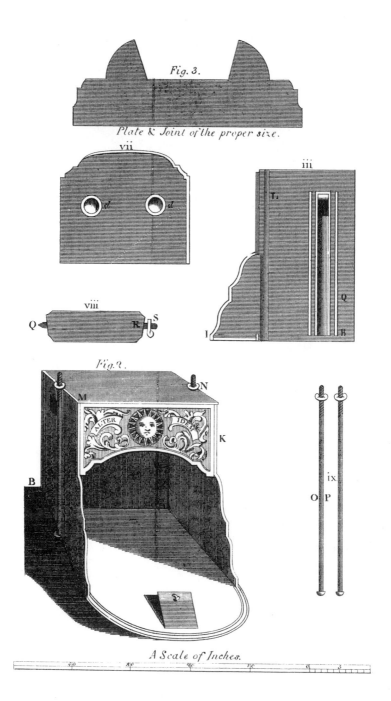

Fig. 3.

Plate & Joint of the proper size.

A Scale of Inches.

The Pennsylvanian Fireplace (Franklin Stove)

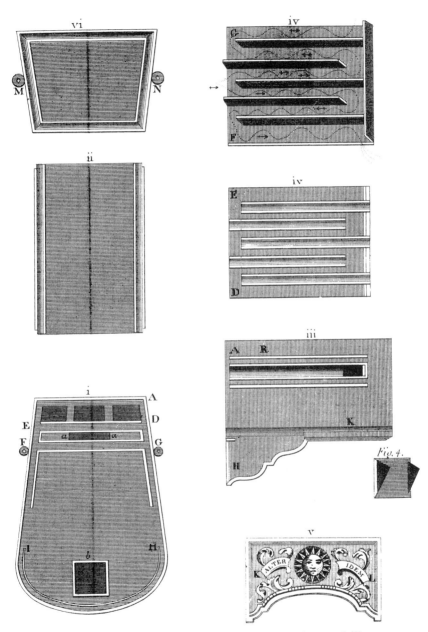

These drawings show the details of construction, and illustrate the famous pamphlet written by Benjamin Franklin to assure a wide sale and use of his superior housewarming method. Reproduced from The Works of Benjamin Franklin, *Published by William Duane, Philadelphia, 1809.*

217

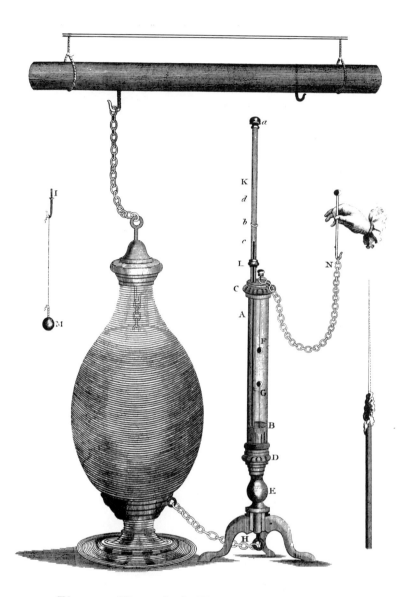

Ebenezer Kinnersley's Electrical Thermometer

*While serving the Colonies in England, Franklin relied on Kinnersley and
others to keep him posted concerning advances in electrical knowledge. Pic-
tured is the* Electrical Thermometer *devised by Kinnersley and reported to
Franklin in a letter on March 12, 1761. Franklin took delight in the new
discoveries made by his former subordinate. He was unstinting in praising
and when opportunity presented repeating the experiments himself. "I am
much pleased with your electrical thermometer," he wrote from London on
February 20, 1762. (Taken from the* Electrical Experiments, The Works of
Benjamin Franklin, *Published by William Duane. Philadelphia, 1809.)*

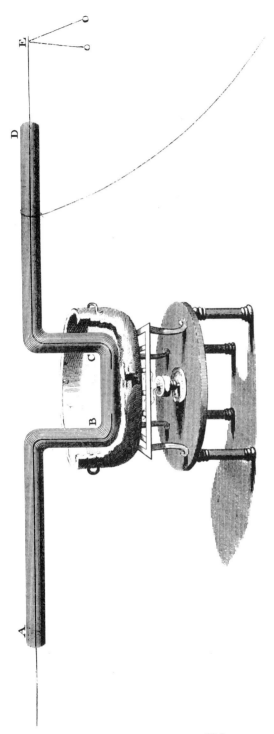

An Experiment by Lord Charles Cavendish

The science of electricity that Benjamin Franklin helped provide with impetus attracted the greatest scientists of the age. In his letter of February 20, 1762, to Kinnersley in America, Franklin enthusiastically wrote of the work being done in both Europe and America. He took a father's pride, perhaps, in the achievements of younger men who had been inspired by his earlier efforts. This illustration, from The Works of Benjamin Franklin (Published by William Duane, 1809), shows the apparatus used by "Lord Charles Cavendish," reported Franklin, who "by a very ingenious experiment, has found the heat of 400 requisite to render thicker glass permeable to the common current." After describing the experiment, Franklin concluded, "It were to be wished, that this noble philosopher would communicate more of his experiments to the world, as he makes many, and with great accuracy."

The able Doctor, or America Swallowing the Bitter Draught.

This 1770 political cartoon is a satirical plea for justice to America. The British ministers are cruelly forcing innocent America to swallow tea while the spirit of Britain mourns the injustice. Smilingly watching on the left are a Frenchman and a Spaniard. Controversy over tea helped to start the Revolution. And during the Revolution, Benjamin Franklin in France questioned the thirsts of his countrymen for the beverage. Even during the hard times of the Revolution, when he was forced to use all his persuasion and wiles to obtain loans, an estimated half a million dollars per year were being spent on tea by Americans. This was true despite the fact that Franklin often had to resort to pleading letters, as in his letter of February 13, 1781 to the French foreign minister Vergennes: "If I were to speak on topics of the kind, it would be to show that our present situation makes one of two things essential to us—a peace, or the most vigorous aid of our allies, particularly in the article of money." Franklin nearly always found the money . . . and some Americans must also usually have found their tea.

Philad.ª July 5. 1775

Mr Strahan;

You are a Member of Parliament, and one of that Majority which has doomed my Country to Destruction. — You have begun to burn our Towns, and murder our People. — Look upon your Hands! — They are stained with the Blood of your Relations! — You and I were long Friends: — You are now my Enemy, — and

I am,

Yours,

B Franklin

Doctor Franklin at Home in Philadelphia

*The print of this portrait by Mason Chamberlin was made in France after
1776 and is rich with symbolism. This was Franklin about the time of the
Declaration of Independence. Is the scientist, quill in hand, making minor
amendments to Jefferson's draft? Through the window, lightning flashes, but
a lightning rod stands serenely by to do its duty. Suspended on the left, like
anthers from an upturned flower, is the electric bell devised by Franklin for
his house. It frightened Deborah and she had it disconnected when Franklin
was in England on extended business for the Colonies.*

222

Natural Philosopher, "Cher Papa," Leader
of the "Insurgents" in France, &c.

This famous portrait by Carmontelle was made in France. Franklin's simple
Quaker homespun dress and manner would (with modest calculation and
cunning) become his trademarks. They would help make him lionized by
the elegant ladies and gentlemen of France, and in turn help a young nation
survive. His hat rests on the Laws of Pennsylvania. The ship in the background may be the Reprisal which landed him at Auray on December 3, 1776
with an assignment as important as Washington's. His task for their joint
enterprise in liberty was the essential aid and active amiability of France.
Neither paused during Franklin's sojourn. Or perhaps the ship is the Bon
Homme Richard, named after Poor Richard in Franklin's honor. Franklin
had obtained the ship from the French to use for the American cause, and
Captain Jones might be hurrying to Franklin for another strategy session.
Subjects: How to harass and humble the British at sea in the places that
hurt most, English prides and pocketbooks.

A Perspective of Paris & the River Seine from Passy

This view could be seen from Franklin's terrace at Passy. His house at Passy became in effect the capital of the United States in Europe, as well as one of the intellectual capitals of the eighteenth century. Near the ferry in later years, the aristocracy of France would lose its head as the price of a "new politics." This drawing was inspired by the successful balloon ascensions of the Montgolfier brothers and others in 1783. Franklin was drawn to each effort and vigorously praised the experiments. He sensed a new threshold for man—the skies above—and was eager to step over.

Walk up Arch Street in Philadelphia and you arrive at the place where
Benjamin Franklin entered eternity. He was placed in the burying ground at
Christ Church beside Deborah Franklin. "Are you done travelling, Ben?"
she asked. "We'll see, we'll see," replied Doctor Franklin, a far look in his
eyes. Twenty thousand gathered for his funeral, the greatest crowd Philadelphia had ever known. Meeting in New York, the House of Representatives
agreed unanimously to wear mourning for a month. Praise words by Washington, Mirabeau, and Turgot were fixed to the stone at his gravesite. Not
everyone believed he was dead. He wasn't.

225

MEMOIRS

OF THE

LIFE AND WRITINGS

OF

BENJAMIN FRANKLIN,

L. L. D. F. R. S.

MINISTER PLENIPOTENTIARY

FROM THE UNITED STATES OF AMERICA TO THE COURT OF FRANCE,

AND FOR THE TREATY OF PEACE AND INDEPENDENCE

WITH GREAT BRITAIN, &c.

WRITTEN BY HIMSELF, TO A LATE PERIOD,

AND CONTINUED TO THE TIME OF HIS DEATH

BY HIS GRANDSON,

WILLIAM TEMPLE FRANKLIN.

NOW FIRST PUBLISHED

FROM THE ORIGINAL MANUSCRIPT,

COMPRISING

THE PRIVATE CORRESPONDENCE & PUBLIC NEGOTIATIONS

OF

DR. FRANKLIN:

TOGETHER WITH THE WHOLE OF HIS

POLITICAL, PHILOSOPHICAL, & MISCELLANEOUS WORKS.

PHILADELPHIA: PRINTED BY T. S. MANNING.

The Vicissitudes of Famous Papers

This is a reproduction of the title page from Volume I of William Temple Franklin's edition of his grandfather's papers. Franklin bequeathed all his papers to his grandson, who selected several thousand special items and left the remainder, perhaps 15,000 items, with Dr. George Fox in Pennsylvania. Those items were haphazardly stored and handled in the Fox stables until 1840. Then Historian Jared Sparks was instrumental in approximately 13,000 of them going to the American Philosophical Society which Franklin founded. Other valuable Franklin materials remained unnoticed in the Fox stables. They were finally saved for scholarship and the historical record about 1903. The items taken by William Temple Franklin disappeared in London after his three volume edition of Franklin's works was published in 1818. They were lost for twenty years or so and were discovered at last in a tailor shop where they were being cut up and used for patterns by a London tailor. Probably Franklin would have been fascinated and amused by the troubled but ultimately triumphant adventures of his words.

XII. Music Maker

ROMANCE IN G

Those who are inclined to dismiss Benjamin Franklin as merely a fresh air fiend, businessman, publisher, statesman, organizer, planner, intriguer, inventor, tinkerer, author, lover, theoretician, scientist, sitdown comic, etc., should realize the inadequacy of their inclinations. Our most versatile Founding Father can also provide convincing credentials as a man of the very highest artistic and cultural importance.

"Straightforward old Ben Franklin?" some might question doubtfully.

Precisely, and his credentials will meet the austere requirements of those at the pinnacle of snobbery, breathing only scented air and thinking light blue thoughts about ethereal aesthetic subjects, languidly.

Straightforward old Ben Franklin invented a musical instrument, the glass harmonica or *Armonica* as he called it. The Armonica became immensely popular in the eighteenth century, inspired the development of several concert virtuosos, and was considered worthy of music composed specifically for it by the outstanding composers of the time, *including Mozart and Beethoven.* The poignant and ingratiating *Romance in G* Beethoven composed for Johann Duncker's 1814 play *Leonora Prohaska* called specifically for the glass harmonica. Franklin's instrument with a few later refinements is still used today. Recordings are available, and modern performers such as Bruno Hoffmann, specialize in the instrument.

The sound made by the glass harmonica is haunting, delicate, and unforgettable. Hearing contemporary stereo recordings, it is not difficult to understand why composers were moved to ensnare some of their melodies in that romantic sound.

Franklin studied music as he did everything else, intensely, and made himself something more than an amateur enthusiast. Of course, inventing an instrument appreciated and used by Mozart eliminates any hints of amateurism. He was genuinely fond of music, and typically was not content simply to seat himself and listen. He wanted to make sounds as well, understand them, analyze them, and decide why one was preferable to another. Why did some prefer *Bach,* or *Handel,* or *Gluck,* or the music of *Piccinni,* one of his neighbors at Passy, while he rather preferred, if you don't mind, the familiar tunes of Scotland? Those were questions of aesthetic judgment, but they were also physiological and psychological questions that curiosity might enjoy trying to answer.

Franklin's interest in music should not in any way seem strange. Music has a natural and direct relationship with science. Both deal in harmonies, and music has a long history as the preferred art form of scientists, up to modern times with Albert Einstein pursuing abstract equations in his head while playing one of Beethoven's quartets with his fingers. Sir Thomas Browne writing in *Religio Medici* united science and music when he wrote:

> For there is a music wherever there is a harmony, order or proportion; and thus far we may maintain the music of the spheres; for those well ordered motions, and regular paces, though they give no sound unto the ear, yet to the understanding they strike a note most full of harmony . . . For even that vulgar and tavern music, which makes one man merry, another mad, strikes in me a deep fit of devotion, and a profound contemplation of the first Composer, there is something in it of divinity more than the ear discovers.

Franklin's concern about the "music of the spheres" or what

serves to make a functioning cosmos sent him appreciatively to music. He approached music with the analytical interest of a scientist, and the artistic impulses of a composer, performer, and listener. Franklin tried and did all three, in addition to inventing the first musical instrument credited to an American. While the other events of his life were busily taking place, Franklin also found time to learn, after a fashion, to play the harp, guitar, and violin. He even extended his innate practicality to music by composing a string quartet that stressed easy playing. The quartet was constructed for simplicity of performance by musicians. This was no doubt a personal bow to the skills of Franklin the violinist, who never quite had time for the hours of daily practice needed to make himself a musical performer of ability. He played, nevertheless, for himself, his friends, and presumably, anyone who would listen. Franklin's "Simplicity" string quartet is still extant and occasionally played for curiosity's sake and as a tribute to a Founding Father. The quartet does not deserve, even remotely, to stand beside any one of the sixteen Beethoven string quartets, but the fact that it exists is wonder enough. It is a variation on Samuel Johnson's observation that, "Sir, a woman's preaching is like a dog's walking on his hinder legs. It is not done well; but you are surprised to find it done at all." Such statements allow the reflection that if Johnson visited the modern world, he would be positively aghast with surprise. Franklin, however, would be likely to say "Hmmm," thoughtfully, and not be surprised at all.

A letter Franklin wrote to *Lord Kames* on June 2, 1765, makes clear that he had thought about music considerably, and that he had specific preferences. He was more comfortable with familiar music than with the "modern" music of 1765. The music that was modern to Benjamin Franklin is today part of the classical Baroque period changing into the Romantic. Is familiarity the key to appreciation? It was to Benjamin Franklin.

> I only wished you had examined more fully the subject of music, and demonstrated that the pleasure artists feel in hearing much of that composed in the modern taste, is not the natural pleasure arising from melody or harmony of sounds, but of the same kind with the pleasure we feel on seeing the surprising feats of tumblers and rope-dancers, who execute difficult things ... I have sometimes, at a concert, attended by a common audience, placed myself so as to see all their faces, and observed no signs of pleasure in them during the performance of a great part that was admired by the performers themselves; while a plain old Scotch tune, which they disdained, and could scarcely be prevailed on to play, gave manifest and general delight.

Franklin was unashamedly partial to Scotch tunes, and thought their appeal was due to their combination of melody and harmony. *Melody he called an agreeable succession of sounds, and harmony the coexistence of agreeable sounds.* Harmony works, he wrote, because "the memory is capable of retaining for some moments a perfect idea of the pitch of a past sound, so as to compare with it the pitch of a succeeding sound, and judge truly of their agreement or disagreement."

He preferred agreement, since the particular satisfaction of the old Scotch tunes was that "almost every succeeding emphatical note is a third, a fifth, an octave, or in short some note that is in concord with the preceding note." The credit for this cautious harmony he gave to the minstrels with their harps who created or preserved the tunes and the beauty "that has so long pleased, and will please for ever, though men scarce know why." In admitting his musical preference, Franklin anticipated the automatic critics of his own time and today.

> The connoisseurs in modern music will say, I have no taste; but I cannot help adding, that I believe our ancestors, in hearing a good song, distinctly articulated, sung to one of those tunes, and accompanied by the harp, felt more real pleasure than is communicated by the generality of modern operas.

Franklin wrote before Wagner's often unmelodic explosions of consummate emotion appeared, but one can imagine him echoing the solemn comment of *Bill Nye*: "I'm told that Wagner's music is better than it sounds."

Franklin's observations about past sounds coalescing with present ones to create a concord are subtle and acute. They aptly explain one reason for the appeal of music. They even explain why for most people a "nice tune" with reliable successions of familiar notes is preferable to a demanding symphony.

He was obviously involved in the London musical scene during the 1760's, and familiar with what he liked as well as what he didn't. He didn't like songs that neglected "all the proprieties and beauties of common speech." A song by *Handel*, "The additional favorite Song in Judas Maccabeus," was criticized on this score. It had "*with their vain mysterious art,*" twice repeated: "*this alone can ne'er deceive you,*" two or three times; "*magic charms can ne'er relieve you,*" three times. He wanted familiar words artfully arranged, and the singer should make them distinctly understandable. To his brother Peter, he wrote:

If ever it was the ambition of musicians to make instruments that should imitate the human voice, that ambition seems now reversed, the voice aiming to be like an instrument. Thus wigs were first made to imitate a good natural head of hair; but when they became fashionable, though in unnatural forms, we have seen natural hair dressed to look like wigs.

THEY LAUGHED WHEN
I SAT DOWN AT THE ARMONICA

Franklin began developing his new musical instrument in the 1750's and it was perfected by 1761. The instrument was manufactured and sold for forty guineas in London. It was quickly popular.

When he developed the glass harmonica, Franklin was familiar with musical glasses and various ways of arranging and playing them. He may have known that the German composer *Gluck* with a full orchestra accompanying had played one of his own concertos on musical glasses.

Franklin's idea was to improve the musical quality and convenience of musical glasses by making an improved and compact integrated unit.

On July 13, 1762, he wrote to the Italian scientist *Giambattista Beccaria*, who had zealously supported Franklin's electrical researches in Europe, about the new instrument.

You have doubtless heard the sweet tone that is drawn from a drinking glass by passing a wet finger round its brim. One Mr. Puckeridge, a gentleman from Ireland, was the first who thought of playing tunes, formed of these tones. He collected a number of glasses of different sizes, fixed them near each other on a table, and tuned them by putting into them water more or less, as each note required. The tones were brought out by passing his fingers round their brims. He was unfortunately burned here, with his instrument, in a fire which consumed the house he lived in. Mr. E. Delaval, a most ingenious member of our Royal Society, made one in imitation of it, with a better choice and form of glasses, which was the first I saw or heard. Being charmed by the sweetness of its tones, the music he produced from it, I wished only to see the glasses disposed in a more convenient form, and brought together in a narrower compass, so as to admit of a greater number of tones, and all within reach of hand to a person sitting before the instrument, which I accomplished, after various intermediate trials and less commodious forms, both of glasses and construction, in the following manner.

Franklin then explained that the glasses were blown in the shape of hemispheres, each with an open neck or socket in the middle. The glass was thickest at the neck, narrowest at the brim; and the glasses ranged in size from nine inches diameter to three. Between the nine inch glass and the three inch glass were twenty-three different sizes, stepping down in size a quarter inch from one size to another.

To make a single instrument, he said, six glasses of each size would be blown, and from those thirty-seven glasses would be chosen to provide three octaves with all the semitones. The glasses when selected should taper smoothly from large sizes to small. Thirty-seven different sizes were not required since glasses of the same size because of variations in thickness, would vary in tone by as much as a note.

When selected, each glass was marked for a particular note and then tuned to that note by careful grinding and polishing. After tuning, the glasses were arranged in a case approximately three feet long. There was to be no skimping in the composition. The spindle was hard iron, attached to a mahogany wheel which was turned by foot pressure on the treadle. The treadle was attached by a strong cord tied to an ivory pin fixed in the wheel.

Displaying the same attention to detail he had shown in his earlier instructions for the Pennsylvanian Fireplace, Franklin meticulously spelled out exactly how the glasses should be attached to the spindle, one glass inside another, neck to socket. Sound was produced from the instrument as the player operated the foot treadle to turn the wheel and thereby the glasses, while touching the protruding glass circumferences with his fingers. The largest glass was G, and there was a full range of notes for three octaves with the visible parts of the glasses in prismatic colors to differentiate notes.

THEY DON'T COMPOSE THE OLD SONGS ANYMORE
Do not imagine that I mean to depreciate the skill of our composers of music here; they are admirable at pleasing practised *ears, and know how to delight* one another; *but in composing for songs, the reigning taste seems to be quite out of nature, or rather the reverse of nature, and yet, like a torrent, hurries them all away with it . . . A modern song . . . neglects all the proprieties and beauties of common speech, and in their place introduces its* defects and ab-surdities *as so many graces.*

(To Peter Franklin)

ARMONICA.

Benjamin Franklin's "Armonica," reproduced from The Complete Works of Benjamin Franklin, *Edited by John Bigelow, G. P. Putnam's Sons, New York, 1887.*

This instrument is played upon, by sitting before the middle of the set of glasses as before the keys of a harpsichord, turning them with the foot, and wetting them now and then with a sponge and clean water.

The fingers should be first a little soaked in water and quite free from all greasiness; a little fine chalk upon them is sometimes useful, to make them catch the glass and bring out the tone more readily. Both hands are used by which means different parts are played together. Observe, that the tones are best drawn out when the glasses turn *from* the ends of the fingers, not when they turn *to* them.

The advantages of this instrument are, that its tones are incomparably sweet beyond those of any other; that they may be swelled and softened at pleasure by stronger or weaker pressures of the finger, and continued to any length; and that the instrument, being once well tuned, never again wants tuning.

In his letter to Beccaria, Franklin reveals that Italy in the eighteenth century had a musical reputation similar to today's. "You live in a musical country," he wrote in praise, and added that his instrument "seems peculiarly adapted to Italian music, especially that of the soft and plaintive kind."

"In honor of your musical language," he concluded, "I have borrowed from it the name of this instrument, calling it the Armonica."

The Armonica enjoyed a wide sale and popularity through the last decades of the eighteenth century. By 1830 the vogue had largely disappeared, but during its heyday the *"instrumento di musica"* that was known to everyone as an invention of the *"celebre Dottore Franklin"* inspired outstanding compositions and virtuoso performers such as *Marianne Davies* (1744-92) and *Marianne Kirchgessner* (1770-1809). Marianne Davies gave concerts in England as early as 1762 and was soon making tours on the continent. At Vienna she taught Princess Marie Antoinette how to play. Franklin, of course, learned to play his own instrument and did so for his friends in both London and Paris. Music, the same as science, was one of the activities that Franklin cherished above others. The enthusiasm with which he wrote about the glass harmonica, attended concerts on his instrument, and enjoyed its fame indicates that he was fully as proud of it as of any other among his inventions and scientific achievements.

He was zealous in defending "my manner of playing on my instrument" against innovations such as the idea of playing it with keys, put forward by *Abbé Perno* and adapted on various later versions of the Armonica. Franklin preferred the intimacy of touching the glass rims directly with moistened fingers.

It was equally important to assemble the instrument properly so that "the glasses are ranged on the horizontal spindle, or, to make use of your expression, *enfilés*, and each one is definitely fixed in its place." Thus he wrote to Barbeu Dubourg on December 8, 1772, and emphasized that each glass must be closely contained in another down the row of descending sizes, but without the resonance portions of the glasses actually touching. They had to be just near enough "as not to admit a finger to pass between them; so that the interior border is not susceptible of being rubbed."

ARMONICA DIRECTIONS (RAINWATER A MUST)

Thoroughness prescribed, naturally, that he would make a careful study of the best ways to assure optimum performance and then offer a list of specific directions. Like most of Franklin's instructions, they read delightfully. And they awaken an urge to acquire a glass harmonica to practice on.

> Before you sit down to play, the fingers should be well washed with soap and water, and the soap well rinsed off.

> You must be provided with a bottle of rainwater (spring water is generally too hard and produces a harsh tone), and a middling sponge in a little slop-bowl, in which you must keep so much of the water that the sponge may be always very wet.

At the same time there should be a teacup filled with fine scraped chalk. All of these accessories assembled, the performer could sit at the instrument and begin by making certain that the fingers were soaked from the sponge. Next he passed the sponge along the glasses, largest to smallest, "suffering it to rest on each glass during at least one revolution" to achieve moderate wetness.

> If the instrument is near a window, let the window be shut or the curtain drawn, as wind or sunshine on the glasses dries them too fast.

> When these particulars are all attended to, and the directions observed, the tone comes forth finely with the slightest pressure of the fingers imaginable, and you swell it at pleasure by adding a little more pressure, no instrument affording more shades, if one may so speak, of the forte piano.

Franklin noted that one wetting of the sponge would be sufficient for music "twice as long as Handel's Water-piece, unless the air be uncommonly drying."

For extended playing, slices of sponge could be inserted behind the glasses to keep them permanently wet. This anticipated the later improvement of adding a permanent water trough to the glass harmonica, which undoubtedly eased the pressures of performance, but erased the rather charming ploy of stroking ones instrument with a sponge before and during a concert.

The chalk, noted the musical doctor, had two uses.

> Fingers, after much playing, sometimes begin to draw out a tone less smooth and soft, and you feel as well as hear a small degree of sharpness. In this case, if you dip the ends of your wet fingers in the chalk, so as to take up a little, and rub the same well on the skin, it will immediately recover the smoothness of tone desired. And, if the glasses have been sullied by handling, or the fingers not being just washed have some little greasiness on them, so that the sounds cannot easily be produced, chalk so used will clean both glasses and fingers, and the sounds will come out to your wish.

The sounds might come out to your wish, but it seems probable that the many variables involved essentially prevented them from coming out the same way twice. Rubbing glasses to make sound somehow lacks the precision and reproducibility of a well-tuned piano. For some musicians, and for Benjamin Franklin, that may have been the special charm of the glass harmonica. It was a complicated, unpredictable, highly personal instrument with tone qualities dependent as much on the "touch" of the performer as on the instrument itself. Modern program notes by R. D. Darrell for a contemporary Bruno Hoffmann Glass Harmonica recording (Candide Vox Record, CE31007) described the sound as "distinctively pulsating, wheezing, ringing, strangely unfocused and other-worldly *timbres*." The sound is all of that, plus benignly and beautifully crazy. It conveys an impression that the performer is literally caressing and coaxing harmonies from his instrument.

The hypnotist Mesmer must have heard the other-worldly quality of the instrument, since he used the glass harmonica to provide background music for the treatments in his clinics. The haunting music was probably as therapeutic as the scrap metal in the treatment trough and the lilac-colored silk cloak worn by the mesmerist.

As previously mentioned, Franklin attended his first session at the Mesmer clinic in Paris with Madame Brillon to hear the Armonica played as part of the complex production.

Among Madame Brillon's activities was the custom of writing descriptions of paradise. On November 1, 1779, she wrote that in heaven Mesmer "will content himself with playing the Armonica and will not bother us with his electrical fluid."

The glass harmonica was celebrated in France during Franklin's years there. This may have been due as much to the quality of the inventor as to the quality of the invention, although the music is ingratiating. It is a source of sounds that seem rather appropriate for a slightly off-beat paradise.

In the drawing of the Armonica, note the drawers on each side to hold chalk, sponges, etc. A performer had serious and elaborate preparations to make before he sat down to play. It was not a casual instrument, and the results were far from casual.

Franklin had helpful tips for performers in their manner of touching the glasses. Chiefly it was a matter of practice and experience as with any other instrument.

> . . . you will also find by trials what part of the fingers most readily produces the sound from particular glasses, and whether they require to be touched on the edge chiefly, or a little more on the side; as different glasses require a different touch, some pretty full on the flat side of the brim, to bring out the best tone, others more on the edge, and some of the largest may need the touch of two fingers at once.

According to *O. G. Sonneck*, publishing in 1900 on the relations of Benjamin Franklin to music, the glass harmonica went out of style as a popular home and concert instrument because the vibrating glasses were trying on the nerves of performers. That may have been a factor. Yet it seems possible that equally important after 1790 was the absence of Benjamin Franklin from the world scene except as a historical figure. The original motive to play Doctor Franklin's special instrument gradually dissipated with time. And no doubt it was more convenient to master an instrument that could be carried around comfortably in a case and never have to worry at the last minute about finding rainwater and a suitable sponge.

But the glass harmonica still uniquely offers what R. D. Darrell calls the "sensitive finger-control common to the musical glasses and non-keyboard types of the glass harmonica."

Franklin never flagged in his enthusiasm for the instrument. During the Paris years he played it often, writing once about a visit from a violin virtuoso: "M. Pagin did me the honor of coming to see me yesterday. He must certainly be one of the best people in the world, for he was patient enough to listen to me play a tune on the armonica, and to hear me through to the end."

There is still a near compulsion to hear the glass harmonica through to the end, and not only because it is our first scientist's curious contribution to music. The sound is insistent.

In a familiar Ode, Arthur William Edgar O'Shaughnessy wrote:

> We are the music makers,
>   We are the dreamers of dreams,
> Wandering by lone sea-breakers,
>   And sitting by desolate streams;—
> World-losers and world-forsakers,
>   On whom the pale moon gleams:
> We are the movers and shakers
>   Of the world for ever, it seems.

"Music maker" clearly has to be added to the list for this particular mover and shaker. He would insist on it and at the same time invite us, with an irresistible smile and gesture at a chair, to hear him play a few amiable Scottish tunes on the Armonica.

Aye, Doctor Franklin, gladly, and a bonny pleasure it is.

1976

Dear Doctor Franklin, Sir,

When you come to the Bicentennial Party, we may have a special task for you: Opening the Libraries.

If present trends continue in our American cities, the hours libraries are open may be drastically reduced. It has already started in New York City. And they warn us that what happens there, eventually happens everywhere, perhaps even in Philadelphia where *your* library still serves the public need.

When you started your library in Philadelphia, and hired one of America's first librarians, young Louis Timothée, the hours were limited: Two until Three on Wednesdays, and Ten to Four on Saturdays. Those hours were sufficient for 1732, since you began with relatively few books and the number of individuals using them was also small.

But as the population increased and libraries expanded to contain millions of volumes, what, in your view, Sir, should have been the result? The answer seems obvious to anyone informed about your feelings concerning the *necessity* of books. "Libraries *must* be open longer and longer hours, preferably *all* the time, so that a person with an irrepressible need for a book at Four A.M. will not be frustrated!" Of course. Who in reason could fail to agree!

That is why the present trend is disturbing. Are you familiar with the great New York Public Library—the one with two giant lions out front? "Go right in," they used to roar, even on Sundays. This treasure palace, with a large collection of *your* works and memorabilia, could be trusted to stay open daily, including Christmas, the Fourth of July, &c. "Just as it should be," you would echo our insistence. Wouldn't you?

On Summer nights and weekends, all in the city could feel themselves millionaires because they had access to the *books,* including those of Doctor Franklin. You might assume that nothing would be allowed to tamper with so necessary and felicitous a formula for human happiness. Metropolitan budgets have tampered, Sir; and the great library was on a lean diet of hours through the Summer of '75. The lions were allowed to sleep during vital weekend hours. The doors to learning were locked.

Frankly, it seemed a wanton and desperate instance of extinguishing the lights. When one arrives to investigate some aspect of human knowledge, and hears the snoring instead of the roaring of the lions, it is as if an eternal freeze were starting. You created libraries where there were none. Help us open the doors of those we have, and keep them open before the minds of America begin to freeze beyond hope of thaw.

We Are, &c.,

YOURS, THE PEOPLE

XIII. Ingenious Men

FOUNDERS, KEEPERS

In 1800, ten years after the death of Franklin, Philadelphia had a population of 70,000, ten thousand more than New York; and it enjoyed stature as one of the outstanding cosmopolitan areas in the world. This was true not only for its population but for its cultural attainments and institutions. In that year of a new century's beginning, wherever one turned in Philadelphia he ran into the work of Benjamin Franklin.

In *The World of Washington Irving*, Van Wyck Brooks paid this genial compliment to the man whose spirit loomed large in the city of his adoption:

> Over the town still brooded the many-sided mind of Franklin, who had so amplified this creation of Penn,—the genius of the colonies whose motto might have been *fiat lux* and who was all "jollity and pleasantry" as Boswell found him. As a bookseller, he had introduced all the great works of the time, before he drew light from the clouds with his kite-string and key; and, while organizing a hospital, a police-force and a

241

fire-company, he had brought in the first Scotch cabbage and the first kohlrabi. He had added three fables to Aesop, and, perfecting the musical glasses, for which Mozart and Beethoven wrote compositions, he had all but invented as well the American republic.

Much of what Brooks wrote about had been established by Franklin fifty and sixty years earlier, yet most of his social and cultural works were still going strong when the new century arrived. It would have been impossible, of course, to prevent Franklin from submerging up to his glasses in such activities. He complained at times about lacking sufficient free time for science and self-improvement in such arts as music, but one of the chief culprits was himself. It was in his blood and in the need of the times to do all possible for the improvement of his community, and with that done or doing, to extend human knowledge in the sciences and arts as broadly as possible throughout the American Colonies. In 1800, and 1900, and on the second centennial of the founding of the American republic, three of the institutions established by Franklin to assist in the quest for knowledge still not only existed but were thriving. More than two centuries later, all three are functioning, serving people, science, the arts, and human knowledge, in pretty much the way that their founder intended. When Benjamin Franklin planned, he planned well. When he founded, he did it solidly.

THE PHILOSOPHER SAID, LET THERE BE BOOKS

If you think it is easy to found a Public Library for the benefit of your neighbors and yourself, try. Where do you get the money for a building, from the neighbors, from frightened politicians who turn pale at the mention of printed words? Where do you get the books, if perchance you live in Colonial Pennsylvania and most books have to cross an ocean to reach you? Even if your circumstances are less complicated, and you live in a pleasant residential suburb, and the stationwagon finally keeps running after the last tuneup, and the telephone is working both in and out, could you establish a community library that would flourish for nearly two and a half centuries? You could? Go to it! And power to you.

Benjamin Franklin could and did.

In assessing the contributions of Benjamin Franklin to the cause of American science, it would be negligent to omit comment on his bibliophilic inclinations from childhood, culminating in the Library and his printing press.

Science does not always end in a library, but much of it undoubtedly begins there. Science began for Benjamin Franklin as he poured through the books of his childhood and youth. Exploring those books, the vital "uneasiness" that could be satisfied only with true answers to the puzzles of the world came to him. At 19, he wrote in his *A Dissertation on Liberty and Necessity,* "Thus is *Uneasiness* the first spring and cause of all action; for till we are uneasy in rest, we can have no desire to move, and without desire of moving there can be no voluntary motion. The experience of every man who has observ'd his own actions will evince the truth of this; and I think nothing need be said to prove that the *Desire* will be equal to the *Uneasiness.*"

"To cease to think is but little different from ceasing to be," asserted the young philosopher. Ergo, the necessity of books. Each was the repository of one man's uneasiness and thinking. Each provided a vital outlet for the uneasiness and thoughts of others.

With the flowering of audio and visual technology in the solid-state and transistor age, perhaps new generations of scientists can be trained through the use of film, cassettes, and television. But they probably will not be. To iron out thoughts and come to terms with that sublime private uneasiness, a book no doubt will still serve each seeker best. Lights will burn and heads will bend above the printed pages, as eyes blink and neurons struggle, across many a future midnight. Young scientists, poets, artists, uneasy seekers of all the arenas where minds journey to find the truth will begin largely in books obtained with Borrower Cards from local libraries. One of those libraries, still operating, proudly claims Benjamin Franklin as a founder.

From childhood books were more than simply a way of life for Benjamin Franklin, they were a love affair. How did he escape Boston for the richer adventure of Philadelphia at the age of seventeen? He reluctantly sold some of the books from a personal library he was assembling. In Philadelphia, those books were replaced many times over. Later in his life, Franklin's library would be recognized as one of the major private libraries in the world, especially in the sciences.

But a private library was not enough. No home was large enough for all the books a man of curiosities and uneasiness required. The women insisted on tables and stoves and other items of furniture that took up incorrigible amounts of space books could otherwise have occupied. In addition, no individual pocketbook could handle the financial challenge of acquiring all the necessary

books. Others in the family always seemed to prefer such question-
able luxuries as clothes and fuel and food. *Chacun à son goût.*

As indicated earlier, one thing that Franklin could do to make
certain important books were available was to publish them himself. He was a practical man, and to make the press profitable, he
published everything, from handbills to almanacs. He gave the
public what they wanted, and more than they knew they wanted
until Franklin's press had helped educate them. In 1744, he published an American edition of Samuel Richardson's *Pamela,* that
benign account of persistence in efforts to seduce virtue (and preserve it). *It was the first novel printed in America.* The venture
made money. So did his practice of importing books from England
and selling them to his friends and printing customers.

But in addition to serving public taste, he also tried to shape it
beneficially by publishing classics, such as James Logan's translations of Cicero. Logan's *Cato Major,* published in 1744, was an
excellent example of colonial bookmaking. In 1918 the American
book collector and essayist A. Edward Newton, with both chagrin
and cheer, wrote: "I have long wanted Franklin's *Cato Major.*
A copy was found not long ago in a farmhouse garret in my own
country; but, unluckily, I did not hear of it until its price, through
successive hands, had reached three hundred dollars." Newton
paid the price cheerfully. He knew it was a good buy.

In the introduction to Logan's translation of Cicero, Franklin
the publisher modestly concluded:

> I shall add to these few lines my hearty wish, that this first transla-
> tion of a *classic* in this *western world,* may be followed with many oth-
> ers, performed with equal judgment and success; and be a happy
> omen, that *Philadelphia* shall become the seat of the *American* Muses.

Cato Major actually was not the first classic published in the
Colonies. Others preceded it. But the American Muses undoubt-
edly were quite content in Philadelphia, thanks to Benjamin
Franklin, assuming they had no difficulty obtaining a library card.

Publishing the works of American scientists was also an active
concern and commitment of Franklin. Bringing the works of American scientists to the attention of other Americans and to their
peers in Europe was a fundamental goal, and it was accomplished
through the Franklin press or the presses of other printers whom
he financed and helped to establish in different parts of the Colonies. On November 28, 1745, he wrote to Cadwallader Colden

concerning his *An Explication of the First Causes of Action in Matter,* eventually published by Franklin's partner, James Parker, in New York.

Sir: I shall be very willing and ready, when you think proper to publish your piece on gravitation, etc., to print it at my own expense and risk. If I can be a means of communicating anything valuable to the world, I do not always think of gaining, nor even of saving, by my business; but a piece of that kind, as it must excite the curiosity of all the learned, can hardly fail of bearing its own expense ... If I was clear that you are anywhere mistaken, I would tell you so, and give my reasons with all freedom, as believing nothing I could do would be more obliging to you. I am persuaded you think, as I do, that he who removes a prejudice or an error from our minds contributes to their beauty, as he would do to that of our faces who should clear them of a wart or a wen.

In the long run, Franklin probably removed more errors and mental warts with his library scheme than with any other. When he arrived in Philadelphia, it was still essentially a frontier community, though it had wise and ambitious citizens such as James Logan. Not many miles beyond Philadelphia, the American outback or wilderness began. Under such conditions, the citizens generally were too preoccupied with surviving, building, and getting on individually to invest time in scientific or literary enterprises. Frankln brought a mammoth load of what was needed if an Athens of America was to emerge from a wilderness village: An eagerness to learn and the public spirit to share the learning. The Junto was one obvious expression, but by the 1730's, the young man knew that something more was needed to encourage learning. People couldn't be rodded or pressured into mastering their "R's" and their "ologies." But there was a way to make knowledge available for voluntary consumption—a Philadelphia Library.

AND THERE ARE BOOKS

Franklin started the process in 1730 at the Junto with a book lover's proposition:

About this time our club meeting, not at a tavern, but in a little room of Mr. Grace's set apart for that purpose, a proposition was made by me that since our books were often referr'd to in our disquisitions upon the Queries, it might be convenient to us to have them all together where we met, that upon occasion they might be consulted:

and by thus clubbing our books to a common library, we should, while we lik'd to keep them together, have each of us the advantage of using the books of all the other members, which would be nearly as beneficial as if each owned the whole. It was lik'd and agreed to and we fill'd one end of the room with such books as we could best spare.

The Junto experiment lasted a year. Then each member retrieved his books and took them home. Franklin learned from the experience. Trying to share privately owned books in a public way had its problems. There was the problem of care and the problem of going slowly insane when a Friend, unwittingly becoming Enemy, could be seen complacently dog-earing a favorite book. Some of the problems might be eliminated if the books were jointly or publicly owned.

Thus in 1731 Franklin began his efforts to establish the *first subscription library in America.* It was through necessity a subscription library, and conditions have not substantially altered with the intervening centuries. Today major libraries operate, tenuously and anxiously, on penurious government funds, donations from the public, and inevitable deficits.

And now I set on foot my first project of a public nature, that for a subscription library. I drew up the proposals, got them put into form by our great scrivener Brockden, and by the help of my friends in the Junto, procur'd fifty subscribers of 40s. each to begin with and 10s. a year for 50 years, the term our company was to continue. We afterwards obtain'd a charter, the company being increas'd to 100. This was the mother of all the N American subscription libraries now so numerous. It is become a great thing itself, and continually increasing. These libraries have improv'd the general conversation of the Americans, made the common tradesmen and farmers as intelligent as most gentlemen from other countries, and perhaps have contributed in some degree to the stand so generally made throughout the Colonies in defence of their privileges.

In 1742 the institution, substantially grown—whatever Benjamin Franklin touched seemed to grow—became the Library Company of Philadelphia.

Logan Pearsall Smith in his memoir *Unforgotten Years* wrote about one major source of books for the library, his ancestor James Logan, whose translations of Cicero, Franklin published with pride. Logan was one of the most distinguished early Pennsylvanians. He served as secretary to William Penn and later was an agent in the colony for Penn and his sons. Logan held every important office available in the commonwealth, became a noted linguist, mathematician, astronomer, and even a botanist credited with contributions to the theory of sexuality in plants. Logan and the younger Franklin inevitably met and recognized, each in the other, a kindred spirit.

According to Logan Pearsall Smith, James Logan left his library with the stipulation that his descendants beginning with his son, should have the position of librarian. Smith notes that his family held the position for half a century and that he was next in line for the job, the only "hereditary office in America." But Smith like the founder of the Library Company saw fit instead to spend much of his adult life, not in Philadelphia, but in Europe looking back.

Before the Logan gifts came along, Franklin gave the honor of being the first librarian in Philadelphia, perhaps America, to a young Frenchman, *Louis Timothée*, who opened the institution on Wednesdays, two to three P.M., and on Saturdays, ten A.M. to four P.M., for an emolument of three pounds sterling every three months. By agreement between Timothée and the Library Company, a room in Timothée's house served as the place "where the said books are reposited."

Franklin got the library going and kept it going. He was the driving force because he had an insatiable impulse to feed his own and the new world's appetite for knowledge. If the appetite was largely his at first, books would help it grow in others and serve to satisfy his personal needs.

"Reading became fashionable," he wrote in the *Autobiography*, "and our people having no public amusements to divert their attention from study became better acquainted with books." As for himself, the library provided the keys needed to unlock many doors.

> This library afforded me the means of improvement by constant study, for which I set apart an hour or two each day; and thus repair'd in some degree the loss of the learned education my father once intended for me. Reading was the only amusement I allow'd myself. I spent no time in taverns, games, or frolics of any kind. And my industry in my business continu'd as indefatigable as it was necessary.

He saw to it that the library contained the books he needed and wanted to read, assuming rightfully that his tastes would not harm the other subscribers.

Mathematicks.
Ward's Introduction. 2 ofèm
Dechales Euclid. —
L'Hospitals Conic Sections A
Ozanam's Course Math ½ Vol.
Hayes upon Fluxions.
Keil's Astronomical Lectures.

Morality
Spectators.
Guardians
Tatlers ——
Puffendorf's Law of Nature &
Addisons Works in 12
Memorable Things of Socrates.
Turkish Spy

Anatomy.
Drakes Anatomy

Nat. Philosophy
Abridg of Phil. Tran. 5 Vol. A
Graves end Nat Philosph. 2 fs
Boerhaave's Chymistry.

Politicks
Sidney on Governm't
Cato's Letters
Sieurs du Port Royal Mor. Essays

The Compleat Tradesman

Logic
Crouza's Art of Thinking
Locke's Essay

Catalogues ——

Philology
Bayley's Dictionary
English Gramar. Brighland's
Homer's Iliad & Odyssey
Greenwood's Grammar —
monsr. Bayles Critical Dictionary
Drydens Virgil

List of Books in Benjamin Franklin's Handwriting for the Library Co.

But Franklin did not try to monopolize the library. It was an experiment in public sharing of the human assets most worth sharing: Books and the ideas within them. James Logan, as one of the patrons, suggested appropriate books, and for that service was exempted from the rule that *only a subscriber could borrow books.* Louis Timothée's instruction, however, was to "permit any civil gentleman to peruse the books of the library in the library-room." Another patron and generous donor of books was Peter Collinson, a Quaker merchant in England, introduced to the Junto by Robert Grace. Collinson in time became Benjamin Franklin's close friend and his chief contact with the scientists of England at the Royal Society of London. Collinson supplied books from London through the years to help the new library become a useful institution.

In 1731 a careful list of books was compiled. The forty-five books included nine scientific works, eight on history, eight on politics and morals, six on law and philosophy, three on the English language, two on geography, five on arts and crafts, two dictionaries, and two classics (translations of Homer and Virgil). Frivolous items were conspicuously absent. It was an intellectual listing for men bent on knowledge, not diversion. It was, in short, a Benjamin Franklin approved list. The initial order for the library was sent to England on March 31, 1732.

THIS QUAKING EARTH

The earth itself may sometimes be the cause of its own shaking; when the roots or basis of some large mass being dissolved or worn away by a fluid underneath, it sinks into the same and with its weight occasions a tremor of the adjacent parts . . . The air may be the cause of earthquakes; for, the air being a collection of fumes and vapors raised from the earth and water, if it be pent up in too narrow viscera of the earth, the subterraneous or its own native heat rarefying and expanding it, the force wherewith it endeavours to escape may shake the earth . . . Thunder, which is the effect of the trembling of the air, caused by the same vapors dispersed through it, has force enough to shake our houses; and why there may not be thunder and lightning underground, in some vast repositories there, I see no reason; especially if we reflect that the matter which composes the noisy vapor above us is in much larger quantities under ground . . . An earthquake is defined to be a vehement shake or agitation of some considerable place or part of the earth from natural causes, attended with a huge noise like thunder, and frequently with an eruption of water, or fire, or smoke, or winds, &c.

(Pennsylvania Gazette, *Dec. 15, 1737)*

MEMOIRS

OF THE

LIFE and WRITINGS

OF

BENJAMIN FRANKLIN

L.L.D. F.R.S.

WRITTEN BY HIMSELF.

PHILADELPHIA:

PRINTED AND PUBLISHED BY WILLIAM DUANE

1818.

The Philadelphia Library shown on a title page from The Works of Benjamin Franklin, *Published by William Duane, Philadelphia, 1808-18.*

In August 1789, fifty-seven years later, Franklin was asked to write an inscription for a new Library Company building. Franklin was the only survivor from the original group of organizers and subscribers.

Advised of the 1789 project, Franklin objected to having his name included as part of the inscription. He had his way. It was still not fame and public recognition that Benjamin Franklin wanted. The library had been built not to push himself forward but to make books available to the youth and citizens of Philadelphia. When he wrote the inscription for a library cornerstone, he must have thought of the thousands past and the tens of thousands future who would benefit from the books there deposited and waiting.

This is the inscription Franklin wrote for the cornerstone of the Library Company building which would continue to serve long beyond his death a few months after the time of writing.

Be it Remembered
In Honour of the Philadelphia Youth
(Then chiefly Artificers)
That in MDCCXXXI,
They cheerfully
INSTITUTED THE PHILADELPHIA LIBRARY
which, tho' small at first,
Is become highly valuable
And extensively useful;
And which the Walls of this Edifice
Are now destined to contain and preserve;
The first Stone of whose Foundation
was here placed
The thirty-first day of August,
An: Dom: MDCCLXXXIX

BOOKS INSTEAD OF BELLS

An event that revealed much about Benjamin Franklin developed in 1785 when a town in Massachusetts named itself Franklin in his honor. Perhaps the citizens of the town genuinely wanted to honor the man still serving his country in France. Or perhaps they saw the move as a clever way to get a new church bell. A bell is what they asked Doctor Franklin to donate.

They didn't get the bell. They got books.

Franklin contributed twenty-five pounds and asked his friend Richard Price to choose suitable books for the community. He advised the town that he was sending books instead of a church bell, "sense being preferable to sound." The books chosen by Price would be "the commencement of a little parochial library for the use of a society of intelligent, respectable farmers such as our country people generally consist of."

Franklin, Massachusetts probably turned out both quieter and wiser than it originally intended. If the temptation was resisted to try other names until someone would send a bell, and if the books were accepted in good faith and used, the town probably turned out about as its namesake intended: A place where he could feel at home. A place where he could get a book to read.

CORRECTING A MISFORTUNE TO YOUTH

If a list were compiled (and it has been frequently) of all those during the past two+ centuries at the University of Pennsylvania who have contributed significantly to scientific knowledge, scholarship, and general learning, it would be a long one. The first name on the list, of course, should be—can you guess—Benjamin Franklin. The institution that reigns in Philadelphia today as the *University of Pennsylvania* developed by gradual but clearly recognizable stages from a brainchild of citizen Franklin. In 1749 he published a pamphlet entitled "Proposals Relating to the Education of Youth in Pennsylvania," which began with this Advertisement to the Reader:

> It has long been regretted as a misfortune to the youth of this province, that we have no Academy, in which they might receive the accomplishments of a regular education. The following Paper of Hints towards forming a plan for that purpose, is so far approv'd by some public-spirited gentlemen, to whom it has been privately communicated.

Alone or in discussion with his Junto friends and others, Franklin developed the idea of an Academy. Massachusetts had Harvard which Mrs. Silence Dogood with scanty camouflage had accused of delivering "after abundance of trouble and charge, as great blockheads as ever." The Philadelphia Academy could and would do much better, if Franklin had his way.

So first the idea, then acquiring associates to support the idea at the Junto and elsewhere, next distributing the pamphlet of proposals or "Paper of Hints" "among the principal inhabitants gratis."

> As soon as I could suppose their minds a little prepared by the perusal of it, I set on foot a subscription for opening and supporting an aca-

demy; it was to be paid in quotas yearly for five years; by so dividing it I judg'd the subscription might be larger, and I believe it was so, amounting to no less (if I remember right) than five thousand pounds. In the introduction to these proposals, I stated their publication not as an act of mine, but of some *public-spirited gentlemen*; avoiding as much as I could, according to my usual rule, the presenting myself to the public as the author of any scheme for their benefit.

The public must have known that it was a Benjamin Franklin project, conceived by, organized by, and run by the author. And the last lines of the Advertisement to the Reader in his initial Proposals would have settled any doubt. Readers favoring the design or having advice to offer were "desired to communicate their sentiments as soon as may be, by letter directed to B. Franklin, *Printer*, in Philadelphia."

The Proposals were representative, vintage Franklin thought, careful, practical, thorough.

> The good education of youth has been esteemed by wise men in all ages, as the surest foundation of the happiness both of private families and of commonwealths.

> ... the best capacities require cultivation, it being truly with them, as with the best ground, which unless well tilled and sowed with profitable seed, produces only ranker weeds.

> That we may obtain the advantages arising from an increase of knowledge, and prevent as much as may be the mischievous consequences that would attend a general ignorance among us, the following *Hints* are offered towards forming a Plan for the Education of the Youth of Pennsylvania.

> It is propos'd, that some persons of leisure and public spirit apply for a charter, by which they may be incorporated, with power to erect an academy for the education of youth.

The author predictably would be hoisted by his own well-meaning petard. He was retired by then with, he hoped, "leisure during the rest of my life, for philosophical studies and amusements" but Robert Burns warning about the best-laid schemes of mice and men was confirmed once more. "The public," wrote Franklin, "now considering me as a man of leisure, laid hold of me for their purpose." One of those purposes was the new Academy.

> That a house be provided for the Academy, if not in the town, not many miles from it; the situation high and dry, and if it may be, not far from a river, having a garden, orchard, meadow, and a field or two.

That the house be furnished with a library (if in the country, if in the town, the town libraries may serve) with maps of all countries, globes, some mathematical instruments, an apparatus for experiments in natural philosophy, and for mechanics; prints, of all kinds, prospects, buildings, machines, &c.

That the Rector be a man of good understanding, good morals, diligent and patient, learn'd in the languages and sciences, and a correct pure speaker and writer of the English tongue....

That the boarding Scholars diet together, plainly, temperately, and frugally.

... As to their studies, it would be well if they could be taught *every Thing* that is useful, and *every Thing* that is ornamental: But Art is long, and their Time is short. It is therefore propos'd that they learn those Things that are likely to be *most useful* and *most ornamental.*

In another paper Franklin wrote out in detail the courses he would offer as the curriculum of the Academy for a school program based on six classes. English composition and grammar received heavy emphasis. "Writing one's own language well is the next necessary accomplishment after good speaking." A broad range of practical knowledge in science and mechanics was also recommended. "Thus instructed, youth will come out of this school fitted for learning any business, calling or profession, except such wherein languages are required," he predicted.

His efforts served to make the predictions true. Twenty-four trustees were chosen from the Academy subscribers, and Franklin continued as one of the trustees for life. The school was opened for classes on January 7, 1751. By September 12th of that year Franklin could write to *Jared Eliot*, "Our Academy flourishes beyond expectation. We have now above one hundred scholars, and the number is daily increasing. We have excellent masters at present; and, as we give pretty good salaries, I hope we shall always be able to procure such."

The Academy was first chartered on July 13, 1753, with Franklin continuing as president of the board until 1756. A charter for the institution as an Academy and College was given May 14, 1755, and the first college class graduated in 1757. In 1779, fears that the school might become sectarian, led the state legislature to confiscate the college and charter a new corporation "the Trustees of the University of the State of Pennsylvania." Finally, in 1791 it was officially named the University of Pennsylvania, and Benjamin Franklin's Academy had emerged as an important fountainhead of learning. The boy from Boston with something less than two years of schooling was the clear and unchallenged ancestor of a major university. Writing in the *Autobiography* late in life, pride spoke justly in these words:

> ...thus we established the present University...I have been continued one of its Trustees from the beginning, now near forty years, and have had the very great pleasure of seeing a number of the youth who have receiv'd their education in it, distinguish'd by their improv'd abilities, serviceable in public stations, and ornaments to the country.

In *The Outline of History*, 1920, H. G. Wells wrote, "Human history becomes more and more a race between education and catastrophe." Franklin certainly understood that one sure way to affect history favorably was education of the young. He could have found no better way to affect and shape the future beneficially in terms of human welfare and knowledge than to start a school or found a library. For double effect, he did both. The cultural and scientific dividends for America since the eighteenth century are immeasurably large. They could not help but be. Philadelphia was one of the pacesetting cities of the Colonies, and what was done there led to comparable actions elsewhere. If it didn't happen automatically, perhaps a little nudge was possible from Benjamin Franklin through the printing establishments and other business enterprises he financed and encouraged throughout the Colonies. Yet in addition to the examples of the Philadelphia Academy and the Library Company, Franklin had still a third institution to set in motion that would serve, not just Philadelphia, but the whole of America, and, eventually, the whole of mankind.

SEVERAL MEETINGS TO MUTUAL SATISFACTION

Among Franklin's many friends and correspondents there were few more important than Peter Collinson, the Quaker merchant and botanist in London. As noted earlier, Collinson became Franklin's contact with the Royal Society of London and was instrumental in communicating many of Franklin's scientific writings to that eminent body. Equally significant, he helped to bring Franklin, years before his own scientific celebrity, into contact with other scientists in America. Collinson had wide scientific interests and a correspondence to match. Thus, though an ocean away, he was in touch with men in America whom Franklin did not know but should. One of them was the outstanding botanist *John Bar-*

tram with whom Franklin established a scientific collaboration lasting many years. When Franklin was in London, Bartram supplied American seeds for transplanting in England. Franklin in turn sent Bartram the first Chinese rhubarb, Scotch cabbage, and kohlrabi for planting in American soil. They grew.

It was John Bartram who probably made the original recommendation that resulted in Franklin's establishment of what is now the *oldest continuous scientific society in America, the American Philosophical Society.* If Bartram supplied the initiating suggestion, as in so many such matters it was Franklin who became the prime mover.

His impulse to know what was happening in other parts of the Colonies provided a strong incentive to launch the Society. Correspondence and publications had established that there were learned men throughout the Colonies, but they were not united and effectively in touch for their mutual benefit. Franklin became *Postmaster of Pennsylvania* in 1737, and this position had brought him into direct contact with the other Colonies. He began to think not just of Philadelphia, but of America. Knowledge had no interest in either state or national boundaries. It travelled wherever men, books, or letters travelled. Franklin wanted men of learning, whether actual or aspiring, to be in direct contact with one another for the benefit of all and for the furtherance of knowledge.

His idea formed in good Lockean style, Franklin did next what was natural for him in such matters. He wrote a detailed proposal, then printed and distributed it. The Society, patterned after the prestigious Royal Society of London, as described by Franklin in his proposal of 1743, was envisioned as an intercolonial organization devoted predominantly to science. It was dated May 14th and carried an impressive title: *A Proposal for Promoting Useful Knowledge Among the British Plantations in America.*

... The first drudgery of settling new colonies, which confines the attention of people to mere necessaries, is now pretty well over; and there are many in every province in circumstances that set them at ease, and afford leisure to cultivate the finer arts and improve the common stock of knowledge. To such of these who are men of speculation, many hints must from time to time arise, many observations occur, which if well examined, pursued, and improved, might produce discoveries to the advantage of some or all of the British plantations, or to the benefit of mankind in general.

But as from the extent of the country such persons are widely separated, and seldom can see and converse or be acquainted with each other, so that many useful particulars remain uncommunicated, die with the discoverers, and are lost to mankind; it is, to remedy this inconvenience for the future, proposed,

That one Society be formed of *virtuosi* or ingenious men, residing in the several colonies, to be called *The American Philosophical Society*, who are to maintain a constant correspondence.

He suggested that Philadelphia because of its central location among the Colonies, its proximity to the sea, and its growing library should be the center of the organization. At Philadelphia there were to be at least seven members, including a physician, botanist, mathematician, chemist, mechanician, geographer, and a general natural philosopher, in additon to a president, treasurer, and secretary. Meetings were to be held monthly for the reading of papers and reports from the Colonies on scientific developments.

That the subjects of the correspondence be: all new discovered plants, herbs, trees, roots, their virtues, uses, &c., methods of propagating them, and making such as are useful, but particular to some plantations, more general; improvements of vegetable juices, as ciders, wines, &c.; new methods of curing or preventing diseases; all new-discovered fossils in different countries, as mines, minerals, and quarries; new and useful improvements in any branch of mathematics; new discoveries in chemistry, such as improvements in distillation, brewing, and assaying of ores; new mechanical inventions for saving labour, as mills and carriages, and for raising and conveying of water, draining of meadows, &c., all new arts, trades, and manufactures, that may be proposed or thought of; surveys, maps, and charts of particular parts of the seacoasts or inland countries; course and junction of rivers and great roads, situation of lakes and mountains, nature of the soil and productions; new methods of improving the breed of useful animals; introducing other sorts from foreign countries; new improvements in planting, gardening, and clearing land; and all philosophical experiments that let light into the nature of things, tend to increase the power of man over matter, and multiply the conveniences or pleasures of life.

The meetings, obviously, if conscientiously attended and held, would be important scientific forums. Correspondence among members would be encouraged, and the American Philosophical Society would have direct contact with the Royal Society of London and the Dublin Society. Knowledge should be promoted in the Americas, but the rest of the world was not to be neglected.

To the secretary of the Society he assigned the duty of receiving letters, bringing them to the attention of the other members, abstracting, correcting, and methodizing papers requiring it, making copies for distant members, answering correspondence at the president's direction, and keeping all the records.

After writing an exhausting description of the secretary's functions, the busiest man in America then ended the document with this remarkable and voluntary offer:

> Benjamin Franklin, the writer of this Proposal, offers himself to serve the Society as their secretary, till they shall be provided with one more capable.

The American Philosophical Society was slow getting started, but it did start, with a certain "B. F____" as secretary. On April 5, 1744, Franklin wrote to Cadwallader Colden with news that the "Society, as far as it relates to Philadelphia, is actually formed, and has had several meetings to mutual satisfaction." In his letter, Franklin listed the first members with their areas of authority.

> Dr. Thomas Bond, as Physician.
> Mr. John Bartram, as Botanist.
> Mr. Thomas Godfrey, as Mathematician.
> Mr. Samuel Rhoads, as Mechanician.
> Mr. William Parsons, as Geographer.
> Dr. Phineas Bond, as General Nat. Philosopher.
> Mr. Thomas Hopkinson, President.
> Mr. William Coleman, Treasurer.
> B.F. _____, Secretary.

Only a Chemist was missing from the originally projected seven, and one can imagine that the secretary was taking steps either to procure one or to become one.

FIRST POOL OF AMERICAN BRAINS

Franklin took the most demanding job in the new Society because by 1744 his business was thriving and the pressures implicit in making it thrive were lessening. He already perhaps could see the end of his business career, by his own option, and was beginning what he hoped would be a lifelong commitment to science. Carl Van Doren in his Pulitzer Prize biography of Franklin expressed his probable attitude effectively:

> Most men as prosperous as he would have lost interest in philosophy. He was more interested than ever. Most philosophers with as many irons in the fire as he still had would have thought themselves distracted. Franklin was specialized to versatility. His inquiring temper

did not call for isolation. It was important that new things should be known, not that he himself should find them out. He was philanthropist and publicist as well as scientist. Let as many men as possible pool their knowledge for the good of all men, and he would serve them in any way that might be needed.

Franklin wanted men to pool their brains as well as their books for the use of others. The Society was simply an effort to bring it about effectively. Unfortunately, the distances involved in the Colonies made it difficult to hold meetings with more members than those locally available. Thus, at first the Society did not become the scientific clearing house Franklin had hoped. But it did allow him to correspond officially with other scientists and acquainted him with distinguished colleagues throughout the Colonies.

The initial members of the Society were scientists in many cases of international repute. Thomas Godfrey, a self-taught mathematician, invented a reflecting quadrant in 1730, comparable with the one invented independently by Hadley in England. Linnaeus praised John Bartram as the world's outstanding natural botanist. Thomas Bond, representing medicine, would join with Franklin in establishing the Pennsylvania Hospital.

Through the Society during its formative, water-treading years, Franklin learned about and encouraged the scientific work of others in the Colonies including that of the versatile New Yorker Cadwallader Colden, botanist, physicist, student of Indian lore, etc. Colden's papers on light, motion, and gravitation had been read with appreciation by scientists in Europe. Men such as Colden of New York and Logan of Pennsylvania made ludicrous the view of some Europeans that America was inhabited exclusively by paupers, religious fanatics, and savages.

The members of the original Society may have lacked academic credits and distinctions, but they made up for the lack in shrewdness, curiosity, and originality of thought. They turned self-education and cooperative instruction into a learning mode notable for its success and unequalled since on this continent, despite universities and colleges sprinkled ubiquitously across the land.

The theoretical speculations of Colden and other Americans even resulted in Franklin and various members of the Society daring to question the untouchable Newton's theories of light. Modern physics has refined and corrected Newton's basic theories without shaking his foundation to pieces, but Franklin in the eighteenth century found it judicious to remark, "It is well we are not as poor Galileo was, subject to the Inquisition for philosophical heresy." He referred to the disposition of himself and his colleagues to challenge the great "unchallengeables."

By the 1740's when Franklin conducted his first electrical experiments, science was taking place in the Colonies. It was good science too, sharp, practical, and even theoretical. Europeans began to be impressed in spite of themselves. How much of the progress was due to the dynamic needs of a new continent and the instinctive responses of "ingenious men," and how much came from the ceaseless efforts of the ebullient and irrepressible Franklin can only be speculated. There was probably a symbiotic combination of the two, a manifest destiny beginning to express itself in the practical sciences of the new world and the gadfly services of B. F____, Secretary.

He was openly interested in anything, and interested in everybody informed about anything. As noted previously, not only his mind but his purse was open. He was ready to publish Colden's scientific papers, and those of other scientists, with no promise of a return on his money. For a sure profit he could have concentrated on almanacs, political and governmental documents, and religious tracts. But he genuinely *did not mind losing money* if thereby something of value could be communicated to the world. For all his Poor Richard maxims about thrift, the record shows that Franklin saw money as something one made to spend, and that there was nothing better than books, science, or scientists on which to spend it.

It was during the early years of the Society, that Franklin made one of the few published plans in his life that he did nothing about. Some of his plans were long delayed. The plan for the Academy, for instance, was first drawn up in 1743, but it was 1751 before a school was opened. On November 28, 1745, Franklin wrote to Cadwallader Colden about his determination to publish an *American Philosophical Miscellany*, monthly or quarterly, starting in 1746. Franklin intended to take full responsibility on himself for the publication, hoping this would free contributors to say what they pleased. Care would be taken "to do exact justice to matters of invention, &c." Franklin was highly qualified for such a project, but the *Miscellany* never appeared. The logical assumption is that Franklin's own experiments, especially in electricity, began consuming the time he might otherwise have devoted to editing the scientific writings of his contemporaries. By March 28, 1747, he was writing to Peter Collinson of his total absorption in the electrical experiments and admitted that he "during some months past, had little leisure for anything else." The suspicion is that the world did not receive any issues of the *American Philosophical Miscellany* because it did receive Franklin's electrical findings.

The world also received, despite initial apathy and a period of interfering politics, a functioning and enduring American Philosophical Society. During the early period, the Society was not everything Franklin had hoped, but it was the chief scientific organization in the Colonies, by the simple fact of its existence and membership.

With Franklin's experiments taking more and more of his time, members of the Proprietary Party, a political group led by *James Hamilton* and cooperating with corrupt heirs of William Penn who were bent on exploiting Pennsylvania for what they could take away in profit, tried to pack the membership of the American Philosophical Society and assume control. Franklin supported the *Popular Party* and resisted all efforts to bribe him away including his son William being appointed Governor of New Jersey at the age of thirty-one.

Soon though the atmosphere of science was poisoned by political dissensions. Franklin and his followers simply stepped aside, revived the old Junto name, and called themselves the Society for the Promotion of Useful Knowledge. Franklin's preoccupation with his private scientific work and his absences in England during the 1750's and 1760's doubtlessly contributed to a relative lack of success by the new Junto. On September 23, 1768, after a series of vicissitudes, the group reorganized, changed its rules, confirmed Franklin as President though he was in England at the time, and named itself *The American Society Held at Philadelphia for the Promotion of Useful Knowledge*. The original Society, controlled by the *Proprietary Party* and under the patronage of *Governor John Penn* who found Franklin's ideals a nuisance, continued to exist and to duplicate the efforts of the competitive group. The situation was untenable, and the two societies were finally united after stormy negotiations. On January 2, 1769, Franklin was elected president of the reunited American Philosophical Society, over his rival, Hamilton. Governor Penn was furious that "the greatest enemy of my family" had triumphed; but Franklin's victory was symptomatic of the democratic spirit beginning to surge through the Colonies, eventually to wash out to sea the proprietary pretensions of aristocrats such as Penn.

The reorganized Society could then begin doing what Franklin had intended for it all along and done with it when he could, encouraging science and scientists throughout the Colonies. It had to be aloof from party politics. From London, Franklin wrote to Cadwallader Evans on September 7, 1769, "I should be very sorry that anything of party remained in the American Philosophical Society after the union. Here the Royal Society is of all parties, but party is entirely out of the question in all our proceedings." Science was clearly a function of truth, not party. Of shared knowledge, not exploitation. Of fact, not emotional propaganda.

Franklin remained President of the Society until his death. After the Revolution and his return to Philadelphia, he took an active role in the organization again and lived to see it firmly established, the same as his Library Company and the University of Pennsylvania.

He was pleased to offer his new scientific writings, including those written during his highly productive return voyage in 1785, to the Society. The voyage papers were published in the American Philosophical Society *Transactions*. That made it indisputable. The ancient voyager was truly home.

By the time of Franklin's return from France, the Society was well on its way to the impeccable respectability and authority that would give it a look of almost unFranklinlike solemnity in later years. For instance, *John Winthrop*, mathematics and natural history professor at Harvard, in collaboration with the Society, studied transits of the planet Venus in the 1760's. In 1769, to study Venus, the first observatory in the Colonies was built in Philadelphia at the behest of the Society. A transit telescope designed and constructed by *David Rittenhouse*, astronomer and member of the Society, was used. American science was no longer the "country mouse," if it ever was. Winthrop founded the first experimental physics laboratory at an American college, and Rittenhouse in addition to discovering a new comet, made original findings concerning the physics of magnetism.

The achievements of these and other scientists were individual accomplishments. They were also seen as American accomplishments, and they were associated with the American Philosophical Society.

During his last years, meetings of the Society were often held in the dining room of Franklin's house. By then it was obvious that the third and hardest-borning of the three institutions he had founded would endure and serve the new country. The future, beckoning with promise from beyond the horizons of his own life, was sending back echoes impossible to mistake. Franklin once wrote to *Benjamin Webb,* "I am not rich enough to afford *much* in good works, and so am obliged to be cunning and to make the most of a little." His cunning took the form of giving to those in need and expecting them in turn, when they could, to help others in need. Thus each gift was enormously multiplied, and the chain of good works could circle the earth several times.

The most cunning of all his good works were the three institutions he launched, like rowboats on a river that grew and grew into giant ships upon an ocean. His effort to encourage useful knowledge multiplied to fill the whole vast ocean of the future. Franklin must have heard the echoes and sensed the spreading waves.

1976

Dear Doctor Franklin, Sir,

In a letter to your friend Barbeu Dubourg, you once expressed a touching wish and compelling idea. "I wish it were possible," you wrote, "to invent a method of embalming drowned persons in such a manner that they may be recalled to life at any period however distant; for having a very ardent desire to see and observe the state of America a hundred years hence, I should prefer to any ordinary death the being immersed in a cask of Madeira wine with a few friends till that time, to be then recalled to life by the solar warmth of my dear country!"

Be assured, my dear Sir, that we never approach a cask of Madeira without a hopeful expectation that somehow you found a way. Yours was a special genius for finding a way.

When you do emerge, slightly soggy but cheerful from your Madeira resting place, learning what has been done with electricity may interest you more than other things.

Electricity is easily our busiest and finest Workman in these times. We are thirsty . . . we open the electric refrigerator and extract a cold bottle of Yoo Hoo. Madeira? Oh no, Sir, it's a nonspiritous sweet drink, and the advertising is intended to energize and refresh the consumer. Since our chocolate doughnut would taste better warm, we heat it in the electric oven. In the background, our electric stereo set is playing "As Time Goes By." Tiring of time going by, we put Anthony Newley on, and snap our fingers merrily while we eat our doughnut. Electricity magnificently handles the whole of it.

It is time for the news, and electricity brings the very latest instalments. Oh, precisely Sir, much faster than producing a *Gazette*. However copies of your *Gazette* have existed more than two hundred years. That is not likely with the electric news provided between commercials. "Old news is cold news?" Aptly expressed, Sir.

Distressed by the news, if we choose to communicate our displeasure to a politician or statesman, we sit at our electric typesetting device and write a few well-chosen electricized words. An electric calculator helps us fail to balance our bank book, and an electric battery encourages the spark plugs to start the fuel ignition cycle in our automobile. Electricity is our constant companion, Sir. It operates our electric clock to tell us the time and our electric blanket to keep us warm. Oh, yes, Sir, many do still prefer a warm companion for that purpose, though an electric blanket even at such times may still be used to keep the chill away. Doctor Franklin, Sir, why are you climbing back into your cask of Madeira? You've seen enough for now and will try again in another hundred years? We'll be waiting, Sir.

We Are, &c.,
YOURS, THE PEOPLE

XIV. Strange Fires

THE ELECTRICAL SECRETS OF MATTER

There are those who have found it difficult to believe that Benjamin Franklin, printer, booster, paramour, and colonial comedian, *could* have made significant, original, and basic scientific discoveries in physics. The idea simply offends their expectation that great scientists must be university men—Newton and Galileo qualified—and certified geniuses with an intellectual mien and a serious manner. Franklin had no beard. Didn't old-style scientists have to display distinguished beards? He was cheerful most of the time, laughed a lot. How could such a man be a genius in physics? A genius at go-getting, perhaps, but physics?

Yes, physics. The evidence is in and no longer convincingly questioned. Franklin did make basic discoveries in physics, write them up brilliantly, and display the full inventive and imaginative flair associated with scientific genius.

A late nineteenth century biographer, *Sydney George Fisher,* performing what he saw as a humanizing reevaluation, couldn't accept Franklin as anything more than a "minor discoverer." To explain the esteem that Franklin enjoyed as a scientist in his own and later centuries, Fisher decided with some logic that it was Franklin's acknowledged ability as a writer rather than as a scientist that explained his popularity. In *The True Benjamin Franklin*, which is a zealous catalog of shortcomings, Fisher wrote:

> Almost every event of his life has been distorted until, from the great and accomplished man he really was, he has been magnified into an impossible prodigy. Almost everything he wrote about in science has been put down as a discovery. His wonderful ability in expressing himself has assisted in this; for if ten men wrote on a subject and Franklin was one of them, his statement is the one most likely to be preserved, because the others, being inferior in language, are soon forgotten and lost.

This is true enough. Franklin's gifts as a writer did make him one of the most readable and understandable scientific writers in history. But Fisher misses an important point, that Franklin's effectiveness as a writer would have gone unused if he had not found solid subjects to write about and explained them with hard, factual data. Art helped make his scientific writings readable, but the science made them worth reading; and in his own time, the chief readers of his scientific materials were other scientists. Could they have been deceived by clever verbal footwork, signifying nothing?

In connection with the electrical experiments, again Fisher compliments the language rather more than the work that inspired the language.

> His command of language had seldom been put to better use than in explaining the rather subtle ideas and conceptions in the early development of electricity. Even now after the lapse of one hundred and fifty years we seem to gain a fresher understanding of that subject by reading his homely and beautiful explanations; and modern students would have an easier time if Franklin were still here to write their text-books.

Fisher's book was published in 1898. His tribute to the electrical writings of Franklin still holds true more than three-quarters of a century later, with no signs of change.

What about Franklin's electrical experiments and conclusions? Did he accomplish something important, or was his work relatively minor in the context of world science?

Certainly the world of the eighteenth century did not consider it minor. By the 1740's a vigorous interest in science was evident throughout Europe and the Americas. Even *Voltaire,* Franklin's great contemporary, was inspired by natural philosophy and at the age of forty-one began an intensive period of scientific experiments. Franklin was about the same age when he devoted himself with increasing concentration to his electrical experiments.

The intellectual climate of the eighteenth century was ripe for scientific popularity, but it was electricity in general that sparked the greatest interest and excitement, and Benjamin Franklin's work in particular that became a sort of central lightning rod about which the other activities whirled.

In Volume IX, *The Age of Voltaire,* of their vast study, *The Story of Civilization,* Will and Ariel Durant wrote that "All Europe was alive, after 1750, with electrical theories and experiments." It was in that period that Voltaire, harassed by government and ecclesiastical pygmies, considered migrating to Pennsylvania, attracted by freedom and the work of Franklin. "If the sea did not make me unsupportably sick, it is among the Quakers of Pennsylvania that I would finish the remainder of my life."

Of Franklin the Durants wrote: "Here was one of the great minds and hearts of history, whose creative curiosity ranged from such proposals as daylight-saving time, rocking chairs, and bifocal glasses to lightning rods and the one-fluid theory of electricity."

Yet even if it is accepted that Franklin served a vital popularizing service in connection with electrical knowledge and set off a wave of further experiments in other countries, this still does not prove that charming words and a flair for publicity were largely responsible, rather than the innate quality of his science.

For an objective assessment of his work in physics, twentieth century spokesmen must be consulted. Fortunately they are available. Considering modern electrical, electron, and atomic theories, one twentieth century scientist, *Sir Joseph Thomson,* admitted being struck by the "similarity between some of the views which we are led to take by the results of the most recent researches with those enunciated by Franklin in the very infancy of the subject."

An American Nobel Prize winning physicist, *Robert Millikan,* some historians might view as America's twentieth century equivalent in science of Benjamin Franklin, because of his distinguished contributions to scientific knowledge as well as his services to government and education. Millikan directed military research during World War I, made the *California Institute of Technology* one of the world's leading centers for science, and at the same time did breakthrough work in physics. He isolated and measured the charge of the electron, studied light, photoelectricity, and cosmic rays, confirmed Einstein's photoelectric equation, and analyzed Planck's constant. Millikan more than any other man became synonymous with American science during the first half of the twentieth century. He wrote generously in recognition of Benjamin Franklin's contributions to physics. And specifically, not just abstractly. In his *Encyclopedia Britannica* article on the "Electron," Millikan wrote that "one of the most important generalizations of all time is that of the electrical constitution of matter, for this conception underlies practically the whole of 20th century physics." He admitted that the conception took place, as does most progress in science "by a process of infinitesimal accretion" with "each experimenter adding a little to the structure reared by his predecessors." In crediting those who contributed to the process of establishing that *"matter itself is electrical in origin,"* he began with Benjamin Franklin:

> In the year 1756 Franklin, upon contemplating the phenomenon of electrostatic induction, said with amazing insight, "The electric matter consists of particles extremely subtle since it can permeate common matter, even the densest, with such freedom and ease as not to receive any appreciable resistance."

This was a profound "Hint," and yet, as Millikan notes, "for fully a hundred years, electrical *particles* were hardly again mentioned. Franklin was intellectually close to the atomic theory of electricity. His words in fact throw beacons of light onto that plateau. But it was almost the twentieth century before Thomson in England studying the mass of particles in cathode rays and other researchers adding their "infinitesimal accretions" brought about general scientific admission of the electrical nature of matter. In recounting the history of this momentous development, Millikan gave Franklin the priority position as the scientist who started the chain reaction leading to the universe's largest wonder, the *electron*. Franklin's contribution in this area was simply one of many speculative byproducts of his electrical experiments.

Perhaps the scientists and public of the eighteenth century were not too far wrong in celebrating the exciting experiments taking place at Franklin's house in Philadelphia. Perhaps they, like Robert Millikan, were looking at the science as well as the man. Perhaps they had more reason than simply the bubbling good spirits of Benjamin Franklin to go on when they turned away from ancient superstitions about electricity and decided all that inviting power could be put to work for man. Perhaps praising Franklin for his work with electricity is not entirely or even importantly a matter of hero worship for a Signer of the Declaration and the Constitution. Which was more significant in the long run, the signings or the experiments? Now *that* is a heavy question.

SOME PARTICULAR PHENOMENA
THAT WE LOOK UPON TO BE NEW

His most important scientific work began in Boston with a vaudeville type science demonstration about 1743. He was still several years away from the time when he felt that he could afford to retire and concentrate on science exclusively.

In 1743 Franklin was a well-known merchant, printer, and man about Philadelphia. He was known to be clever, interested in books, philosophy, ideas, and discussions on an infinite range of topics from the ethereal to the natural. If his fellow citizens of Philadelphia, or even his friends in the Junto had been asked to choose words descriptive of Franklin, scientist would not have been one of them in all probability. True, he had written to many scientists on technical subjects. He was known to be quick and logical in analyzing technical matters. He was also known to be good with his hands, skilled at making tools and things of his own design. He had invented a fireplace (the Franklin Stove) that would be successfully marketed. And in May of that year he had put forward his proposal for an American Philosophical Society to provide a forum where men could share scientific and philosophic ideas. *But to call Benjamin Franklin a scientist or natural philosopher equal to Isaac Newton?* In 1743 those who chose to think so would have earned the friendly response of laughter and wise words from Poor Richard: "Who has deceived thee so oft as thyself?"

Little more than a decade after 1743, Franklin's name would be known to all scientists and most people in Europe and America. By that time there would be nothing strange about an association of the names Newton and Franklin. Then it was being done. Then it was taken for granted.

Looking back historically we may think of Franklin as a Founding Father, Signer, &c., who also did some science. In the eighteenth century, the science came first. His contemporaries thought of him as one of the greatest scientists in the world who also happened, probably by mistake, to become involved in politics. If Franklin had never stumbled, fallen, or been pushed into politics and statesmanship, his stature as a scientist probably would be more widely and accurately recognized. *The Declaration of Independence* keeps getting in our way when we try to understand that he *was* one of the most reasonable men in the *Age of Reason* and a contributor to the advancement of science on an equal footing with such scientists as Priestley and Lavoisier. Certainly *they* thought so.

The first mention of the electrical experiments came in the letter of March 28, 1747 to Peter Collinson. Collinson previously had sent the Library Company of Philadelphia an electrical glass tube with instructions for its use.

> Your kind present of an electric tube, with directions for using it, has put several of us on making electrical experiments, in which we have observed some particular phenomena that we look upon to be new. I shall therefore communicate them to you in my next, though possibly they may not be new to you, as among the numbers daily employed in those experiments on your side of the water, it is probable some one or other has hit upon the same observations. For my own part, I never was before engaged in any study that so totally engrossed my attention and my time, as this has lately done; for what with making experiments when I can be alone, and repeating them to my friends and acquaintance, who, from the novelty of the thing, come continually in crowds to see them, I have, during some months past, had little leisure for anything else.

That was 1747 and the experiments had begun in full earnest, but the interest went back several years. In the *Autobiography* he noted meeting *Dr. Archibald Spencer* in Boston and seeing a series of "imperfectly performed" but curiosity-arousing electrical experiments. Archibald Spencer was himself a curious individual. A male midwife from Edinburgh, Scotland, he was touring the Colonies giving demonstration-lectures on "Experimental Philosophy." Franklin probably saw him in Boston in 1743 and perhaps the following year as well when he was in Philadelphia.

Of the Boston demonstration, Franklin wrote in the *Autobiography*, "Dr. Spence, who was lately arrived from Scotland,... show'd me some electric experiments. They were imperfectly perform'd, as he was not very expert; but being on a subject quite new to me, they equally surpriz'd and pleas'd me."

Spencer's electrical program included among other events suspending a boy in the air with a silk cord and drawing sparks from his ears and nose. Boys presumably were plentiful or dispensable in those days.

Though Spencer's tricks were not very successful in Boston's pervading dampness, Franklin nevertheless saw the possibilities; and his speculations can be presumed to date from that time. Interest in electricity was mounting in many parts of the world during the 1740's. It was an idea whose time had almost come.

The exact date that Franklin's work commenced cannot be fixed, except that it was some time between the Spencer demonstrations with his purchase of Spencer's equipment (perhaps 1744 when Spencer was in Philadelphia) and his letter to Collinson of March 28, 1747. At first he may have engaged simply in tentative experiments, background reading in the limited literature, and reflection. But soon enough the phenomena of electricity commanded his attention fully; and he began the concentrated, all-out onslaught that was characteristic of him in business, self-improvement programs, &c.

Spencer's apparatus was acquired. The electric tube was sent by Peter Collinson. Whatever else could be commandeered to experiment with the mysterious sparks was commandeered. Then Franklin and his three friends were ready to borrow fire from heaven.

Other friends came and went through the years of the experiments, but his three main partners in the work were *Thomas Hopkinson, Ebenezer Kinnersley,* and *Philip Syng.* Hopkinson was a lawyer who originally came to America as an agent for London firms. He was a member of the Junto and the first President of the American Philosophical Society. Kinnersley, ordained as a Baptist minister, became a teacher and scientist instead. He lectured on electricity and was considered Franklin's main associate in the experiments. Philip Syng, originally from Ireland, was a silversmith by profession and an early member of the Junto. Syng engraved the original seals for the Library Company, and for those who delight in the footnotes of history, his inkstand was on duty for the official signing of the Declaration of Independence and the Constitution.

It would be charged later, not by his coworkers but by historical trouble seekers, that Franklin had pushed himself forward and taken credit for group achievements at the expense of his associates. The charges are not convincing and there is no persuasive evidence. Kinnersley was the most gifted and knowledgeable experimenter after Franklin, and earned a tribute from Joseph Priestley in 1767 to the effect that his name, following Franklin's, might be "second to few in the history of electricity."

In the *Autobiography*, Franklin wrote about the first experiments and his principal coworker:

> I eagerly seized the opportunity of repeating what I had seen at Boston, and by much practice acquir'd great readiness in performing those also which we had an account of from England, adding a number of new ones. I say much practice, for my house was continually full for some time, with people who came to see these new wonders. To divide a little this incumbrance among my friends, I caused a number of similar tubes to be blown at our glass-house, with which they furnish'd themselves, so that we had at length several performers. Among these the principal was Mr. Kinnersley, an ingenious neighbour, who being out of business, I encouraged to undertake showing the experiments for money, and drew up for him two lectures, in which the experiments were rang'd in such order and accompanied with explanations in such method, as that the foregoing should assist in comprehending the following. He procur'd an elegant apparatus for the purpose, in which all the little machines that I had roughly made for myself, were nicely form'd by instrument-makers. His lectures were well attended and gave great satisfaction; and after some time he went thro' the Colonies exhibiting them in every capital town, and pick'd up some money.

When it came to picking up some money, it obviously did no harm to be a scientific colleague of Benjamin Franklin. The two lectures he prepared sound like the first programmed learning course in electricity.

The "little machines" Franklin mentioned were improvised to meet the moment's need, and they hearkened back to his childhood when he admired workmen with their tools and learned from them so that later he could "construct little machines for my experiments while the intention of making the experiment was fresh and warm in my mind."

It was written of Franklin that "he could make an experiment with less apparatus and conduct his experimental inquiry to a discovery with more ordinary materials than any other philosopher we ever saw." "Philosopher" was used in its eighteenth century context as a catchall for science, experimentation, and theorizing about nature.

Kinnersley was important to the experiments during the 1740's and 1750's. He continued to experiment and to correspond with Franklin on the subject after the press of public duties prevented Franklin from doing the same. But it was evident that Kinnersley as well as the others considered Franklin the leader of the team. In their correspondence, it was Franklin who was fertile with new ideas for experimental directions that Kinnersley might explore. Franklin was clearly eager to try them himself. Kinnersley settled the question of leadership in the conclusion of his letter to Franklin on March 12, 1761. The letter reported Kinnersley's current findings and ended thus:

> And now, Sir, I most heartily congratulate you on the pleasure you must have in finding your great and well grounded expectations so far fulfilled. May this method of security from the destructive violence of one of the most awful powers of nature meet with such further success, as to induce every good and grateful heart to bless God for this important discovery! (The lightning rod) May the benefit thereof be diffused over the whole globe! May it extend to the latest posterity of mankind and make the name of Franklin, like that of Newton, *immortal!*

At a distance of two centuries, it seems that the relationship of the four experimenters was that of three useful graduate students with their professor. The professor, Franklin, gave credit freely to his associates whenever it was due. Yet even the most active of the associates never tried to take over the class or criticize the professor. "Kinnersley became very skillful," wrote Bernard Faÿ in *Franklin The Apostle of Modern Times*, "but none of them, not even the most shrewd, could achieve the art of understanding it like Franklin." The letters, the use of Franklin's house, his leadership throughout tend to confirm Faÿ's supposition. There is one other confirmation, Franklin's consistent refusal in all his scientific work to be ambitious or care a fig about his personal fame. Whatever the truth was, he didn't invent it; he was simply trying to find it out. He had no secrets from his coworkers or his friends. No great scientific work was ever done more openly than the electrical experiments of Benjamin Franklin. The neighbors were welcome to come watch, or the Junto, or the Russians, or anyone. And he did not hesitate to look foolish if he happened to be wrong. He wrote of certain electrical theories that in spite of doubts he was publishing them because "even a bad solution read, and its faults discovered, has often given rise to a good one in the mind of an ingenious reader."

He had no fear of ingenious readers or associates. They were in fact welcome, since they might help get at the truth faster. Franklin was grateful for his collaborators, whom he personally invited to participate. He was never jealous. It was Franklin who sent Kinnersley on the lecture tour through the Colonies in an effort to popularize the new field of science and make money. When Kinnersley objected that it was difficult to experiment while travelling, Franklin responded with a suggestion for an unbreakable portable electrical apparatus. *Franklin sought answers, not kudos.*

There is no doubt that the years beginning with 1747 were scientifically absorbing for Franklin, with electricity dominating. In 1748, he turned the business over to his partner David Hall and moved from Market to quieter Race Street. Considering the fury and intensity of his "retirement" efforts, the name of his new street seems touched with poetic irony.

On Race Street, he had more leisure and found the tools, many of his own devising, to dissect the mystery. It wasn't simply ambition to enter the name Franklin in the encyclopedias of science that drove him to answer the nagging question: "What is electricity?" It was something more compelling, a driving itch to know. There was a great deal to know, as well as popular superstitions to overcome. Many thought of electricity as the tricks of witchcraft, the devil's nasty work, the bright games of the Dark One. But Franklin put no credence in Dark Ones, devils, or witchcraft. Superstition was simply the veil of ignorance over a natural truth that hadn't been adequately explained.

Devising the means of drawing nature's electrical secrets from her bag of tricks would be no easy task. Men had been trying for a long time, and little had been learned. But Franklin was "totally engrossed." The message to nature was that she had better watch the drawstrings closely unless she was reconciled to letting her secrets be known.

QUEEN ELIZABETH'S DOCTOR, &c.

Static electricity had not just been discovered. It was known about, played with, and guessed about for a considerable period. *Thales of Miletus* as early as 600 B.C. was thought to have discovered that rubbing substances such as amber and jet gave them the "authority" to attract tiny objects. *Pliny the Elder* also mentioned the curious fact in his scientific writings before he was a victim during the destruction at Herculaneum and Pompeii following the eruption of Vesuvius on August 24, 79 A.D.

William Gilbert, Queen Elizabeth's physician, studied magnetism and in a book on the subject called the phenomenon *"vis electrica"* after the Greek word for amber.

Walter Charleton found a word for it. He first used the word "electricity" in his *Ternary of Paradoxes* (1650).

In the eighteenth century before Franklin became involved, discoveries were made by other experimenters. Science in the field was inching forward slowly thanks to the separate efforts of individual searchers. Each pushed the totality of knowledge slightly higher than before so that it grew like a stalagmite, *drop by drop.* Each new discovery was an act of cooperation and collaboration with all the discoveries that preceded it. It was the design of science for the present and future to build on the accrued past.

In electricity, *Du Faye*, gardener to Louis XV of France, established that there are two "kinds" and that likes attract, while unlikes repel.

Stephan Gray learned that the power to attract can be transferred through other bodies. Such bodies Desaguliers called conductors in 1736.

Insulators were materials which would not transmit electrical energies. It was established that if a conductor were charged with electricity through contact with a source, its charge would disappear completely if the conductor touched the earth. Thus it was "grounded."

Once hypothesized and proved, such details can be taken for granted. They become pages of common knowledge, postulates, part of each individual's basic information about nature. But consider the times when they were not known at all. Consider in the absence of all knowledge how one might proceed to learn about electricity. Consider the meticulous thought, effort, care, and no doubt, worry, needed to piece together slowly each separate morsel of fact that becomes simple and elementary only after it is known.

Researchers proved that electricity could be induced in other ways than by rubbing amber. Glass rods, hard rubber, and sealing wax could also be electrified to repel or attract items such as a pith ball. Friction electrical machines, common from the start of the eighteenth century, were used to supply stronger electrical charges than before. *Hauksbee* devised a friction machine that could be turned rapidly to produce sparks. It could also generate intense electrical charges in insulated conductors. The mechanics of making electricity available to researchers or showmen was being solved.

In 1745 an important breakthrough came. Independently, two men made the same discovery. Simultaneous discoveries by independent workers are not uncommon in science. It is as if nature herself had inspired a certain momentum in researches and decreed disclosure of a secret.

E. Von Kleist of Pomerania, a clergyman, and *Pieter van Mus-schenbroek* of Leyden separately established the technical basis of the condenser. It was called a Leyden jar because of Musschen-broek rather than a Pomerania jar, showing the etymological good sense of scientists in the eighteenth century.

At first the Leyden jar was used for dramatic show. Charged with electricity, the jar could shock people, give off exciting sparks, cause strange lights, kill small animals. But scientists knew that there was a grave force present. What was it? Could it be harnessed? Was it more than a vigorous toy to make men jump as *Abbé Nollet* managed with several hundred monks, connected by wires to a condenser at one end, a conductor at the other. The monks gave a healthy, united leap which was impressive and brought pleasure to *King Louis XV*. Was that the ultimate purpose of the force, to make kings laugh?

In 1746, *William Watson* of London published a paper concerning his experiments with the Leyden jar and his conclusions that *all bodies contain electricity*. Electricity he thought was a sort of elastic fluid which could be transferred as an actual substance from one body to another. Uncharged bodies contained their electricity in a state of equilibrium. A charged body had either more vitreous or less resinous electricity than the uncharged body.

Watson's concept was muddled, but it was moving closer to the truth. Then it was Benjamin Franklin's turn.

THE NEW SCIENCE OF POINTS

Franklin used the glass tube sent to him by Collinson as a generator, and he went to work devising the apparatus he needed for his experiments. There was no consultation of a scientific catalog. He rummaged through the house and appropriated such things as a vinegar cruet, a pump handle, a saltcellar, even gold that had been used in the binding of a book.

Bernard Faÿ provided a good description of Franklin's electrical experiments and the reasons for their success in this paragraph from *Franklin The Apostle of Modern Times*:

> After he received this tube, he bought the instruments which Spence had used and settled down to steady work. He made excellent progress while his contemporaries in Europe were merely groping, for he was superior to them in two ways: he was a skillful manual workman and quick at seeing his way out of a fix. This he had learned from his father, and he was able to make much of his apparatus himself. When almost all the European experimenters, with their white hands and

lacy cuffs, could do no more than the simplest experiments, employing workmen to manufacture their instruments and for the dirty work in general—that is to say, exposing themselves to innumerable causes of error—Franklin, thanks to his manual skill and his habit of physical labor, was able to make the most complicated experiments all by himself. Being a journalist gave him another advantage, for as he was not familiar with the technical jargon of science and had to use clear, simple English, he avoided the absurd errors of the European scholars, who used the old-fashioned expressions for their new-fashioned discoveries. Franklin, who had no other basis for his theories than his experiments, and no other way to explain them but in common everyday words, began from the beginning and remained constantly logical and intelligible. It was precisely this quality which the study of electricity demanded.

Between March 28 and July 11, 1747, Franklin experimented furiously as if he could see a goal ahead and was getting closer. Actually he was experiencing a veritable orgy of discoveries, and who was ever able to stop or even slow down in the midst of an orgy. It was not a time for philosophical detachment, but for adding fact to fact ceaselessly.

There was the astonishing matter of *points* that could *throw off* as well as *draw off* electrical fire. There was positive and negative electricity. The "electrical kiss." And much more.

Franklin was increasingly conscious of his distance from what he still considered the center of the action, Europe. Were the things he observed commonplaces there? It was all so simple, the suspicion was that others too must have made the the same observations and reached the same conclusions. He could not know and dared not assume that he was entering a *terra incognita* of science with every new experiment, each tentative supposition. Franklin was deep into new science yet didn't know it for certain.

On July 11, 1747, he wrote again to Collinson, bringing him up-to-date.

In my last I informed you that, in pursuing our electrical enquiries, we had observed some particular phenomena, which we looked upon to be new, and of which I promised to give you some account, though I apprehended they might not possibly be new to you, as so many hands are daily employed in electrical experiments on your side the water, some or other of which would probably hit on the same observations.

The first is the wonderful effect of pointed bodies, both in *drawing off* and *throwing off* the electrical fire.

Franklin gave a number of examples. If an iron shot about three inches in diameter was placed at the mouth of a clean dry glass bottle and a cork ball suspended by a silk thread from the ceiling until it touched the shot slightly, the cork ball would be repelled when the shot was electrified.

Then the phenomenon of points. "When in this state, if you present to the shot the point of a long, slender, sharp bodkin, at six or eight inches distance, the repellence is instantly destroyed, and the cork flies to the shot." A blunt object had to be brought to within one inch of the shot and draw a spark before the cork ball would cease to be repelled.

One experiment proved little. Franklin tried many others "to prove that the electrical fire is *drawn off* by the point." The report to Collinson was not the report of an amateur or gifted dilettante. There was no doubt that a scientist, an exceptionally careful and thorough one, was at work.

There was also the capacity of points to throw off the electrical fire. Franklin later credited one of his coworkers with this information. "This power . . . was first communicated to me by my ingenious friend, Mr. Thomas Hopkinson, since deceased, whose virtue and integrity, in every station of life, public and private, will ever make his memory dear to those who knew him, and knew how to value him."

They learned that if a long sharp needle was placed on the shot it could not be electrified to repel the cork ball. If a needle was fixed to the end of a gun barrel or iron rod, the electrical fire continually ran silently out the point of the needle; and the barrel or rod could not be electrified.

POSITIVE AND NEGATIVE

The July 11, 1747 letter continued with accounts of another fundamental experiment that has helped make the letter a significant document in the history of science.

> We had for some time been of opinion that the electrical fire was not created by friction, but collected, being really an element diffused among, and attracted by other matter, particularly by water and metals. We had even discovered and demonstrated its afflux to the electrical sphere, as well as its efflux, by means of little, light windmill-wheels made of stiff paper vanes fixed obliquely, and turning freely on fine wire axes; also by little wheels of the same matter, but formed like water-wheels.

The purpose of the experiment was to determine whether or not electricity was created anew when glass was rubbed with silk, or if it was just transferred. Franklin from the beginning favored the transfer idea. It was his theory that all matter contained the fine fluid or "particles extremely subtle" that constituted electricity. His theory concerning these "particles" was one of the inspired scientific leaps that Robert Millikan considered a basic contribution to the field of electricity.

The experiment Franklin devised with the cooperation of his friends was simple and effective. Knowing that wax was not a conductor, experimenters were stationed on cakes of wax. When one of them, A, rubbed a glass tube, he could pass electrical fire to B, also insulated on a cake of wax. Variations on this performance led to clear conclusions that electricity was an "element diffused among matter," and it necessitated some original terminology, used by Franklin for the first time.

Hence have arisen some new terms among us: we say B (and bodies like circumstanced) is electrized *positively*; A, *negatively*. Or rather, B is electrized *plus*; A, *minus*. And we daily in our experiments electrize bodies *plus* or *minus*, as we think proper. To electrize *plus* or *minus*, no more needs to be known than this, that the parts of the tube or sphere that are rubbed, do, in the instant of the friction, attract the electrical fire, and therefore take it from the thing rubbing; the same parts immediately, as the friction upon them ceases, are disposed to give the fire they have received to any body that has less.

We can thank Benjamin Franklin for the simplicity of "positive and negative," "plus and minus," in describing the phenomena of electricity. Imagine the terminology, formulae, and elaborate symbols that would have inevitably and insatiably been applied if a modern, technical syllablizer had been faced by the same opportunity. There is no need to wonder. The opportunity for new terminology is frequent, and contemporary experts respond with gosh-awful clots of numbers, words, and symbols, where a gentle plus or a maidenly minus could serve perhaps more easily and tidily. Does modern science strive for calculated complexity in order to keep the Benjamin Franklins out? The suspicion rises like an electrified point.

"As the vessel is just upon sailing," continued Franklin on July 11th, "I cannot give you so large an account of American electricity as I intended; I shall only mention a few particulars more."

One was the *electrical kiss*. "Let A and B stand on wax, or A on wax and B on the floor; give one of them the electrized phial in hand; let the other take hold of the wire; there will be a small spark; but when their lips approach they will be struck and shocked." "An intimation," poets and lovers might insist, "of the electrical fires in human ardor."

Another was the counterfeit, lead-weighted spider constructed from burnt cork and suspended by a silk thread. The spider could be made to leap back and forth from an electrified phial to an upright wire as if it were alive.

There were more curiosities and finally a number of practical tips to help European experimenters take advantage of the useful machines and practices developed by the Americans. Then the remarkable July letter ended with: "I am, &c., B. Franklin."

Some years passed before the letter and those to follow had complete effect in Europe, but when attention was given, it was recognized that Franklin's "positive and negative" description was a useful breakthrough in electrical thinking. It represented a major departure from the traditional point of view. The older conception of electricity was that there were two different types, *vitreous electricity* and *resinous electricity*. Du Faye, gardener to the King of France, made a number of correct observations, plus that incorrect one.

Franklin fixed on a *one-fluid theory*, with positive and negative attributes depending upon the charge. This was a neat, logical theory. If something possessed too much electricity, it was charged positively. A less than normal amount meant a negative charge. The theory was not correct, in all details, but Thomson, who discovered the electron, admitted that "a collection of electrons would resemble in many respects Franklin's electric fluid." Franklin was on the edge and looking over at an explanation which came in another century and a half, *the proton and electron composition of matter.*

FIRE—THE SUBTILE FLUID
I see your philosophers are in the way of finding out at last what fire is. I have long been of opinion that it exists everywhere in the state of a subtile fluid; that too much of that fluid in our flesh gives us the sensation we call heat; too little, cold; its vibrations, light; that all solid or fluid substances which are inflammable, have been composed of it; their dissolution in returning to their original fluid state, we call fire. This subtile fluid is attracted by other substances, thermometers, etc., variously; has a particular affinity with water, and will quit many other bodies to attach itself to water and go off with it in evaporation. Adieu.

(To Benjamin Vaughan, April 29, 1784)

Franklin's terms and ideas described electrical phenomena more thoroughly and accurately than they had ever been described before. And he hadn't finished. There were more experiments to do, more reports for Collinson.

M. MUSSCHENBROEK'S WONDERFUL BOTTLE

The summer of 1747 was a warm one in Philadelphia. It was also the wettest summer in thirty years, making it difficult to harvest crops. Nevertheless, the harvest was a good one. In July, Franklin wrote to Jared Eliot about the weather, agriculture (valuable grass seed Eliot had provided proved to be timothy grass, persuading Franklin that it was taken "out of a wrong paper or parcel"), and politics ("to a friend one may hazard one's notions, right or wrong; and as you are pleased to desire my thoughts, you shall have them and welcome. I wish they were better.")

The letter to Eliot made no mention of the electrical experiments which meant that Franklin did not share the main burden of his thoughts. Through the whole summer he was busy with electricity. And on August 14, he seemed to be having trouble, even to the point of dispatching a hurried note to Collinson telling him not to expose the letters he had previously sent on electrical subjects.

> On some further experiments since I have observ'd a phenomenon or two, that I cannot at present account for on the principle laid down in those letters, and am therefore become a little diffident of my hypothesis, and asham'd that I have express'd myself in so positive a manner. In going on with these experiments how many pretty systems do we build which we soon find ourselves oblig'd to destroy! If there is no other use discover'd of electricity this however is something considerable, that it may *help to make a vain man humble.*

But by September 1st, confidence was back in full surge and the experiments were going forward.

> The necessary trouble of copying long letters, which perhaps, when they come to your hands, may contain nothing new, or worth your reading (so quick is the progress made with you in electricity), half discourages me of writing any more on that subject. Yet I cannot forebear adding a few observations of M. Musschenbroek's wonderful bottle.

The Leyden jar was precisely the instrument he needed to extend his experiments and hopefully to prove his one fluid theory of electricity. When they obtained the jar, the first experiments were repetitions of those done in Europe to familiarize themselves with the device. But Franklin soon was making observations and reaching conclusions the Europeans had not recorded. The assumption until Franklin reported his experiments was that when electricity was present the electrical fluid had to pass from one medium to another. Franklin established that electrical attraction occurred without the passage of anything. It could take place, mysteriously and remarkably, at a distance.

He noted that when a Leyden jar is charged, the two coatings of the glass become differently charged, with the glass between them. Since glass was an insulator, the electrical charge from one side could not pass as a fluid through the glass to the coating on the other side. He found that positive and negative charges could attract each other even through glass. If there was no way for an electrical fluid to pass, the attraction must be operating at a distance. At that juncture, Franklin abandoned the previously held view of electrical fluids around charged bodies. He concluded the electrical force was held within the charged body and acted at a distance on other charged bodies. It was strange, simple, and beautiful at the same time. Nature was an odd one who seemed to delight in giving the searchers a merry chase. And a happy ending.

The work continued. It was found that the "wire and the top of the bottle, &c., is electrized *positively* or *plus*, the bottom of the bottle is electrized *negatively* or *minus*, in exact proportion; that is, whatever quantity of electrical fire is thrown in at the top, an equal quantity goes out of the bottom."

> The equilibrium cannot be restored in the bottle by *inward* communication or contact of the parts; but it must be done by a communication formed *without* the bottle, between the top and bottom, by some nonelectric, touching or approaching both at the same time; in which case it is restored with a violence and quickness inexpressible; or touching each alternately, in which case the equilibrium is restored by degrees.
>
> . . . So wonderfully are these two states of electricity, the *plus* and *minus*, combined and balanced in this miraculous bottle! situated and related to each other in a manner that I can by no means comprehend! . . . here we have a bottle containing at the same time a *plenum* of electrical fire and a *vacuum* of the same fire, and yet the equilibrium cannot be restored between them but by a communication *without*, though the *plenum* presses violently to expand, and the hungry vacuum seems to attract as violently in order to be filled.

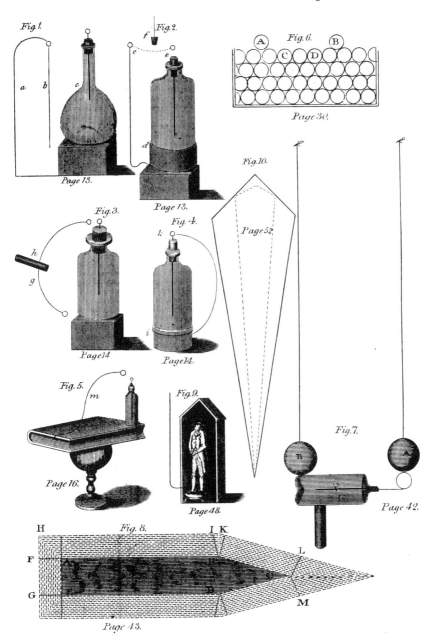

Fig. 1.

Fig. 2.

Fig. 6.

Page 30.

Page 13.

Page 13.

Fig. 3.

Fig. 4.

Fig. 10.

Page 52.

Page 14.

Page 14.

Fig. 5.

Fig. 9.

Fig. 7.

Page 16.

Page 48.

Page 42.

Fig. 8.

Page 43.

Reproduced from The Works of Benjamin Franklin, *Published by William Duane, Philadelphia, 1809.*

The September first letter contained meticulous details on various experiments, eleven of them, some displaying an imaginative complexity proving Franklin's increasing command and confidence. He was learning to manage the strange force and to manipulate it. And he was approaching fundamental characteristics of the force as he studied its behavior. The force was orderly and predictable and as consistent as the sunrise.

Experiment XI involved passing electricity from the inside to the outside of the bottle, or from one coating to another through the glass, and it was "rendered strongly visible by the following pretty experiment." Figure 5 in the illustrations shows the arrangement. A wire 8 or 10 inches in length was slipped around the cover of a book filleted with gold, so that the wire touched the gold. The book was placed on glass or wax "to show that the visible electricity is not brought up from the common stock of the earth." At the other end of the book's gold line, an electrified Leyden jar was placed, and a ring on the end of the wire was brought close to the ring of the jar.

> Instantly there is a strong spark and stroke, and the whole line of gold, which completes the communication between the top and bottom of the bottle, will appear a vivid flame, like the sharpest lightning . . . If you would have the whole filleting round the cover appear in fire at once, let the bottle and wire touch the gold in the diagonally opposite corners.

AN ELECTRICAL BATTERY

The rest of 1747 inescapably brought him other concerns than the confounding but compelling riddles of electricity. Government and civic duties, as always, laid effective siege to his energies and time. The world of the Colonies was learning more and more to beat a path to the door of Benjamin Franklin. No one was busier, so the adage that when something needed to be done, a busy man should be found to do it, led straight to Franklin. In July came his *Plain Truth* plea to Pennsylvania and the Colonies for self-defense against French and Spanish privateers. In November there were the pressures and responsibilities of organizing the Association formed for defense of Pennsylvania. On December 3, 1747, the *Gazette* published his remarks on the *Proposals for a Volunteer and Republican Military Force*. Among other logical, reasonable, and revolutionary remarks was the observation that "ill consequences" resulted from allowing the Governor to appoint the Officers of the Militia. He wanted the Militia to elect its own officers. "It is to be presumed the choice will naturally fall on men of the best character for their military skill; on such too, from whose prudence and good-nature there may be no fear of injustice or military oppression." He pointed to the "Old Romans" for historical support while insisting that "frequent elections secure the liberty of the people. And what can give more spirit and martial vigour to an army of FREEMEN, than to be led by those of whom they have the best opinion?" In three decades, militias made up of Freemen and officered by equals they respected would defeat the best of European armies led by hereditary officers and political appointees. Clearly there was something to be said for *Freemen.* Men looked at the record and found that Franklin had already said it.

Thomas Penn, the Proprietor of Pennsylvania, cared not for *Plain Truth,* the Proposals, or their author.

> This Association is founded on a contempt to government, and cannot end in anything but anarchy and confusion ... tho very true in itself, that obedience to governors is no more due that protection to the people, yet it is not fit to be always in the heads of the wild unthinking multitude.

Franklin, a developing leader of the wild unthinking multitude, was called "a dangerous man" by Proprietor Penn, who added, "I should be very glad he inhabited any other country, as I believe him of a very uneasy spirit."

The displeasure of the Proprietor may have been more an encouragement than a hindrance to the Association. In December 1747 Franklin could write to James Logan that "near eight hundred have signed the *Association,* and more are signing hourly. One company of Dutch is complete."

Such activities were not hospitable to the peace of mind or the tranquillity needed for "ingenious science." The evidence is strong, however, that Franklin needed far less of peace and tranquillity for effective labors in science than most men. The descriptions provided of the throngs arriving to see his electrical experiments convey the sense of a "madhouse" rather than a laboratory. Whatever the tumult, apparently he managed to keep working. Perhaps preceding the move to Race Street, he was *sometimes* aware of the surrounding confusion. Before the end of 1747 he wrote to Thomas Hopkinson that "the din of the Market (Philadelphia Market) increases upon me; and that, with frequent interruptions, has, I find, made me say some things twice over."

In addition to the din, it should be remembered that he was still probably the busiest printer in the Colonies, and voluntary Secretary to the American Philosophical Society, and ... The list was no modest one.

He kept up his business, his civic activities, maintained his correspondence, and simultaneously continued a program of basic scientific research that was astonishingly, against odds, delivering new knowledge to the world.

In letters during the period to Cadwallader Colden and James Logan, he wrote of scientific matters but made no mention of electricity. Discussion of electrical fire at that time was still reserved for Peter Collinson who could bring the information to the attention of European researchers and the Royal Society, which, being a Society, predictably neglected at first to listen very well.

The demands of the electrical experiments served to precipitate a decision Franklin had been contemplating a long time. He wrote to Cadwallader Colden of his decision on September 29, 1748.

> The share I had in the late Association, &c., having given me a little present run of popularity, there was a pretty general intention of choosing me a representative of the city at the next election of Assembly men; but I have desired all my friends who spoke to me about it, to discourage it, declaring that I should not serve if chosen. Thus you see I am in a fair way of having no other tasks than such as I shall like to give myself, and of enjoying what I look upon as a great happiness, leisure to read, study, make experiments, and converse at large with such ingenious and worthy men as are pleased to honor me with their friendship or acquaintance, on such points as may produce something for the common benefit of mankind, uninterrupted by the little cares and fatigues of business.

But he didn't wait for his reprieve from worldly cares to continue experimenting. They went on despite all competing claims, and before midcentury, he had important reports to deliver.

In one of these, describing experiments with Leyden jars and electrified phials, he added two new words to the vocabulary of electricity, simple words describing the movement of the force. The words explained an apparent effect graphically, but scientifically they were inexact. Franklin the scientist wanted that understood.

> When we use the terms of *charging* and *discharging* the phial, it is in compliance with custom, and for want of others more suitable. Since

we are of opinion that there is really no more electrical fire in the phial after what is called its *charging*, than before, nor less after its *discharging*; excepting only the small spark that might be given to, and taken from, the non-electric matter, if separated from the bottle, which spark may not be equal to a five-hundredth part of what is called the explosion. For if, on the explosion, the electrical fire came out of the bottle by one part, and did not enter in again by another, then, if a man, standing on wax, holding the bottle in one hand, takes the spark by touching the wire hook with the other, the bottle being thereby *discharged*, the man would be *charged*; or whatever fire was lost by one, would be found in the other, since there was no way for its escape; but the contrary is true.

The experiments slowly were providing intimations concerning the true nature of electricity. The unfathomable was being fathomed. The mask was being lifted from the inscrutable. And as Franklin was certain all along, the occult force was showing itself to be natural and pervasive. He had never expected in his experiments to bump headlong into angry and offended little satans, bent on revenge. He expected electricity simply to be established as a basic part of the universal scheme, and it was. In 1751, broadening his correspondence, he wrote to Cadwallader Colden, who in turn forwarded the information to Collinson in London, that he no longer thought it accurate to speak of some objects having electricity and some not.

> ... some of my experiments show, that glass contains it in great quantity, and I now suspect it to be pretty equally diffused in all the matter of this terraqueous globe. If so, the terms *electric per se,* and *non-electric,* should be laid aside as improper, and (the only difference being this, that some bodies will conduct electric matter, and others will not) the terms *conductor* and *non-conductor* may supply their place. If any portion of electric matter is applied to a piece of conducting matter, it penetrates and flows through it, or spreads equally on its surface; if applied to a piece of non-conducting matter, it will do neither. Perfect conductors of electric matter are only metals and water. Other bodies conducting only as they contain a mixture of those; without more or less of which they will not conduct at all. This (by the way) shows a new relation between metals and water heretofore unknown.

PAYING DEAR
If I see one fond of appearance, or fine clothes, fine houses, fine furniture, fine equipages, all above his fortune, for which he contracts debts, and ends his career in a prison, Alas! say I, he has paid dear, very dear, for his whistle.
(The Whistle, *To Madame Brillon, 1779*)

Franklin *generalized too broadly concerning metals and water as the only conductors*, but he was again close to the cosmic secret and the core of all matter when he surmised the electrical content of matter throughout the globe.

Such conclusions were built up to gradually by the force of evidence during the experiments. In his third major accounting to Collinson, he was already reporting that glass contained a great quantity of electrical fire in proportion to its mass. Here too his mind was flirting with the edges of the microcosmic atomic universe with its unimaginable reservoir of cohesive energies.

The experiments were becoming more elaborate and sophisticated, also more daring. He had learned that phials could be charged in series with the same effort needed to charge one. Serial charging meant a corresponding multiplication of the available power.

Experimenting with the jar directly, he found that electricity was in the glass, not the coatings of the glass. The coating of a charged jar could be removed and another added with a shock resulting. "The whole force of the bottle and power of giving a shock is in the *glass itself*," he concluded, and described the proof. If water was placed in the Leyden jar, the water gave off a strong spark when the jar was electrified. But when water was removed from an electrified jar the water gave off no shock. This contradicted the earlier opinion that electricity was "crowded into and condensed" in the water, with the glass serving only as a confining medium.

Experiment showed, however, that the electricity remained in the glass of the bottle, not in the water or the coatings of the bottle. This was new information to Franklin. He did not know that it was also new to the world.

With his associates, he then electrified a piece of sash-glass between two pieces of lead. Removed from the lead, the glass emitted a series of tiny sparks, but placed again between the lead plates, and "completing a circle between the two surfaces, a violent shock ensued, which demonstrated the power to reside in glass as glass."

That finding illuminated the way to another innovation of great significance. It was as if a peephole had been made in the curtains to the modern world.

Upon this we made what we called an *electrical battery*, consisting of eleven panes of large sash-glass, armed with thin leaden plates, pasted on each side, placed vertically, and supported at two inches distance on silk cords, with thick hooks of leaden wire, one from each side, standing upright, distant from each other, and convenient communications of wire and chain, from the giving side of one pane to the receiving side of the other, that so the whole might be charged together, and with the same labor as one single pane; and another contrivance to bring the giving sides, after charging, in contact with one long wire, and the receivers with another, which two long wires would give the force of all the plates of glass at once through the body of any animal forming the circle with them. The plates may also be discharged separately, or any number together that is required.

ELECTRICAL CONSPIRATORS AND A FEAST

Frank Donovan in *The Benjamin Franklin Papers* wrote of followup experiments to this one that Franklin "was well on the way to inventing the electric chair." Seeking practical applications, Franklin did consider the use of electricity to kill turkeys, and small animals for food; but it is unlikely that he would have approved the other use. Like his Quaker friend James Logan, Franklin tended to oppose capital punishment as a weapon of society. It was an effort to protect property at the expense of humanity, and thus an abuse of power and the commencement of tyranny.

Continuing his third report to Collinson, Franklin described some of the electrical recreations being indulged in. He created a *"magical picture"* of the "King (God preserve him)" in which a gilded frame and crown were electrified, and anyone holding the frame who tried to remove the crown would receive a "terrible blow and fail in the attempt." "If the picture were highly charged," added Franklin, "the consequence might perhaps be as fatal as that of high treason; for when the spark is taken through a quire of paper laid on the picture by means of a wire communication, it makes a fair hole through every sheet, that is, through forty-eight leaves, though a quire of paper is thought good armour against the push of a sword, or even against a pistol bullet, and the crack is exceedingly loud ... If a ring of persons take the shock among them, the experiment is called *The Conspirators*."

This experiment in royal protection stirs a sense of amused irony when Franklin's future exploits are placed beside it. He had no wish to remove the crown of a king, but he did quite effectively remove a crown colony from a king. And there was a shock involved, a shock that shook the world.

After detailing further experiments in his report, Franklin concluded with a startling plan that serious scientists in all ages might view askance as frivolous, capricious, fraught with levity. But it is necessary to remember that this particular scientist was Benjamin Franklin, who was not a sober man, though he was a practical one.

Chagrined a little that we have been hitherto able to produce nothing in this way of use to mankind; and the hot weather coming on, when the electrical experiments are not so agreeable, it is proposed to put an end to them for this season, somewhat humorously, in a party of pleasure on the banks of the Schuylkill. Spirits, at the same time, are to be fired by a spark sent from side to side through the river, without any other conductor than the water; an experiment which we some time since performed to the amazement of many. A turkey is to be killed for our dinner by *electrical shock*, and roasted by the *electrical jack*, before a fire kindled by the electrified bottle; when the healths of all the famous electricians in England, Holland, France, and Germany are to be drunk in *electrified bumpers*, under the discharge of guns from the *electrical battery*.

If Benjamin Franklin learned the secrets of the universe, he intended to have fun with them, or what the good?

The electrical feast presumably took place when the hot weather was near, during that season when Benjamin Franklin's city between the Schuylkill and Delaware Rivers was subject to sudden storms. The weather on the day of the feast is not known, but perhaps an additional spectacle was provided in the skies to rival the electrical games being played out upon the river banks. If so, Franklin would have paused to look at the sky, to compare, and think. The significance and nature of the explosions that took place in the sky during a thunderstorm were already beginning to take the shape of *new experiments and theories in his mind*. It would have been appropriate during the electrical sports if celestial forces had chosen to join in, if javelins of lightning had been thrown earthward in challenge to the electricians.

Whether the instigating moment occurred at that time or another, it was a challenge Benjamin Franklin was preparing himself to accept.

—

RECALL TO LIFE OF THE THREE DROWNED FLIES
They had been drowned in Madeira wine, apparently about the time it had been bottled in Virginia, to be sent to London. At the opening of one of the bottles, at the house of a friend where I was, three drowned flies fell into the first glass that was filled. Having heard it remarked that drowned flies were capable of being revived by the rays of the sun, I proposed making the experiment upon these. They were therefore exposed to the sun, upon a sieve which had been employed to strain them out of the wine. In less than three hours two of them began by degrees to recover life. They commenced by some convulsive motions of the thighs, and at length they raised themselves upon their legs with their forefeet, beat and brushed their wings with their hind feet, and soon after began to fly, finding themselves in Old England, without knowing how they came thither. The third continued lifeless till sunset, when, losing all hopes of him, he was thrown away.

(To M. Dubourg)

1976

Dear Doctor Franklin, Sir,

Sharing your adventures, experiments, and achievements at a distance, today we get the definite impression that you were a pundit, a rationalist, a man of original reason and unquestionably pixilated. That's a friendly old word for someone who is whimsical, unconventional, mischievous.

The European scientists of your day must have been badly shaken by the news out of Philadelphia. They labored solemnly to discover nature's truths and prayed for divine guidance to be worthy. You labored merrily, sometimes prankishly, often puckishly; and when you were making remarkable progress, you didn't assemble a dignified group to tell you in what ways you must be mistaken. Instead you went on an electrical picnic.

Pixilated, Sir, that must have been the decision of your peers among the scientists of the time. Perhaps one of them even whispered, "Franklin? Genius of course, but daffy. Make no mistake of it, daffy. He *enjoys* everything, no matter how serious."

When the time came for your most remarkable demonstration, what did you do? Why you and your son found an open field in which you could fly a kite! And you produced one of the memorable events in the history of world science.

We should be as accurate as we can be sir. You had something, frequently lacking in modern science, and in the science of your own time for that matter. The something we mean, of course, is: Fun.

Whether you were taking the temperature of the Gulf Stream, experimenting with the sensations of Madeira wine, inventing electric bells, or theorizing about light from the stars, you maintained a sense of perennial fun. Whatever else you might conclude about them, the universe to you was always amusing and its Author had a sense of humor.

Sir, we need mirth again in our science and our lives. Perhaps you can give us fresh pointers at the celebration, our bicentennial electric picnic, even if you disguise them as maxims from Richard Saunders, Silence Dogood, Polly Baker, Historicus, or one of the other living characters you invented to tell a truth, teach a lesson, deflate a lie, and have some fun. Make us pixilated too. It sounds great.

We Are, &c.,
YOURS, THE PEOPLE

XV. Lightning: An Extreme Subtle Fluid

LET THE EXPERIMENT BE MADE

In a memorandum on November 7, 1749, Franklin listed a number of intriguing comparisons and came to a conclusion:

> Electrical fluid agrees with lightning in these particulars: 1. Giving light. 2. Color of the light. 3. Crooked direction. 4. Swift motion. 5. Being conducted by metals. 6. Crack or noise on exploding. 7. Subsiding in water or ice. 8. Rending bodies it passes through. 9. Destroying animals. 10. Melting metals. 11. Firing inflammable substances. 12. Sulphurous smell.

> The electrical fluid is attracted by points. We do not know whether this is a property of lightning. But since they agree in all particulars wherein we can already compare them, is it not probable that they agree likewise in this? Let the experiment be made.

The experimenter had reached a bolder threshold in his speculations. He had studied the electrical forces available for mastery on the surface of the earth more intently and closely than anyone before him. Now he lifted his eyes and glanced throughtfully at the sky.

Lightning!

Celestial theatre on a scale awesome and terrifying. A dangerous and yet magnificent fury seeking desperate solutions to its fiery tensions. Lightning flashed above Philadelphia turning darkness into twilight, eerie and yet magnificent. The flash was only a moment, but it seemed unmistakably to be the concentrated essence of fury. "Lightning that mocks the night, brief even as bright," wrote the poet Shelley. But it was a character in Shakespeare's *Macbeth* that came closer to expressing the general fear about lightning. "When shall we three meet again," said the First Witch to her two sisters, "In thunder, lightning, or in rain?" Lightning was a thing of witches, of devils, and of gods angry beyond argument. Franklin and his neighbors were intimately acquainted with the force. They had seen it strike capriciously and harmlessly. They had seen it destroy. And they had seen it kill.

In the *Gazette* for June 17, 1731, the strange antics of lightning had been reported:

> From Newcastle we hear, that on Tuesday the 8th Instant, the Lightning fell upon a House within a few Miles of that Place, in which it killed 3 Dogs, struck several Persons deaf, and split a Woman's Nose in a surprizing Manner.

June 1st of the following year brought another account of lightning's talent for terror to the pages of the *Gazette*.

Three miles from the city the house of the Widow Mifflin had been savagely wounded in a lightning storm. Her chimney was partially struck down, her roof shattered, plaster knocked from part of a brick wall, a window broken, and a boy badly burned.

The newspaper did not accuse, but the Widow Mifflin's neighbors no doubt viewed the event in the fashion of the times as a judgment of God. Lightning was an unconquerable and inescapable force. In the absence of natural explanations, inevitably it was made an object of fear and superstition. From one view it was divine wrath. From another it was the diabolical plaything of witches and devils. In either case it was a power to treat with respect, approach cautiously, and never take for granted.

In the *Gazette* for July 10, 1732, there were more lightning-fostered tribulations to report. Lightning did its mischievous worst and in seconds was gone, like an unstoppable thief. There was no point calling the constable. An arrest was never made.

> We hear from Allenstown, that on Tuesday last the House of Mr. James Rogers was struck by Lightning. It split down Part of the Chimney, went through the Room where he was sitting with his Children, but without hurting any of them; and entring into the Cellar, fir'd a full Hogshead of Rum which stood under an Arch, and bursting out the Head, the whole Cellar was instantly fill'd with Flames which pour'd out at the Windows. There was several hundred weight of Butter in Tubs, which melted and took fire also; but by the timely Assistance of abundance of People, and the Help of a large Quantity of Water just gathered from the Rain in a Hollow near by, the House was happily preserved... 'Tis said that tho' they fill'd the Cellar with so much Water as to be near a Foot deep, yet after the Fire was out, it was so hot as not to be tolerable to the Feet and Legs of those who would have gone in.

Had Mr. Rogers or Mrs. Mifflin irked an angel or miffed a witch? Whatever the reason or motive for lightning, whether natural or supernatural, it was a spectacular wildness that needed controlling if there was any way. Many had thought about the matter before Franklin, but none had suggested an answer.

Among scientists the similarity in appearance and behavior between lightning and electricity had been noted for some time. The possibility of a relationship between them had been suggested by Sir Isaac Newton, which gave the idea credibility and authority. In 1743, the Abbé Nollet, science teacher to the Royal Family of France, again hypothecated a similarity between lightning and electricity in his *Leçons de Physique*. About the time Franklin began his electrical experiments, a German scientist, Winkler, reported that electricity in thunderstorms and the spark generated by a friction machine are fundamentally the same, differing only in intensity. Winkler explained lightning as the result of friction between air particles and water vapor.

It required a printer from Boston turned scientist to prove what others only guessed. Franklin was the one who designed an experiment not just to speculate but to establish whether or not there was a relationship between lightning and electricity. Franklin dated his own reflections on the subject from his memorandum of November 7, 1749. In his March 18, 1755 letter to *Dr. John Lining* he quoted the memorandum noting that "by this extract you will see that the thought was not so much 'an out-of-the-way one,' but that it might have occurred to an electrician."

It can be presumed that Franklin was familiar with the speculations of other scientists on the subject. He kept himself up-to-date
on what others, especially the Europeans, were doing and thinking
in the field. At that point, such information served only to confirm
his own developing theories. These in turn were based on careful
observations and bold experimentation. Ahead of him were experiments even bolder to *prove the similarity of lightning and electricity.* Accusations of recklessness have been leveled against Franklin
for some of his experiments in electricity; but in fairness it is necessary to keep in mind that he and his friends were entering a totally
new and unknown area of science. Timid scientists rarely seem to
make progress in such areas. Hesitant about the way ahead, they
pause before taking the first step to weigh carefully every possible
danger and to map the route. More often than not, the first step is
never taken. Scientists who develop cures rather than theories eventually inoculate themselves and take their own chances.

Franklin can be called reckless for daring to attempt certain
things without knowing the consequences. But the word does not
seem useful or fair. If he wanted safe and easy science, he could
have busied himself analyzing chemically and poetically the fra-
grances of flowers. But electricity, for all its perils, was more interesting and more promising for a man who wanted to explore nature's
lustier profiles.

Looking back in 1755, he told Dr. Lining matter-of-factly about
the experiment in which six men were knocked down simultaneously with the partial charge from two Leyden jars. The discharging rod was placed on the head of the first man. He put his hand
on the head of the second, as if he were blessing him, and so on to
the last man who held the chain connected to the jars. "When they
were thus placed, I applied the other end of my rod to the prime
conductor, and they all dropped together. When they got up, they
all declared they had not felt any stroke, and wondered how they
came to fall . . . You suppose it a dangerous experiment; but I had
once suffered the same myself, receiving, by accident, an equal
stroke through my head, that struck me down, without hurting me."

Franklin could have been seriously, even critically hurt during
some of his experiments. So could his friends. They were not naively
unaware of the dangers, and they were as prudent as the capricious
force they were struggling to understand allowed them to be. But
electricity was not a child's innocent toy. Chances had to be taken
if anything was to be learned. Franklin was never seriously hurt,
nor any of his immediate associates. That says something about

the intelligence with which they proceeded. "Too great a charge might, indeed, kill a man," wrote Franklin to Dr. Lining, "but I have not yet seen any hurt done by it. It would certainly, as you observe, be the easiest of all deaths."

The word "death" didn't stop him from proceeding with his electrical experiments on the ground. And it didn't stop him from continuing to study the lightning and to continue asking "how". It was certain that when he had settled on the method, he would try it. After a method is determined, a scientist reduces the risk to the extent he can, and then proceeds. Or he is someone other than a scientist.

TEN THOUSAND ACRES OF ELECTRIFIED SKY

During the 1747-1749 period, Franklin began methodically attempting to establish a hypothetical connection between lightning and electricity. In 1749 he sent a report to Collinson, containing materials dating back to 1747, in which he speculated at length about oceans as the parents of thundergusts and lightning. His conclusions were off in some particulars. But the broad assumption was that lightning and electricity are different aspects of the same phenomenon.

> Water being electrified, the vapors arising from it will be equally electrified, and floating in the air, in the form of clouds, or otherwise, will retain that quantity of electrical fire, till they meet with other clouds or bodies not so much electrified, and then will communicate.

He reasoned that electrified particles of water, rising in vapors, would attach themselves to particles of air, and form electrified clouds "ten thousand acres" vast. Clouds formed over oceans would be intensely electrified because of the electrical fire inherent in the ocean, and when such clouds approached mountains or clouds formed over land, there would be an exchange of electrical fire (lightning) between them to equalize the charges. The lightning when heavily concentrated electrical charges are involved "flashes brightly and cracks loudly."

When Franklin wrote this report on thunder and lightning, he was obviously already drawing useful analogies between the behavior of lightning and experimental electricity. A vital clue was provided in item 43:

> As electrified clouds pass over a country, high hills and high trees, lofty towers, spires, masts of ships, chimneys, &c., as so many promi-

nences and points draw the electrical fire, and the whole cloud discharges there. 44. Dangerous, therefore, is it to take shelter under a tree during a thunder-gust. It has been fatal to many, both men and beasts. 45. It is safer to be in the open field for another reason. When the clothes are wet, if a flash in its way to the ground should strike your head, it may run in the water over the surface of your body; whereas, if your clothes were dry, it would go through the body, because the blood and other humours, containing so much water, are more ready conductors. Hence a wet rat cannot be killed by the exploding electrical bottle, when a dry rat may.

Even the wet rat, of course, should be wary of electrical storms or more heavily charged electrical bottles. Franklin was dealing with facts in these observations, and from the facts to practical suppositions was not a long or especially difficult journey for the experimenter.

His basic arguments concerning the known mechanics of lightning were surprisingly close if not exact. Lightning research has been taking place more than 220 years since Franklin's experiments, and all the answers are not yet known. *The conditions that cause different types of lightning—forked, sheet, ball—are still being analyzed for full understanding. Ball lightning, for instance, that among other things has been considered a possible explanation for UFO (Unidentified Flying Object) sightings, is still being subjected to fundamental research in an effort to learn all its whys and wherefores.* Is it a sign of sport among the celestial forces? Is it a Universal Series in the Cosmic Baseball League, or something more unusual than that? By the late 1740's Franklin knew lightning's behavior, the "what" of it, virtually as well as it is now known. He also understood the basic "why" of it simply from the arguments of logic if he did not precisely grasp all the technical details. He knew that tremendous electrical conditions built up in clouds, that these sought relief through electrical discharges, when passing near other electrified clouds, or when a pointed object on the earth offered a suitable target.

The basic modern explanation of lightning is not radically distant in its conjectures from the hypotheses Franklin sent to Collinson in 1749. Today we simply have more details.

When thunderclouds develop, this is taking place: Positive and negative particles separate in the clouds as they become charged, positive charges moving to the summit of the clouds, the negative charges preferring the bottom portions. Why they separate in charged clouds is a continuing puzzle. Modern scientists, in essence, suggest that the curious should "interview" the particles. On the surface of the earth, positive charges also strive to reach the highest points; and the electrical attraction commences between these positive charges on the surface and the negative charges in clouds.

The air between cloud and ground serves as an insulating medium until the electrical buildup becomes sufficiently large to overcome the resistance. In order to effect a link between the positive charges on the surface, streams of negative charges from the clouds streak in narrow columns toward the earth. These columns can be miles in length and yet only a few hundred millimeters in diameter. Linkage is effected with the earth when the negative charges from the cloud come close enough to the aspiring positive charges, built up at high points, to force the positive charges to leap upward in response. When this occurs, lightning can be said to have struck. Flashes of lightning in the sky are streams of negative charges, travelling in different streams and giving the jagged, forked effect characteristic of lightning storms. When a bolt of lightning is said to strike the earth, in effect what has happened is that positive electrical current has shot up from the earth to neutralize or embrace the negative forces coming down. In a matter of seconds, there may be a negative flash downward, and a much brighter flash upward from the positively charged point on earth. The visual effect may seem to be a sword of electricity thrust out of the sky into the earth, but actually the main part of the lightning bolt flashes up not down. Since the event is close to instantaneous and since people being struck by lightning are seldom psychologically alert enough to pay meticulous attention to the intricate details, it is not strange that we think of the earth and ourselves as targets for lightning from the heavens, rather than as revolvers firing at the sky, which is technically closer to the truth.

Thunder occurs following the lightning flash as a result of rapidly expanding hot gases coming in contact with colder air. Because of lightning activity, the formation of raindrops is speeded up in clouds; and thunder following lightning is one of the triggers that tends to start precipitation.

That, in brief, is the current explanation of "what" occurs. It is not impressively remote from many of Franklin's eighteenth century conceptions.

... If air thus loaded be compressed by adverse winds or by being driven against mountains, &c., or condensed by taking away the fire that assisted it in expanding, the triangles contract, the air with its

water will descend as a dew; or if the water surrounding one particle
of air comes in contact with the water surrounding another, they co-
alesce and form a drop, and we have rain.

... If much loaded, the electrical fire is at once taken from the whole
cloud; and, in leaving it, flashes brightly and cracks loudly, the particles coalescing for want of that fire, and falling in a heavy shower.

Later in his reflections Franklin decided that he had been mistaken in his first assumption that the sea was the source of lightning. Writing to Collinson in September, 1753, he readily admitted
that he had been misled by the luminescence of the ocean in places.
assuming this was "owing to electric fire produced by friction between the particles of water and those of salt." "Living far from
the sea," he added, "I had then no opportunity of making experiments on the sea-water, and so embraced this opinion too hastily."
In 1750 and 1751 when he had greater opportunity to investigate
bottled water from the sea, he soon rejected the earlier theory.
Even with agitation it was impossible to create a condition of light
in the sea water. The scientist didn't struggle, as some have, against
the facts. Admitting that the "luminous appearance in sea-water
must be owing to some other principles," he immediately began
looking for the true explanation of electrified clouds, and in the
process advanced many leagues through the unknown to the heart
of modern theory.

*It was typical of Franklin not to cling to a wrong theory or a
false position. His commitment to truth was too great, and his
scientific ego was in no way damaged by ready admission of error.
Quite the contrary. He was always clearly eager to admit a mistake so that it could be corrected and he could move on.*

In his letter to Dr. Lining on March 18, 1755, he made this revealing comment, responding to a question he could not answer:

The fact is singular. You require the reason; I do not know it. Perhaps
you may discover it, and then you will be so good as to communicate
it to me. I find a frank acknowledgement of one's ignorance is not only
the easiest way to get rid of a difficulty, but the likeliest way to obtain information, and therefore I practice it: I think it an honest policy. Those who affect to be thought to know everything, and so undertake to explain everything, often remain long ignorant of many things
that others could and would instruct them in, if they appeared less
conceited.

After escaping the error about the sea as the source of lightning,
Franklin decided that it might result (though the curious should

continue to examine the matter) from air particles rubbing against structures, trees, and earth extensions such as mountains, hills, etc. The resulting friction might "draw the electric fire from the earth" in rising vapors which would electrify the clouds.

That wasn't the final answer, but it was correctly focused and provided a theoretical foundation for the "opinions and conjectures" concerning lightning and electricity that brought the name Franklin to the attention not just of scientists but the world. From 1747 on, it seems clear that Franklin never doubted the relationship of lightning and electricity. From all the parallels between the two, he simply took their similarity for granted. With that truth as a goal, the challenge was to prove it, which required nothing more than a little ingenuity. Josiah Franklin's son could provide it.

LIGHTNING POINTS

Scientific breakthroughs in one direction could result in a whole chain of breakthroughs. Truth has a tendency to be multidirectional.

One of the first important discoveries by the Philadelphia School had been "the wonderful effect of pointed bodies both in *drawing off* and *throwing off* the electrical fire." Franklin had scrupulously credited Thomas Hopkinson with initiating this vein of research, and then had gone on in experiments and speculation to make it a fundamental building block in electrical science.

If lightning and electricity were the same, then the significance of points could be predicted in that direction as well. Franklin boldly made the surmise in 1749 or 1750 and reported to Collinson:

> The doctrine of points is very curious, and the effects of them truly wonderful; and, from what I have observed on experiments, I am of opinion that houses, ships, and even towers and churches may be effectually secured from the strokes of lightning by their means; for if, instead of the round balls of wood or metal which are commonly placed on the tops of weathercocks, vanes, or spindles of churches, spires, or masts, there should be a rod of eight or ten feet in length, sharpened gradually to a point like a needle, and gilt to prevent rusting, or divided into a number of points, which would be better, the electrical fire would, I think, be drawn out of a cloud silently, before it could come near enough to strike."

This was his first allusion to a practical application of the electrical discoveries. If what had been learned could be applied to protect the Widow Mifflin, Mr. James Rogers, and thousands of others

annually from the destruction of lightning, there was no doubt
about the practicality of what he had been doing. When he began
to realize the possibilities, Franklin was pleased; but he knew that
his experiments had not begun with that useful end in view. They
had begun, urged on by scientific curiosity, for truth's sake and
continued for the same reason. Utility was a pleasing dividend and
one of the earliest illustrations of how pure science can eventually
lead to practical results. Franklin may have had this in mind when
he wrote to Cadwallader Colden on April 23, 1752: "Frequently,
in a variety of experiments, though we miss what we expected to
find, yet something valuable turns out, something surprising, and
instructing, though unthought of."

His realization about the possibilities of points in connection
with lightning brought Franklin to a brilliant epidemic of conclusions which he conveyed to Collinson with a note on July 29, 1750,
again apologetic that it might include nothing new "considering
the number of ingenious men in Europe continually engaged in the
same researches" but that it would show Collinson the apparatus
he had sent the Library Company had not been neglected.

The report carried an impressive title to match even more impressive contents: *Opinions and Conjectures concerning the Effects of the Electrical Matter, and the Means of Preserving Buildings, Ships, &c., from Lightning, arising from Experiments and
Observations made at Philadelphia, 1749.*

"The electrical matter consists of particles extremely subtle,
since it can permeate common matter, even the densest metals,"
began Franklin in his report. He continued with a detailed accounting of what had been learned about the properties of electricity,
giving special emphasis to the greater electrical sensitivity displayed by pointed objects over blunt objects. The author provided
reasons for the phenomenon, though he was not certain that he
had the full or correct explanation. But even an inadequate answer
might propel someone else in the direction of the right one.

> Nor is it of much importance to us to know the manner in which na-
> ture executes her laws; it is enough if we know the laws themselves.
> It is of real use to know that china left in the air unsupported will
> fall and break; but *how* it comes to fall, and *why* it breaks, are matters
> of speculation. It is a pleasure indeed to know them, but we can pre-
> serve our china without it.
> ... Thus, in the present case, to know this power of points may possi-
> bly be of some use to mankind, though we should never be able to ex-
> plain it.

Franklin proceeded to expand and refine his original idea of using metal rods for protection against lightning. Now he specified "upright rods of iron made sharp as a needle" and remembered to provide a goundwire from the base of the rods "down the outside of the building into the ground, or down round one of the shrouds of a ship, and down her side till it reaches the water."

"Would not," asked Franklin, "these pointed rods probably draw the electrical fire silently out of a cloud before it came nigh enough to strike, and thereby secure us from that most sudden and terrible mischief?"

In addition to this practical application of experimentally derived knowledge, he was also ready to suggest an audacious means of proving once and for all that lightning and electricity are equally bona fide members of the electrical fire family.

On the top of some high tower or steeple, place a kind of sentry-box, big enough to contain a man and an electrical stand. From the middle of the stand let an iron rod rise and pass bending out of the door, and then upright twenty or thirty feet, pointed very sharp at the end. If the electrical stand be clean and dry, a man standing on it when such clouds are passing low might be electrified and afford sparks, the rod drawing fire to him from a cloud. If any danger to the man should be apprehended (though I think there would be none), let him stand on the floor of his box, and now then bring near to the rod the loop of wire that has one end fastened to the leads, he holding it by a wax handle; so the sparks, if the rod is electrified, will strike from the rod to the wire and not affect him.

The state of electrical knowledge was not then sufficient to realize the dangers of electrocution inherent in such an experiment. Before trying it, Franklin luckily thought of an even more dramatic method (also dangerous) of proving his theory, involving a kite and a key.

The "Opinions and Conjectures" summary contained new data concerning the conductivity of glass, further technical explanation of the Leyden jar, details of another experiment in electrical aesthetics, the *"golden fish,"* and finally concluded that "I shall never have done, if I tell you all my conjectures, thoughts, and imaginations on the nature and operations of this electric fluid, and relate the variety of little experiments we have tried."

Whatever was not included in the report, the two main items were included—development of the lightning rod concept, suggestion of a dangerous but definitive experiment to confirm the lightning theory.

During the same general period, the electrical experiments gave Franklin two personal interviews with danger. One occurred on December 23, 1750 when he tried to use two large electrified jars to execute a turkey for Christmas dinner. He estimated that the jars contained "as much electrical fire as forty common phials."

The turkey, whom Franklin later would pay the tribute of recommending as a national emblem because it was more respectable and more naturally American than the lazy eagle with its filthy habits and bad moral character, was unharmed. Franklin took the full charge through his arms and body, and upon recovering remarked that he had "nearly killed a goose" while trying to kill a turkey. He described the effect as "a universal blow throughout my whole body from head to foot, which seemed within as well as without; after which the first thing I took notice of was a violent quick shaking of my body." His sense gradually returned, though the hand where the shock had entered was like "dead flesh" for several minutes, and there was numbness in his neck and arms until the following day.

Another time while treating a paralytic patient, he was struck down by the charge from two large jars. "I neither saw the flash, heard the report, nor felt the stroke ... A small swelling rose on the top of my head, which continued sore for some days; but I do not remember any other effect good or bad."

With such results possible from Leyden jars, special caution was called for in connection with lightning. But that was at the beginning of electrical understanding and information. Franklin's own experience with shock suggested to him "that a man can without great detriment bear a much greater electrical shock than I imagined."

The problem was that in equating such electrical forces with lightning, the difference in intensity could not then be sufficiently guessed. In the case of lightning they were experimenting with *forces that could reach temperatures surpassing that of the sun's surface and delivering currents involving millions of volts.* Franklin was quite correct in his reasoning about the lightning rod, and its ability to ground lightning bolts safely. The force follows the most direct route to reach earth. Franklin simply did not quite comprehend the scope and peril of the force. Even had he known, it is possible that his experiments would have proceeded anyway, though they might have been amended to suit the untamed caprices of the electrical fire waiting for harvest in the sky.

"The Lightning reached a fiery rod," declaimed *Joaquin Miller*, the poet, "And on Death's fearful forehead wrote—The autograph of God."

Franklin chose not to be fearful of that autograph. He wanted to understand it and to make it safe, which meant reaching up into the skies, not oblivious but superior to dangers.

PUBLICATION OF THE ELECTRICAL LETTERS

The letters Franklin sent to Peter Collinson concerning the electrical experiments, the conclusions, and hypotheses were communicated by Collinson to the Royal Society. That august body listened, but sceptically, to the results from Philadelphia. Some members were openly dubious and critical. The body as a whole tended to assume a "wait and see" stance concerning the astonishing information that Collinson seemed to receive with every ship's arrival from the Colonies.

The Royal Society's hesitation was fully understandable. Who, after all, was Benjamin Franklin? What did a Philadelphia printer know about a science that had puzzled Sir Isaac Newton and occupied many of the best minds of Europe for long periods. Abbé Nollet in France, who had done basic research in electricity and hypothecated the similarity of lightning and electricity, among others was destined to be a vigorous critic of Franklin's experiments and conclusions. When the Abbé's criticisms were followed up, however, by David Colden of New York, it seemed that he had either been careless in repeating Franklin's experiments, deficient in understanding them, or professionally envious. William Watson, the respected British experimenter in electricity and a regular contributor to the Royal Society, reported positive and negative electricity some months after Franklin's 1747 priority paper on the subject. Watson in subsequent matters occasionally disputed Franklin's conclusions, such as the Philadelphia argument that electrical fire accumulates in the electrical glass rather than in the nonelectric matter connected with the glass. In nearly all of these disputes it was the printer in Philadelphia who was proved to have observed and reasoned correctly.

Dr. Stuber, one of his first biographers, may have expressed the problem of Europe's initial reception when he wrote as follows:

By these experiments Franklin's theory was established in the most convincing manner. When the truth of it could no longer be doubted, envy and vanity endeavored to detract from its merit. That an American, an inhabitant of the obscure city of Philadelphia, the name of which was hardly known, should be able to make discoveries, and to frame theories, which had escaped the notice of the enlightened philosophers of Europe was too mortifying to be admitted. He must certainly have taken the idea from someone else. An American, a being of an inferior order, make discoveries!—Impossible.

Nevertheless, that embarrassing possibility eventually had to be faced and then accepted. Collinson kept bringing in the persistent letters. When the letters were not accepted in full for inclusion in the Transactions of the Royal Society, pressures mounted for other outlets.

The letters were given by Collinson to *The Gentleman's Magazine* and its imaginative, original editor *Edward Cave*. Founded in 1731, Cave's publication was the first to call itself a magazine, and its brief article format had proved highly successful. Cave's journal was exceptionally hospitable to news of American science. It published an article on the Philadelphia experiments in January 1750, plus an excerpt from one of the letters to Collinson in May 1750. Franklin read *The Gentleman's Magazine*, contributed to it through the years in other ways. Cave was even more receptive of Franklin's writings than he knew, having printed the satirical Polly Baker speech, written by Franklin, in the edition of April 1747. It was Cave's version that chose to reward Polly for her honesty and directness by allowing her fifteen legitimate children fathered by one of her admiring judges. This apropos embellishment has been perpetuated.

EARTH'S FLUID CENTRE

... at the lowest part of that rocky mountain which was in sight, there were oyster shells mixed in the stone; and part of the high country of Derby being probably as much above the level of the sea, as the coal mines of Whitehaven were below it, seemed a proof that there had been a great bouleversement in the surface of that island, some part of it having been depressed under the sea, and other parts, which had been under it, being raised above it. Such changes in the superficial parts of the globe seemed to me unlikely to happen, if the earth were solid to the centre. I therefore imagined, that the internal parts might be a fluid more dense, and of greater specific gravity than any of the solids we are acquainted with, which therefore might swim in or upon that fluid. Thus the surface of the globe would be a shell, capable of being broken and disordered by the violent movements of the fluid on which it rested.

(To the Abbé Soulavie, September 22, 1782)

The *Gentleman's Magazine:*

St JOHN's GATE

London Gazette
Read's Jour.
Craftsman
Daily Adver-
tiser.
St James's Œ
bening Post
London Even-
ing Po:
Gen. Evening
Post
Daily Gazet-
teer
Gen. Adver-
tiser
Westminster
Journal.
Old England
Anatomist.
Lon. Courant
Whitehall Eb
Post

Ingh 3 News
Dublin 4
Edinburgh 2
Bristol :: 2
Norwich 2
Exeter 2
Worcester
Northampton
Gloucester 3
Stamford :
Nottingham:
Chester Jour
Derby ditto
Ipswich 1 1
Reading 1 1 2
Leed's Merc.
Newcastle 3
Canterbury
Colchester.
Sherborn
Birmingham
Manchester
Bath
Cambridge

For A P R I L 1747.

C O N T A I N I N G,
[More in Quantity and greater Variety than any Book of the Kind and Price.]

I. Account of the behaviour and execution of lord *Lovat*, with further particulars of his life.
II. History of *Genoa*, an account of the expulsion of the *Austrians*, and the oftentatious infcription on } occafion.
III. Remedy for fizy blood.
IV. Method to prevent fhips from leaking.
V. Method of warming all the rooms in a houfe by the kitchen fire, with a cut.
VI. Description of *Ijeland* and manners of its inhabitants.
VII. Speech of *Polly Baker*.
VIII. The abbe *de la Ville's* memorial, and the *French* king's curious declaration at length to the *Dutch* ftates.
IX. Essay on female education.
X. Emendation of a paffage in *Shakespear*.
XI. Office of a Stadtholder.

XII. Description of *Dutch Brabant*, and *Dutch Flanders*.
XIII. Letter from the mafter of *Lovat*, Mr *Painter's* letters, with lord *Lovat's* remarks on him.
XIV. Electrical experiments propofed, and problems anfwered.
XV. An account of the taking fort St *George* and *Madrafs*.
XVI. Charge againft *Milton* continu'd.
XVII. List of fhips taken.
XVIII. Poetry. Specimen of a new tranflation of *Tafo* ; the father, a tale ; to the duke of *Cumberland*, French and *English* ; in memory of Mr *Chubb*.
XIX. Historical chronicle.
XX. List of births and marriages.
XXI. Each day's price of ftocks.
XXII. Foreign hiftory.
XXIII. Register of books.

With a Plan of G E N O A, fhewing its remarkable places by above 100 references, alfo another curious Plate.

By *S Y L V A N U S   U R B A N*, Gent.

LONDON: Printed by E. Cave, jun. at St *John's Gate*.

Title page from *The Gentleman's Magazine*, April 1747. Note item VII. Edward Cave published this Franklin piece for entertainment, and later issued the first edition of Franklin's scientific writings on electricity, a work of epochal significance.

On the title page of his publication, Cave used the pseudonym Sylvanus Urban, Gent. Cave was credited with coining the motto *E. Pluribus Unum,* one out of many, which faithful reader Franklin may have helped to be adopted as the U.S. motto.

In the *Autobiography,* Franklin summarized the steps that led to the publication of the electrical papers by Edward Cave.

> Oblig'd as we were to Mr. Collinson for his present of the tube, &c., I thought it right he should be inform'd of our success in using it, and wrote him several letters containing accounts of our experiments. He got them read in the Royal Society, where they were not at first thought worth so much notice as to be printed in their Transactions. One paper which I wrote for Mr. Kinnersley, on the sameness of lightning with electricity, I sent to Dr. Mitchell, an acquaintance of mine, and one of the members also of that Society; who wrote me word that it had been read but was laughed at by the connoisseurs: The papers however being shown to Dr. Fothergill, he thought them of too much value to be stifled, and advis'd the printing of them. Mr. Collinson then gave them to Cave for publication in his Gentleman's Magazine; but he chose to print them separately in a pamphlet, and Dr. Fothergill wrote the preface. Cave it seems judg'd rightly for his profit; for by the additions that arriv'd afterwards they swell'd to a quarto volume, which has had five editions, and cost him nothing for copy-money.

John Fothergill, whose pressure and preface helped bring about the publication of the papers, was an Edinburgh physician who served Franklin professionally in 1757 and became his close friend. Fothergill worked with Franklin to seek a peaceful settlement of the differences between the Colonies and Great Britain. After Fothergill's death in 1780, Franklin wrote to *Dr. Lettsom,* Fothergill's biographer, "If we may estimate the goodness of a man by his disposition to do good, and his constant endeavors and success in doing it, I can hardly conceive that a better man has ever existed." In a letter to *David Barclay* from Passy on February 12, 1781, Franklin gave another encomium for his friend: "He was a great doer of good. How much might have been done, and how much mischief prevented, if his, your, and my joint endeavors in a certain melancholy affair, had been attended to."

Fothergill and Franklin failed in their struggle to prevent war, but the first did great good for the world and earned honor for himself when he worked to see the scientific papers of the second through the press and into distribution. Eventually, one way or another, Franklin's papers would have presumably found their audience. But it was Peter Collinson who made them available, Dr.

Fothergill who prefaced and supported them, and Edward Cave who published them. All three Englishmen deserve credit for their services to a then unknown American and to electrical science in general. Science benefited because, like it or not, the pamphlet reported breakthroughs that British and continental scientists had not made. Entitled *Experiments and Observations on Electricity*, the pamphlet appeared in April 1751, and included all the Philadelphia reports on electricity since 1747. Supplements to the pamphlet appeared in 1753 and 1754 with later materials, and in 1769 an enlarged edition included other scientific writings by Franklin.

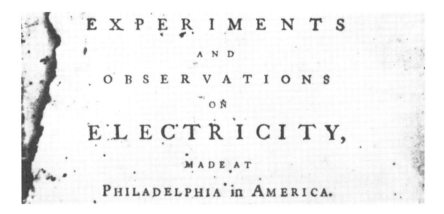

Fragment of cover for Franklin's 1769 London edition of the electrical letters, &c.

In June 1751, Dr. Watson abstracted the pamphlet for the Royal Society, admitting that Franklin was correct in his conclusions but emphasizing for members that the Philadelphia findings largely coincided with his own communicated results. Watson seemed to be using Franklin largely in support of his own observations, and he made no mention in his abstract of the lightning rod suggestions

SIX WAYS OF LOSING A SHIP
There are six accidents, that may occasion the loss of ships at sea. We have considered one of them, that of foundering by a leak. The other five are: 1. Oversetting by sudden flaws of wind, or by carrying sail beyond the bearing. 2. Fire by accident or carelessness. 3. A heavy stroke of lightning, making a breach in the ship, or firing the powder. 4. Meeting and shocking with other ships in the night. 5. Meeting in the night with islands of ice.
(To David Le Roy, Aboard the London Packet, August, 1785)

or the experiments for proving the connection between lightning and electricity.

Thus, even with publication, the reception of the experiments in Britain continued to be tepid and somewhat limited for a while longer. Watson's lukewarm and incomplete abstract probably helped to curtail enthusiasm, though Dr. Fothergill and a minority in the Royal Society from the start were impressed by the experiments. *Dr. John Mitchell* had reported "laughter by the connoisseurs" in response to the letter Franklin sent to him concerning lightning and electricity. The letter had been read to the Royal Society and extracted in the *Philosophical Transactions*, XLVI (1749-50). Some members of the Society had received the letter with admiration for its "clear intelligent stile" and also for "the novelty of the subjects." They were a minority destined to become a majority.

Perhaps it was simply that the British Royal Society in the eighteenth century was slow to absorb and accept the new, although a few individual members were capable of a readier reception.

PROOF ON THREE WINE BOTTLES

The more ebullient and volatile French were quicker to accept the experiments and to admire the experimenter. A copy of the electricity pamphlet came to the attention of the *Comte De Buffon*, the keeper of the Jardin du Roi and a naturalist with broad interests in science including electricity. Buffon's classification of animals paralleled that of Linnaeus's classification of plants, and his work laid the foundation for later studies in zoology. He also wrote the first study of the earth dividing the planet's history into geological ages. It was Buffon's alertness that caught the significance of the Franklin work on electricity and recommended it to colleagues in France. He specifically suggested that *Thomas-François D'Alibard* prepare an effective translation, which was published in Paris in 1752.

Only the Abbé Nollet was upset by the result. Franklin later wrote of this rival that he was "an able experimenter, who had form'd and publish'd a Theory of Electricity, which then had the general vogue. He could not at first believe that such a work came from America, and said it must have been fabricated by his enemies at Paris, to decry his system. Afterwards having been assur'd that there really existed such a person as Franklin of Philadelphia, which he had doubted, he wrote and published a volume of letters, chiefly address'd to me, defending his theory, and denying the verity of my experiments and of the positions deduc'd from them."

In the *Autobiography*, Franklin indicated his initial impulse to answer the Abbé in detail, but then decided against it, since most of his electrical writings were descriptions of experiments which were easy to verify or of "observations, offer'd as conjectures, and not delivered, dogmatically, therefore not laying me under any obligation to defend them." There was no need for the author of *Experiments and Observations* to mount his own defense. Other capable scientists, David Colden in America, Giambattista Beccaria in Italy, and Abbé Nollet's own countrymen, Buffon, D'Alibard, and Jean-Baptiste Le Roy were eager to confirm the Philadelphia experiments. The difficulty of carrying on an argument sensibly in two languages was one of Franklin's reasons for refusing to dispute a technical matter with the Abbé. ". . . much of one of the Abbé's letters being founded on an error in the translation, I concluded to let my papers shift for themselves; believing it was better to spend what time I could spare from public business in making new experiments, than in disputing about those already made."

The decision was a wise one. His experiments and the papers describing them shifted very well for themselves, since most turned out to be accurate and reproducible.

Franklin's translator D'Alibard was one of the first to move. He set up the iron rod experiment Franklin had suggested in a garden at Marly, a suburb near Paris.

He erected a forty foot iron rod, one inch in diameter, insulating it from the ground, not with resin, but with a wooden plank resting on three wine bottles. (*Vive la France!*)

At 2:20 in the afternoon on May 10, 1752, a thunderstorm visited Marly. D'Alibard was absent, but *Coiffier*, a guard, carrying an electric phial, rushed to the iron rod. The rod was giving off electric sparks and making a crackling noise. A child was sent running for *Raulet*, the prior of Marly. That worthy also hurried to the experiment site, took over, and drew off electricity into the guard's phial. Then using Coiffier as the messenger, Raulet dispatched a letter to D'Alibard reporting the success. D'Alibard in turn promptly reported to the *Academie Royale des Sciences* that Franklin's theories were proved. On May 18th, the experiment was repeated by *DeLor*, an electrical showman, in Paris, with positive results again. DeLor performed the *Philadelphia Experiments* for King Louis XV and "all the curious of Paris flocked to see them." The King had commendations for Franklin directed to the Royal Society in London. An English physician, *Dr. Wright*, notified a member of the

Royal Society of the success of the experiments in Paris. On July 20, 1752, an electrical experimenter and London schoolmaster named *John Canton* also performed the iron rod experiment successfully. His findings were supported by the experiments of *Benjamin Wilson* and *John Bevis*. These results coupled with confirmations from the continent made it impossible for the Royal Society to withhold full recognition. "They soon made me more than amends for the slight with which they had before treated me," wrote Franklin. At the same time his achievements were being recognized and acclaimed in other parts of Europe. "He was famous in Europe," wrote biographer Carl Van Doren, "before he knew it in America."

Sometime after the successful experiment at Marly, Franklin in Philadelphia, unaware that his theories had already been proved, apparently went outside one day with his son William to fly a kite.

REACHING FOR THE FIRE

The exact date of the kite experiment is not known, though June 1752 has generally been accepted as the likeliest time. The experiment would have taken place before ships arrived with news from Europe of the successful French experiments. It is unlikely that Franklin would have performed the experiment, knowing the dangers and uncertainties, if the news of D'Alibard's and DeLor's results had reached him. Franklin rarely showed any personal ego in such matters. He would have made the experiment only because he considered it relevant to his theory and would have dropped it when that condition no longer held true.

Since the precise time of the kite experiment cannot be fixed and since it was no longer actually needed, it has been speculated that the famous kite experiment actually took place only as an idea in Franklin's head. It was one way to test his theory, but circumstances made it unnecessary. Such speculations, however, are contradicted by Franklin's own writings.

In the *Autobiography*, Franklin explicitly stated that he had derived infinite pleasure from a successful experiment with a kite at Philadelphia. And in a letter to Collinson on October 19, 1752, he gave details of the kite experiment. Another account of the experiment was provided in 1767 by Franklin's scientist friend, Joseph Priestley the chemist. It has been assumed that he had the details directly from Franklin.

According to Priestley, Franklin abandoned the idea of waiting for the erection of an iron rod on Christ Church in Philadelphia when he thought of something even better that required waiting only for a storm. Before the French scientists proved that the iron rod did not have to be at an exceptional height, it had been Franklin's belief that a moderate height would not be sufficient. His new idea was simple, dramatic, and typically Franklin. He would use a kite to go even higher than a spire and meet the thunder on its own battlegrounds.

The idea of flying a kite, a child's toy, to capture lightning and prove a scientific theory, may have brought apprehensions and inhibitions even to the outspoken Franklin. He said nothing about the experiment in advance, hence the delay between the probable occurrence of the experiment in June and his report to Collinson in October. According to Priestley, Franklin "dreading the ridicule which too commonly attends unsuccessful attempts in science, he communicated his intended experiment to nobody but his son," who had been recruited as a volunteer to help raise the kite. In the letter to Collinson, Franklin gave details of the kite's construction:

> Make a small cross of two light strips of cedar, the arms so long as to reach to the four corners of a large thin silk handkerchief when extended; tie the corners of the handkerchief to the extremities of the cross, so you have the body of a kite; which, being properly accommodated with a tail, loop, and string, will rise in the air, like those made of paper; but this being of silk is fitter to bear the wet and wind of a thunder-gust without tearing. To the top of the upright stick of the cross is to be fixed a very sharp-pointed wire, rising a foot or more above the wood. To the end of the twine, next the hand, is to be tied a silk ribbon, and where the silk and twine join, a key may be fastened.

When a thunderstorm of promising proportions and vehemence appeared, Franklin and William took shelter under a shed in a field. When the storm seemed sufficiently fierce, the kite was launched. Soon the fibers of the hemp cord began to repel one another and to spread apart. Franklin received an encouraging spark when he touched the metal key with a knuckle.

That spark was the scientist's payment for long thought, experiment, and apprehensive trial. It was confirmation that lightning and electricity were identical kinds of energy. The lightning had been summoned to the metal point the same as electricity would be if the source had been a Leyden jar instead of the stormy sky. "When the rain had wet the string, he collected electric fire very copiously," wrote Joseph Priestley.

Franklin found that an electric phial could be charged from the key at the end of the silk ribbon. No more proof was needed. Lightning flashes had been used to supply a traditional electrical charge, and thereby "the sameness of the electrical matter with that of lightning" was "completely demonstrated."

Today the great danger of such experiments is better known. But "not knowing" was the inevitable peril at the beginning of a new science. If they dwelt exclusively on possible dangers, searchers entering that unknown could not advance. Some of them, the Franklins, went ahead, hoping for the best and learning as they advanced.

If the hemp cord of his kite had been completely soaked, *Franklin might have been electrocuted* when he flew his kite in the thunderstorm. One scientist was killed performing a Franklin experiment. Swedish *Professor G. Rikhman* of the Imperial Academy of Sciences, St. Petersburg, was electrocuted by lightning while he was holding a wire from an experimental rod erected in accordance with Franklin's instructions.

Despite the danger, Franklin was not through with lightning. He had proved its identity, but he wanted to learn more about it and if possible, prevent its doing destructive mischief. He made progress in both.

THE BELL AND THE ROD

Franklin's report to Collinson in September 1753 contained important data, both practical and theoretical, in addition to the correction of his erroneous idea that the sea was the source of lightning. The letter gave details of an iron rod Franklin erected at his house to draw lightning and two electrical bells he had set up inside the house to ring when electrical conditions developed. The bells would sometimes ring simply at the appearance of a dark cloud, and on occasion there would be streams of sparks between the two wires on which the bells were suspended. A further description written in 1772 noted that between the bells there was a small brass ball on a silk thread which would jump and strike the bells when clouds containing electricity passed overhead.

One night this apparatus may have given Franklin an unexpected glimpse of the world's first indoor electric light. Hearing a loud cracking noise from the vicinity of the wires, he investigated.

I perceived that the brass ball instead of vibrating as usual between the bells, was repelled and kept at a distance from both; while the fire passed sometimes in very large quick cracks from bell to bell; and sometimes in a continued dense white stream, seemingly as large as my finger, whereby the whole staircase was enlighted as with sunshine, so that one might see to pick up a pin.

This passage was written to prove the effectiveness of pointed rods as the ideal conductors "for securing buildings from damage by strokes of lightning," when Franklin served on a Royal Society committee studying the subject during one of his stays in England.

In April 1753, Franklin used the iron rod on his house to conduct an experiment designed to establish experimentally whether electrified clouds were positively or negatively charged. He took two phials, charged one with lightning from the iron rod, and charged the other positively with an electric glass globe. When a cork ball was suspended between the phials, its behavior would indicate whether the lightning charged phial was positive or negative.

In the April experiment, "having placed them properly, I beheld, with great surprise and pleasure, the cork ball play briskly between them; and was convinced that one bottle was electrised *negatively*." He had already established in other experiments that the glass globe was positively charged. Thus, the clouds responsible for the charge in the other phial had to be negatively charged.

The fact was a basic scientific finding. Other experiments, with one exception, confirmed the results. When he brought the positively charged phial close to the ringing bells, activated by lightning through the iron rod, the bells would stop until the phial was discharged. This indicated negative electricity in the passing clouds. Once, however, the bells rang more vigorously, indicating positive clouds.

That exception compelled Franklin to qualify his conclusion: "*That the clouds of a thunder-gust are most commonly in a negative state of electricity, but sometimes in a positive state.*"

His colleague Kinnersley, then travelling on his lecture tour, told Franklin that his experiments always showed clouds to be in a negative state. Franklin decided that clouds in a positive state were a rare exception. Reasoning from this general truth and the

PERSPIRATION IN THE NUDE
... having some suspicions that the common notion, which attributes cold to the property of stopping the pores and obstructing perspiration, was ill founded, I engaged a young physician, who is making some experiments with Sanctorius' balance, to estimate the different proportions of his perspirations, when remaining one hour quite naked, and another warmly clothed. He pursued the experiment in this alternate manner for eight hours successively, and found his perspiration almost doubled during those hours in which he was naked.
(To M. Dubourg, March 10, 1773)

known habits of electricity, the corollary conclusion was reached that in thunder-strokes, *"it is the earth that strikes into the clouds, and not the clouds that strike into the earth."* Modern science has not wandered very far beyond these fundamental insights.

The success of the rod on his house both for electrical studies and protection paralleled the positive action he was taking to make the rods available to the public for the protection afforded against the violent caprices of lightning.

In the *Gazette* for October 19, 1752, there was an article about his kite experiment, the information that he sent to Collinson for presentation at the Royal Society. The same issue contained an advertisement for *Poor Richard's Almanac* of 1753. That almanac provided Franklin's first public instructions on a practical method to apply what he had learned about lightning and electricity in guarding houses.

> It has pleased God in his goodness to mankind, at length to discover to them the means of securing their habitations and other buildings from mischief by thunder and lightning. The method is this: Provide a small iron rod (it may be made of the rod-iron used by the nailers) but of such a length, that one end being three or four feet in the moist ground, the other may be six or eight feet above the highest part of the building. To the upper end of the rod fasten about a foot of brass wire, the size of a common knitting-needle sharpened to a fine point; the rod may be secured to the house by a few small staples. If the house or barn be long, there may be a rod and point at each end, and a middling wire along the ridge from one to the other. A house thus furnished will not be damaged by lightning, it being attracted by the points, and passing thro the metal into the ground without hurting any thing. Vessels also, having a sharp pointed rod fix'd on the top of their masts, with a wire from the foot of the rod reaching down, round one of the shrouds to the water, will not be hurt by lightning.

MYSTERIOUS PARTICLES

It is very curious. But I must own I am much in the dark about light. I am not satisfied with the doctrine that supposes particles of matter, called light, continually driven off from the sun's surface, with a swiftness so prodigious! Must not the smallest particle conceivable have, with such a motion, a force exceeding that of a twenty-four pounder discharged from a cannon? Must not the sun diminish exceedingly by such a waste of matter; and the planets, instead of drawing nearer to him, as some have feared, recede to greater distances through the lessened attraction? Yet these particles, with this amazing motion, will not drive before them, or remove the least and lightest dust they meet with. And the sun, for aught we know, continues of his ancient dimensions, and his attendants move in their ancient orbits.

(To Cadwallader Colden, April 23, 1752)

Mayor's Courts for the City

ARE held quarterly at *Annapolis*, viz The laſt tueſ-day in *Janvary*, *April*, *July* and *October*.

How to ſecure Houſes, &c. *from* LIGHTNING.

IT has pleaſed God in his Goodneſs to Mankind, at length to diſcover to them the Means of ſecuring their Habitations and other Buildings from Miſchief by Thunder and Lightning. The Method is this : Provide a ſmall Iron Rod (it may be made of the Rod-iron uſed by the Nailers) but of ſuch a Length, that one End being three or four Feet in the moiſt Ground, the other may be ſix or eight Feet above the higheſt Part of the Building. To the upper End of the Rod faſten about a Foot of Braſs Wire, the Size of a common Knitting-needle, ſharpened to a fine Point ; the Rod may be ſecured to the Houſe by a few ſmall Staples. If the Houſe or Barn be long, there may be a Rod and Point at each End, and a middling Wire along the Ridge from one to the other. A Houſe thus furniſhed will not be damaged by Lightning, it being at-tracted by the Points, and paſſing thro the Metal into the Ground without hurting any Thing. Veſſels alſo, having a ſharp pointed Rod fix'd on the Top of their Maſts, with a Wire from the Foot of the Rod reaching down, round one of the Shrouds, to the Water, will not be hurt by Lightning.

QUAKERS *General Meetings are kept*, AT Philadelphia, the 3d Sunday in March. At Che-ſter-River, the 2d Sunday in April. At Duck-Creek, the 3d Sunday in April. At Salem, the 4th Sunday in April. At Weſt River on Whitſunday. At Little Egg-Harbour, the 3d Sunday in May. At Fluſh-ing, the laſt Sunday in May, and laſt in Nov. At Se-tacket, the 1ſt Sunday in June. At New-town, (Long-Iſland) the laſt Sunday in June. At Newport, the 2d Friday in June. At Weſtbury, the laſt Sunday in Au-guſt, and laſt in February. At Philadelphia, the 3d Sun-day in September. At Nottingham, the laſt Monday in September. At Cecil, the 1ſt Saturday in October. At Choptank the 2d Saturday in October. At Little-Creek, the 3d Sunday in October At Shrewſbury the 4th Sunday in October. At Matinicok the laſt Sunday in October.

FAIRS *are kept*,

At Noxonton April 29, and October 21. Cohanſie May 5, and October 27. Wilmington May 9, and November 4. Salem May 12, and October 31. Newcaſtle May 14, and Nov. 14. Cheſter May 16, and Oct. 16. Briſtol May 19, and Nov. 9. Burlington May 21, and Nov. 12. Philadelphia May 27, and November 27. Lancaſter June 12, and Nov. 12. Marcus-Hook Oct. 10. Annapolis May 12, and Oct. 10. Charleſtown May 3, and Oct. 29.

A page from *Poor Richard's Almanack* for 1753 with the first instructions on *"How to Secure Houses, &c. from Lightning."*

Again, as with his other inventions, Franklin made no effort to exploit the lightning rod or to profit from it. With his writing skills, he could have advertised "A Proven Method, Approved by Provi-dence, of Guarding Your Property Against Violent Bolts of Mali-cious Lightning," and sold the Franklin Lightning Rod widely.

The assurance about Providence might have been needed at first to persuade the superstitious that the rod was not a dangerous interference with the "will of Heaven." In his lectures on electricity during the period, Kinnersley at Franklin's suggestion took the trouble to explain that the use of lightning rods was not an act of impiety.

Franklin sought no monetary income from the lightning rod, but he did seek the psychic income of improving it, making it work better, and thus contributing to the greater security of houses against sudden wrath from the skies. He seemed to derive genuine personal pleasure from such intangible satisfactions. Was it a pose, an inexpensive way for a man in comfortable circumstances to earn respect from his peers and esteem from his fellow citizens through the largesse of his hobbies? That is a possible way to view the matter, but Franklin was too consistent in his generosity for the view to persuade or seem especially important. One of his teachers, *Robert Boyle*, rather grandly described the principles of mathematics and mechanics as "the alphabet in which God wrote the world." Franklin in practice extended this to mean that scientific knowledge, wherever and by whomever acquired, was the property of all mankind. In the introduction to their 1936 collection of Franklin's writings, Mott and Jorgenson wrote: "As a discoverer of nature's laws and their application to man's use, Franklin, the Newton of electricity, appealed to fact and experiment rather than authority and suggested that education in science may serve, in addition to making the world more comfortable, to make it more habitable and less terrifying."

Both were excellent goals in Benjamin Franklin's benign, happy, and intellectual cosmos, and both were splendidly served by the lightning rods. They would make the houses of men safer. And the men who pushed through the underbrush of superstition and theological warnings to use them, would be overcoming a residue of terror, misguided dogma, and dread of the unknown. *Power to them.*

ROD OF FEAR OR ROD OF REASON?

The lightning rod was openly attacked by some churchmen in America. Their reaction may have been due in part to the enthusiasm with which philosophers, anti-church men, and men of learning in general greeted the invention.

The lightning rods standing silently and serenely above houses throughout the Colonies pointed toward the heavens. Whether

*they did so aggressively, accusingly, insultingly, impiously, or rev-
erently, depended on individual interpretation. To Franklin they
simply guarded against destructive bolts of lightning and were
metal rods, not pointing fingers.*

Franklin helped Kinnersley prepare the lectures with which he
tried to separate electricity from superstitition, and to counter the
diatribes of some ministers that the Eternal Father would take
offense.

In New England, the *Reverend Prince* even attempted to associate himself with science in order to attack the "points of iron."

> The more points of iron are erected round the earth, to draw the elec-
> trical substance out of the air, the more the earth must needs be
> charged with it. And therefore it seems worthy of consideration,
> whether any part of the earth being fuller of this terrible substance
> may not be more exposed to more shocking earthquakes... O! There
> is no getting out of the mighty Hand of God. If we think to avoid it
> in the air, we cannot in the earth: Yea it may grow more fatal; and
> there is no safety anywhere, but in his Almighty Friendship.

Doctor Winthrop of Harvard answered for science that lightning
and earthquakes were not connected, that Reverend Prince clearly
knew little of lightning rods and science, that lightning and thunderstorms instead of being expressions of divine anger could more
logically be seen as useful means of freeing "the atmosphere from
a certain unwholesome sultriness, which often infects it."

Another of Franklin's teachers in his youth, Cotton Mather,
could also be quoted to the religious and fearful. Mather, perhaps
nervously, had called reason "the voice of God" and insisted that
the discoveries of science were not an enemy but "a mighty and
wondrous incentive to religion."

Franklin did not want to undermine the ancient faith of Chris-
tians with ungodly devices. But he did want them to understand
that if a God made lightning, he also made the possibility of science to understand, guard against, and even use the lightning as
Franklin used it to ring bells near his staircase. Men used the animals of the earth for food and to aid their labors. Why not use the
lightning of the skies in whatever way possible?

Perhaps all of these conditions, the need for enlightenment, the
attacks of the ministers, the disputes that arose with some scientists concerning the efficacy of the lightning rod, and if efficacy
were accepted, the validity of pointed versus rounded rods, helped
make the lightning rod the best known, most controversial, and
most demanding of all his inventions and contributions to science.

Whatever the difficulties, Franklin maintained an unvarying generosity with this, as with other scientific achievements. He had the fun of doing the experiments. His was the private pleasure of lassoing thunderbolts for the first time and drawing them, tame as tigers, into his phials. Further benefits belonged to everyone.

Superstitions, predictably, didn't survive long when some citizens ventured to protect their houses with the Franklin rods and no dire celestial consequences were seen to happen. Eventually even ministers had lightning rods on their houses, hopeful hands of iron reaching up to embrace the sparklers of eternity.

In both England and the Colonies the use of lightning rods spread quickly once the initial theological clamors had been dismissed. Rather oddly, since Franklin's celebrity was always greatest there, use of the lightning rods caught on more slowly in France and the rest of the continent. Scientists, philosophers, and thinkers, of course, used it as a symbol of reason, enlightenment, and the progress of human knowledge. They flaunted it on their houses, sometimes elaborately decorated in ways that made the rods seem more like temptresses to lure the lightning than mere points of entry.

Among the religious, however, acceptance was slow. Time was needed to convince stern traditionalists that the Glory of God was not diminished by fixing a thin metal rod to the roof. In Europe the controversy continued through much of the eighteenth century. During 1782, *Maximilian de Robespierre*, who would be heard from again both nobly and ignobly, was a defense lawyer in a case involving the lightning rod. A man had been charged with blasphemy for erecting a lightning rod on a house rented from a canon of the church. He and his defender Robespierre lost the case, though perhaps they contributed unknowingly to the slow inching forward of knowledge and reason into the catacomb kingdoms of conventional dread.

The French epigrammatist, *Antoine de Rivarol*, described the intellectual vs. superstitious climate in France when he wrote, "You may distinguish the learned and the superstitious man when it thunders. One seeks protection in sacred relics, the other in a lightning rod." But many Frenchmen, fearful of "stealing divine fire," had to be reassured they were not trying to escape the judgment of God.

Whatever the rod's true effectiveness, and this is still disputed, it became a symbol of advancement during the eighteenth century. A certain pride was achieved in a man's mind when he overcame reluctance to defy tradition and positioned the iron point on his roof. He wasn't trying to escape judgment but to assert truth.

The lightning rod more than any other object served as a mark of punctuation, an exclamation point at the summit of a structure, saying: Here science is accepted. Here the benefits of knowledge are not dreaded. Here the courage of wisdom is nourished.

POINTED RODDERS VERSUS ROUND RODDERS

Franklin's inventions, especially the lightning rod, were rather like children. He could not always successfully bring them into the world, wish them well, and go on to other projects without a further thought for their welfare. When they cried for attention, they received it.

He continued to feel a responsibility for their correct use. His correspondence through the years contained references to the stove, the Armonica, and the lightning rod, usually with suggestions to make them serve better or to improve their functioning. In a letter to *Joseph Huey* on June 6, 1753, Franklin wrote, "For my own part, when I am employed in serving others, I do not look upon myself as conferring favours, but as paying debts." The kindnesses he had received, he felt an obligation to repay, if not to the original donors, then to other men generally.

This sense of debt was carried through in connection with his inventions. He was never quite finished with the lightning rod, and through the years had to continue explaining and instructing. He did so because of his original conviction that if properly used it would do an effective job of protecting property and lives.

For example, in his letter of June 29, 1755, sent to D'Alibard in Paris by way of Peter Collinson, he commented on Père Beccaria's strong defense of Franklin's electrical experiments in general, but his tendency to question the effectiveness of lightning rods.

> I find I have been but partly understood in that matter. I have mentioned it in several of my letters, and except once, always in the *alternative*, viz., that pointed rods erected on buildings, and communicating with the moist earth, would either prevent a stroke, *or,* if not prevented, would *conduct* it, so as that the building should suffer no damage. Yet whenever my opinion is examined in Europe, nothing is considered but the probability of those rods *preventing* a stroke or explosion, which is only a *part* of the use I proposed for them.

He described the great damage effected by lightning in a New England church, although the lightning had done no damage in the part of the church where it could follow a metal pendulum and a small wire leading to a clock. Conclusion: "That lightning, in its passage through a building, will leave wood to pass as far as it can in metal, and not enter the wood again till the conductor of metal ceases." *A lightning rod on the steeple would have saved the church.* So said the facts.

In 1762, to the philosopher *David Hume*, he sent his latest thoughts on securing buildings from the "mischiefs of lightning." The steel rod should be five or six feet long, half an inch thick at its biggest end, tapering to a point at the other. The big end should contain an eye half an inch in diameter. The rod should be steadied with staples against the chimney or highest part of the structure being protected, pointed end up and extending at least three or four feet higher than the structure. Another iron rod, ten to twelve feet long, with an eye in one end, should be driven into the ground no closer than ten feet from the house. Then one-half inch iron rods should be fastened from the rod planted in the ground to the rod on the roof. This iron chain should have all its joints securely closed in with lead to guard against rust and to seal the passage where lightning would travel to the ground. "And though the iron be crooked round the corner of the building, or make ever so many turns between the upper and the lower rod, the lightning will follow it, and be guided by it, without affecting the building."

Typically thorough, Franklin gave the philosopher precise details on applying lead at joints, fixing the extended chain of iron to the house, and even erecting a post to carry it above the heads of people when it left the house to reach the buried iron. And he concluded: "If I have not been explicit enough in my directions, I shall, on the least intimation, endeavour to supply the defect."

The letter is that of an expert in a corporation Customer Consultation Department working overtime to make certain a company functions beautifully so the customer will pay his bill and end another orgy of frivolous complaint. Franklin's consultation was gratuitous, he had no company, and his only return would likely be another letter asking him to explain again that business about jointing the iron rod with lead.

From the beginning, Franklin knew that the lightning rod "like other new instruments" had not yet achieved perfection and he counted on "improvement from experience." To help in this process, Franklin had a notice in the *Gazette* for October 19, 1752 that effectively made him once more a volunteer secretary, this time in the unofficial lightning information institute.

Those of our readers in this and the neighboring provinces who may have an opportunity of observing, during the present summer any of the effects of lightning on houses, ships, trees, etc, are requested to take particular notices of its course, and deviation from a strait line in the walls or other matter affected by it, its different operation or effects on wood, stone, bricks, glass, metals, animal bodies, etc and every other circumstance that may tend to discover the nature and complete the history of that terrible meteor. Such observations being put in writing and communicated to Benjamin Franklin in Philadelphia will be very thankfully accepted and acknowledged.

Such details did come to him, and not just for the summer of 1752. He collected the information, thought about it, and disseminated it through his scientific correspondents and the Royal Society. The world unanimously elected him head Professor of Pointed Lightning Rods. He accepted the position, which was without salary. And he had to pay his own postage.

In 1767, at the request of Parisians trying to overcome Gallic fears of the lightning rod, he wrote a lucid, straightforward paper: *Of Lightning, And the Methods now used in America for securing Buildings and Persons from its mischievous Effects.* It was a charming introduction to the fundamentals of electricity and to the efficacy of an iron rod on the outside of a building to provide a safe harbor for transient bolts of lightning. If perchance one found oneself in a house without the security of an iron rod, "the safest place is the middle of the room (so it be not under a metal lustre suspended by a chain) sitting in one chair and laying the feet up in another. It is still safer to bring two or three mattresses or beds into the middle of the room, and, folding them up double, place the chair upon them; for they not being so good conductors as the walls, the lightning will not choose an interrupted course through the air of the room and the bedding, when it can go through a continued better conductor, the wall. But where it can be had, a hammock or swinging bed, suspended by silk cords equally distant from the walls on every side, and from the ceiling and floor above and below, affords the safest situation a person can have in any room whatever; and what indeed may be deemed quite free from danger of any stroke by lightning."

So felicitously did Franklin write of the swinging bed on a silk cord, speculation starts whether sales of lightning rods or the sales of those items followed the publication of his paper. Hopefully both were snapped up by the grateful people of Paris.

In the city of London Franklin also encountered lightning rod difficulties, though politics in the long run seemed to offer more difficulties than science.

The amazing scientific quarrel that began as an intellectual dispute at the Royal Society and ended as a political squabble with George III bluntly interfering might be called the *Affair of the Pointed versus the Rounded or Knobbed Rods.* British scientist J. J. Thomson aptly described it as the battle of the sharps and the flats.

The affair began when Franklin was requested by the British Board of Ordnance to offer his views on the best way to protect powder magazines at Purfleet from the dangers of lightning. The inventor of the lightning rod not surprisingly suggested the erection of lightning rods. *Pointed* lightning rods.

The Royal Society was then invited to give its views on this recommendation. A five man committee was appointed by the Royal Society to investigate and report. With Franklin on the committee was *Benjamin Wilson,* a painter and electrician for the Board of Ordnance. It was Wilson's advocacy of blunt conductors to protect the magazines, following destruction of a powder-mill by lightning, that challenged Franklin's stand for pointed conductors and started the controversy on its way. Other members of the committee were William Watson, Franklin's distinguished rival and co-genius in the early days of electrical research, John Robertson, and *Henry Cavendish.* Aside from Franklin, Cavendish was the greatest scientist of the group and the most interesting. The discoverer of hydrogen, Cavendish was one of the marvellous individualists of the eighteenth century. Indifferent to dress, fearful of women to the point of misogyny, superior to any sort of social diversion, Cavendish was the epitome of the ivory tower recluse. He shut himself in his laboratory, accepted food only through a hole in the laboratory wall without looking at the providers, and cloistered himself to perform such basic experiments as uniting oxygen and hydrogen to form water.

By most standards it was a remarkable committee, with a rather bizarre assignment, to choose between pointed and rounded lightning rods.

Franklin prepared the committee's report and wrote a supporting paper, *Experiments, Observations, and Facts, Tending to Support the Opinion of the Utility of Long, Pointed Rods, for Securing Buildings from Damage by Strokes of Lightning.* The paper was read to the committee on August 27, 1772.

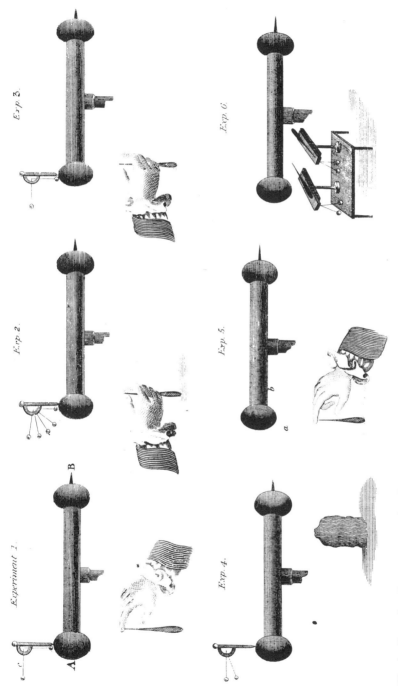

Illustrations for the report to the Committee of the Royal Society considering erection of conductors to secure the magazines at Purfleet, August 27, 1772. Reproduced from *The Works of Benjamin Franklin*, Published by William Duane, Philadelphia, 1809.

Franklin outlined with scrupulous detail and illustrated for his colleagues six experiments on the subject. He described his long experience with lightning rods, including details of the electric bells safely used for years in his Philadelphia home while hooked to a pointed rod. He referred to the instances in America where pointed rods had protected houses from destruction by lightning. He predicated that a one inch diameter conductor would be sufficient for any stroke of lightning ever likely to be encountered. But he added a warning: "It is true that, if another deluge should happen wherein the windows of heaven are to be opened, such pipes may be unequal to the falling quantity; and, if God for our sins should think it fit to rain fire upon us, as upon some cities of old, it is not expected that our conductors, of whatever size, should secure our houses against a miracle."

Franklin's arguments for pointed lightning rods, plus his careful defense against legal suits if divine forces ran miraculously amok, were accepted by three members of the committee, Watson, Robertson, and Cavendish, but Benjamin Wilson still dissented. The majority were Pointed Rodders. He was an unconvinced, unregenerate Round Rodder, with, as it turned out, royal backing.

INVENTORS BEWARE

It was one of those situations where the reason of the majority could not sway the emotions of the minority. A classic line from *Punch*, the British humor magazine, seems to fit some of the participants: "You surely don't suppose I am going to allow mere *proof* to sway my opinion."

The majority of the Royal Society committee reported their support for pointed rods, and their view prevailed. Pointed rods were used at the magazines. But Wilson defiantly published his counter argument that the pointed rods would serve to attract or *solicit* lightning directly *into* the magazines with devastating results. Franklin followed his earlier practice when he was criticized by Abbé Nollet. He said nothing and left the matter for the ultimate disclosures of truth.

But politics wasn't finished with the affair. Benjamin Wilson captured the attention of King George III. During the Revolution, when the King was angry at the Colonies for their militancy and inclined to condemn Franklin for the entire imbroglio, he became contemptuous of pointed rods and a relentless advocate of blunted rods. To the King, only traitors preferred the pointed rods of that man Franklin. It was an indispensable mark of patriotism to be a Round Rodder.

George III ordered John Pringle, the Royal Physician and President of the Royal Society, to favor blunted rods. Pringle politely insisted that he could not "reverse the laws and operations of nature."

This reply was good science. It was bad politics. Pringle was asked to resign as Royal Physician and as President of the Royal Society. He did so.

George III refused to have the unpatriotic pointed rods on Kew Palace. Since the unpatriotic rods were already in place, they were removed and blunted ones installed.

Franklin, as a verse of the period suggested, "kept to the point" and took no umbrage. He knew what his experiments had proved. There was no permanent way to argue successfully with the truth. It could be set aside by fiat, but it could not be changed. The truth was not substantively affected if a monarch chose to decree scientific error. For himself, Franklin had no ambition to protect and thus no inclination to quarrel with those who insisted on taking a stand against the evidence. Eventually, if they were capable of accepting truth, the evidence would convince them. In either case, Franklin's concern or irritation would serve no purpose. His scientific views were developed conscientiously with all the skill he could bring to them. When they were finally offered to the world, it was his custom to let them rise or fall on their own merits. He would assist with further information and explanations when they were useful, as with his inventions. Beyond that point of defense he seldom ventured.

If his ego was hurt or worried by attacks, he seldom showed it. Once he let a certain portion of resentment show through, but that was a general statement applied to inventors as a group, rather than to himself specifically. In his March 18, 1755 letter to Doctor Lining, he wrote:

There are everywhere a number of people, who being totally destitute of any inventive faculty themselves, do not readily conceive that others may possess it: they think of inventions as miracles; there might be such formerly, but they are ceased. With these, everyone who offers a new invention is deemed a pretender: he had it from some other country, or from some book: a man of *their own acquaintance*; one who has no more sense than themselves, could not possibly, in their opinion, have been the inventor of anything.... Thus, through envy, jealousy, and the vanity of competitors for fame, the origin of many of the most extraordinary inventions, though produced within but a few centuries past, is involved in doubt and uncertainty. We scarce know to whom we are indebted for the *compass*, and for *spectacles*, nor have even *paper* and *printing*, that record everything else, been able to preserve with certainty the name and reputation of their inventors. One would not, therefore, of all faculties, or qualities of the mind, wish, for a friend, or a child, that he should have that of invention. For his attempts to benefit mankind in that way, however well imagined, if they do not succeed, expose him, though very unjustly, to general ridicule and contempt; and, if they do succeed, to envy, robbery, and abuse.

This passage is one of the few in Franklin's correspondence or other writings that expresses a sense of regret and sadness at injustices to inventors. Perhaps he was remembering at that moment and regretting the spiteful attacks of the Abbé Nollet or the competitive challenges of William Watson. Perhaps he was simply realistically appraising the fate of creators who have the audacity to challenge their neighbors by introducing something new in the world. Just for a moment he looked on the dark side of that particular human moon. And a sigh was heard.

Usually it was the bright side that attracted his instinctive optimism. And optimism could trust that truth would prevail and that merit would be recognized. If perchance it was not recognized, at any rate the creator had the satisfaction of the creative act and the creative result. A more typical Franklin statement, consistent with his actions, explained his attitude toward his scientific findings this way:

I leave them to take their chance in the world. If they are right, truth and experience will support them; if wrong, they ought to be refuted and rejected. Disputes are apt to sour one's temper and disturb one's quiet. I have no private interest in the reception of my inventions by the world, having never made, nor proposed to make, the least profit by any of them.

The admission to Dr. Lining does imply that he may sometimes have hoped with his inventions at least to earn the profit of recognition, respect, and perhaps gratitude.

Other inventors as he indicated might have occasion to complain on these points, but Doctor Franklin was not among them. From the 1750's to the present, his electrical experiments have earned him stature as one of the world's great scientists. It was more, perhaps, than a printer's apprentice in Boston had imagined for himself when he first discovered the explosive ideas of Newton and Locke and began to ask new questions about the world's old ways.

1976

Dear Doctor Franklin, Sir,

Modern scientific technologies keep us so busy reading dials, they often leave us remarkably little time for thinking or creative leisure. You were the world's leading expert on the full and pleasurable use of time, and perhaps can assist us.

It is true that some believe you went too far in your penchant for praising the virtues of keeping busy, even to the dangerous extreme of advising gullible youth that "time is money." (It is, of course, no doubt about that.)

Good as such advice may have been for young men of the Colonies with work to do and a nation to build, easier times have brought criticism.

Possibly you have met one of your better known critics, Mark Twain. You would get along swimmingly since each of you had a congenital habit of speaking or writing with his tongue planted firmly in his cheek. Mark Twain once wrote about you, earnestly and facetiously, about half and half:

> With a malevolence which is without parallel in history, he would work all day, and then sit up nights, and let on to be studying algebra by the light of a smoldering fire, so that all other boys might have to do that also, or else have Benjamin Franklin thrown up to them. Franklin said once, in one of his inspired flights of malignity: "Early to bed and early to rise —Makes a man healthy and wealthy and wise." As if it were any object to a boy to be healthy and wealthy and wise on such terms. . . . The sorrow that that maxim has cost me, through my parents experimenting on me with it, tongue cannot tell.

Obviously Mark Twain had you confused with your friend, Poor Richard Saunders, a very different individual from yourself. Poor Richard was given to saying things such as "Rather go to bed supperless than rise in debt." You didn't hesitate to go into debt for your business or your country. With his cautious ideas, how would Poor Richard have fared in France trying to finance a Revolution?

Mark Twain meant somebody else, Sir, not Benjamin Franklin.

We Are, &c.,

YOURS, THE PEOPLE

XVI. Living Usefully

THE VOCATIONS OF LEISURE

Harry Truman, man from the people, President of the United States, and self-made intellectual, had the distinction of never graduating from one of the major academies for America's traditional aristocracy and elite. Truman did graduate, however, with highest honors from a lifelong habit of reading whatever he could get his hands on and his mind around. One of the books he admitted having a special fondness for and finding particularly useful was Benjamin Franklin's *Autobiography*. Franklin's book helped him organize his time and spend it wisely.

From *Moses* to psychoanalyst *Lawrence Kubie*, one persistent message concerning the human race has been that most humans are what they are (limited) and do what they do (little), because they utilize only a tiny portion of their energies, their minds, or their leisures. According to Dr. Kubie (*Harvard Alumni Bulletin*, September 29, 1956), the typical man uses only a meager fraction of his brain power because the brain's "psychological products are so organized that almost from birth we are continuously blocked by conflicts among internal factions. Each man grows up to resemble a pair of moose with horns locked in battle. He dies of a struggle which he wages with himself."

Not Franklin.

He escaped being a moose with locked horns because he possessed genius, because of the program he set for himself as a youth to accomplish the utmost with his time, and because he did not grind his guts together like unlubricated wheels when set upon by each day's snarling trifles. He kept perspective, and he learned to concentrate. He was in effect superior to trifles, which helped to make him efficient and highly productive.

Inaccurately, this carefully nurtured aspect of Franklin's character has been read as a lesson in frugality and temperance, doggedness and self-reliance, plus business sharpness coupled with an "onward and upward" philosophy. These *could* have been derivatives of his character, but not all of them were. He developed very different interests in his thirties, so that "onwarding and upwarding" in conventional social and business terms became relatively unimportant to him. In reality, his main goal was to prove such a blistering success in business, he could afford the leisure to concentrate on what he liked more, science.

Irwin Edman, the American philosopher, wrote that "the best test of the quality of a civilization is the quality of its leisure." Franklin used his to establish fundamental truths about the universe. With an intense and creative use of his "leisure," Franklin in the words of *Carl Van Doren* "found electricity a curiosity and left it a science."

In this sense perhaps he was not what he has been called, the first modern man, but the *new* man still to come. He represented the next stage of development that *Mortimer J. Adler* implied when he wrote, "The ultimate aim of pure capitalism, beyond the establishment of economic justice, is the enjoyment of leisure for all men in the major portion of their life's time."

If that millennium were reached, how would the major portion of life's time be used, for beer and skittles, or for fundamental truths? For getting and spending or for squeezing new light from primeval darkness? Which formula did Franklin choose?

Some historians have considered Franklin incurably committed to getting and spending, America's original Babbitt, the champion of boosters. The historians have been wrong. Whatever verifications can be read into these assumptions based on Franklin's writings, especially the Almanacs, and his long, highly successful public service, they are bad readings of truth when seeking the mother lode of Franklin's character. Wise prospectors pass them by as copper pyrites or fool's gold and look further for paydirt.

Great profits were available to be made from Franklin's scientific achievements. A tradesman astute as Franklin could not fail to see them. He saw. But he chose not to take them. This fact throws doubt on the personal applicability of his earlier maxims about frugality and making hay while the sun shined. The Franklin Stove could have made him wealthy. He gave it away. His printed advice sometimes seemed to advocate pinching pennies as good sense for young men and young nations groping for economic stability. For himself, he couldn't be bothered. In his early forties, he turned aside from business full-time. He took the fertility of ideas and gift for invention that could have made him America's wealthiest man and went about his real business of studying nature and teaching the world. Others were welcome to profit from his ideas. Happiness to them. Franklin was hurrying on to fresh ideas.

His enthusiasm and commitment as a teacher of both natural philosophy and practical morality may have helped cause him to be misjudged. He has been criticized as the classic example of materialistic America. *A case can be made only by stopping short of the truth.*

ANOTHER FEUD WITH A NONEXISTENT BEN

In an imaginatively personal study of American literature, D. H. Lawrence managed with his mystic fervor to misread Franklin completely. "Oh, Franklin was the first downright American," wailed Lawrence, "He knew what he was about, the sharp little man." Lawrence decided that Franklin was the "snuff-coloured little man" who raised America on a pillar of dollars and destroyed Europe.

A few aromas of truth came through to Lawrence. The process of "Americanizing and mechanizing" that Franklin helped to start, Lawrence rightfully saw as overthrowing the past. He thought he saw a terrible danger too:

And now look at America, tangled in her own barbed wire, and mastered by her own machines. Absolutely got down by her own barbed wire of shalt-nots, and shut up fast in her own "productive" machines like millions of squirrels running in millions of cages.

If the words cut, it is because they contain those aromas of truth. But they were never truths about Benjamin Franklin. The America he wanted and worked to achieve had no barbed wire or shalt-nots. Both were as inimical to Franklin as to Lawrence.

Franklin was never Richard Saunders, the Poor Richard of the Almanacs, any more than he was Silence Dogood, or Alice Addertongue, or Anthony Afterwit, or Polly Baker, or any of the other identities he assumed for entertainment and instruction. He was none of them, but he was in a way, *all* of them, and much more. The record shows that Franklin listened to Poor Richard, for instance, only when it was convenient. Lawrence should have been subtle enough to see behind the facades. Then he would have written differently:

> Now if Mr. Andrew Carnegie, or any other millionaire, had wished to invent a God to suit his ends, he could not have done better. Benjamin did it for him in the eighteenth century. God is the supreme servant of men who want to get on, to *produce*. Providence. The provider. The heavenly store-keeper. The everlasting Wanamaker.

Had he seen more clearly, he could not have written with such searing contempt that "Benjamin fenced a little tract that he called the soul of man, and proceeded to get it into cultivation."

Poor Lawrence. He never did see Benjamin Franklin at all, did he? And if Lawrence could not see him, what of other men? Do they too chiefly notice a tidy little rulemaker putting strait jackets on the spirit and ordering each man to find a grindstone for his nose and there to fix it firmly?

Richard Saunders, Philom.,* was forced on Poor Lawrence when Lawrence was a child. He bristled at the memory.

> And probably I haven't got over those Poor Richard tags yet. I rankle still with them. They are thorns in young flesh. Because although I still believe that honesty is the best policy, I dislike policy altogether; though it is just as well not to count your chickens before they are hatched, it's still more hateful to count them with gloating when they *are* hatched. It has taken me many years and countless smarts to get out of that barbed wire moral enclosure.

---

*"Philom." always appears after Richard Saunders name on the title pages of the Almanacs. It is the abbreviation for "Philomath," which literally meant "love of learning," and was popularly applied to the makers of almanacs. Having a distinguished philomath was essential for a successful almanac. Franklin invented his own philomath and had the most successful almanac in history.

Poor Lawrence, Poor America, Poor World, struggling to escape an enclosure that Benjamin Franklin never entered. It is sad that Lawrence could not locate the real Franklin outside the barbed wire. He would have found him, if not a cousin of the spirit, at least an amiable uncle willing to listen.

Franklin himself was perhaps knowingly responsible for his own concealment behind Poor Richard's maxims on industry and frugality. During a voyage to England in 1757, Franklin extracted the maxims relevant to those matters from the previous Almanacs. They were published in a pamphlet entitled "The Way to Wealth" that was phenomenally successful. Franklin's grandson in the 1818 edition of Franklin's works wrote that the pamphlet had "greatly contributed to the formation of that national character they (the American people) have since exhibited." "The Way to Wealth" has gone through hundreds of editions and is almost routinely included in general collections of Franklin's writings. Lindsay Swift, one of Franklin's biographers, wrote that it bears "the stamp of our national spirit." This is no doubt true. Historically it represents an aspect of American character as it developed from Franklin's time through the "Do or Die" days of *Horatio Alger* heroes. Alger seems virtually a twin brother, though less clever, of the philomath charting "The Way to Wealth." Both vigorously preached what Lawrence and others have attacked as the sermon of American industry. *Clifton Fadiman* once wrote nostalgically of the irresistible appeal of such sermons: "I suppose my generation is the last to have been brought up on the Algerine Virtues," he wrote in *Any Number Can Play*. "From his books I learned that wealth is the direct consequence of honesty, thrift, self-reliance, industry, a cheerful whistle, and an open, manly face. Today (now they tell me) I know this to be untrue. But somehow I feel that there just might be something in it."

"The Way to Wealth" dared to be humorous, but it delivered much the same "early to bed" wisdom. "The sleeping fox catches no poultry." "He that lives upon hope will die fasting."

It was a sententious, clever, cheerful aria in praise of hard work. In the context of the Colonies, it was both useful and practical. And even today, with Clifton Fadiman, we feel that there just might be something in it.

However, the admission can be made that if "The Way to Wealth" had been *all* that Franklin offered, there might be more reason to pay attention when Lawrence protests, "I'm not going to be turned into a virtuous little automaton as Benjamin would have me."

The truth was that "The Way to Wealth" was only a small portion of Poor Richard's quarter-century of wit, wisdom, and good advice. It was a single village on the continent of Franklin's total work. Franklin certainly did not think of the pamphlet as a vade mecum for success. It contained amiable suggestions, not holy commandments. He always intended Poor Richard's maxims to be: First, amusing. Second, useful to young people trying seriously to make something of their lives.

HOW "BENJAMIN" WAS "POOR RICHARD?"

Franklin was never shallow enough to value the making of money for its own sake (one of Lawrence's mistakes). He didn't even value work for its own sake, but for the sake of *what* could be accomplished for human good. To *do* something worth doing was what drove Benjamin Franklin to save his money and to respect Poor Richard's dictum that "diligence is the mother of good luck."

He needed money so he could give the major portion of his life to the productive enjoyment of science. That he was frustrated in achieving his goal was the fault of history, George III, and the Continental Congress, not the fault of Benjamin Franklin.

Poor Lawrence focused myopically on a meager aspect of Franklin's life when he concluded that Franklin was trying to remake the world in the image of Richard Saunders for whom "one today is worth two tomorrows" and "fools make feasts and wise men eat them."

Richard Saunders, in fact, nearly always expressed himself with pithy cleverness. His wit usually sounds true if not profound. "Drink water; put the money in your pocket, and leave the dry bellyache in the punch-bowl." "Fish and visitors smell in three days." "Necessity never made a good bargain." "Three may keep a secret, if two of them are dead." "God heals, the doctor takes the fee."

Poor Richard also has thoughts with a serious ring, as if special Franklin echoes are entering in: "The noblest question in the world is, what good may I do in it?" Exactly what is wrong with that, Poor Lawrence? Or with this? "Industry need not wish." Or this? "Serving God is doing good to man, but praying is thought an easier service, and therefore more generally chosen."

They are glib, elementary, aptly worded, sometimes playful, sometimes serious, memorable, useful. Through such maxims and "The Way to Wealth," Franklin had influence on the development of the American character. This was in spite of himself to an extent, since the development went farther in the wealth direction than he might have wished.

His influence is still strong in this respect, often without our knowledge. He has turned most of us into quoters, like it or not. Franklin's Poor Richard sayings long ago entered the general idiom. "It is the little writer," said *Havelock Ellis*, "rather than the great writer who seems never to quote, and the reason is that he is never really doing anything else." We quote Franklin all the time, as much perhaps as Shakespeare or the *Bible*, without being aware. Perhaps unwitting plagiarism is the ultimate tribute of posterity to a great man.

True or not, Poor Richard's maxims are too simple and obvious to convey the broader complexity of Benjamin Franklin. They stop short in the valley before the mountain is reached. Lawrence may have detected a truth, not about Franklin, but about America which seemed to adopt the superficial aspects of materialism without fully grasping what Franklin was driving at.

His own actions were crystal clear, speaking louder it may be than Poor Richard's words. He retired from work to concentrate on science. He moved from the hubbub of the inner city, taking a house with gardens reaching to the Delaware River. He could swim in the river to relax or to work out the maddening, fascinating puzzles of electricity. Despite all the manifold opportunities, he stopped working directly for money, and let his money work for him. He financed other printers, invested in paper companies, bought property. But such activities were sidelines, not central pursuits. Scientific work "to produce something for the common benefit of mankind" occupied the center.

It was a sincere program, but he could not hold to it because of the long interruptions imposed by the needs of his country during its first and greatest trial. Please explain, Poor Lawrence, if he was an automaton of little rules priggishly devoted to business and the pursuit of pennies, why was it that only duty, not profit, could interfere with his regimen of scientific study?

On October 11, 1750, Franklin wrote to Cadwallader Colden, telling himself as well as his friend that the country and the public rightfully had claims on the time of a philosopher:

... let not your love of philosophical amusements have more than its due weight with you. Had Newton been pilot but of a single common ship, the finest of his discoveries would scarce have excused, or atoned for, his abandoning the helm one hour in time of danger; how much less if she had carried the fate of the commonwealth.

Finally, to correct history's full portrait of Benjamin Franklin, accuracy is served by quoting from a letter to his mother when he was young, and a letter to his sister when he was old. The letter written to his mother on April 12, 1750 reveals more, somehow, than the apothegms for youth's instruction and maturity's amusement sprinkled through the Almanacs.

... so the years roll round, and the last will come, when I would rather have it said "He lived usefully" than "He died rich."

Funny thing. He apparently meant it. And lived it.

On July 13, 1785, Franklin, weary of his struggles in France, wrote to his sister Jane Mecom, the day after his departure. "I have continued to work till late in the day; 'tis time I should go home, and go to bed."

He went home, but he did not go to bed, not yet. At the age of eighty-one, he helped write the *Constitution of the United States.* Heaven knows, there was no money in that.

True, as previously noted, his contribution to the Constitutional Convention chiefly was to provide a patriarchal presence. But when James Wilson after the Convention's long struggles in many directions proposed that the executive should be a single person, there was, as Madison wrote in his notes, a "considerable pause." Then into the silence, Benjamin Franklin spoke. Wilson's point was important. They should discuss it thoroughly. They did. The *American Presidency* was established. Is it naive to assume that Franklin's support at a critical moment helped to shape the decision? Had he not been the greatest living American, with the single debatable exception of Washington, his contribution to a pregnant pause might have meant little. He was Benjamin Franklin. His words meant everything. He did not abuse his power by speaking often during the Convention, but he was there.

What sort of wealth was he aiming at that summer of 1787? Was it bankable? If the old man was by his special lights obeying the maxims of Poor Richard, then there must be something gritty in them, something strong to say in their favor. D. H. Lawrence and the critics may have remained too long on "The Way to Wealth." They should have looked further. They might have been surprised.

1976

Dear Doctor Franklin, Sir,

When fame came your way, it came in flood. But you were an aquatic expert. No danger of drowning.

The fame is still very much at the flood. Kites with your picture front and center are being offered for the bicentennial festivities, and Franklin medallions, Franklin stamps, Franklin this, and Franklin that. You would no doubt ask to be excused. You always became uncomfortable when the praise was too fulsome. Perhaps it sounded as if they thought you should have the courtesy to enter eternity prematurely so the eulogies could pop and crackle with unembarrassed vigor.

At the bicentennial, we'll try to be reasonable, Sir. The feeling around the nation these days is that we could use several additional Franklins right now, not just kites, medallions, and stamps with your picture.

Consider that a request if you please.

Before you left port after eighty-four years to explore remoter latitudes, you admitted a willingness to live your years again, though you would appreciate permission to correct a few *errata*.

Actually your life has been lived through again and again in the pages of books, and you are officially one of the leading Founding Fathers. As for the *errata*, they have been consumed in the confusion. Biographers and historians have clustered around the eighteenth century for two hundred years staring at the details of your life. And running merrily around in many circles.

Instead of a Founding Father, perhaps you would feel easier and more comfortable as a Great Uncle. Certainly you were the Great Uncle of American science, as well as a Founding Father.

Uncle Sam would welcome an "Uncle Benjamin."

We could use you again, Sir, *errata* and all. Please visit and bring your friends.

We Are, &c.,
YOURS, THE PEOPLE

XVII. A New Scientific Star

THE ROYAL SOCIETY

Is it only in retrospect that we can look at an event and, knowing that it captured the imagination of the public, remark that it couldn't miss? Research in electricity was not new when the French dramatically seized lightning, following Doctor Franklin's instructions, and thus proved its electrical nature.

The earlier experiments in Philadelphia and Europe had stirred no comparable response. When *Georg Bose* in Germany in 1742 suggested the electrical origin of the aurora borealis, there was no dancing in the streets, no special acclaim. When William Watson proved the existence of an electrical "circuit" and used the name in that connection for the first time, he received attention at the Royal Academy, but he was not raised on the shoulders of the members and carried down the Strand to the lusty huzzas of excited Londoners. In 1745 when *E. G. von Kleist* of Pomerania made the significant discovery that an electrical charge could be stored in a glass tube by inserting a liquid containing a nail hooked to a friction electricity machine, the fact was considered worthy of remark without being remarkable. The use of electricity to ignite inflammable materials at the Berlin Academy in 1744 by *Christian Ludolff* proved electricity was a dramatic force, but didn't everyone know that already?

For reasons that seem reasonably obvious, *in retrospect*, Franklin became the first celebrity scientist since Isaac Newton, and electricity was the start. "She has star qualities," we say thoughtfully, focusing on the natural talents of the latest in a long line of healthy young actresses. Without being that different from those who passed before, she comes along at the right moment with suitable endowments, and a star is born.

Franklin came along at the right moment. He wrote with calm, nontechnical ease to make a complicated subject understandable. Also, the rods summoning violent electricity from the clouds were dramatic. And the amazing kite with key attached was clearly, in every possible way, *box office*. Once celebrity began, the fact that he was a simple printer in Philadelphia helped enormously rather than hindered. The old school tie tradition that earlier had kept him from gaining an audience among traditional scientists became meaningless when those scientists began rushing to honor the printer with all the symbolic ties he could possibly wear.

Instead of holding back and ho-humming when Collinson arrived with a new report from Philadelphia (the situation that had prevailed until D'Alibard's proof), the Society leaned forward expectantly when Franklin's letter on the electrical kite was read December 21, 1752. Franklin had worried about the reception the kite experiment would receive, but it seemed to complete the celebrity package. Sir Isaac Newton's successor had arrived and was ready to be crowned with honorary degrees (Harvard, July 1753; Yale, September 1753; William and Mary, April 1756) and with distinguished tributes from his scientific peers. The Royal Society of London, chary before with its approval, became generous and genial.

> Without my having made any application for that honour, they chose me a member, and voted that I should be excus'd the customary payments, which would have amounted to twenty-five Guineas, and ever since have given me their Transactions gratis. They also presented me with the Gold Medal of Sir Godfrey Copley for the year 1753, the delivery of which was accompanied by a very handsome speech of the President Lord Macclesfield, wherein I was highly honoured.

The Copley Medal was bestowed, November 30, 1753, in recognition of Benjamin Franklin's electrical experiments and observations. It was the highest award in science at the time. On April 29, 1756, Franklin was unanimously elected to membership in the Royal Society.

In 1767 as a member of the Royal Society Council, while investigating "one Dacosta, a Jew, who, as our clerk, was entrusted with collecting our moneys, has been so unfaithful as to embezzle near thirteen hundred pounds in four years," Franklin had a chance to look at the minutes concerning his election eleven years earlier. He described the findings to his son William on December 19, 1767:

> You must know it is not usual to admit persons that have not requested to be admitted; and a recommendatory certificate in favor of the candidate, signed by at least three of the members, is by our rule to be presented to the Society, expressing that he is desirous of that honor, and is so and so qualified. As I never had asked or expected the honor, I was, as I said before, curious to see how the business was managed . . . the election was by a unanimous vote; and, the honor being voluntarily conferred by the Society, unsolicited by me, it was thought wrong to demand or receive the usual fees or composition.

The Royal Society is still important, but it has competition among a number of comparable bodies. In the eighteenth century it was the supreme council, the major leagues, the highest court of science. It was, after all, Newton's organization and the oldest scientific society in the world.

The Royal Society of London for Improving Natural Knowledge was officially founded according to the records in 1660. But meetings were held since 1645 of "divers worthy persons" interested in natural philosophy, learning, and the new *Experimental Philosophy*, a special empirical branch of natural philosophy.

Many of the first participants were associated with Oxford College, but the meeting on November 28, 1660 was held at Gresham College, London. At that meeting the first journal of the Society was started with a notice of a lecture by *Christopher Wren*. At the November 28th meeting, it was decided to hold weekly lectures on Wednesdays, and to formalize the proceedings of the Society. Royal approval was given (hence the name), and the Royal Society was committed to the service of natural knowledge.

The journals of the Royal Society make a who's who of international and historical science. The record for December 21, 1671 shows that "the lord bishop of Sarum proposed for candidate Mr. Isaac Newton, professor of the mathematicks at Cambridge."

Newton was elected a Fellow on January 11, 1671. In 1703, three years before the birth of Benjamin Franklin, Newton became President of the Royal Society, and held the post until his death in 1727, the year that Franklin and his friends formed the Junto.

The Royal Society's recognition of achievement became one of the supreme accolades in science. The annual Copley Medal and other awards by the Society became measures of high accomplishment.

As a member of the Royal Society, Franklin was in direct contact with the scientific summits. During his stays in London, he attended meetings, served on committees, took an active part. When away from Great Britain, Franklin corresponded with *Sir Joseph Banks*, President of the Royal Society. He delivered papers on his continuing scientific studies and speculations. Even the American Revolution did not stifle his ties with the Society. On September 9, 1782, with the war continuing, he wrote to Sir Joseph Banks, from Passy:

> I have just received the very kind, friendly letter you were so good as to write to me by Dr. Broussonnet. Be assured, that I long earnestly for a return of those peaceful times, when I could sit down in sweet society with my English philosophical friends, communicating to each other new discoveries, and proposing improvements of old ones; all tending to extend the power of man over matter, avert or diminish the evils he is subject to, or augment the number of his enjoyments. Much more happy should I be thus employed in your most desirable company, than in that of all the grandees of the earth projecting plans of mischief, however necessary they may be supposed for obtaining greater good.

On August 30, 1783, Franklin sent a science news report to Banks concerning the "aërostatic experiment" or balloon ascension he had witnessed in Paris with excitement and admiration, together with nearly fifty thousand Parisians who gathered to witness the event.

Science for Franklin took precedence over war and the bitter controversies of politics, as his letters to Banks attest. Scientific curiosity summoned him to witness the first balloon ascension in Paris at the Champ-de-Mars on August 27, 1783. The *Montgolfier brothers* in June of that year had launched a linen balloon inflated with smoke from burning straw near Lyons, France. The Paris attempt was directed by the physicist *Jacques Charles*. A silk balloon filled with hydrogen gas lifted off at five P.M. and to Franklin made an impressive sight.

With his usual attention to details, Franklin described the balloon as a twelve foot diameter hollow globe, "formed of what is called in England oiled silk, here *taffetas gommé*, the silk being impregnated with a solution of gum elastic in linseed oil." Still wet with gum, the parts were sewn together, and the seams regummed for greater tightness. Filled with the "inflammable air that is produced by pouring oil of vitriol upon filings of iron," the globe was "found to have a tendency upwards."

After watching the balloon disappear into the clouds, Franklin listened to the various members of the crowd speculating on potential uses of the invention. He expressed his own view to Banks that "possibly it may pave the way to some discoveries in natural philosophy of which at present we have no conception." "I thought it my duty, sir," he concluded, "to send an early account of this extraordinary fact to the Society which does me the honor to reckon me among its members."

THE STARS APPLAUD WHEN PHILOSOPHERS EMBRACE

In spite of war the Academy valued Franklin's membership, and English scientists regretted that he gave of his energies to politics. Perhaps there was envy too as Franklin, in spite of political intrigues, appropriated time during his years in France to engage in some natural philosophy, the affairs of the Academy of Sciences in Paris, and even such celebrated events as an official public meeting with the *other* distinguished philosopher of the eighteenth century, Monsieur Voltaire. They met on April 29, 1778 at the Academy of Sciences. John Adams' diary provides a description of the event. Voltaire and Franklin were present at the meeting of the Academy, and a cry arose that they must be introduced. Then the shouting would not subside until they had embraced in the French manner.

> The two aged actors upon this great theatre of philosophy and frivolity then embraced each other by hugging one another in their arms and kissing each other's cheeks, and then the tumult subsided. And the cry immediately spread throughout the kingdom, and I suppose all over Europe: *Qu'il est charmant de voir embrasser Solon et Sophocle.*

What happiness to see Solon and Sophocles embrace. At the Royal Society in London there was no doubt disapproval and jealousy. Doctor Franklin had been theirs for twenty years. The mad French were endeavoring to steal him away. Drat politics!

There was further regret in England when Franklin chose the Paris Academy of Sciences to read his paper, "Aurora Borealis, Suppositions and Conjectures towards forming an Hypothesis for its Explanation," on April 14, 1779.

> May not then the great quantity of electricity brought into the polar regions by the clouds, which are condens'd there, and fall in snow, which electricity would enter the earth, but cannot penetrate the ice; may it not, I say (*as a bottle overcharged*) break thro' that low atmosphere and run along in the vacuum over the air towards the equator, diverging as the degrees of longitude enlarge, strongly visible where densest, and becoming less visible as it more diverges; till it finds a passage to the earth in more temperate climates, or is mingled with the upper air?

The theory was carefully thought through and written. Modern science believes cosmic rays and/or geomagnetism may have something to do with the polar auroras, but it isn't certain of the precise details. The aurora is still among the mysteries.

Despite hostilities and the fact that Franklin's name had become anathema to George III, his paper on the Aurora Borealis was published in England. In 1779 a collection of his writings entitled *Political, Miscellaneous and Philosophical Pieces* was also published there. A likeness of the philosopher was used as the frontispiece, and Franklin's sister in 1786 wrote to him of this picture that it was "Your profile done more to your likeness than any I have heretofore seen."

LUNCHING ON THE SUN
I have heard that chemists can by their art decompose stone and wood, extracting a considerable quantity of water from the one and air from the other. It seems natural to conclude, from this, that water and air were ingredients in their original composition; for men cannot make new matter of any kind. In the same manner may we not suppose that, when we consume combustibles of all kinds, and produce heat or light, we do not create that heat or light, but only decompose a substance which received it originally as a part of its composition? ...I can conceive that in the first assemblage of the particles of which this earth is composed, each brought its portion of the loose heat that had been connected with it, and the whole, when pressed together, produced the internal fire that still subsists.

(To the Abbé Soulavie)

B.FRANKLIN, L.L.D. F.R.S.

Born at Boston in New England, Jan 17ᵗʰ 1706.

NON SORDIDUS AUCTOR NATURÆ VERIQUE.

Benjamin Franklin, "Enemy of England,"
1779

This likeness, which his sister Jane Mecom considered the most accurate profile of her brother she had seen, was used as the frontispiece to Political, Miscellaneous, and Philosophical Pieces, 1779. *Printed in London, the work was attributed to "The Minister Plenipotentiary at the Court of Paris for the United States of America." At the time Britain had been waging a fitful war for three years to prove that there was no such thing as a United States of America. It turned out there was.*

Clearly, in spite of war, his admirers in England and the Royal Society kept faith with Benjamin Franklin. Keeping the scientific faith was, of course, a fundamental obligation for the Society whose traditions Newton helped establish. The Society's commitment to natural truth was more important than any other commitment, including those to party and country. Historically the list of scientific projects sponsored by the Society ranges from Captain Cook's Antarctic expeditions in the eighteenth century to the latest solar eclipse. Current events in science do not escape the attention of contemporary members, Benjamin Franklin's spiritual descendants, when they convene at Burlington House in London.

NEWTON AND FRANKLIN IN THE GUEST BOOK

In 1943, Carl Van Doren in *Meet Dr. Franklin*, wrote of a fascinating disclosure by *Dr. Simon Flexner.* Flexner told Carl Van Doren of his experience in London signing the Guest Book of the Royal Society.

Flexner asked to see the signature of Sir Isaac Newton. He found that people tracing their fingers under the signature of Newton had worn away the name directly beneath his.

He asked to see Benjamin Franklin's name, and found that there too the name beneath had been erased by the pressing fingers of the curious through the decades.

"Newton and Franklin were the only names so eminent as to have caused this obliteration of their neighbors," wrote Van Doren.

Through Franklin, worthy Americans became members of the Royal Society. He served as a bridge for the exchange of scientific knowledge back and forth across the Atlantic. The irony of war in the eighteenth century was dramatized by the contact and friendship maintained by the scientists on both sides. They were quite capable of being adversaries in war and simultaneously collaborators in the peaceful sciences. Learning and scientific knowledge transcended war because they could be viewed as human rather than national enterprises. There is evidence that Franklin sincerely managed to view science in that remarkably international fashion, and that he helped teach the view to America, England, France, and perhaps the rest of the world.

COMMON FRIENDS TO MANKIND

The lesson has experienced ups and downs, but it has prevailed into relatively modern times. Even amid the total wars of the twentieth century, significant scientific studies and explorations have gone on, sponsored by governments caught up in war's destruction. The spirit of Benjamin Franklin is sensed in the decision of the British government to encourage *Ernest Shackleton* and his volunteers to go ahead with their planned 1914 scientific exploration of Antarctica, despite war in Europe. The decision was made that the researches to be conducted in the frozen South were important to scientific knowledge and mankind, and should be encouraged.

During the Revolution, Franklin supplied a personal example of extraordinary hospitality to science, and he did so with a matter-of-factness that makes the episode seem inevitable and natural, though it was neither.

In the second half of the eighteenth century, despite revolutions, scientific work continued. One of the men leading voyages of discovery was *James Cook*, whom Franklin had met in London. During the 1770's, Captain Cook made three voyages for science in the south Pacific and in the Southern Ocean surrounding Antarctica. Sir Joseph Banks, later President of the Royal Society, accompanied Cook on his first voyage which resulted in the discovery of Australia. His second voyage led to the first crossing of the Antarctic Circle and the first astronomical and meteorological observations by man from the austere perspective of the Antarctic. Cook's astounding second voyage proved what had only been conjecture before for the entire history of mankind—the existence of Antarctica. Equally astounding was the fact that during the second voyage, only one man in a company of 118 was lost during a voyage of three years. Dietary practices during Cook's voyage proved that scurvy, scourge of the sea theretofore, could be controlled and prevented. Franklin was intrigued by the voyages and interested in the research.

With his ships *Resolution* and *Discovery*, Captain Cook began his third voyage from England on July 12, 1776. The signing of the Declaration of Independence eight days earlier theoretically made James Cook and his Royal Academy scientists "enemies."

Nonsense. They were scientists in quest of knowledge for mankind. They were not Benjamin Franklin's enemies. Reason dictated rising above the passions of politics and war. In 1779, aware that the voyagers were expected to return soon to European waters from the Pacific, Franklin acted officially, using his powers as Minister Plenipotentiary to France, to issue a directive that when the ships of Captain Cook appeared, they were not to be attacked by American vessels. They were designated noncombatants, guaranteed "free passage" through the sea lanes where American captains and vessels harassed and fought to bankrupt Britain. That was all right. That was war. *But Cook and his men were not war. They were science. Let them through.*

To All Captains and Commanders of Armed Ships Acting by Commis-
sion from the Congress of the United States of America, now in War
with Great Britain
Gentlemen:—A ship having been fitted out from England before the
commencement of this war, to make discoveries of new countries in
unknown seas, under the conduct of that most celebrated navigator,
Captain Cook; an undertaking truly laudable in itself . . . this is,
therefore, most earnestly to recommend to every one of you that, in
case the said ship, which is now expected to be soon in the European
seas on her return, should happen to fall into your hands, you would
not consider her as an enemy . . . but that you would treat the said
Captain Cook and his people with all civility and kindness, affording
them, as common friends to mankind, all the assistance in your power,
which they may happen to stand in need of.

This generosity, rare between opponents in war, was not lost on
the leaders in Britain. Even though Cook had been killed by Ha-
waiians on February 14th that year, Franklin's hospitality to science, rising above war, impressed the British. In 1784 when Cook's
account of the third voyage was published in two volumes, *Voyage
to the Pacific Ocean*, even George III approved bestowing on
Franklin one of the gold medals the Royal Society struck to honor
Captain Cook. Through Lord Howe, Franklin's correspondent and
friend, the Admiralty sent Franklin a copy of Cook's work; and
Franklin thanked Howe, insisting that the good will he had shown
in protecting the "illustrious discoverer" was "no more than a duty
to mankind."

He was sincere and consistent in thinking of science as a duty
to mankind. This commitment was not set aside to accommodate a
war. Indeed, during the French years, he used science as a welcome
relief from the pressures of statecraft and the business of revolution.

He kept up his scientific correspondence to the extent possible
with Jan Ingenhousz in Holland, Joseph Priestley in England, and
Father Beccaria in Italy, among others. Throughout Europe,
Franklin's researches were known and scholars were eager to discuss them. Beccaria, the Italian priest-physicist, was a devoted follower of Franklin, and it was Franklin's influence that encouraged
Beccaria in experiments that significantly helped extend electrical
knowledge.

Franklin's international reputation as a scientist and his sociable reception of new ideas, theories, inventions, etc., made his house
at Passy a scientific crossroads. Every new invention was sent to
him for inspection and verdict. He gave freely of his time, too

freely for John Adams who felt that Franklin should concentrate totally on the business of the Colonies, just as Ingenhousz and other scientists thought he should forget war and politics to concentrate on science.

But Franklin did what he had done all his life, he contrived to do both, without cheating either. The work of scientific societies in England and France was work that he wanted to see carried on in spite of war, and he did all that he could to help. That was the reason—one of them—for taking such trouble to report on the balloon ascensions to the Royal Society. The other reason was that the aeronautical events were enormously stimulating and fascinating curiosities.

As the experiments continued, Franklin conscientiously informed the Royal Society through Sir Joseph Banks. Eventually he chided England's slowness in failing to undertake such experiments.

> I am sorry this experiment is totally neglected in England, where mechanic genius is so strong ... Your philosophy seems to be too bashful. In this country we are not so much afraid of being laughed at. If we do a foolish thing, we are the first to laugh at it ourselves ... This experiment is by no means a trifling one. It may be attended with important consequences that no one can foresee. We should not suffer pride to prevent our progress in Science.

Franklin's reports to Banks proved that he reciprocated the warmth and respect that the Society had shown him. Both Franklin and the Royal Society apparently considered their relationship superior to, or at least unrelated to the raging conflict of revolution.

Governments could hate and send their citizens to kill in the name of that hate. Science did not hate. It served truth, not with weapons, but with experiments and rigorously proven facts.

END OF A CRISIS

Eventually, governments too could learn, if not from science, then perhaps from scientists such as Benjamin Franklin. The government of Great Britain during that same year of the balloon ascensions finally realized and admitted what Franklin had said repeatedly since the 1760's, that a war in America would be impossible for Britain to win and too expensive to continue long.

All the Americans had to do to assure ultimate victory was to maintain an army in the field, no matter the size of the army, no matter the field. And General Washington had proved his ability to hold an army together, to preserve it from confrontations that threatened defeat, to keep going. That was enough, because it prevented Britain from suppressing the rebellion, and it meant a continuing burden on the strained exchequer of England.

August 1783, as the balloon went up, completed nearly seven years—seven years of war—since Franklin arrived in Paris with his grandsons and began waging his part of the struggle in the capital of France. To keep an army in the field was his task no less than Washington's, and all his skills had been needed. Seven years!

Just two days after Franklin arrived in Paris on December 21, 1776, Thomas Paine, with Washington's army of less than six thousand men (their commander described many of them as "entirely naked and most so thinly clad as to be unfit for service") sat down to write his first *Crisis Paper*. He was carrying on a tradition of pamphleteering for freedom and survival that some thought Franklin had started with his *Plain Truth* paper in 1747. Legend has it that Paine wrote the paper at the behest of the General, the soldiers gathered round as he used a drumhead for his writing desk.

> These are the times that try men's souls. The summer soldier and the sunshine patriot will in this crisis, shrink from the service of his country; but he that stands it now, deserves the love and thanks of man and woman.

That August of 1783 did Franklin think of Thomas Paine and the part he had played in introducing the intense young Englishman to the Colonies? Two days after the writing of the *Crisis*, on Christmas Day, Washington and his thinclads, many shoeless, crossed the ice-clogged Delaware, the same river that had passed Franklin's house on Race Street in Philadelphia. Those American winter soldiers and icetime patriots attacked the Hessian mercenaries at Trenton, New Jersey. It took an hour to give the Colonies perhaps their most important victory and to capture nine hundred prisoners.

It was established that December night in New Jersey that Great Britain would not win if the semblance of an army could be maintained. If Washington could summon the personal strength to keep going? He could. If Franklin could charm and wheedle and connive to provide the money, arms, and international backing essential for the struggle? He could.

But if Britain was slow to move in science as in the case of balloon technology, it was slow to see or admit the truth in connection with the war that went on and on, as an old man in Paris connived, and wheedled, and charmed.

Then the day following his first letter to Banks at the Royal Society concerning the new science of aërostatics, Franklin finally could write a letter to the President of Congress, saying:

> Sir: After a continued course of treating for nine months, the English ministry have at length come to a resolution to lay aside, for the present, all the new propositions that have been made and agreed to, their own, as well as ours; and they offer to sign again as a definitive treaty, the articles of November the 30th, 1782, the ratifications of which have already been exchanged. We have agreed to this, and on Wednesday next, the third of September, it will be signed, with all the definitive treaties, establishing a general peace, which may God long continue. I am, with great respect, &c.,   B. Franklin.

Thus at the Court of Versailles on September 3, 1783, Benjamin Franklin signed the third great American document of his country's young history, the treaty of peace with Great Britain. Joining him as signatories were John Adams and John Jay for the United States, with David Hartley, Franklin's long time friend, representing Britain. *The war was over.*

On September 6, Franklin wrote to Hartley about rumors that America was verging on anarchy and would soon welcome "returning to the obedience of Britain." Anyone who so believed, he wrote, would be "like one who, being shown some spots on the sun, should fancy that the whole disk would soon be overspread with them, and that there would be an end of daylight."

The United States of America was not going to disappear. Neither wish nor fantasy could make it go away. On the following day, Franklin wrote to *Mrs. Mary Hewson*, commenting on her fear that the country had been badly hurt by the war.

> Parts of it have indeed suffered . . . but the body of the country has not been much hurt, and the fertility of our soil, with the industry of our people, now that the commerce of all the world is open to us, will soon repair the damages received, and introduce that prosperity which we hope Providence intends for us, since it has so remarkably favored our Revolution.

The war was over. There would hopefully be more time for new science, new ideas, and old clubs, such as his favorite in London, the *Honest Whigs*. Less than a fortnight after the settlement, Franklin was writing to *Dr. Richard Price* about each of the three.

All the conversation here at present turns upon the balloons filled with light inflammable air, and the means of managing them, so to give men the advantage of flying . . . I have now a little leisure, and long to see and be merry with the club, but I doubt I cannot undertake the journey before spring . . .

At the end of the letter he was zooming off into the ethereal again, seeking a way to control the new balloons, seeking a way for another scientific curiosity to become a practical aid to man, seeking a way to master the grand new possibility of flying. "If a man should go up with one of the large ones, might there not be some mechanical contrivance to compress the globe at pleasure, and thereby incline it to descend, and let it expand when he inclines to rise again?" Benjamin Franklin's antennae were alert. There was a new age coming, and in it *men would fly. He knew it.*

1976

Dear Doctor Franklin, Sir,

Few topics of speculation failed to catch your eye, and the suspicion is that your *other* profession (printing) served to bring them to your attention. Curiosity about everything must have been one reason that other profession was perfect for you and pridefully upheld.

You even began your will with the words. . . . "I, Benjamin Franklin of Philadelphia, printer . . ." And you never suggested altering the famous epitaph that identified you with the inky enterprise.

In the eighteenth century, a printer was often a journalist, publisher, bookseller, typesetter, newspaper editor, educator, and a dozen others all at once. You mastered the arts and sciences of printing young and kept them green your long life through.

Biographers delight in the visit you made to Francois Didot's lavish printshop in Paris. To the surprise of the printers, you took over a press, letting them know with expert action that the distinguished Doctor Franklin was a member of their profession.

When that infuriating gout prevented you from continuing any printing on your own, you wrote to Mrs. Catherine Greene that "loving the business, I have brought up my grandson Benjamin to it, and have built and furnished a printing-house for him, which he now manages under my eyes." The grandson, Benjamin Franklin Bache, trained under Didot thanks to your influence.

You were as skilled with tools as you were with words, and in your time handled every aspect of printing from writing, to casting type and setting it in pages, to mixing inks and applying them to the plates, to building presses, to introducing and improving copper-plate printing, to engraving and stereotyping. All aspects of printing were advanced under your influence. You made printing a more workmanlike and respected craft than ever before. You helped other printers open their own shops, providing them with equipment and financial backing, as well as encouragement. Young America needed printers to spread the words . . . such words as liberty, and justice, and the United States. Printers took your advice about what to print and even how. You encouraged the use of type by John Baskerville and it was used widely in the Colonies.

Today anything printed on your press in Philadelphia is greatly valuable. This includes items that you thought little of yourself. You printed them in accord with the view that a responsible printer must serve other tastes than his own. You published books your customers wanted. But you also published books *you* wanted, such as scientific works by American scientists or translations of classics by James Logan and others.

Also popular are the "Bagatelles" and light pieces done on the private press you established at your home in Passy. Those especially bear the Franklin touch. Was it the influence of Paris, Madeira, or the ladies, Sir? You wrote, designed, and printed the Passy items, making them sometimes risqué if not risky.

You would be amused and perhaps flattered at the steps taken to identify with you and your Philadelphia press. Consider the case of our popular long-running journal, *The Saturday Evening Post*. For decades it claimed to be "Founded A.D. 1728 by Benjamin Franklin." Is that news to you, Sir? Mott and Jorgenson wrote that the *Post* actually started in 1821. Apparently a clever promotion person found a thread of connection with you in the fact that the *Post's* first location was 53 Market Street, near the place where your printing business was located. Thus are historical dreams born and sent rolling down the corridor of time.

It hasn't been lost on history that your *General Magazine* (1741) was the second in America. Andrew Bradford's *American Magazine* preceded you by three days. He appropriated your idea and ran with it. Your magazine lasted six issues, Bradford's three. But it was a beginning.

Printing establishments such as yours were custodians of both news and knowledge during the eighteenth century. The printer's tools were the surest preservers of the past as well as architects of the future.

Today printers are proud of the traditions you served and helped establish. They do splendid work. You would delight in the technical advances. But modern printers find it necessary to specialize. Few are still "Benjamin-of-all-trade" capable of everything from "quill to bindery." So something has been lost—or misplaced—in our age of specialization.

Your curiosity would have made you a scientist of note even if you had never become a printer; but the printing profession, the contacts it brought, and the means it provided to communicate, served to broaden the scope of your scientific activities. The columns of the *Pennsylvania Gazette* had to be filled twice a week. You filled them with a wide-ranging correspondence on a multitude of subjects, especially the sciences.

The habit of curiosity never stopped. Throughout your life, you wanted to *know*, whatever the subject. In the eighteenth century, printing was an excellent profession for anyone with such an appetite. Printer's ink was the perfect beverage for appeasing, or at least pleasing the thirst to know.

Fate did well for you, Sir, when it put you to press. At the same time, it also did remarkably well for us.

We Are, &c.,

YOURS, THE PEOPLE

EARTH OR HELL?
A young angel of distinction being sent down to this world on some business, for the first time, had an old courier-spirit assigned him as a guide. They arrived over the seas of Martinico, in the middle of the long day of obstinate fight between the fleets of Rodney and De Grasse. When, through the clouds of smoke, he saw the fire of the guns, the decks covered with mangled limbs and bodies dead or dying; the ships sinking, burning, or blown into the air; and the quantity of pain, misery, and destruction the crews yet alive were thus with so much eagerness dealing round to one another, he turned angrily to his guide and said: "You blundering blockhead, you are ignorant of your business; you undertook to conduct me to the earth, and you have brought me into hell!" "No, sir," says the guide, "I have made no mistake; this is really the earth, and these are men. Devils never treat one another in this cruel manner; they have more sense, and more of what men (vainly) call humanity."
(To Joseph Priestley, June 7, 1782)

XVIII. The Long Arm of Science

QUOI BON L'ENFANT?

During the first exhibition of balloon ascensions in Paris, Franklin delivered the famous reply that has become a sort of whimsical credo for scientists engaged in researches for which immediate practical uses are not apparent.

Someone near Franklin in the crowd observing the ascension asked the inevitable question: "What good is it?"

Franklin immediately responded in his rough but ready French, "Eh, à quoi bon l'enfant qui vient de naître?"

What good is a newborn baby?

The *bon mot* was widely circulated because it was a clever answer, and because it had been made by the venerable Doctor Franklin. Time made it a cliché for the idea that science, whatever its immediate relevance, eventually found its own applications and justifications. Knowledge, whether clearly practical or not, was valuable for its own sake.

Other scientists picked up Franklin's response. *Michael Faraday*, his successor in the study of electricity, remembered the comment and used it in 1816:

Before leaving this substance, chlorine, I will point out its history, as
an answer to those who are in the habit of saying to every new fact,
"What is its use?" Dr. Franklin says to such, "What is the use of an
infant?" The answer of the experimentalist would be, "Endeavor to
make it useful." When Scheele discovered this substance it appeared
to have no use, it was in its infantine and useless state; but having
grown up to maturity, witness its powers, and see what endeavors to
make it useful have done.

Joseph Montgolfier was in Paris sixteen days after the signing
with Britain. He gave an ascension demonstration at Versailles for
the court. Several weeks later, Franklin observed the initial use of
balloons to raise human passengers. Not the first living passengers.
A previous liftoff for the royal family had sent aloft as airborne
creatures from earth, a duck, rooster, and sheep. On November 20,
1783 at Passy, *Pilatre de Rozier* and the *Marquis d'Arlandes*
crossed the threshold into space for man. They wore frock coats
and carried champagne, as the balloon rose approximately five
hundred feet, crossed the Seine, and landed safely in Paris. The
two flyers, first of the human race, hearing the sound of the river,
later admitted regret that they had not taken their flutes. The flyers were uninjured, but there was a tragedy in the course of the
landing. De Rozier's frock coat was accidently ripped, and he refused, naturally, to join the celebration parade in such a state of
disarray.

Otherwise it went splendidly. And Franklin was present. He was
present on December 1, 1783, when Jacques Charles who considered himself a disciple of Franklin's lifted off from the Garden
of the Tuileries and reached an altitude of two thousand feet. "Nature cannot say no to him!" exclaimed Franklin of Charles.

Franklin saw the balloon ascensions as the opening of another
door in man's power over matter, which he believed was a basic
criterion of progress. He considered that it obviously might become
a means of transport to relieve men from the tedium and hardship
of conventional travel modes. The military possibilities were also
clear, both for attack, and if men could be wise, for defense against
war itself. To Jan Ingenhousz he wrote:

It appears, as you observe, to be a discovery of great importance, and
what may possibly give a new turn to human affairs. Convincing sovereigns of the folly of wars may perhaps be one effect of it, since it
will be impracticable for the most potent of them to guard his domin-
ions.

Alas, sovereigns and their colleagues have too seldom been capable of Franklin's rational good sense in recognizing the impracticable until they have bludgeoned themselves to a bloody pulp with the facts.

In December 1783, air travel was used for a more beneficent purpose than combat. *John Jeffries* and *Jean-Pierre Blanchard* for the first time flew a balloon across the English Channel and symbolically delivered the first letter by air to Benjamin Franklin.

Later in Philadelphia, hampered by gout during the year of the Constitutional Convention, Franklin thought of a highly practical personal use for the balloon which he described in a letter to Jean-Baptiste Le Roy in France:

> ... sometimes wished I had brought with me from France a balloon sufficiently large to raise me from the ground. In my malady it would have been the most easy carriage for me, being led by a string held by a man walking on the ground.

Franklin's attitude to balloon ascension was that of a man whose long life, experience, and habit of hope had convinced him that sometimes a very unpromising baby could turn out fantastically well. His mind instinctively began leaping forward to postulate practical applications almost before the first balloon had safely landed. He would not have worried about the landing. Making it work effectively was simply a technical challenge. That could be handled. What to do with it, how to use it, that was the larger challenge.

It was a characteristic of his mind to be curious about everything, whether abstract or concrete, preposterous or serious, fanciful or genuine. Thus, the range of his scientific speculations tended to encompass anything he could see or sense, near and far. Oil and water, whirlwinds, shooting stars, seashells on mountains ... all were curiosities cheerfully to puzzle over, and perhaps find an answer or the beginnings of an answer.

CAST YOUR OIL UPON THE WATERS

It was said of Franklin that he could devise a serious and important experiment with the most unimpressive of materials and the simplest of apparatus. This was because the whole world, oceans, land, and the air above them, were his laboratories. His curiosity went to work when he looked at a rock or the sun or agitated water.

Simplicity was his touchstone in both life and authorship. "Simplify, Simplify," urged a later American philosopher, Thoreau. He could have learned such wisdom from Doctor Franklin. In his writing, Franklin worked hard to achieve simplicity. From Daniel Defoe's essays he learned to be *"as concise as possible,"* and to strive for a language that was "explicit, easy, free, and very plain." A lucid, tranquil, lighthearted Franklin style was the result, and it made his scientific writings works of art as well as science. *Sir Humphrey Davy* took time off from chemistry experiments and inventing the miner's safety lamp to write that Franklin's language "was almost as worthy of admiration as the doctrine" contained.

One among the multitudes of topics he considered was the effect of oil on water. During passage to Madeira in 1762, he noted that in a makeshift oil lamp with the oil above a lower layer of water, the water became agitated until the oil was burned away. Then the water was calm again.

Ashore, he carried oil in a hollow portion of his cane in order to experiment when an occasion presented itself. What would be the effect of oil on waters in commotion due to weather? " . . . the oil, though not more than a teaspoonful, produced an instant calm over a space several yards square." With his trick cane, he also performed water calming "magic" to amuse his companions when confronted with a stream made choppy by the wind.

He remembered that the Roman Pliny had recorded the use of oil by the seamen of ancient times to still ocean waves in a storm. But Pliny, being "ancient," was not taken seriously. Writing to *Dr. Brownrigg* on November 7, 1773, he made a point about tolerance for all legitimate sources of learning: ". . . it has been of late too much the mode to slight the learning of the ancients. The learned, too, are apt to slight too much the knowledge of the vulgar."

The puzzle of oil and agitated water was one that neither the learned nor the vulgar could answer. He had to study the matter carefully himself. He was surprised to note the "sudden, wide, and forcible spreading of a drop of oil on the face of water."

It seems as if a mutual repulsion between its particles took place as soon as it touched the water . . . the quantity of this force, and the distance to which it will operate, I have not yet ascertained; but I think it is a curious enquiry, and I wish to understand whence it arises.

He decided that because of a mutual repulsion between the particles of oil, and no attraction between oil and water, "oil dropped on water will not be held together by adhesion to the spot whereon it falls; it will not be imbibed by the water; it will be at liberty to expand itself." When this occurs, the wind "blowing over water thus covered with a film of oil, cannot easily *catch* upon it, so as to raise the first wrinkles, but slides over it, and leaves it smooth." "Wrinkles" are the "elements of waves" and when the wind is frustrated in its efforts to raise them, water is calmed. This might be useful to ships in trouble as Pliny had claimed for the ships of antiquity. Writing in a century when the vast oceans seemed untouchable by the pollutions of man, Franklin was oblivious for the time being that oil on water might calm the waves and yet stifle the life beneath them.

His letter to Dr. Brownrigg on the use of oil to calm water was printed in the *Transactions* of the Royal Society after its presentation on June 2, 1774. All hesitation was gone at the Royal Society concerning the experiments and speculations of Benjamin Franklin. A quick hearing was automatic for any contributions from the scientist who captured and controlled lightning, and who was not shy about seeking answers to other terrifying natural forces.

WHIRLWINDS AND WATERSPOUTS

On February 4, 1753, Franklin continued a correspondence with *Dr. John Perkins* of Boston concerning those impressive mysteries, waterspouts and whirlwinds. Both earned Franklin's careful attention over many years, and he devoted considerable space in his scientific writings to their explication. In response to his earlier comments on the subject, Dr. Perkins had entered a number of objections; and Franklin readily answered with thanks.

FOOT OUT DISPELS THE GOUT
You inquired about my gout, and I forgot to acquaint you, that I had treated it a little cavalierly in its two last accesses. Finding one night that my foot gave me more pain after it was covered warm in bed, I put it out of bed naked; and, perceiving it easier, I let it remain longer than I at first designed, and at length fell asleep leaving it there till morning. The pain did not return, and I grew well . . . this method requires to be confirmed by more experiments, before one can conscientiously recommend it. I give it you, however, in exchange for your receipt of tartar emetic; because the commerce of philosophy as well as other commerce, is best promoted by taking care to make returns.
(To Alexander Small, July 22, 1780)

Nothing certainly, can be more improving to a searcher into nature, than objections judiciously made to his opinion, taken up, perhaps, too hastily: for such objections oblige him to restudy the point, consider every circumstance carefully, compare facts, make experiments, weigh arguments, and be slow in drawing conclusions.. And hence a sure advantage results; for he either confirms a truth, before too lightly supported; or discovers an error, and receives instruction from the objector.

Considering his friend's objections, Franklin hopes they may "sift out the truth between us." There was a great amount of truth to deal with since Franklin had read the extensive literature on the subject and observed more. He had studied whirlwinds and their tendency to form a whirl of air about a vacuum, shaped "like a speaking trumpet, its big end upwards." His meteorology observations had helped him understand the prevailing winds and the reasons for aberrations, as dramatically demonstrated in whirlwinds. The anatomy of waterspouts was equally fascinating.

"Whirlwinds generally arise after calms and great heats," he noted. The same is true of waterspouts. Thus both are more frequent in warm latitudes. "The wind blows every way towards a whirlwind, from a large space around." It was Franklin's thesis from observation, reflection, and reading, that whirlwinds and waterspouts were caused by the same interaction of forces involving heat, the earth's rotation, and local climatic conditions. The difference, still to be proved, was that while whirlwinds could be of the ascending or descending variety, waterspouts seemed exclusively to ascend. "I have not met with any accounts of spouts, that certainly descended; I suspect they are not frequent."

THE SCIENCE OF STARTING TO MAKE SOAP
Set a leach or leaches that will contain eighteen bushels of ashes and one bushel of stone lime two hogsheads will do they must be very tight made clean a hole bored in the bottom near the chine but not close, nor near a seam in the head, with a large tap-borer, fit a pine plug to prevent its leaking. Let your leach be set high enough to set a tub under and with a very small descent towards the tap, surround the hole inside with bricks leaving a passage between for the lye to run and lay more bricks over or a flat stone on part of a barrel head to prevent the ashes pressing & some light sticks around also a handful of hay that will cover the bottom but thickest about the tap to keep the lye clear as possible . . . lay with a small descent towards the middle then fill with water till the water stands on the top and let them stand ten or twelve days. Draw off your first run of lye & fix your copper over night see that your lye is strong enough to bare an egg . . .
                    (Part of the Recipe for Crown Soap from Jane Mecom to her Brother Benjamin at his request)

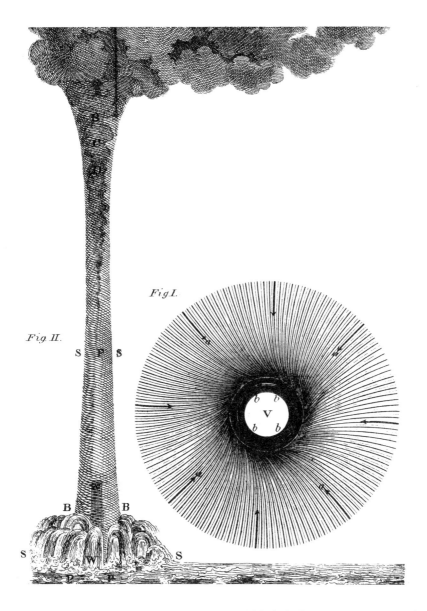

Figure I Shows the ground plan of a whirlwind. Between a a a a and b b b b I suppose a body of air, condensed strongly by the pressure of the currents moving towards it, from all sides without, and by its centrifugal force from within, moving round with prodigious swiftness ... it is this whirling body of air between a a a a and b b b b that rises spirally; by its force it tears buildings to pieces, twists up great trees by the roots, &c ...

Figure II is to represent the elevation of a waterspout, wherein I suppose P P P to be the cone, at first a vacuum, till W W, the rising column of water, has filled so much of it. S S S S, the spiral whirl of air, surrounding the vacuum, and continued higher in a close column after the vacuum ends in the point P, till it reaches the cool region of the air. B B, the bush described by Stuart, surrounding the foot of the column of water.

One of the questions posed by Dr. Perkins was why, if water was carried into the clouds by waterspouts, salt rains did not result. Franklin's theory was that when water containing salt was raised, the water and salt quickly separated. The water adhered to particles of air, and the salt fell back to the sea again.

> So the water quits the salt, and embraces the air; but air will not embrace the salt, and quit the water, otherwise our rains would indeed be salt, and every tree and plant on the face of the earth be destroyed, with all the animals that depend on them for subsistence.

Why was this so?

"It has pleased the goodness of God so to order it."

He gave the answer of a scientist who could not at the moment answer why. Variations on the same answer are still used, of course. "That's just the way it is," is another method of saying the same. Einstein credited a celestial force he called the "Old One" for universal order.

In his letter to Dr. Perkins, as if sensing that some of his hypotheses were sufficiently intrepid to need support from "Higher Authority," Franklin added his own defense for frankness, if not for accuracy: "If my hypothesis is not the truth itself it is at least as naked for I have not, with some of our learned moderns, disguised my nonsense in Greek, clothed it in algebra or adorned it with fluxions. You have it in *puris naturalibus*."

Franklin relished the process of manufacturing hypotheses. That was one of the better games of science. And he could engage in the sport to his heart's content with whirlwinds and waterspouts, which would go on whirling whatever theories were addressed to them.

Actually, his speculations on the whole were broadly correct. He identified whirlwinds and waterspouts as related phenomena. This is acceptably accurate since waterspouts are thought to be due to sea tornadoes. He reasoned convincingly that both must be

SAILORS PROVERBALIZE ON MEAT AND COOKS
The most disagreeable thing at sea is the cookery; for there is not, properly speaking, any professional cook on board. The worse sailor is generally chosen for that purpose, who for the most part is equally dirty. Hence comes the proverb used among the English sailors, that God sends meat, and the Devil sends cooks.
(Precautions to be Used by Those Who are About to Undertake a Sea Voyage)

caused by convective currents set in motion through the violence with which heated surface air could be forced upward by colder, heavier air descending.

On these subjects as on others, his contemporaries made him their official expert. People noting anything special in waterspouts or anything meteorologically unusual in whirlwinds reported to Benjamin Franklin. When the answers to peculiarities involving wind movements were needed, Franklin was automatically consulted.

Cadwallader Colden in 1754 noted his personal failure to receive satisfaction "from the attempts of others on this subject." He told Franklin that "it deserves then your thoughts, as a subject in which you may distinguish yourself and be useful."

Colden, reflecting on the wind and its relationship to hot and cold air masses, thought Franklin also was the scientist to follow up a question in physics that would be controversial and puzzled over until the twentieth century: Is there an invisible elastic medium filling the universe and serving as a substance for transporting heat, cold, and light? In the twentieth century Einstein would eliminate the fluid and establish time as a more meaningful dimension, but in the eighteenth century it was a century and a half too early for the Theory of Relativity.

"I agree with you," Franklin wrote to Colden, "that it seems absurd to suppose that a body can act where it is not. I have no idea of bodies at a distance attracting or repelling one another without the assistance of some medium, though I know not what the medium is, or how it operates." His uncertainty was closer to the truth than the certainties of those who insisted dogmatically on "ether."

Franklin felt as Colden did that problems such as whirlwinds and waterspouts were important matters of study. Nor could he abandon eighteenth century rationalism and conceive a universe without an elastic fluid holding it all together. Eighteenth century logic needed a fluid, and there would have to be a time and a science less committed to formal logic before a less mechanistic view of the universe might be conceived and accepted.

Franklin was a man of his age; but in a larger sense than most of his contemporaries, he was a man of all ages. The scientific revolutions of the twentieth century would have earned his attention, his arguments, and finally his complacent acceptance. He was always optimistic about the truth and had no fear of it, whether in waterspouts or the mystical mechanics of the outer stars.

SHOOTING STARS

His correspondents sought his views on many subjects, assuming that the conqueror of lightning could easily be master of any topic. Shooting stars, for instance.

In answering a request for information, he had to admit knowing little about them, but he was willing to theorize.

> I imagine them to be passes of electric fire from place to place in the atmosphere, perhaps occasioned by accidental pressures of a non-electric circumambient fluid, and so by propulsion, or elicited by the circumstance of a distant quantity *minus* electrified, which it shoots to supply, and becomes apparent by its contracted passage through a non-electric medium.

The "shoots" as he called them develop as a result of the "usual commotions and interchanges" of earth's atmosphere. They are an aspect of the always active electric fire present everywhere.

"I believe I have now said enough of what I know nothing about," he concluded his report on the shoots, "If it should serve for your amusement, or any way oblige you, it is all I aim at, and shall, at your desire, be always ready to say what I think, as I am sure of your candor."

More was left to be said concerning shoots, and Franklin knew it. But he had the pleasure of seaming together an explanation which if not true was at least plausible.

The peril, of course, with a scientist of Franklin's stature was that even his mistaken conclusions would be accepted as natural truth. There is evidence, as in his unhesitating admissions that he was uninformed on various subjects, that he tried to guard against such acceptance. He sought to encourage learning, not to camouflage it.

Always the teacher, what he most wanted was to stimulate other scientists into seeking fuller explanations as a result of his own preliminary observations.

BIFOCALS

A problem often encountered by people, old and young, including this author, is that of seeing clearly with myopic eyes at a distance as well as close up. The same spectacles that serve one need, may not serve another.

Franklin had the problem. Unlike most men with an affliction, and no solutions available, he did not choose to grin and bear it with all the equanimity he could muster. He chose to do something about it. Franklin could not see as well as he would like. So he invented bifocals.

He explained the new invention graphically as part of a long letter to *George Whately*, a London economist, on May 23, 1785. Franklin jested with his "dear old friend" concerning the problems of age. Whatley was "rising seventy-five" while Franklin was "rising (perhaps more properly falling) eighty." He wrote of an old man's wishes, including that of outliving the gout and the stone; yet recognized the folly of wishing. "Things happen, after all, as they will happen."

Wishing would serve little purpose. Doing, on the other hand, could sometimes stimulate happenings in the right direction. The urge to see had prompted Franklin to do something, and he informed his friend of the matter.

> I imagine it will be found pretty generally true that the same convexity of glass through which a man sees clearest and best at the distance proper for reading, is not the best for greater distances. I therefore had formerly two pair of spectacles which I shifted occasionally, as in travelling I sometimes read, and often wanted to regard the prospects. Finding this change troublesome, and not always sufficiently ready, I had the glasses cut, and half of each kind associated in the same circle, thus,

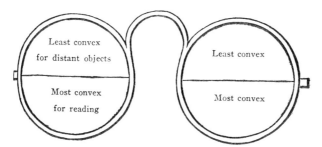

> By this means, as I wear my spectacles constantly, I have only to move my eyes up or down, as I want to see distinctly far or near, the proper glasses being always ready.

One hundred and ninety years after Benjamin Franklin wrote those words about his brilliantly simple and eminently useful invention, the words are copied by the author wearing similarly constructed glasses. Adjustments from one glass to the other are made automatically without reflection. Those who wear bifocals today doubtless give few thoughts to the inventor of this instrument for their visual liberation. But Franklin made the first pair and wore them.

In addition to reading, they were valuable in France at the sacred ritual of eating. With the "most convex" glass he could see what he was consuming. With the "least convex" he could see the people opposite. "And when one's ears are not well accustomed to the sounds of a language, a sight of the movements in the features of him that speaks helps to explain; so that I understand French better by help of my spectacles."

The glasses were essential, because without them he wrote that he could not "distinguish a letter even of large print." They could also be considered essential for identification purposes. Although there are many pictures representing him without glasses at various stages of his life, the classic picture of Benjamin Franklin that occupies an immortal place in the memory of mankind shows him with a gentle smile, equally close to seriousness and laughter, and with the glasses in position. The glasses are part of the memory portrait, impossible to revise, and therefore necessary.

Carl Van Doren described Franklin as he looked in Paris about the time he invented bifocals. "Some of his compatriots thought him lavish, and he himself said in June 1782 that frugality was 'a virtue I never could acquire in myself.' But, economical for his country, he lived more plainly than any other ambassador in Paris. His sober unembroidered brown coat, with a fur collar in cold weather, became almost his uniform. He carried his crab-tree stick wherever he went, and always wore glasses."

His simple dress in Paris also has become a permanent part of the world's memory. There are portraits showing an elegant Franklin, the Sumner portrait of Franklin at twenty, and the Martin portrait of Franklin at sixty; but such portraits are history, not emotional human memory. Memory has him in his modest Quaker garb, and always wearing the glasses of his own invention.

DAYLIGHT SAVING TIME

In the United States when a historical event such as a centennial anniversary is celebrated in the summer, it is usually one hour off the original historical timing. The blame can in part be assigned, where else, to Benjamin Franklin. The United States and many other countries apply the formula of "Spring Forward, Fall Back" to their clocks and call it Daylight Saving Time.

Franklin introduced the idea when he wrote his tongue-in-cheek

1784 essay, "An Economical Project." The essay expatiated concerning the great savings in candles if people would only get up earlier. In the *Autobiography* he wrote about summer observations in London that may have led, years later, to the origin of Daylight Saving Time.

> For in walking thro' the Strand and Fleet Street one morning at 7 a clock I observ'd there was not one shop open tho' it had been daylight and the sun up above three hours. The inhabitants of London choosing voluntarily to live much by candlelight, and sleep by sunshine; and yet often complain a little absurdly, of the duty on candles and the high price of tallow.

"An Economical Project" was one of the pieces he wrote in his house at Passy for Madame Brillon, Madame Helvétius, and others he wished to amuse in Paris. The essay was addressed "To the Authors of the Journal of Paris" and emphasized that Franklin, being accidentally awakened at six one morning, found it "extraordinary that the sun should rise so early." He assured those who had never in their lives so much as glimpsed the sun before noon, that with his own eyes he had seen the sun not only up but giving light as soon as it arose. He admitted it was difficult to find anyone in Paris who would believe him. But he was certain of his facts and calculated the economies that would result if the people of Paris used sunshine instead of candles, by rising when the sun rises instead of sleeping until noon.

Calculating 7 hours of candle burning time for each of the 183 nights between March 20th and September 20th, there were 1,281 hours, at half a pound of wax and tallow per hour, for the 100,000 population, or 64,050,000 pounds of candles, for a total cost of 96,-075,000 livres which could be saved by getting up with the light and sleeping with the dark. "I believe all who have commonsense," wrote the public benefactor, "as soon as they have learnt from this paper that it is daylight when the sun rises, will contrive to rise with him, and, to compel the rest."

Franklin consoled those who adopted his suggestion with the promise that it would be easier after the first two or three days, for *"ce n'est que le premier pas qui coute.* Oblige a man to rise at four in the morning, and it is more than probable he will go willingly to bed at eight in the evening."

With his usual modesty, Franklin did not want credit or reward for his discovery that the sun gives light as soon as it rises, even though the fact obviously was unknown to the moderns, especially

Parisians. It could not have been known, or such a sensible people as the Parisians would not have "lived so long by the smoky, unwholesome, and enormously expensive light of candles, if they had really known that they might have had as much pure light of the sun for nothing."

It was satire, but serious; and Franklin sincerely believed that other men, not necessarily himself, should make use of sunlight more intelligently. In the modern world, he would, we can speculate, be in the forefront of the scientific effort to develop practical ways to use solar energy. As for his own hours, they were too full and to irregular for a personal attendance at the daily rising of the sun. But then, of course, it was the business of a philosopher to pass along good advice, not necessarily to take it. This practical scheme, like others of Benjamin Franklin's, the world needed a little time to carry out. When implemented, it was somewhat more timidly than the philosopher intended, and for a reason that would not have delighted him. During World War I most countries began the practice of putting clocks ahead one hour during spring, summer, and autumn months for the logical reason Franklin had suggested, *to save fuel*. In Great Britain, where *William Willett* in 1907 suggested "Summer Time" to provide longer evenings, the practice of advancing clocks an hour began officially on May 21, 1916. Daylight saving was instituted in the United States during World War I, but after the war was used only sporadically across America on a state and community basis chiefly because the cows didn't like it. Apparently Franklin was right about it becoming easier, even for livestock, since daylight saving in the twentieth century gradually became a permanent national custom for the United States as well as other countries.

Franklin's "Economical Project" was not an isolated contribution to the science of economics. He was quite active as both writer and student in economic areas. From his youth he opposed Negro slavery in America on economic as well as humanitarian grounds, proving arithmetically that the labor of slaves "can never be so cheap here as the labor of working men in Britain." Depending on slaves, enfeebled their white owners, made white children "proud, disgusted with labor, and being educated in idleness, are rendered unfit to get a living by industry." Slavery undermined and debilitated the character of owners while being economically unprofitable in comparison with free labor.

Franklin also thought and wrote extensively on currency, agriculture, manufacturing, free trade (he favored it), &c. He may, while in London, have been consulted by Adam Smith and contributed to his *Wealth of Nations*. Deborah Logan in an 1829 letter noted that Franklin had informed Dr. Logan that "Adam Smith, when writing his 'Wealth of Nations,' was in the habit of bringing chapter after chapter as he composed it, to himself, Dr. Price, and others of the literati; then patiently hear their observations, and profit by their discussion and criticism—even sometimes submitting to write whole chapters anew, and even to reverse some of his propositions."

When his friend George Whately published his *Principles of Trade*, Franklin was believed to have participated certainly in the thinking and possibly in the composition. The Whately work detailed for English and Colonial readers the origin of the phrase *"Laissez-faire"* which became and remains a fundamental economic doctrine.

When Colbert, French diplomat of the seventeenth century, asked the merchants what he should do to promote commerce, they answered with three words: *"Laissez-nous faire."* Let us alone.

This phrase, as well as the other French expression, *pas trop gouverner*, warning governments not to govern *too* much, were in general supported by Franklin and effectively popularized by him. Economics, that benign confusion still struggling to become a science, assumed its modern directions in the eighteenth century, with Franklin as one of the surveyors and mapmakers for the way ahead.

Franklin's economic views combined with his political views in accord with the Lockean precept that men have certain natural rights, including "the mutual preservation of their lives, liberties, and estates, which I call by the general name, property." Those natural rights took precedence over manmade laws, and *in extremis* justified disobedience and revolution. Natural rights might be in part set aside to achieve civil rights, but if civil rights were abused, natural rights again applied with full force. In *Plain Truth*, Franklin warned that "Protection is as truly due from the government to the people, as obedience from the people to the government." The statement seems innocent enough, but what it implied frightened Thomas Penn into declaiming that such dangerous ideas were "not fit to be in the heads of the unthinking multitude."

But Franklin was part of the multitude, and he was thinking. Eventually, together with others, he began to think that governments must exist for the people, not the people for governments. The principle of *pas trop gouverner* was used to impose the politics of revolution and the economics of freedom. Daylight savings expanded into life savings, and not even the cows complained.

CORN

Agriculture and what the earth did with seeds inevitably attracted the scientific attention of Benjamin Franklin. The Colonists had virtually an entire fertile continent to cope with, and agriculture would be the first and principal means of conquering the continent. Guns could subdue natives. Only agriculture could subdue the land. Franklin, Washington, and Jefferson belonged to the Philadelphia Society for Promoting Agriculture, whose motto was "Venerate the Plough."

In one of his economic papers, *Positions to be Examined, Concerning National Wealth*, Franklin wrote that a nation could acquire wealth by war (robbery), by commerce (cheating), or by agriculture which was the only *honest* way. In 1766 for the *London Chronicle*, he began a defense of agriculture with these words: "I am one of the class of people that feeds you all, and at present is abused by you all; in short, I am a *farmer*." There are indications in Franklin's writings that he cherished the familiar dream of many city people, to escape the hurly-burly of town and live on a farm. In Franklin's case, agriscience might have been given an early push forward if circumstances had allowed him to concentrate his scientific talents and insight on the challenges of growing food.

Even with little time to spare, he still applied himself to a variety of agricultural topics and became an expert on such matters as corn, the growing, cooking, and marketing of it. European farmers first arriving in North America tended to "despise and neglect the culture of maize, or Indian corn; but, observing the advantage it affords their neighbours, the older inhabitants, they by degrees get more and more into the practice of raising it; and the face of the country shows, from time to time, that the culture of that grain goes on visibly augmenting."

He knew about hominy and how to make it. The ripe, hard grains were to be soaked overnight, then pounded in a mortar with a wooden pestle so that "the skin of each grain is by that means skinned off, and the farinaceous part left whole, which, being boiled, swells into a white soft pulp." The corn expert could report authoritatively that the result was delicious when eaten with milk, butter, and sugar. If corn were ground into a fine meal, it could be boiled into a hasty-pudding, called *bouilli*, resembling what the Italians call *polenta*.

Six to eight ounces per day of parched corn, he noted, could sustain an Indian in hard travel. How do you parch corn? You fill an iron pot with sand, put it on the fire; and when very hot you mix in two or three pounds of grain. "Each grain bursts and throws out a white substance of twice its bigness." A wire sieve is used to separate the sand which is returned to the pot for another parching. The result of the parching sounds like what is needed, with a little butter, for a double-feature at the Rialto. But there is still one more step for this popped corn. It is pounded to a powder in mortars, sifted, and is then ready for the long trail.

> The flour of *maize*, mixed with that of wheat, makes excellent bread, sweeter and more agreeable than that of wheat alone.

Benjamin Franklin, historians take note, liked cornbread.

> To feed horses, it is good to soak the grain twelve hours; they mash it easier with their teeth, and it yields them more nourishment.

> The stalks, pressed like sugar-cane, yield a sweet juice, which, being fermented and distilled, yields an excellent spirit; boiled without fermentation, it affords a pleasant syrup.

Corn liquor and corn syrup!

Franklin invested in agricultural properties, experimented in mulching and natural fertilization. He tried proportional crop control, watched the results, and corresponded with Jared Eliot on the subject, even in the midst of his electrical experiments. He knew the vital importance of agriculture to America and the world and wanted the subject taught in the academy he was helping to create in Philadelphia. In agriculture as in other arenas of natural philosophy, men had to be made aware of and receptive to new ideas.

In 1747 he wrote to Jared Eliot of the problem:

> Sir:—I have perused your two essays on field husbandry, and think the public may be much benefited by them; but, if the farmers in your neighborhood are as unwilling to leave the beaten road of their ancestors as they are near me, it will be difficult to persuade them to attempt any improvement. Where the cash is to be laid out on a probability of a return, they are very averse to the running any risk at all, or even expending freely, where a gentleman of a more public spirit has given them ocular demonstration of the success.

Franklin indulged his appetite for agricultural experiments with a three hundred acre farm at Burlington, New Jersey. This took the form of improving it "in the best and speediest manner." He studied the land to choose the seeds best suited for particular soils, ditched and drained a pond to reclaim land, and measured results with care ("I have found by experiment, that a bushel of clean chaff of timothy or Salem grass will yield five quarts of seed.")

From his account to Eliot of the experiments at Burlington, the conclusion is tempting that if Benjamin Franklin had been allowed to follow one of his inclinations to become a farmer, a "green revolution" would have paralleled the American Revolution.

SEA SHELLS ON MOUNTAINS
AND THE GIFT OF A TOOTH

"It is certainly the *wreck* of a world we live on!" he wrote to Jared Eliot on July 16, 1747. Franklin was excited about the fact that the strata of sea shells, clearly marked in solid rocks, had been found many places, including near the summits, through the Appalachian Mountains. Specimens of the "sea shell rocks" had been "broken off near the tops of these mountains, brought and deposited in our library as curiosities."

The antiquity of earth's rocks and the innumerable creatures that had left evidences of their lives in those rocks continued to fascinate Franklin with each new discovery through the eighteenth century.

In 1768 he was writing to *Abbé Chappe* about the skeletons of thirty elephant-like creatures found near the Ohio River.

> I sent you sometime since, directed to the care of M. Molini, a bookseller near the Quay des Augustins, a tooth that I mention'd to you when I had the pleasure of meeting with you at the Marquis de Courtanvaux's. It was found near the River Ohio in America, about 200 leagues below Fort Du Quesne, at what is called the Great Licking Place, where the earth has a saltish taste that is agreeable to the buffaloes & deer, who come there at certain seasons in great numbers to lick the same.

Grinding knobs on the jaws of the mammal skeletons were not found on elephants. This suggested beasts with carnivorous habits; but Franklin reasoned that the animals, like elephants, were probably "too bulky to have the activity necessary for pursuing and taking prey." He thought the knobs "might be as useful to grind the small branches of trees, as to chaw flesh."

One discovery, in April, 1782, at a limestone quarry near Paris, required a considerable suspension of disbelief. Workmen, presumably both sober and honest, had reported finding toads concealed alive in ancient limestone. Franklin with Monsieur Chaumont saw the toads, one dead, but another for the moment sassy with life. If concealed in the inaccessible limestone until the quarriers came, the toads would be thousands of years old. Franklin didn't close his mind to the possibility.

Soon the living toad appeared dead as well, but when it and its companion were put in a wine bottle to preserve them, the spirits again revived the one that had been alive. "He flounced about in it very vigorously for two or three minutes, and then expir'd."

"It is observed, that animals who perspire but little," Franklin concluded, "can live long without food ... Toads shut up in solid stone, which prevents their losing any thing of their substance, may perhaps for that reason need no supply; and being guarded against all accidents, and all the inclemencies of the air and changes of the season, are, it seems, subject to no diseases, and become as it were immortal."

Immortal, that is, until excessively inspired with the spirits of wine on very, very empty stomachs.

THE LONG ARM

Franklin's inventiveness did not wane with the years. In 1785 when he was nearly eighty, expediency again led him to a practical innovation as it had in the case of bifocals. Gout made it impossible to be physically agile, but his brain was agile as ever.

He was back at his house on Market Street in Philadelphia trying to find a convenient disposition for a library of four thousand books. Arranging so many books inevitably meant some had to go on high shelves. Franklin could no longer climb ladders or leap like a gazelle to get them down. He applied logic to the problem and devised an answer: *The Long Arm.*

On January 26, 1786, he sent a description of the device to Jonathan Williams in Boston. Williams was the young friend who had helped him with scientific observations and sea temperature recordings during his 1785 voyage home from France.

THE FRUGAL MRS. FRANKLIN
Frugality is an enriching virtue; a virtue I never could acquire myself; but I was once lucky enough to find it in a wife, who thereby became a fortune to me. Do you possess it? If you do, and I were twenty years younger, I would give your father one thousand guineas for you. I know you would be worth more to me as a ménagère, but I am covetous, and love good bargains.
(To Miss Alexander, June 1782)

Noting in his description the inconvenience of ladders or steps for old men "their heads being sometimes subject to giddinesses," he had remedied the matter with another "simple machine."

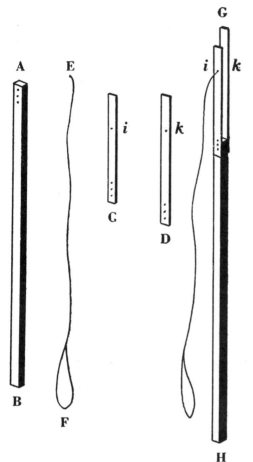

AB, the **Arm**, *is a stick of pine, an inch square and 8 feet long. C, D, the* Thumb *and* **Finger**, *are two pieces of ash lath, an inch and a half wide, and a quarter of an inch thick. These are fixed by wood screws on opposite sides of the end A of the arm AB; the finger D being longer and standing out an inch and half farther than the thumb C. The outside of the ends of these laths are pared off sloping and thin, that they more easily enter between books that stand together on a shelf. Two small holes are bored through them at i, k. EF, the sinew, is a cord of the size of a small goosequill, with a loop at one end. When applied to the machine it passes through the two laths, and is stopped by a knot in its other end behind the longest at k. The hole at i is nearer the end of the arm than that at k, about an inch. A number of knots are also on the cord distant three or four inches from each other.*

With such a recipe, anyone with the need and will should be able to make himself a Long Arm. Franklin noted that "All new tools require some practice before we can become expert in the use of them. This requires very little." The instrument is used by fitting the "finger and thumb" around the book desired, pulling the "sinew" cord EF which will cause the "finger and thumb" to pinch the book tightly enough to remove safely. "As it leaves the other books, turn the instrument a *quarter* round, so that the book may lie flat" as it is worked down to the hands by means of the successive knots on the "sinew."

Practice and experience proved that the Long Arm was excellent for duodecimo or octavo size books. Quartos and folios were too heavy, but Franklin suggests that those are or should be located on lower shelves for easier access. Furthermore, "the book taken down, may, when done with, be put up again into its place by the same machine."

The "machine" which Franklin considered of "practical utility" is still seen today in various stores, and even in those areas for which he specifically intended it, libraries.

WITHOUT BOUNDARIES

Anything in the natural world could command his attention. He would give liberally of his time during the months or years required to puzzle it through satisfactorily. In his sixties he was doing research in hydrodynamics, using boat models and miniature canals to check the relationship between depth of water and the speed of sailing craft.

During that same sexagenarian decade when most men of his age begin slowly subsiding or estivating into a torpor, he became curious about the Gulf Stream. That was when he persuaded his cousin, Nantucket Captain Timothy Folger, to record observations in and out of the Gulf Stream. Franklin himself took and recorded whatever facts he could from the durations of eclipses to temperatures of the sea whenever and wherever possible until his eighties.

He wanted to know whether ants and other insects held conversations. Did they have some process of thought and communication inaccessible to man because of his limited means of observation?

What about marine fossils at elevations thousands of feet above sea level? When had the mountains been raised above the sea, or when had the sea been above the mountains?

He recognized no boundaries in science. The questing mind could and should go anywhere... everywhere. It was a natural impulse and a natural right. The modern tendency for scientists of one type to turn back when close to the forbidden boundaries of another science... "I can't go in there, that's *chemistry*," moans the physicist... would have seemed impossible and ridiculous to Franklin. A neglect of duty. Truth was the only goal. No barricades were allowed.

He studied smoking chimneys and their waste. Then he invented a stove. He studied the problem of seeing, and invented bifocals. He needed a book without becoming a giraffe, and grew a longer arm. Agriculture, ventilation, disease, economics, the electrical fire, each had corridors of curious fact, new knowledge, and intriguing truth. So each_of the corridors, as far as he could, he wanted to explore.

                                                              1976
Dear Doctor Franklin, Sir,

Take heart, Sir, your tradition lives on, and pranks are still possible in Pennsylvania. The spirit of spoof survives there.

Your clear and present influence was unmistakable in events that took place during the summer of 1975 at the school you helped create, the University of Pennsylvania. The details were reported in a story by reporter James Wooten on July 20, 1975 for *The New York Times*. The *Times,* by the way, might startle you with its size and range of interests. A regiment of "pullers and beaters" would be needed to print an issue with the methods you had available for the *Pennsylvania Gazette.*

Pennsylvania Gazette is the name adopted for the University of Pennsylvania's monthly alumni magazine. Borrowed from your newspaper, of course.

The back cover of the *Gazette's* modern offspring contained a 1975 appeal in the form of an advertisement for "immediate reunion of the United States with England," followed by a vigorous "God Save the Queen!"

The advertisement was the inspiration of two young men you might claim as godchildren, Mr. John N. Ambrose and Mr. David A. Gambill, founders and only members of "The Committee for Reunion with England."

"The whole Bicentennial celebration was so—so vainglorious," said Mr. Ambrose, "we decided to pop a few balloons."

They succeeded. Ire was inspired. Subscriptions were cancelled. Editors were even reminded that *you* were one of the Founders of the University. The protesters were misguided if they think you would be upset by such a spoof. It would be entirely to your taste, a chuckle in the craw, and right down your alley. "Good way to wake up the affair," you probably would observe with a laugh.

You used the same method again and again to wake people up, and to amuse them in the process. Perhaps your theory was that if they could wake up laughing, they wouldn't so much mind being awake.

But seriously, on this matter of reunion with England, what do you think? Would they take us back? If so, would it be a case of the minnow swallowing the whale and in effect becoming its own dinner? Perhaps, on the whole, America and England are beter as they are. What is your view? Mr. Ambrose, Mr. Gambill, and the rest of us would still find it prudent to heed your suggestions.

We Are, &c.,
YOURS, THE PEOPLE

PROLIFIC IN THE SHADE OF WHOLESOME TREES

That the vegetable creation should restore the air which is spoiled by the animal part of it, looks like a rational system, and seems to be of a piece with the rest . . . We knew before, that putrid animal substances were converted into sweet vegetables, when mixed with the earth and applied as manure; and now it seems that the same putrid substances, mixed with the air, have a similar effect. The strong, thriving state of your mint in putrid air seems to show that the air is mended by taking something from it, and not by adding to it. I hope this will give some check to the rage of destroying trees that grow near houses, which has accompanied our late improvements in gardening, from an opinion of their being unwholesome. I am certain, from long observation, that there is nothing unhealthy in the air of woods; for we Americans have everywhere our country habitations in the midst of woods, and no people on earth enjoy better health, or are more prolific.

(To Joseph Priestley)

XIX. The Lasting Revolution

THE FRIENDS OF FRANKLIN

Perhaps the most critical measure of Franklin's contribution as a scientist is the extent of his influence on others, both in his own time and later.

His value in the eighteenth century in this respect stands out clearly. But youths in following generations who read about Benjamin Franklin, his electrical experiments, the celebrity they brought him among the ladies of Paris, and who decided that careers in science were for them, are not so easy to trace or count. We suspect they existed and exist now.

There is no doubt that Franklin's dedication to science combined with his eminence in many fields helped make science more respected and popular than before. Even more certainly, he gave the world an identifiable American scientist. With Franklin, American science first became internationally recognized. His influence brought American researchers to the attention of the Royal Society, and also the reverse. By his good offices, scientific knowledge journeyed across the Atlantic in both directions.

His associations formed a comprehensive biography of eighteenth century science. It was Franklin who encouraged English minister Joseph Priestley to concentrate on science. This led to Priestley's 1774 discovery of oxygen ("dephlogisticated air"), one of science's milestones.

At Lavoisier's laboratory in France, the printer-electrician from Philadelphia saw Priestley's work extended and the foundations of modern chemistry established block by block.

Through Lavoisier, Franklin met *E. I. du Pont de Nemours,* a scientist to whom he wrote through the years. In 1770 he planted a thought which may have dramatically contributed to the history of future Amrican commerce and industry. He expressed the wish that Du Pont and others of his friends in France "with their good ladies" could be settled in Philadelphia to "form a little happy society that would prevent my ever wishing again to visit Europe."

During the French Revolution, Du Pont acted on this "invitation" to emigrate to America. Later, back in France, he helped negotiate the Louisiana Purchase. That was the first great movement of the new country in the direction of continental expansion. Meanwhile, Du Pont's sons in 1802 started a little business, a powder mill, on the banks of the Delaware River. The Du Pont Company flourished. It grew. And grew. When last seen, it was still growing.

Du Pont became part of what might be called the Lasting Revolution of the eighteenth century.

Three revolutions took place during the century of Benjamin Franklin. Two were essentially political involving the natural rights of man and the struggle against congealed old orders. Franklin helped lead one, the American Revolution, and to influence the other, the French Revolution.

He was also involved in the Lasting Revolution, which affected the future of man as much or more than either political revolution.

Various dates have been suggested for the start of this Industrial or Scientific Revolution in the eighteenth century. March 1747 when Franklin began reporting his electrical experiments is one of them. But *June 1775* seems to have special symbolic relevance for the beginning of the third revolution.

June 1, 1775 was the date of partnership between *James Watt,* inventor of an improved, practical, and effective steam engine, and British industrialist, *Matthew Boulton.* Watt held a patent on a condensing steam engine that worked. Matthew Boulton owned the Soho Engineering Works in Birmingham, England. The Watt-Boulton partnership produced 496 steam engines. Many were used to pump out coal mines. Over three hundred provided power in factories for industrial production. Those successful engines were followed by thousands. This inaugurated what has become the longest lasting revolution in the history of man. It is still occurring and apparently permanent.

Ironically, June 1775 was important in both the Industrial and American Revolutions. Watt and Boulton that month united their scientific and financial resources. And on June 17th, the *Battle of Bunker's Hill* took place to warn the British without success that they were undertaking an impossible adventure in the American Plantations.

Long before either revolution, Franklin met Matthew Boulton in England. In 1759 on a tour of England with his son William, Franklin performed electrical experiments with Boulton in Birmingham. He also knew *William Small*, Scotch mathematician and physician, who like Boulton helped Watt make further refinements in the steam engine.

Perhaps no one, including the principals, appreciated the significance of the Lasting Revolution that began in 1775. Yet if it had not occurred, the meaning of the American Revolution would be different. Because of the Lasting Revolution, America was able to create a nation achieving levels of unparalleled well-being and power for a larger number of people than at any time previously in history.

Given the energy figures in America for 1975, Franklin could have quickly figured (as he did in the case of candle savings for France if rising with the sun became a habit) that the Lasting Revolution provides energy equal to over one hundred healthy and enthusiastic slaves working for each of America's more than two hundred million inhabitants. Such figures could be seen as vindicating his belief that human slavery is an economic as well as a humane mistake. The steam engine and its energetic successors have proved far more tractable and productive than poor creatures activated by whips.

Eventually Franklin saw to it that one of the collaborators in perfecting the steam engine, William Small, was invited to become the *Natural History Professor at William and Mary College in Virginia*. Small accepted, emigrated to Williamsburg, and there became an important influence on a rather special student, Thomas Jefferson. Jefferson's enthusiasm and hospitality for science could be traced to Professor Small. And Professor Small's presence in America could be traced to Benjamin Franklin.

THE PRESS OF STEAM

He did not live to see it, but as a scientist and life-long printer using the screw-type hand press, Franklin would have cheered the phase of the Lasting Revolution that was inaugurated November 29, 1814. On that date, *The Times* of London delivered the first newspaper "printed by steam power" on the flat-bed press with a revolving cylinder invented by *Frederick Koenig* and *Andrew Bauer* Steam power on the new press could produce approximately eleven hundred impressions an hour, more than four times better than the best that could be accomplished with strenuous effort on a hand press.

Once begun, there was no stopping progress. By 1827, engineers at *The Times, Applegarth and Cowper,* had perfected a press capable of four thousand impressions an hour. In 1848, Applegarth introduced a new press with vertical cylinders and vertical feeding that delivered eight thousand impressions per hour. It in turn was replaced by the Hoe revolving machine, and that by the Walter rotary press in 1868. And so on.

None of these advances would have surprised Franklin. He expected them, and would have been pleased by the confirmation.

On February 8, 1780, in a letter to Joseph Priestley, Franklin wrote the often-quoted words that made him the philosopher-prophet of the Lasting Revolution. He wrote prophetically of possibilities which still seem genuine, and some which have become dramatic realities. In the same letter he emphasized a particular limitation of man and science, which also is still regrettably with us.

> ...I always rejoice to hear of your still being employed in experimental researches into nature, and of the success you meet with. The rapid progress *true* science now makes, occasions my regretting sometimes that I was born so soon. It is impossible to imagine the height to which may be carried, in a thousand years, the power of man over matter. We may perhaps learn to deprive large masses of their gravity, and give them absolute levity, for the sake of easy transport. Agriculture may diminish its labor and double its produce; all diseases may by sure means be prevented or cured, not excepting even that of old age, and our lives lengthened at pleasure even beyond the antediluvian standard. O that moral science were in as fair a way of improvement, that men would cease to be wolves to one another, and that human beings would at length learn what they now improperly call humanity!

So spake, Franklin, the prophet of science, natural and moral.

Priestley was one of the scientists eventually drawn to America. After eight years as librarian and literary companion to Lord Shelburne, a position he was helped to accept by Franklin's charming exercise in "prudential algebra," Priestley settled at Birmingham where he could be near such friends as Boulton and Watt. But in the 1790's, when his championing of the French Revolution, an outgrowth of his support for the American Revolution, led to mob violence in the burning of his chapel and the ransacking of his home, Priestley, with his possessions and the work of years destroyed, took his family to America. Considering his long friendship with Benjamin Franklin it was natural that he should settle in Pennsylvania where he lived until his death in 1804.

Both scientists and science found their way to Pennsylvania because of Benjamin Franklin. His American Philosophical Society was one of the magnets, but his own enthusiasm was even more important.

BUGLE BOY

Benjamin Franklin was entangled in all the major revolutions of the eighteenth century. His role in the American Revolution and effect on the French Revolution are part of the popular Founding Father image. His contributions to the *Lasting Revolution of Science* are not as well known but may be even more significant.

In a June 1782 letter to Priestley, Franklin wrote wistfully of his desire to "recover the leisure to search with you into the works of nature."

The very fact that he esteemed science so highly, even when leisure could not be recovered as he wished, played a part in preparing and furthering the Lasting Revolution. It helped promote a climate in which more and more men were persuaded to set their superstitions aside and to depend on reason, observation, and experiment as surer means of reaching useful truth. It was only in such a climate that machine power could be developed to replace human power in production.

Franklin believed in the Lasting Revolution, And he repeatedly said so with all the authority of the man who had mastered electricity and conquered lightning (Franklin's biographer *Mason Weems* wrote that with "equal ease" he "could play the Newton or the Chesterfield, and charm alike the lightnings and the ladies."). People listened, the ordinary as well as the exceptional. When a man such as Franklin values something and insistently points at it, all the world watches. He pointed at the natural universe and marvelled, making himself one of the rare men qualified to call reveille for the minds of other men. When he did so, many of them awakened to see the sun rise. For the first time. But once it was seen there was no going back to darkness. An awakening came in Europe and America. Franklin was one of the buglers.

He managed the impressive achievement of doing electrical experiments and daring to manipulate the lightning without being burned alive as a warlock. The awakening was not overnight. It took time. Among some it is still in process. But gradually scientists were able to do their experiments without being smashed by superstitious neighbors worried about the reaction of easily angered gods. "Natural philosophy" came to be accepted or at least tolerated even by nervous theologians with presumably close personal pipelines to the brain cells of the divine. Maybe the gods weren't all that frightened of man's learning and using natural truth. Maybe they were even pleased, or at least amused.

He came to epitomize both hospitality for science and hospitality for freedom. Each was eagerly awaited at Benjamin Franklin's door, and the door was open. Perhaps they were the same visitor, and when they arrived only one bed was needed for the traveller's rest.

He asked men to do something difficult, but not impossible, to keep their minds alive and questioning. To keep their doors and windows open. To keep their pathways free from the blockades some men build to guard against the unfamiliar.

Science had to welcome the unfamiliar. It could not fear the unknown. Banishing fear was one of his functions, and he did it well. Even lightning could be controlled if approached carefully, cautiously, and imaginatively, without fear.

Science did not start in the eighteenth century. But it was continued, enlarged, and advanced with less fear to inhibit and slow it. Modern science actually began to take shape in the century before Franklin's birth. He was the beneficiary of the century that *Alfred North Whitehead* said had supplied an "accumulated capital of ideas."

Before the seventeenth century, the Scholastics, defending the views of the Mediaeval Church, insisted that reality should be accepted, right or wrong, for what *Aristotle* and the Church said it was.

This was not possible for Francis Bacon, John Locke, Isaac Newton, Robert Boyle in England, for Galileo and Giordano Bruno in Italy, for Rene Descartes in France, during the seventeenth century. It was not possible for their distinguished predecessor Nicola Copernicus during the sixteenth century. For each of them, scientific evidence challenging scholastic dogmas kept insisting on a hearing.

These men established the steel framework of modern science by choosing the precision of mathematics and the accuracy of experiment as their methods. Galileo followed Copernicus in proving that the earth could not be at the center of the universe like a king on a royal throne. Descartes sought a mathematical interpretation of nature and said, "Give me extension and motion, and I shall construct the universe."

With experiment as the method of science, each step became the prelude to the next. "Ideas will string themselves like ropes of onions," wrote Franklin to Jared Eliot. One advance led to the following advance, as certainly if not as imperturbably as gravity. Each idea felt incomplete until a later idea was attached.

Franklin's friend Lavoisier wrote, "I have imposed upon myself the law of never advancing but from the known to the unknown, of deducing no consequence that is not immediately derived from experiments and observations."

In that manner, with diligent care, the eighteenth century used the tools passed on by the seventeenth century: *experiment—mathematics—reason—proven fact.* Franklin and his friends took the accumulated capital they had received and made it multiply. Finding the right answers was the intellectual credo of the eighteenth century. It was their method of investing the capital of received ideas, and the earned interest was high.

This slow process was difficult to recognize while it was occurring. There was nothing dramatic about it like war or unmistakable like peace. This special sanity of science was the steady, plodding aspect of its method. So historian *Herbert J. Muller* could write that "the rise of science was the quietest as well as the profoundest revolution in history."

The seventeenth century broke free from the shackles of the scholastic past, and men began asking questions, observing, analyzing, experimenting. The eighteenth century added one more wrinkle, a new tradition of not accepting on faith, but of proving everything empirically from science to politics.

Ironically even the new tradition developed its true believers. By the twentieth century there came a growing inability to question anything with the authoritative label of "science." If an "expert" with the proper degrees and titles insists that "it must be so," then so it must be for those properly trained to swallow the properly baited hooks.

Franklin and his friends would regret such obedience and suggest that their Lasting Revolution needs a fresh injection of the approach to science that Rene Descartes called "systematic doubt." When Francis Bacon in his *Novum Organum Scientiarum* of 1620 advocated "the more perfect use of reason in the investigation of things," he did not mean that reason should be deified or treated as a pet dogmatism with wagging tail. He meant proving all things and holding fast the truth, which involved adding knowledge to knowledge like a gigantic patchwork quilt growing all the time as it passed on from searcher to searcher.

The danger has always been that reason and experiment not only can be used to establish facts but can be misused to prove guesses or to support doctrinaire positions, just as college science students can learn to go futilely through the motions by doing exercises backward from the answers.

This may have been what Franklin had in mind when he wrote to Priestley about the progress of *true* science with special emphasis on a troublesome four-letter word.

ELECTRIFYING

Benjamin Franklin had been part of history more than three decades when *Matthew Arnold* was born in 1822. More decades would pass before Arnold, as a British poet and critic, would write what was still true, "Franklin's is the weightiest voice that has yet sounded from across the Atlantic."

Now centuries have passed, and Franklin's voice is still not one that has been lost among the bric-a-brac of curious but irrelevant antiquity. From Constitution-writing to soap-making, from hominy to harmony, Franklin speaks to the point and the point is still with us, applicable alike to minds and lightning rods. For true effectiveness, neither should be blunted.

He tried to mine many scientific veins, perhaps too many for big strikes. Some of his guesses were inspired as when he came within whispers of the modern electron theory. Some were just exuberant hypotheses or inventions by a man too busy to keep digging for the deeper facts. In 1782 he wrote to the Abbé Soulavie with his view concerning the formation of the earth (when "the almighty fiat ordained gravity" the separate particles, confused and widely spread, would "move to their common centre"). In the letter he said, "You see I have given a loose to imagination; but I approve much more your method of philosophizing, which proceeds upon actual observation, makes a collection of facts, and concludes no further than those facts will warrant. In my present circumstances, that mode of studying the nature of the globe is out of my power, and therefore I have permitted myself to wander a little in the wilds of fancy."

Sometimes this was true, and sometimes the fancy itself came usefully close to that shy damosel, scientific fact. Yet once certainly he collected facts prodigiously, kept digging until he reached the mother lode, and earned all the applause his peers could muster. First class scientists have admitted that his work with electricity was first class science.

Even the dictionary acknowledges his contribution. The *Oxford English Dictionary* listing the first recorded use of "battery" in connection with electricity quotes Franklin (1748). "Electrify" is credited to Franklin (1747): "We electrify . . . a book that has a double line of gold round upon the covers."

The Lasting Revolution began with the steam engine, but eventually electricity became the real "open sesame" to the *modern world of multiplied power*. Franklin helped with the preliminary preparations. His work was essential. Someone had to do it before the lights could be turned on.

After a near shipwreck on one of his voyages, Franklin sent *a revealing message* to his wife: "Perhaps I should on this occasion vow to build a chapel to some saint; but . . . if I were to vow at all, it should be to build a lighthouse."

Franklin helped men understand electricity. With understanding, they learned to make it work beneficially, and thus houses were lighted all over the world, including the American Scott-Amundsen Base at the South Pole in its six month darkness.

He couldn't know these results when he worked on electricity. But he always hoped for and sought practical applications. The observation by historian *Marc Bloch* in this century is an echo from Benjamin Franklin: "It is undeniable that a science will always seem to us incomplete if it cannot, sooner or later, in one way or another, aid us to live better."

Benjamin Franklin did.

Dear Doctor Franklin, Sir,

Which are you?

We still don't know for certain. The best we can decide is that you are all of them, the entire convention of Benjamin Franklins, concentrated somehow in one person, yourself.

Perhaps when we reach that conclusion, it means we have given up trying to pin you down. But the question keeps coming back. If you were all the members of that multi-faceted, one man Junto of Franklins, which were you mainly?

Do you remember Jeremy Bentham, the English philosopher who admired you as a scientist and statesman? When Bentham died in 1832, as his will directed, he was dissected in the presence of his friends, and his skeleton was wired for permanent display at the Anatomical Museum of University College, London. Bentham wanted to prove with his bones a devotion to science and support of dissection for research.

Probably Philadelphia wasn't quite ready for such a gesture in 1790. But without going to Bentham's extreme, you did help in this matter of identification with the Himalayan collection of letters you preserved and the *Autobiography* which is generally accepted now as the first classic work in American literature.

You allowed us to see Benjamin Franklin full-fleshed. You opened the portals for a look far inside. But that makes it even harder to pin you down. Each of the Franklins stands out vigorously, clamoring insistently. Each says, "Choose me! I'm the true Ben." So it becomes impossible to choose.

Then we come at you another way. What do the various Franklins have in common? Say, that works better. One thing is plain, whatever the ups and downs of time, all the Franklins were receptive to change and new ideas. You became even more receptive with advancing years. Most men as they grow older turn conservative and shudder at new theories and innovations. Not the convention of Benjamin Franklins. You were more radical, to use a sturdy and stubborn word, at seventy and eighty than at twenty and thirty.

You became a revolutionist through the needs of the times. And once you had begun changing old orders, you seemed to decide that most old orders needed changing. Old orders like attics tended to mustiness without periodic airings. And you were a ventilation expert.

"Benjamin Franklin, Maker of Revolutions, apply at the New Printing-Office."

Could that be it, Sir, the central you, the Chairman of all the Franklins?

We Are, &c.,
YOURS, THE PEOPLE

THAT ETERNAL WELFARE QUESTION
For my own part, I am not so well satisfied of the goodness of this thing. I am for doing good to the poor; but I differ in opinion about the means. I think the best way of doing good to the poor is, not making them easy in poverty, but leading or driving them out of it. In my youth I travelled much, and I observed in different countries that the more public provisions were made for the poor, the less they provided for themselves, and, of course, became poorer. And, on the contrary, the less was done for them, the more they did for themselves, and became richer.

(London Chronicle, *1766*)

XX. A Lasting Revolutionist

ABLUTIONS IN AN ERA OF FLEAS

At the end, it should be emphasized that he had what the eighteenth century called "bottom." A gentleman was expected to have "bottom," and Benjamin Franklin had it. The term came from ships. It meant stability, keeping one's head in emergencies, solid.

He had "bottom," no doubt of it, but he was an American, not a gentleman. Make no mistake of that. Gentlemen allowed Britain to blunder into a confrontation with the Americans, which meant a confrontation with him, which meant trouble for gentlemen and Britain.

He took baths, both by air and water, loved them. The gentlemen of England seldom bathed in the eighteenth century. "I hate immersion," confessed Dr. Johnson. Scented powder was used in a long and continuing war against fleas. During the reign of George III, it was calculated that the British Army used six thousand five hundred tons of flour annually for powdering purposes.

There were no fleas on Benjamin Franklin, or powder.

Wigs and powder and fancy dress were all the style when he went to France seeking friends and funds for a little Revolution back home. He appeared in a marten-cap and simple, unvarying homespun he pridefully claimed were made complete by his good wife Deborah. *Was he wily or innocent, calculating or simple?* The French found the whole package irresistible and adored him to a woman. Men too.

Was he a bird lover or simply incurably frugal? Writing to Catherine Ray, with whom he may have had a brief love affair followed by a long and affectionate correspondence, he sensibly suggested that she should kill no more pigeons than she could eat.

Mark Twain pretended not to like him. Or maybe he didn't pretend. It was hard to tell with Mark. He accused Benjamin Franklin of a "vicious disposition" who "early prostituted his talents to the invention of maxims and aphorisms calculated to inflict suffering upon the rising generation of all subsequent ages."

That business of Franklin entering Philadelphia for the first time with only a couple of shillings wasn't so much when you examined it critically, according to Mark. "Anybody could have done it."

But what happened after that made the history books, which took Benjamin Franklin, not just anybody. Mark Twain probably knew that and was simply making a "funny."

Benjamin Franklin had a sense of humor, irony, and sadness too. Once he wrote that people are corrupt and venal because they accept money for their votes at every election. In a letter to Joseph Priestley on June 7, 1782, he said that the greater his knowledge of men, the greater his disgust with them. They enjoyed killing more than begetting, and he wasn't sure the species was worth preserving. There were tears and regrets in Benjamin Franklin.

There was also laughter. When Madame Helvétius complained of his failure to visit, he assured her that he was waiting till the nights were longer. And on another occasion a wise Quaker sought the philosopher's aid: "Friend Franklin, thou knowest everything. Canst thou tell me how I am to preserve my small beer in the backyard? My neighbors, I find, are tapping it." "Put a barrel of old Madeira by the side of it," instructed the Philosopher.

If he did not know everything, he did know a little about women, and was said to be democratically generous with his attentions. His tact was that from which legends often are made. When any lady requested assurances that he loved her the most, he graciously replied, "Yes, when you are nearest me, because of the force of your attraction."

Tact, keeping his temper, calm, and self-control were corner-stones in his technique with other men on the gaming fields of life. "Motionless and silent" he endured a verbal stomping from Wedderburn, the Solicitor-General of England. It was Franklin who came out of the encounter with the greatest credit, and with observers convinced he was the stronger man.

Thomas Jefferson was something of a pupil to Benjamin Franklin, and he wrote of the master: "It was one of the rules which, above all others, made Doctor Franklin the most amiable of men in society, 'never to contradict anybody.' If he was urged to announce an opinion, he did it rather by asking questions, as if for information, or by suggesting doubts."

That was Socrates' method, which made him such a gadfly to the authorities, they swatted him with hemlock. Benjamin Franklin took no hemlock. He did take occasional Madeira for the stomach's and the pleasure's sake.

Another pleasure was corresponding with ladies about science. They seemed to like it as well, perhaps believing as Franklin did that women and knowledge are not instinctive enemies, but indeed go naturally together. He was one of the first to dare seriously urging the "propriety of educating the female sex." He did not fear to encourage developing the abilities of women. Revolutionists were paid to take chances.

He also corresponded with scientists about science. Yet it wasn't about science, but about man and misery that he wrote at first on July 27, 1783 to Sir Joseph Banks, President of the Royal Society:

> I join with you most cordially in rejoicing at the return of peace. I hope it will be lasting, and that mankind will at length, as they call themselves reasonable creatures, have reason and sense enough to settle their differences without cutting throats; for, in my opinion, *there never was a good war or a bad peace.* What vast additions to the conveniences and comforts of living might mankind have acquired, if the money spent in wars had been employed in works of public utility! What an extension of agriculture, even to the tops of our mountains; what rivers rendered navigable or joined by canals; what bridges, aqueducts, new roads, and other public works, edifices, and improvements, rendering England a complete paradise, might have been obtained by spending those millions in doing good, which in the last war have been spent in doing mischief; in bringing misery into thousands of families, and destroying the lives of so many thousands of working people, who might have performed the useful labor!

Then he wrote prophetically about science: "Furnished as all Europe now is with academies of science, with nice instruments and the spirit of experiment, the progress of human knowledge will be rapid, and discoveries made, of which we have at present no conception. I begin to be almost sorry I was born so soon, since I cannot have the happiness of knowing what will be known one hundred years hence."

He was a toolmaker and the most eccentric of inventors.

His eccentricity was that he refused to make a profit from his inventions. For him the fun of doing it was pay a-plenty. He relished the thinking, toolmaking, and experimenting part. The rest was business. He had less interest in business than many have chosen to suppose. Business provided fertilizer for scientific plans.

COME WITH ME TO PHILADELPHIA AND WE WILL MAKE BEAUTIFUL EXPERIMENTS TOGETHER

He would have understood but not have completely agreed with a scientific colleague, *Sir Lawrence Bragg*, who wrote in a later century: "The fun in science lies not in discovering facts, but in discovering new ways of thinking about them."

He was satisfied, deep down, by both. He discovered facts (similarity of lightning and the Leyden spark, positive and negative electricity, the one-fluid nature of the electrical fire) and enjoyed it. But he found time for the other thing too, allowing his thoughts to lope freely through time and space, picking up stardust on the way.

He used rudimentary equipment to prove the boldest of surmises about one of nature's most powerful and terrifying displays. And he lived to tell the tale. When Franklin's tale was heard, the world took a close took at him and liked what it saw. From then on he was an officially recognized great man, and he could always make a living on the banquet circuit if things got tough in the printing business.

He recommended the first school for Negroes in America, frightening some who knew the dangers of education for what *John Quincy Adams* called the "lawless and desperate rabble." To smarten up the blacks and the poor white laborers was seen as desperate folly by many good and comfortable men who preferred things as they were. He ignored the good and comfortable men, and in his eighty-first year accepted the chairmanship of the Pennsylvania Society for Promoting the Abolition of Slavery.

That was in 1787, and from May 28 to September 17 the same year, he participated in the writing of the U.S. Constitution. He "attended the business of it 5 hours in every day from the beginning," and was said to have kept the whole thing together with his serenity and political commitment to the golden mean. Extremists had to meet at a common ground, and when they arrived, they found he was there waiting, camp set up, beans on the fire, ready to work out the moderations and compromises that would make the Constitution acceptable to the people and their delegates.

Debating with politicians around a convention campfire was duty, not pleasure. What he would prefer doing with his remaining years, he spelled out in one of his letters to a fellow scientist, Jan Ingenhousz:

> Rejoice with me, dear friend, that I am once more a free man after fifty years service in public affairs. And let me know soon if you will make me happy the little remainder of my life by spending the time with me in America. I have instruments, if the enemy did not destroy them all, and we will make plenty of experiments together.

"Making plenty of experiments together" was what mattered to the signer of the Declaration of Independence and the Constitution of the United States. The documents mattered too, of course, in their way. He was, after all, Benjamin Franklin. He was many men with many interests.

Electricity had made him the best known scientist in the world, which was all right. But other matters were important also, such as the Franklin family's *"Crown Soap."* He had sold it for years at the New Printing-Office for one shilling per cake. The cakes were green and stamped with a crown to give them special class. It was excellent for the "Washing of Scarlets, or any other bright and curious Colours, that are apt to change by the Use of common *Soap.*"

IN DIVERSITY THERE IS COMPROMISE
An eighth state has since acceded, and when a ninth is added, which is now daily expected, the Constitution will be carried into execution . . . But we must not expect that a new government may be formed, as a game of chess may be played by a skillful hand, without a fault. The players of our game are so many, their ideas so different, their prejudices so strong and so various, and their particular interests, independent of the general, seeming so opposite, that not a move can be made that is not contested; the numerous objections confound the understanding; the wisest must agree to some unreasonable things, that reasonable ones of more consequence may be obtained . . .
(To M. Du Pont De Nemours, June 9, 1788)

He considered it superior soap and continued sending it often as gifts. Lest the formula for its creation be lost, he told his sister, Jane Mecom, on September 21, 1786, "I think you will do well to instruct your grandson in the art of making that soap . . . 'tis pity it should be lost."

His father manufactured candles and soap, light and cleanliness. So he had somehow taken it on himself to light the streets of the human mind and to sweep them clean of old debris with help from the rising wind of freedom.

On March 24, 1790, he again wrote to his sister: "You have done well not to send me any more fish at present. These continue good and give me pleasure."

Freedom was a good tool against tyranny, as good a tool in its way as a kite and a key against lightning. He knew about tools. Franklin Crown Soap was a good tool.

Still, he didn't want to make too much of tools, including soap. They treated more with outsides than insides. "Happiness in this life rather depends on internals than externals," was a discovery he made sometime in his voyage from January 17, 1706 to April 17, 1790, eighty-four years and three months with no time off and no paroles.

He was a busy Benjamin and frankly seemed to want it that way, though he could bemoan the fact occasionally with a friend, as to Le Veillard on April 22, 1788: ". . . in this city my time is so cut to pieces by friends and strangers, that I have sometimes envied the prisoners in Bastille." But in spite of distractions he promised to continue with the project Le Veillard had strenuously urged on him, the third part of the *Autobiography*.

Part II he had written in Paris, that city where many American artists have gone to put their lives on paper, looking back at America across miles and years. Perhaps in that practice Franklin was starting something. He was always starting something.

"Those that feel can judge best," he said in the House of Commons during his interrogation on the Stamp Act in 1766. What a thing to say to the fox-hunters of Parliament. And he added, "No power, how great soever, can force men to change their opinions." Such ideas could start ricochets going that might never stop.

He must have liked cheese, or hated inscriptions on stones, or both. He confessed that finding a recipe for Parmesan cheese during travels in Italy would give more satisfaction than a "transcript of any description from any old stone whatever."

He enjoyed startling the innocent by calming waters with oil, but when an English farmer fell at his feet after a demonstration and begged to know what he should believe, it was too much. "What you have seen, and nothing else," said the philosopher impatiently.

But mostly he was patient. Science could only be done with patience. Truth was shy. The pressures of haste made it run blushingly away. Thus, he was a careful, constant lover until an elopement could be suitably arranged.

A CANE WITH THE CAP OF LIBERTY

He wrote his Last Will and Testament, taking time off from the *Autobiography*, and signed it on July 17, 1788. He had books, lands, houses, and money to distribute properly. On June 23, 1789, he added a Codicil, stipulating among other things the size of the marble stone he would agree to have resting above him. It should be "made by Chambers, six feet long, four feet wide, plain with only a small moulding round the upper edge." The inscription on the stone was to be limited to the names Benjamin and Deborah Franklin with the years. A reasonable guess might be that he did not want the curious bending over to read an elaborate inscription when they could be better occupied seeking cheese recipes.

He had more property to bestow including something special, and he took care of that in the Codicil:

> My fine crabtree walking-stick, with a gold head curiously wrought in the form of the cap of liberty, I give to my friend, and the friend of mankind, *General Washington*. If it were a sceptre, he has merited it, and would become it. It was a present to me from that excellent woman, Madame de Forbach, the Dowager Duchess of Deux-Ponts, connected with some verses which should go with it.

SELLING "SUPERFINE" SOAP
. . . A Parcel of superfine CROWN SOAP. It cleanses fine Linens, Muslins, Laces, Chinces, Cambricks, &c. with Ease and Expedition, which often suffer more from the long and hard Rubbing of the Washer, through the ill Qualities of the Soap they use, than the Wearing. It is excellent for the Washing of Scarlets, or any other bright and curious Colours, that are apt to change by the Use of common Soap. The Sweetness of the Flavor and the fine Lather it immediately produces, renders it pleasant for the Use of Barbers. It is cut in exact and equal Cakes, neatly put up, and sold at the New Printing-Office, at 1s. per Cake.
(From The Pennsylvania Gazette, November 22, 1733)

Together with the crabtree walking-stick he was also giving General Washington the United States of America to look after and see to. The country was still an infant, after all, and infants needed tending. They needed watching. And they needed love. General Washington could be trusted with the task. The walking-stick might help.

To *Henry Hill*, one of his proposed executors, he left the silver cream-pot, with the motto *Keep bright the chain*, that had been given to him by Dr. Fothergill. His reflecting telescope was intended for David Rittenhouse to use in his observatory. His type and printing equipment he left to Benjamin Franklin Bache, his grandson, and most of his books to another grandson, William Temple Franklin.

The will and Codicil were unusual in one conspicuous respect. They contained not a tickle of levity, not a puff of jest. *Lawyers*?

Eventually the time came, of course, when the Will and Codicil went into effect and history took over the life and times of Benjamin Franklin.

He was ready for the journey. Writing to George Whately, he expressed a Deist's confidence/hope in this gentle fashion: "I look upon death to be as necessary to our constitution as sleep. We shall rise refreshed in the morning." Whately was less certain in his reply. He did not understand, and could not accept a consoling argument that was unproven. "We can know nothing of what we were before we existed, nor can we more certainly or more positively say what shall become of us on our dissolution." But Franklin, who had looked deep into the heart of nature and man, believed. With death close enough to see, he said, "What are the pains of a moment in comparison with the pleasures of eternity?"

One of his last letters was to Thomas Jefferson, dated April 8, 1790, an effort to settle a boundary question between Britain and the United States in connection with the Bay of Passamaquoddy. Located between Maine and New Brunswick, the Bay of Passamaquoddy lies at the inlet to the Bay of Fundy. Britain was trying to encroach on the eastern limits of the United States, according to Thomas Jefferson.

Considering the Bays of Passamaquoddy and Fundy may have sent Franklin's thoughts nostalgically back through the years to the Junto. A Junto question in the 1750's had been: "What is the reason that the tides rise higher in the Bay of Fundy, than the Bay of Delaware?" He had been in England then, but in touch, and probably knew the question. Years after the Junto's start, he wrote to Hugh Roberts, "Since we have held that club till we are grown gray together, let us hold it out to the end." Near the end, perhaps he remembered when he was young, drinking wine, and discussing great questions at the Junto with his friends.

The dispute over boundaries could also have reminded Franklin of a brief prayer he had written and sent the previous December to David Hartley:

> God grant, that not only the Love of Liberty but a thorough Knowledge of the Rights of Man, may pervade all the Nations of the Earth, so that a Philosopher may set his Foot anywhere on its Surface, and say, "This is my Country."

It is a good prayer by a man who preferred doing to praying. He did a lot, much more than most. He built a nation to his own specifications. It was a nation with plenty of room where strangers were welcome. Willingness to work and be industrious were his only requirements. "America is the Land of Labour," he wrote, not a place "where the streets are said to be pav'd with half-peck loaves, the houses tiled with pancakes, and where the fowls fly about ready roasted, crying, *Come eat me!*"

America, he wrote, is a place where "people do not inquire concerning a stranger, *What is he?* but, *What can he do?*"

His nation was a place with laws designed to serve the cause of human liberty, a place where people would be important enough to determine their own destinies and to govern themselves. At the Constitutional Convention, Alexander Hamilton wanted to institute a sort of native American aristocracy for ex-presidents because it would be cruel to degrade them after high position.

Not so, declared Franklin. "In free governments the rulers are the servants and the people their superiors and sovereigns. For the former therefore to return among the latter is not to degrade them but to promote them."

He prayed for a world where each philosopher and scientist could be everywhere at home. Of course he knew that his prayer, men being men, might take considerable time to answer. *So he built a nation where philosophers and scientists could leave oppressions behind and say, "I am at home here in Benjamin Franklin's country."*

A scientist named Albert Einstein wrote in a part of Europe that dared not allow him to be free, "My political ideal is democracy.

Let every man be respected as an individual and no man idolized."
*Eventually scientist Einstein came to Benjamin Franklin's country
and felt at home.*

Franklin knew what he was about when he kept his marble head-
stone simple. He had a larger monument surrounding him, a country where exiled scientists and philosophers and the lost, weary
children of oppression could find a living place for themselves and
new ideas.

He was a rotund man, Benjamin Franklin, well-rounded in diverse and special ways. He carried an impish gleam in his eyes, as
if he saw the point of the joke. And he definitely had "bottom" in
the nautical sense of the word.

The future was also his country as it is of every scientist and
philosopher. His urge was to build the future, not simply to let it
happen. Since we are residents in the future that Franklin built,
he has a builder's right to question. How are we treating the house?
Can driven scientists, poets, Messiahs, and other wanderers still
arrive after dark or amid the lightning storm and find a place, if
only one of straw? Are we preserving the roof from leaks? Can men
pass freely among all the rooms? Are we keeping the foundation
sound? How well are we doing in Benjamin Franklin's place?

The questions are hard to escape.

From a Letter to Benjamin Franklin, September 23, 1789.

If to be venerated for benevolence, if to be admired for
talents, if to be esteemed for patriotism, if to be beloved
for philanthropy, can gratify the human mind, you must
have the pleasing consolation to know that you have not
lived in vain. And I flatter myself that it will not be ranked
among the least grateful occurrences of your life to be assured that, so long as I retain my memory, you will be re-
collected with respect, veneration, and affection by your
sincere friend,

GEORGE WASHINGTON

1976

Dear Doctor Franklin, Sir,

As your country and ours begins its third century, we turn instinctively to the place of independence and find you waiting.

In April, 1790, you paused in your journey and settled for rest where you began. Your present place, green and tranquil, is plainly and simply marked as you requested. It is easy to find in the old grounds at Fifth and Arch Streets, Philadelphia.

Today the area is called Independence National Historical Park. Close by are all your familiar places. Now each is a cherished shrine of American independence. Each proclaims the enduring message of America. And you are inseparably part of that remarkable neighborhood where America was remarkably born.

During the bicentennial year, millions will walk slowly and thoughtfully where you lived and hurried two hundred short years ago. Whatever direction they turn, the visitors will see you. There you are . . . rushing with a wheelbarrow loaded with paper for the Franklin press on Market Street. There . . . discussing electricity with friends from the Junto. There . . .

The visitors will cross Benjamin Franklin Bridge. They will visit Washington Square, Independence Square, and of course, Franklin Square. They will enter the great room to the right of the foyer in Independence Hall where you and your fellow partisans of freedom asserted liberty by enacting the Declaration of Independence, and then saved liberty by writing a Constitution.

The guests of independence will stand near you and in a small compass will feel themselves at the historical heart of America. It is a heart beating with the memory of giants, one of them a bespectacled realist named Benjamin Franklin.

A short distance from you down Arch Street is where Betsy Ross and her husband John had their small upholstery shop. Her brother-in-law George Ross was one of your cosigners on the Declaration. Tradition insists it was to the Ross shop that George Washington, Robert Morris, and George Ross went to obtain Mrs. Ross's assistance in sewing a flag. The first for a new nation.

A bit farther away near Market Street is the site of your home. A framework of steel tubes stands there now to represent the Franklin house. The original, we're informed, was burned in the nineteenth century by angry relatives to protest taxes. Your kinsmen must naively have thought that fire could repeal the natural law you expressed to Monsieur Le Roy in November, 1789: "In this world nothing can be said to be certain, except death and taxes."

Thanks to you and your friends, freedom too has been more certain and longer lasting than ever before. The phantom presence of your house, and the memory of what was done and written there, helps keep freedom an official part of the American message. The steel framework symbolizing the Franklin abode seems appropriate. Steel is a vigorous signal of man's progress. You would approve.

Not far from your place of pause is Christ Church with its famous spire reaching upward. That spire once made Christ Church the tallest man-made structure in America. The skyscrapers of metropolitan Philadelphia stand taller now by steel measures, but not by the measures of time.

You'll recall that spire, Sir. In 1753 there were plans to erect an ambitious spire. You intended to use it for your experiments to capture lightning. However, before the spire was in position, you had another idea. You went even higher with a kite . . . and captured lightning in a key fastened to a ribbon of silk.

In the midst of storm, you touched the key with a knuckle and felt a spark. We feel that spark today as fiercely and excitingly as ever. To us it is the spark of liberty that you and your companions set free in the world to illuminate the future. There have been periods of shadow, times of eclipse, but the spark has never vanished. Our lights have not gone out.

Many who pass your way during the 200th birthday year will find themselves in the peaceful rose garden behind Christ Church. Some may stop and listen as the past tells them about the future. Your voice and those of others will speak in the wind as it moves through the trees of independence neighborhood. "Liberty" is one of the words they might hear as the old spire above them yearns upward toward the lightning.

Visitors should feel and know again that liberty is the abiding message of America. They will see and hear it everywhere in your neighborhood. Special bells will ring out with the identical message.

Thirteen seconds before midnight on the last day of 1975, a bell will ring thirteen times. Thus will start the bicentennial year. Earlier on New Year's Eve, another special bell with a crack along its side will be taken from Independence Hall to a glass-enclosed pavilion at Independence Mall, not far from you. You know the bell, Sir. We call it Liberty Bell. Despite the crack it received during testing in 1752, the bell rang in July 1776 to summon Philadelphians for a reading of the Declaration of Independence. You remember . . .

As bells go, it is not especially impressive. There are many larger bells than our little one-ton, cracked symbol of American liberty. The great "Tsar Kolokol" bell in Moscow weighed nearly 180 tons when it was cast in 1733, the year of the first *Poor Richard Almanack*. Another Moscow bell weighed 128 tons, and a 53 ton hanging bell in Peking also dwarfed the tiny Liberty Bell. There have been many great bells, yet none have sounded stronger or farther than the bell of American liberty. Its echoes and reverberations can still be heard throughout the world from that fateful day of ringing in the summer of '76.

The inscription on the Liberty Bell contains words selected from *Leviticus,* Chapter 25, Verse 10: "And ye shall hallow the fiftieth year, and *proclaim liberty throughout all the land unto all the inhabitants thereof*: it shall be a jubilee unto you. . ."

So the Liberty Bell with those words in place . . . Proclaim liberty throughout all the land unto all the inhabitants thereof . . . will be enshrined near you. Liberty will be your companion still, as it was in life. With mind and heart dedicated to the unchanging truths of science, you learned young that truth is found and served best where liberty is constant.

Will you wake up, Sir, when we sound the bell at midnight as our third century begins? Will you help us stay awake to hear the message of America once more and to keep the truths of liberty alive?

We Are, &c.,
YOURS, THE PEOPLE

THE SERENDIPITIES OF SCIENCE
I wish you had the convenience of trying the experiments you seem to have such expectations from, upon various kinds of spirits, salts, earth, &c. Frequently, in a variety of experiments, though we miss what we expected to find, yet something valuable turns out, something surprising and instructing, though unthought of.

(To Cadwallader Colden)

An Afterword on Sources

Benjamin Franklin gave me quite a runaround, through libraries and through those dusty attics of promise, the used and rare bookstores of America. For instance, there was the basement of Dauber and Pine at 66 Fifth Avenue in Manhattan. The Dauber and Pine basement is one of those places where a complete escape can be made into the special world of books. I asked for out-of-print Franklin items.

"Old Ben," said the Bookman with respect and affection, "There were nice sets of Old Ben around the turn of the century. We don't see them often, of course." His message was that anyone fortunate enough to have a set of Old Ben would be mad to let it go. I learned in the course of my quest that few did let them go. Early Franklin materials have become exceedingly scarce outside libraries.

My first long stops on the road to Franklin were at the University of Michigan Graduate Library and the Ann Arbor Public Library. From oceans of material, the libraries supplied most of the words Franklin wrote and a good portion of the millions written about him. Plenty of information was available for literary fishing. But an old problem surfaced. There were too many books to carry away conveniently. Many were "Library Use Only." I needed the books at home. There was no help for it. I promptly became a Franklin collector.

I already possessed two essential sources: The valuable Yale edition of the *Autobiography* and Carl Van Doren's inimitable Pulitzer Prize biography. Much more was desirable. So I found myself doing what one naturally does in such a pickle, contacting book stores around the country.

"Do you have the Smyth edition, 1907, or the Bigelow Collected Works, 1888?"

"We seldom see those," was a reply that became a chorus. I did make finds however. George Brown in Toledo had a nice copy of Russell's sprightly *The First Civilized American*. Kendall G. Gaisser, also Toledo, provided Volume I of Yale's *The Papers of Benjamin Franklin*. In Ann Arbor, the Wooden Spoon, David's Books, Treasure Mart, and Charing Cross Book Store supplied Crane's *Benjamin Franklin and a Rising People*, Fay's imaginative *The Apostle of Modern Times*, as well as useful paperback collections of Franklin's miscellaneous writings and background materials.

It was time to go farther afield. Since persistence is the secret of bargains, as Poor Richard might say, I kept on: Robert Shuhi-Books in Morris, Connecticut, good book providers but with no Franklins. The Byrn Mawr-Vassar Book Store in Pittsburgh, with the Christopher Morley quotation on the wall: *"The most godly diversion known to man ... selling books."* No significant Franklins. The Book Stop in Tucson ... sorry. Maggie DuPriest's Old Book Shop in Coconut Grove, Florida ... sorry.

But there were victories too. For instance, Editions in Boiceville, New York provided *The Ingenious Dr. Franklin*, a useful, charming collection of Franklin's science, and Van Doren's biography of *Jane Mecom*.

Next ... Manhattan, first by phone, then foot. Jack Bartfield had recently sold a Franklin set, but had nothing. He recommended Maggie DuPriest in Coconut Grove. Strand had no rare or special Franklins. Neither did Biblo & Tannen. But Argosy on East 59th Street proved to be a Franklin mother lode.

Argosy's lady in Americana: "Yes, we have some early Franklins." "Sets?" "I think so, wait."

Then came the pleasant business of discussing old books. "The bindings are excellent. The paper is foxed but will last another hundred years." She described a five volume partial set of William Duane's original 1809-1818 six volume edition of the *Works*. Yes, the vital *Electricity* volume was present with all illustrations in good condition. They came west, beautiful books wonderfully preserved nearly a hundred and sixty years. William Duane made books to endure the whips and scorns of time.

A few days later, Argosy reported new and major acquisitions. They had a complete ten volume Bigelow with sick bindings. "Did I want them?" I did. Sick bindings were simply a welcome challenge for Academy Book Bindery in Dexter, Michigan. A complete Bigelow plus 83.3% of a complete Duane afforded credibility to my private collection. I was centuries closer to Benjamin Franklin.

Finally, there was a weekend in New York City for a rooting expedition to Book Row south of 14th Street. We started with a stop at Dauber and Pine for a chat about Old Ben. After that, the search intensified. And in the first store, the Bookman had a Franklin in his hand: Mott and Jorgenson's excellently edited, highly useful 1936 collection! With that seldom encountered book so conspicuously waiting ... in hand ... it rather seemed that fate was cooperating.

At the Strand, an Everest of Americana beckoned, and I emerged begrimed but victorious with several standard items, including Fisher's caustic *The True Benjamin Franklin*.

In the first shop on Fourth Avenue: "Franklin? I have a nice set back here." It was a set of Lincoln. Are great Americans interchangeable? Do the greatest blend into a unique hybrid called AbeTom GeorgeBen JefferFrankLincolnWash?

There were more stores to try. Again rooting paid off. "Browsing" is too meek and tame a word for diligent digging in a used book store worthy of the name. Rooting, not browsing, uncovered two needed volumes from the early Chronicles of America series, Thompson's *The Age of Invention* and Slosson's *The American Spirit in Education*. Each offers good insights on Franklin.

The final store before reaching Astor Place and Cooper's Union provided two excellent finds. Van Doren's important *Benjamin Franklin's Autobiographical Writings* and a particularly congenial print of Franklin based on C. N. Cochin's 1777 drawing. It depicted a chubby, cheerful Franklin. Seeing I was taken, the Bookman began adding decades to the age with historical verve. I accepted hurriedly and ran for Frances Steloff's Gotham Book Mart on West Forty-Seventh.

With an air of international intrigue, the Bookman offered the correspondence of Franklin and Catharine Ray Greene plus Volume X of the Smyth collection from a locked case.

After that furious Saturday, weary but wealthy with Franklins, I returned to Ann Arbor. "There is no moderate life for a Bookman," Lawrence Clark Powell had warned in *A Passion for Books.* But who wants moderation!

The effort had been worthwhile and productive. To complement the libraries, I had Franklin's known scientific writings in several versions, plus broad background and supplementary materials. All were useful for cross-comparisons. Franklin "facts" abound in sometimes contradictory profusion. They advance like army ants from one direction and man-eating tropical fish from another. Diligent care and multiple sources become the obligatory handmaidens of accuracy. But Benjamin Franklin liberally rewards every seeker.

Following are the principal sources consulted for this book. I am grateful to each.

EXPLORERS, WHO WILL BE FIRST TO THE SOUTH POLE OF THE UNIVERSE?
It has long been a supposition of mine that the iron contained in the surface of the globe has made it capable of becoming, as it is, a great magnet; that the fluid of magnetism perhaps exists in all space; so that there is a magnetical north and south of the universe as well as of this globe, and that, if it were possible for a man to fly from star to star, he might govern his course by the compass; that it was by the power of this general magnetism this globe became a particular magnet.
(To the Abbé Soulavie, September 22, 1782)

BIBLIOGRAPHY

The Writings of Benjamin Franklin

1. *Memoirs of the Life and Writings of Benjamin Franklin*, Volume I, Edited by William Temple Franklin, T. S. Manning, Philadelphia, 1818.
2. *The Works of Benjamin Franklin*, William Duane, Philadelphia, 1809.
3. *The Complete Works of Benjamin Franklin*, 10 Volumes, Edited by John Bigelow, G. P. Putnam's Sons, New York, 1887-1888.
4. *The Writings of Benjamin Franklin*, 10 Volumes, Edited by Albert Henry Smyth, The Macmillan Company, New York, 1905-1907.
5. *The Works of Benjamin Franklin, consisting of Essays, Humorous, Moral, and Literary: with his Life, Written by Himself*, S. Andrus and Son, Hartford, 1850.
6. *Benjamin Franklin, Representative Selections*, Edited by Frank Luther Mott and Chester E. Jorgenson, American Writers Series (AWS), American Book Company, New York, 1936.
7. *The Ingenious Dr. Franklin*, Edited by Nathan G. Goodman, University of Pennsylvania Press, Philadelphia, 1931.

411

8. *Benjamin Franklin's Autobiographical Writings*, Edited By Carl Van Doren, Viking Press, New York, 1945.
9. *Benjamin Franklin and Catharine Ray Greene, Their Correspondence*, Edited by William Greene Roelker, Memoirs of the American Philosophical Society held at Philadelphia for Promoting Useful Knowledge, Volume 26, American Philosophical Society, Philadelphia, 1949.
10. *The Papers of Benjamin Franklin*, Volume I, Edited by Leonard W. Labaree, Yale University Press, New Haven, 1959.
11. *Benjamin Franklin, The Autobiography and Other Writings*, Edited by L. Jesse Lemisch, Signet Classic, New American Library, New York, 1961.
12. *The Benjamin Franklin Papers*, Edited by Frank Donovan, Apollo Editions, Dodd, Mead & Company, New York, 1962.
13. *The Autobiography of Benjamin Franklin*, Edited by Leonard W. Labaree, Ralph L. Ketcham, Helen C. Boatfield, and Helene H. Fineman, Yale University Press, New Haven, 1964.
14. *The Political Thought of Benjamin Franklin*, Edited by Ralph Ketcham, The American Heritage Series, The Bobbs-Merrill Company, Inc., New York, 1965.
15. *Benjamin Franklin, A Biography in His Own Words*, Edited by Thomas Fleming, Newsweek Book Division, New York, 1972.
16. *The Letters of Benjamin Franklin & Jane Mecom*, Edited by Carl Van Doren, The American Philosophical Society, Princeton University Press, Princeton, N. J., 1950.

Concerning Benjamin Franklin

1. Crane, Verner W., *Benjamin Franklin and a Rising People*, The Library of American Biography, Little, Brown and Company, Boston, 1954.
2. Currey, Cecil B., *Code Number 72—Ben Franklin: Patriot or Spy?*, Prentice-Hall, Inc., Englewood Cliffs, N. J., 1972.
3. Faÿ, Bernard, *Franklin, The Apostle of Modern Times*, Little, Brown and Company, 1929.
4. Fisher, Sydney George, *The True Benjamin Franklin*, J. B. Lippincott Company, Philadelphia, 1898.
5. Hall, Max, *Benjamin Franklin and Polly Baker*, The Institute of Early American History and Culture, Williamsburg, Virginia, The University of North Carolina Press, Chapel Hill, 1960.
6. Hubbard, Elbert, *Little Journeys to the Homes of American Statesmen*, "Benjamin Franklin," The World Publishing Company, New York, 1928.
7. Keyes, Nelson Beecher, *Ben Franklin*, Hanover House, Garden City, N. Y., 1956.

8. Lopez, Claude-Anne, *Mon Cher Papa—Franklin and the Ladies of Paris*, Yale University Press, New Haven, 1966.
9. Lucas, F. L., *The Art of Living—Four Eighteenth-Century Minds*, The Macmillan Company, New York, 1960.
10. Morse, John T. Jr., *Benjamin Franklin*, American Statesmen Series, Volume 1, Houghton Mifflin Company, Cambridge, 1898.
11. Peattie, Donald Culross, *Lives of Destiny*, "Benjamin Franklin: Multiple Genius," Signet Key Book, New American Library, New York, 1954.
12. Russell, Phillips, *Benjamin Franklin—The First Civilized American*, Brentano's Inc., New York, 1926.
13. Sanford, Charles L., Editor, *Benjamin Franklin and the American Character*, Problems in American Civilization, D. C. Heath and Company, Boston, 1967.
14. Van Doren, Carl, *Benjamin Franklin*, The Viking Press, New York, 1938.
15. Van Doren, Carl, *Jane Mecom—Franklin's Favorite Sister*, The Viking Press, New York, 1950.

Background Sources

Valuable throughout for support, confirmation, and details was the *Encyclopedia Britannica*, 24 Volumes, Fourteenth Edition, 1937, that I wouldn't trade for a more recent encyclopedia. Also of repeated value: *Oxford English Dictionary*, Reproduced Micrographically, Oxford University Press, 1971.

1. Addison, Joseph and Steele, Richard, *The Spectator*, Everyman's Library, J. M. Dent & Sons Ltd., London, 1945.
2. Bacon, Francis, *Essays*, Thomas Nelson and Sons, New York.
3. Bainbridge, John, *Biography of an Idea—The Story of Mutual Fire and Casualty Insurance*, Doubleday & Company, Inc., New York, 1952.
4. Bloch, Marc, *The Historian's Craft*, A Caravelle Edition, Vintage Books, New York, 1953.
5. Boswell, James, *The Life of Samuel Johnson, LL.D.*, Oxford University Press, London, 1924.
6. Brogan, D. W., *The American Character*, Vintage Books, New York, 1956.
7. Cohen, I. Bernard, *The Birth of a New Physics*, Anchor Books, Doubleday & Company, Inc., New York, 1960.
8. Conant, James B., *On Understanding Science—An Historical Approach*, Yale University Press, New Haven, 1947.
9. Descartes, Rene, *Meditations on First Philosophy*, The Library of Liberal Arts, The Bobbs-Merrill Company, Inc., New York, 1960.

10. Dietz, David, *The Story of Science*, The New Home Library, New York, 1942.
11. Durant, Will and Ariel, *The Age of Voltaire*, Volume IX, The Story of Civilization, Simon and Schuster, New York, 1965.
12. Einstein, Albert, *Ideas and Opinions*, Bonanza Books, New York, 1954.
13. Einstein, Albert, *Out of My Later Years*, Philosophical Library, New York, 1950.
14. Farrand, Max, *The Framing of the Constitution of the United States*, Yale University Press, 1965.
15. Fast, Howard, *The Selected Work of Tom Paine and Citizen Tom Paine*, The Modern Library, New York, 1945.
16. Faÿ, Bernard, *Revolution and Freemasonry, 1680-1800*, Little, Brown and Company, 1935.
17. Forster, E. M., *Two Cheers for Democracy*, Penguin Books Ltd., Harmondsworth, Middlesex, England, 1970.
18. Gardner, Martin, *Fads & Fallacies in the Name of Science*, Dover Publications, Inc., New York, 1957.
19. Goran, Morris, *Science and Anti-Science,* Ann Arbor Science Publishers, Inc., Ann Arbor, Michigan, 1974.
20. Hamilton, Alexander, Madison, James, and Jay, John, *Selections from The Federalist*, Edited by Henry Steele Commager, Crofts Classics, Appleton-Century-Crofts, Inc., New York, 1949.
21. Lancaster, Bruce and Plumb, J. H., *The American Heritage Book of the Revolution*, Dell Publishing Co., Inc., 1974.
22. Lawrence, D. H., *Studies in Classic American Literature*, Doubleday Anchor Books, Doubleday & Company, Inc., New York, 1953.
23. Miller, John C., *Origins of the American Revolution*, Little, Brown and Company, Boston, 1943.
24. Muller, Herbert J., *The Uses of the Past*, Mentor Book, New American Library, 1954.
25. Newton, A. Edward, *The Amenities of Book-Collecting and Kindred Affections*, The Atlantic Monthly Press, Boston, 1920.
26. Newton, A. Edward, *This Book-Collecting Game*, Little, Brown and Company, Boston, 1928.
27. Newton, A. Edward, *End Papers*, Little, Brown and Company, Boston, 1933.
28. Newton, A. Edward, *The Greatest Book in the World and Other Papers*, Little, Brown and Company, Boston, 1925.
29. Newton, A. Edward, *A Magnificent Farce and Other Diversions of a Book-Collector*, The Atlantic Monthly Press, Boston, 1922.
30. O'Connor, D. J., *John Locke*, Penguin Books Ltd., Harmondsworth, Middlesex, England, 1952.
31. Padover, Saul K., *Jefferson*, Mentor Book, New American Library, 1952.

32. Peattie, Donald Culross, *Journey into America*, Editions for the Armed Services, Inc., 1943.

33. Plumb, J. H., *England in the Eighteenth Century*, Penguin Books Ltd., Harmondsworth, Middlesex, England, 1951.

34. Rapson, Richard L., Editor, *Individualism and Conformity in the American Character,* Problems in American Civilization, D. C. Heath and Company, Boston, 1967.

35. Schapiro, J. Salwyn, *Liberalism: Its Meaning and History*, Anvil Original, D. Van Nostrand Company, Inc., Princeton, N. J., 1958.

36. *A Short History of Science*, Origins and Results of the Scientific Revolution, A Symposium, Doubleday Anchor Books, Doubleday & Company, Inc., New York, 1959.

37. Slosson, Edwin E., *The American Spirit in Education*, The Chronicles of America Series, Yale University Press, New Haven, 1921.

38. Smith, Logan Pearsall, *Unforgotten Years*, Little, Brown and Company, 1939.

39. Sullivan, J. W. N., *The Limitations of Science*, The Viking Press, New York, 1933.

40. Thompson, Holland, *The Age of Invention*, The Chronicles of America Series, Yale University Press, New Haven, 1921.

41. Tolles, Frederick B., *George Logan of Philadelphia*, Oxford University Press, New York, 1953.

42. Tomlinson, H. M., *The Wind is Rising*, Little, Brown and Company Boston, 1942.

43. Twain, Mark, *The Complete Humorous Sketches and Tales,* Edited by Charles Neider, Doubleday & Company, Inc., 1961.

44. Van Doren, Carl, *The Great Rehearsal*, Time Life Books, New York, 1965.

45. White, T. H., *The Age of Scandal*, G. P. Putnam's Sons, New York, 1950.

46. Wilson, Edmund, *A Piece of My Mind—Reflections at Sixty*, Doubleday Anchor Books, Doubleday & Company, Inc., New York, 1958.

QUESTION OF THE QUESTION
This leads me to mention an old error in our mode of printing. We are sensible that, when a question is met with in reading, there is a proper variation to be used in the management of the voice. We have therefore a point called an interrogation affixed to the question in order to distinguish it. But this is absurdly placed at its end; so that the reader does not discover it till he finds he has wrongly modulated his voice, and is therefore obliged to begin again the sentence. To prevent this, the Spanish printers, more sensibly, place an interrogation at the beginning as well as at the end of a question.
(To Noah Webster, December 26, 1789)

Index

A

Adams, John 48, 111, 351, 353; Comment on BF's love for beauty 6; Diary description of Voltaire and BF meeting in Paris 345

Adams, John Quincy 396

Adams, Matthew, loaned BF books 41

Addison, Joseph, coauthor of *Spectator,* 41, 150, 152

Adler, Mortimer J. 332

Admiralty (Britain), sent BF copy of Cook's Voyage 350

Agriculture, only honest way to wealth 372; experiments 373–374

Alger, Horatio 335

Alice Addertongue, BF pseudonym 334

Ambrose, John N. 378, 379

American Magazine, first in America, 355

American Muses, BF sought them for Philadelphia 244

American Philosophical Miscellany. planned by BF but not developed 260–261

American Philosophical Society, BF chief founder and first secretary 24, 130, 269, 286, 385; Junto, forerunner of 146, 156; Repository of BF papers 226; Proposal by BF 256–257; Initial membership 258; Need to keep out party factionalism 262; BF President for life 262

American Society Held at Philadelphia for the Promotion of Useful Knowledge 261

American Weekly Mercury, published BF Busy-Body letters 97

Anatomical Museum (University College, London), Jeremy Bentham's skeleton 390

417

Animal magnetism, force claimed
by Mesmer 198
Antaeus 139
Anthony Afterwit, BF pseudonym
334
Applegarth and Cowper 384
Aristotle 386
Armonica (*See* Glass harmonica)
Arnauld, Antoine, coauthor of
book on logic, 41
Arnold, Matthew 388
*Articles of Belief and Acts of
Religion* 81
Articles of Confederation 7
Art of Living (F.L. Lucas),
modern British view of BF 160
*Art of Procuring Pleasant
Dreams, The* 109
Association for the Defense of
Pennsylvania, BF proposed
157–158, 284–285
As Time Goes By 263
Atomic theory 268, 280, 288
Aurora Borealis paper 346
Autobiography (*See* Franklin,
Benjamin: Titles)

B
Babbitt 332
Bach, Johann S. 228
Bache, Benjamin Franklin, BF
grandson, accompanied to
France 177; Trained as printer
under Didot 354; Given type and
printing equipment in BF's
will 400
Bache, Sarah, BF daughter, 24,
207; BF letter to on Chinese
system of honor 142
Bacon, Francis 44, 106, 388
Bagatelles, light pieces BF printed
at Passy 66, 169–170, 287, 355
Bailly, Jean, French astronomer
on Mesmer commission with BF
199
Baird, Patrick 157
Baker, Polly (*See* Polly Baker,
BF hoax)
Balloon ascensions, witnessed by
BF and reported to Royal
Society 224, 344–345, 351; Future
possibilities 345; Military
application 358; First air letter
delivered to BF 359
Band, club patterned on Junto 156
Banks, Sir Joseph, President of

Royal Society and BF
correspondent 344, 353; BF
reported balloon ascensions to
344–345; Scientist on Cook's first
voyage 349: BF criticized
England for slowness in balloon
experiments 351; BF letter to on
war and peace 395
Barbon, Nicholas 128
Barclay, David 308
Bartram, John, American
botanist 256; May have
originated idea of American
Philosophical Society 256
Baskerville, John, 355
Baths, 167, 202, 393
Battery, electrical 288–289
Bauer, Andrew, coinventor of
steam press 384
Beccaria, Giambattista, Italian
scientist, BF wrote to on glass
harmonica 231–232; Defended
BF electrical experiments 311,
350; BF sent explanation of
pointed lightning rods 321
Beethoven, Ludwig Van, composed
for glass harmonica 206–207,
228, 229, 242
Ben Davis's Golden Fleece
Tavern 128
Benjamin Franklin Bridge 403
Benjamin Franklin Papers
(Frank Donovan) 289
Bentham, Jeremy 390
Berkshire, BF returned to
Philadelphia aboard 65, 69, 72,
75–79, 80
*Bernier's Travels through
Hindustan* 121
Bevis, John 312
Bifocal glasses 267, 366–367, 378;
BF letter to Whately explained
and illustrated 367
Bigelow, John, BF biographer
and editor 18
Blake, William 57, 95, 101
Blanchard, Jean-Pierre, with
Jeffries ballooned across
English Channel first 359
Bloch, Marc 389
Bohr, Niels 117
Bond, Phineas, among first
members of American
Philosophical Society 258
Bond, Thomas, recruited BF in
founding hospital 179, 202, 259;

Among first members of American Philosophical Society 258

Bon Homme Richard, (named after Poor Richard) 223

Bose, Georg, hypothecated electrical origin of aurora borealis 341

Boston Tea Party 191

Boswell, James, 123, 166, 241

Bottom, individual quality of BF 393, 402

Boulton, Matthew, partner of James Watt 382–383, 385; Performed electrical experiments with BF 383

Boyle, Robert 124–126, 318, 386

Boyle's Law 125

Boyle's Lectures (Robert Boyle) 124–125

Boylston, Zabdiel, used inoculation 187

Bradford, Andrew, Philadelphia printer 51, 55, 57, 88; First magazine in America 355

Bradford, William, New York printer 51

Bradford, William, passenger on *Mayflower* 11

Bragg, Sir Lawrence 396

Brewster, William, passenger on *Mayflower* 11

Brientnal, Joseph, member of Junto 147, 157

Brillon de Jouy, Madame 179, 237, 369; Received Bagatelles from BF 66, 167–169; Chess with BF in her bath 168; Verses sent to BF 168; Heard glass harmonica at Mesmer clinic with BF 199–200, 236

British Museum 64

Brockden, Charles, scrivener for BF's library proposals 246

Brooks, Van Wyck, description of BF and Philadelphia 241–242

Broussonnet, Dr. 344

Browne, Sir Thomas 107; Described "music of the spheres" 228

Brownell, George, BF's teacher in Boston 36, 106, 176

Brownrigg, William 360; BF suggested use of oil to calm waves 361

Bruno, Giordano 386

Bunch of Grapes Tavern 2

Bunker Hill, Battle of 12, 383

Burke, Edmund 7

Burns, Robert 253

Busy-Body letters 97

C

Cabinis, Pierre-Georges 202

Caillot, Blanchette 177

Calendar Act of 1750 30

California Institute of Technology 267

Cambridge University 120, 344

Camel journey, use of evaporation to keep water cool 121

Cancer, superstitious treatment 181

Cane, containing oil to calm waters as a magic trick 360–361, 399

Canton, John, repeated BF electrical experiment 312

Carlyle, Thomas 72

Carmontelle, portrait of BF 223

Carnegie, Andrew 334

Catheter, BF designed first in America 185–186

Cato Major or His Discourse of Old Age (M.T. Cicero, translated by James Logan) published by BF 88, 244

Cave, Edward, editor *Gentleman's Magazine,* 306, 307, 308; Credited with motto *E. Pluribus Unum* 308; Published BF's electrical papers 309

Cavendish, Henry, on Royal Society lightning rod committee 324–326; Scientific recluse 324

Cavendish, Lord Charles, electrical experiment illustrated 219

Cavendish Laboratory 117

Chamberlin, Mason, painted BF's portrait 222

Chambers, BF named to do gravestone 399

Champ-de-Mars, site of first Parisian balloon ascension 344

Chappe, Abbé, 374

Charging and discharging (electricity) 286–287

Charles I 148

Charles, Jacques, French physicist and balloon ascensionist 345, 358

Charleton, Walter, first used word "electricity" 275

Chaucer, Geoffrey 11

Chaumont, Donatien Le Ray de,
  with BF when toads released
  from limestone 375
Chess 167–171; *Morals of Chess,*
  BF Bagatelle 169–170
Chesterfield, Earl of (Philip
  Dormer Stanhope) 385
Christ Church (Philadelphia) 404;
  BF considered for lightning
  experiment 313
Churchill, Sir Winston 166
Cicero 88, 244
City Tavern 2, 13
Civilisation (Kenneth Clark) 117
Clark, Kenneth 117
Clio, Muse of History 54
Cochin, C.N., drawing of BF
  by him 209
Codicil to will 31, 399
Coiffier, guard at Marly during
  historic electrical experiment 311
Colbert, Jean Baptiste, publisher
  of laissez-faire theory 371
Colden, Cadwallader, American
  scientist 163–164, 204, 244, 258,
  259, 260, 286, 302, 337, 365, 405;
  BF letter to on actions of human
  heart 205–206; BF in letter used
  terms conductor and non-
  conductor 287; BF on particles
  of light 316
Colden, David, defender of BF
  electrical experiments 305, 311
Colds, BF views 190–194
Coleman, William, member of
  Junto 157; First Treasurer
  American Philosophical Society
  258
Collins, Anthony, influenced BF
  toward Deism 45
Collinson, Peter, BF contact with
  the Royal Society, received
  major electrical letters 55, 159,
  255, 260, 286, 305, 306, 308, 321,
  342; BF wrote to on magic
  squares and circles 172–176;
  Donated books to Library
  Company 249; First BF mention
  of electrical experiments 270;
  Glass tube for electrical
  experiments sent to Library
  Company 270, 276; BF letters on
  electrical experiments 277–284;
  BF account of thundergust and
  lightning origin 297–298; BF
  admitted non-electrical nature

of ocean luminescence 300;
  Suggestion by BF of pointed
  lightning rods 301–303; Letter
  from BF on kite experiment
  313–314
Committee for Reunion with
  England 378
Comus, associate of Mesmer 200
Conductors and non-conductors 287
Conspirators, BF electrical
  recreation 289
Constitution, U.S., derived in part
  from Locke's theories 43, 338,
  397, 403
Constitutional Convention 1–14,
  397, 401; Signing the Constitution
  10; Closing speech to convention
  by BF, read by Wilson 4–8
Cook, James, captained voyages
  for Royal Society 348–350
Cooper, Anthony Ashley, influenced
  BF toward Deism 45
Copernicus, Nicola 387
Copley Medal, 27, 343
Copley, Sir Godfrey 342
Cosmic rays 346
Courtanvaux, Marquis de 374
Cowper (*See* Applegarth and
  Cowper)
Crabtree walking-stick, bequeathed
  to Washington 399–400
Craven Street, BF lodgings in
  London 72, 197
Crevecoeur, St. John de 18
Crisis (Thomas Paine) 352
Cromwell, Oliver 148
Crooked Billet Inn 54
Crown Soap, Franklin family
  specialty, recipe sent to BF by
  Jane Mecom 362, 397, 398, 399
Cushing, Thomas 95
Cutler, Manasseh 24–26

D
Dacosta, embezzling clerk of
  Royal Society 343
D'Alibard, Thomas-Francois,
  translated BF electrical papers
  into French 310; Defended BF
  electrical methods and results
  311, 312, 321; Successfully
  performed historic electrical
  experiment following BF's
  instructions 311
D'Arlandes, Marquis, he and de
  Rozier were first balloon

passengers 358

Darrell, R.D., notes on glass harmonica 236–237

Darwin, Charles 27

David's Psalms 104

Davies, Marianne, eighteenth century glass harmonica virtuoso 234

Davis, Elmer 109

Davy, Sir Humphrey 360

Daylight saving 267, 368–372

Deane, Silas, commissioner to France with BF and Arthur Lee 7

Death and Taxes, BF quotation 404

De Buffon, Comte, Keeper of Jardin du Roi 310; Defended BF electrical experiments 311

Declaration of Independence 4, 10, 12, 43, 222, 349, 397, 403; Association with BF complicated seeing him clearly as scientist 270

De Coverley, Sir Roger, character featured in *Spectator* 150

Defluctions, problem in badly heated houses 133

Defoe, Daniel 61, 360

DeGrasse 356

Deism, BF religion 45, 400

De La Roche, Abbé Lefebvre 202

Delaval, Edmund Hussey, devised arrangement of musical glasses after Puckeridge 231

Delaware River 290, 337; Crossed by Washington and army 352

DeLor, demonstrated BF electrical experiment for Louis XV 311, 312

Denham, Thomas 65, 69, 80

Depholgisticated air (oxygen), discovered by Priestley 382

Desaguliers, Dr., studied effects on air passed through iron or brass 137, 275

Descartes, René 40, 387, 388

Deslon, associate of Mesmer 200

Dialogue Between the Gout and M. Franklin, Bagatelle for Madame Brillon 167–169

Didot, François, Paris printer 354

Discovery, ship on Cook's third voyage 349

Dissertation on Liberty and Necessity, Pleasure and Pain 62, 69, 243

Divers Ouvrages de Mathématique

par Messieurs de l'Académie des Sciences (Bernard Frénicle) 171

Dogood, Silence (*See* Silence Dogood)

Donovan, Frank 289

Don Saltero's Curiosities 69

Douglass, William, opposed smallpox inoculation in Boston 186–190

Dreams 109

Dry-Belly-Ache (lead poisoning), BF observations 195–196, 206

Dryden, John 62

Dublin Society 257

Dubourg, Barbeu 70–71; BF letter on bracing or tonic bath 166–167; Letter from BF on glass harmonica 235; BF wish for immersion in cask of Madeira 263; BF on flies drowned in Madeira and revived 290; Perspiration experiment reported by BF 315

Duchesse de Bourbon, played chess with BF 171

Du Faye, Gardener to Louis XV, did electrical experiments 275; hypothesis of vitreous and resinous electricities 280

Duncker, Johann, wrote *Leonora Prohaska* 228

DuPont Company 382

DuPont de Nemours, E.I., BF influenced his immigration to America 382; BF letter reported Constitution nearly adopted 397

Durant, Will and Ariel 267

E

Earl of Shelburne, employed Priestley as Librarian 108

Earthquakes, discussed in *Gazette* 249

Economical Project, An 369

Economics, BF views 370–371, 378; *Laissez-faire* policy favored 371; *Pas trop gouverner*, economic stand against excessive government 371

Edgerton, Samuel Jr., criticism of BF stove 138

Edison, Thomas 117

Edman, Irwin 332

Education, BF views 43

Einstein, Albert 118, 228, 268, 364, 365, 401–402; Need for scientific bridges linking nations 99

Electric bell 222
Electric picnic 290
Electrical thermometer 218
Electricity, used by BF to treat paralytics 197; BF experiments 270; Other experimentors 274–276; Points attract and give off electricity 277; Positive and negative 278–280, 396; Electrical kiss 279–280; One-fluid theory of BF 280, 396; Leyden jar experiments 281–284, 396; Electrical experiments illustrated 283; Charging and discharging 286; Conductor and non-conductor 287; Electrical battery 288; Electrical recreations, magical picture, conspirators 289; Golden fish 303; BF injured by 304; Publication of electrical papers in England 306–309; Electrical papers translated into French by D'Alibard 310; BF doesn't answer Nollet's attack 310–311; D'Alibard proved BF thesis in Marly experiment 311; DeLor repeated experiment for Louis XV 311; Electric bell operated using iron rod to draw electricity 314
Electron theory, 268, 280, 388
Electrotherapy 197–198
Eliot, Jared 65, 281, 387; BF reported to on success of Academy 254; BF on agriculture 373, 374
Ellis, Havelock 337
Empiricism, BF philosophical view influenced by Locke 40–44, 192
Epitaph, written by BF at twenty-three 82
E. Pluribus Unum 308
Essay Concerning Human Understanding (Locke) 43, 46, 47, 150
Essay on Criticism (Alexander Pope) 147
Essays to do Good (Cotton Mather) 149
Euclid's Elements 106–107
Evans, Cadwallader, American Philosophical Society 262
Evaporation experiments, with Professor Hadley 120–122
Everlasting Club (*Spectator*) 152
Every Night Club, rich merchants of Philadelphia 147, 157
Experimental philosophy 343; Demonstration-lecture given by Archibald Spencer, witnessed by BF 270
Experimentation, tool of science 387
Experiments, agriculture 373–374
Experiments and Observations on Electricity, BF's principal scientific writings collected under title 309
Experiments, Observations, and Facts. . . , BF report on pointed rods vs. rounded rods for Royal Society committee 324
Explication of the First Causes of Action in Matter (Cadwallader Colden), BF offered to publish 245

F
Faculty of Medicine (Paris), BF on Mesmer investigation committee 199
Fadiman, Clifton 335
Faraday, Michael 27, 357–358
Faÿ, Bernard, BF biographer 61, 210; On openness of BF electrical experiments 273; Value of BF's manual skills 276–277
Fire, problem in Colonies 127–128; BF speculation on 280
Fisher, Sydney George, BF biographer 204, 265
Fletcher, Horace 165
Fletcherism 165
Flexner, Dr. Simon 348
Folger, Abiah (*See* Franklin, Abiah)
Folger, Captain Timothy, Gulf Stream observations for BF 377
Forbach, Madame de 399
Forster, E.M. 110
Fort Duquesne, Skeletons found nearby at Great Licking Place 374
Fothergill, John, wrote preface for BF electrical papers 308–309, 310, 400
Fourteen Points, BF's explanation of Franklin Stove 136
Fourteen Points of Woodrow Wilson 141
Fox, George, BF papers left in Fox stables for decades 226

Franklin, Abiah (Folger), mother
of BF 30–31; BF medical advice
to 181; BF letter to 338
Franklin, Ann, first wife of Josiah
Franklin 30
Franklin, Benjamin: Personal
history; Considered America's
greatest philosopher in eighteenth
century 2; At Constitutional
Convention 2, 3, 5, 6, 9; Last
speech to Convention, read by
James Wilson 4–8; Opposition to
hereditary offices 7;
Impersonated George III in
satirical article 8; Signer of four
major documents of American
history 14; In Hall of Fame as
scientist 15; Voyage home from
France after Revolution 17;
Wrote on water-tight
compartments in ships 18;
Elected President of Pennsylvania 22; Machine to show
circulation of blood 25; Rolling
press for copying letters 25; Birth
on Milk Street, Boston 30, 33;
Move to Union and Hanover
Streets, Boston 33; Schooling
35, 36; Bequest in will to Boston
free grammar schools 36;
Entered family soap and candle
business 37; Apprentice in
brother James's print shop 37;
Wrote Silence Dogood letters
for brother's *New-England
Courant* 38; Scientific and
philosophical reading 40–47;
Extracts from *Pennsylvania
Gazette* 44; Deism, BF's religion
45; Moved from Boston to
Philadelphia 48–52; Sought job
in William Bradford's print shop,
New York 51; Worked to become
established in Philadelphia 52–58;
Visited Boston to display success
58; First trip to London 60;
Experiences in London 60–64;
Considered opening English
Swimming School 65; First
experiments with kite to aid
swimming 68; Return to
Philadelphia aboard *Berkshire*
75–79; Extensive scientific
observations at sea 77–79;
Religious views 80–81; Built first
copperplate press in America 83;

Printing partnership with Hugh
Meredith, soon dissolved 83–84;
Marriage 85–87; Advice for
longevity and health 92; Use of
Gazette to further science in
Colonies 97–112; Considered
scientific progress made by
mankind 101–102; Parable of
father, son, and their ass 104–105;
Editorial giving intentions
of *Gazette* 112; One of
first scientific experiments
reported 119; Evaporation
experiments at Cambridge 120–
122; Treatment of inflammations
with spirit 122; Man defined as
"toolmaking animal" 124; *Gazette*
promoted fire protection 127–128;
Organization and activities of the
Junto 145–161; Steady growth of
human knowledge 159; Studied
languages 164–165; Chess 167–
171; Polly Baker episode 177–178;
Medical contributions 180–206;
First American catheter 185–186;
Inoculation (smallpox)
controversy in Boston 186–190;
Scientific modesty 195; Dry-
belly-ache (lead poisoning) 195–
196; Electrotherapy 197–198;
Pennsylvania Hospital founded
202–204; Invention of Armonica
(Glass Harmonica), musical
interests 227–238;
Composed string quartet 229;
Description of Glass Harmonica
232; Library Company founded
245–251; Books sent instead of
bells requested by Franklin,
Massachusetts 251–252;
University of Pennsylvania
resulted from BF projects 252–
255; Pennsylvania Postmaster
256; American Philosophical
Society proposed and
established 256–262; First
Secretary of the American
Philosophical Society 258; Start
of electrical experiments 269;
Significance of points 276–277;
Positive and negative electricity
278–280; Electrical kiss 279–280;
One-fluid theory of electricity
280; Leyden jar experiments 281–
284; Additions to electrical
vocabulary 279, 282, 286–287,

Franklin, Benjamin (*continued*)
389; Pointed lightning rod 301–
303; Lightning experiments 293,
296, 303, 304; Publication of
electrical papers in England 306–
309; Charging and discharging
286; Conductor and non-
conductor 287; Electrical battery,
first 288; Electrical recreations,
"magical picture," the "conspirators" 289; Kite experiment
during thunderstorm
312–314; BF lightning-electricity
theory proven 314; Lightning
rod instructions in *Poor Richard's
Almanack* 316; Refusal to profit
from lightning rod 318; Member
of Royal Society committee on
lightning rods 315, 324–327;
Pointed rods favored by majority,
opposed by Wilson and George
III 326–327; *The Way to Wealth*
73, 335–338; Contributions to
making of the Constitution 338;
Winner of Copley Medal from
Royal Society for electrical
experiments 343–344; Balloon
ascensions witnessed, reported to
Royal Society 344–345; Embraced
Voltaire at Royal Academy 345–
346; Aurora Borealis paper
presented at Royal Academy, in
1779 BF collection 346; Ordered
American sea captains not to
hinder Captain Cook's scientific
voyage 349–350; Notified
Congress of peace agreement 353;
Began America's second
magazine 355; Military
possibilities of balloons 358; Brisk
treatment for gout 361; Whirlwinds and waterspouts studied
362–365; Bifocals 367–368; Daylight saving 368–372; Influence
on economists and economics 370–
371; Agriculture and farmers
372–373; Agriculture experiments
374; The Long Arm 375–377;
Hydrodynamics 377; Further
study of Gulf Stream 377; International influence on science 378–
389; Education of women 395;
Wrote there was never a good
war or a bad peace 395; Advocate
of first American school for

Blacks 396; Wanted to spend
remainder of life doing experiments 397; Interrupted *Auto-
biography* to write Will 399;
Hoped for time when a philosopher could say of every nation
"this is my country" 401
Franklin Benjamin: Titles
*Account of the New-Invented
Pennsylvanian Fireplaces, An,*
pamphlet to explain and promote
Franklin Stove 131–139; *Advice
to a Young Man on the Choice
of a Mistress* 178; *Advice to a
Young Tradesman from An Old
Tradesman* 112; *Art of Procuring
Pleasant Dreams, The,* BF to
Catherine Shipley 109; *Articles
of Belief and Acts of Religion* 81;
*Aurora Borealis, Suppositions
and Conjectures towards forming
an Hypothesis for its Explanation*
346; *Autobiography* 30, 32, 34,
36, 41, 46, 52, 55, 57, 59, 60, 62,
63, 65, 79. 83. 84–86, 88–91, 93,
97, 98, 106, 129, 139, 142, 148,
150, 152, 155, 164–165, 166, 246,
247, 255, 270, 272, 308, 310–311,
312, 331, 390, 398, 399; *Busy-Body
letters* 97; *Dialogue Between the
Gout and M. Franklin,* BF
Bagatelle to Madame Brillon
167–169; *Dissertation on Liberty
and Necessity, Pleasure and
Pain, A* 62, 69, 243; *Economical
Project, An,* daylight saving plan
369; *Epitaph,* written by BF at
twenty-three 82; *Experiments
and Observations on Electricity*
309; *Experiments, Observations,
and Facts, Tending to Support
the Opinion of the Utility of
Long, Pointed Rods, for Securing
Buildings from Damage by
Strokes of Lightning,* report prepared by BF for Royal Academy
committee 324; *How to Secure
Houses &c. from Lightning* 316–
317; *Maritime Observations* 18;
Illustrations 20–21; *Morals of
Chess,* Bagatelle done in France
169–170; *Nature and Necessity of
a Paper Currency,* presented to
Junto 155; *Observations on My
Reading History in Library,* in-

cluded in *Autobiography* 98, 106; *Of Lightning, And the Methods now used in America for securing Buildings and Persons from its Mischievous Effects,* written to reassure Parisians about lightning rods 323; *On the Causes and Cure of Smoky Chimneys* 18, 130; Illustrated 215; *On the Usefulness of Mathematics* 105; *Opinions and Conjectures concerning the Effects of the Electrical Matter, and the Means of Preserving Buildings, Ships, &c., from Lightning, arising from Experiments and Observations made at Philadelphia, 1749,* important report to Collinson 302; *Plain Truth,* considered forerunner of *Declaration of Independence* 157-158, 284-285, 352, 371; *Political, Miscellaneous, and Philosophical Pieces* 346, 347; *Poor Richard's Almanack* 4, 32-33, 53, 54, 73, 88, 106, 160, 167, 260, 269, 291, 316, 329, 333-338, 405; *Positions to be Examined, Concerning National Wealth,* agriculture called honest way to wealth 372; *Precautions to be Used by Those About to Undertake a Sea Voyage* 364; *Proposal for Promoting Useful Knowledge Among the British Plantations in America,* beginning of American Philosophical Society 256; *Proposals for a Volunteer and Republican Military Force,* defense of Pennsylvania 284-285; *Proposals Relating to the Education of Youth in Pennsylvania,* first step toward the University of Pennsylvania 252-254; *Silence Dogood letters,* first published BF writings in *New-England Courant* 38, 39, 97, 102, 189, 211, 252, 291, 334; *Speech of Polly Baker, The* 177. 291, 306, 307, 334; *Standing Apology for Printers* 104; *Virtues,* list used by BF as guide 90; *Way to Wealth, The,* selected by BF from Poor Richard 73, 335-338; *Whistle, The,* Bagatelle for Madame Brillon 66, 287

Franklin, Deborah (Read), wife of BF 53, 54, 55, 60, 64, 65, 67, 69, 81, 94, 102, 126, 178, 213, 222, 225, 375, 389, 394, 399; Married and separated from John Rogers 79-80; BF letter prescribed journey for himself to relieve giddiness 192

Franklin, James, brother of BF, BF apprentice in his print shop 37, 47, 50, 51, 57, 58, 81; Took stand in *New-England Courant* against inoculation 186-189; Jailed for practising too much freedom of the press 188

Franklin, John, brother of BF 37; BF invented catheter to help 185-186

Franklin, Josiah, father of BF 29, 185, 301, 398; Candle and soap maker 30; Description by BF 32; Representative of English trade traditions 33; Influence on BF 34; Refused funds for BF to start print shop 58; Frugality emphasized 115; Medical advice to 181

Franklin, Josiah, brother of BF 37

Franklin, Massachusetts 251-252

Franklin, Peter, brother of BF 37; BF letter to 230-232

Franklin Square 403

Franklin Stove (*See* Pennsylvanian Fireplace)

Franklin the Apostle of Modern Times (Bernard Faÿ) 273, 276-277

Franklin, William, son of BF 86, 343; Appointed Governor of New Jersey 261; Accompanied BF during kite experiment 312-314

Franklin, William Temple, grandson of BF, accompanied to France 177, 335; Known as Franklinet 177; His handling of BF's papers 226; Inherited most of BF's books 400

Franklinet (*See* Franklin, William Temple) 177

Freemen, BF held they made the best soldiers 285

Frénicle, Bernard, wrote on magic squares 171

Fresh air, BF believed in as useful for health 132, 204, 379; Need for 146, 192

Frugality, virtue BF claimed for Mrs. Franklin 375

Fuel, importance of availability and economical use 130–137
Fulton, Robert 15
Fundy, Bay of 400

G

Galilei, Galileo 40, 259, 265, 386, 387; Studied medicine, invented thermometer 185
Gambill, David A. 378–379
Gasparro, Frank, numismatic sculptor 207
General Advertiser of London, first to print Polly Baker article as genuine 177
General Assembly of Pennsylvania, BF clerk for 171
General Coughs and Colds (Thomas Molyneux), BF quoted in *Gazette* 190–191
General Magazine, started by BF, second in America 355
Gentleman's Magazine, published BF writings on magic squares and circle 176; Polly Baker 306–307; BF on electricity 306
Geomagnetism 346
George I 148
George II 148, 158
George III 4, 8, 148, 158, 336, 346, 350; Denounced pointed lightning rods because of BF and Revolution 326–327
Gerry, Elbridge 24
Gibbs, J. Willard 27
Gilbert, William, Queen Elizabeth's physician 274
Glass harmonica 113; Used for background music in Mesmer clinic 199; Music composed for 206–207; BF invented and named Armonica 227; Description, illustration 232–233
Gluck, Christoph Willibald 228; Played concerto on musical glasses 231
Godfrey (Mrs.) 84
Godfrey, Thomas, American mathematician 84; Member of Junto 157; Invented quadrant 157, 259; Among first members of American Philosophical Society 258
Golden fish, BF electrical recreation 303
Gorham, Nathaniel, delegate to Constitutional Convention from Massachusetts 9

Gout, BF Bagatelle on 167–169; *Le Sage et le Goutte* (Madame Brillon) 168; Brisk treatment for 361
Grace, Robert, sold Franklin Stove 129, 131, 249; Member of Junto 157; Provided room in house for Junto meetings 245
Gray, Stephan 275
Great Licking Place, site of ancient animal skeletons 374
Greene, Catherine (Ray) 354, 394
Gregorian Calendar 30
Gresham College, meeting place of Invisible College, later Royal Society 125, 343
Grogan, George 73
Gronovius, Colden sent him Franklin Stove paper 204
Grub Street (London), later Milton Street 61
Guillotin, Joseph Ignace, member of Mesmer commission with BF 199
Gulf Stream 14, 17–18, 19, 118, 291; BF had observations made by Captain Folger 377

H

Hadley, John, Cambridge chemistry professor 120–122
Hadley's Quadrant 157
Haldane, J.B.S. 45, 109
Hall, David, BF's partner 163, 190
Hall of Fame, New York University 15
Hamilton, Alexander 3, 9, 12, 401
Hamilton, James, BF rival for leadership of American Philosophical Society 261
Handel, George Frederick 228, 230, 235
Hanoverian Georges 148
Harmony, analyzed by BF 230
Hartley, David 353, 401
Harvard Alumni Bulletin, article by Kubie on underuse of brain 331–332
Harvard College 61, 176, 252, 262; Awarded Master of Arts Degree to BF 35, 342; Silence Dogood letter satirized 40; BF bought scientific instruments for in London 125
Harvard, John 35
Hauksbee, made friction machine to produce sparks 275

Heberden, William 190
Helvétius, Madame 179, 202, 369, 394
Hessian mercenaries 352
Hewson, (Mrs.) Mary 353
Hill, Henry 400
Historicus, BF pseudonym for satire against slavery, his last 291
Hoe revolving press 384
Hoffmann, Bruno, glass harmonica virtuoso, modern 206, 228, 236
Homes, Robert, BF's brother-in-law 58
Honest Whigs, BF's London club 353
Honeycomb, Will, character featured in *Spectator* 150
Hopkinson, Francis, letter to from BF on press responsibility 110
Hopkinson, Thomas, first President American Philosophical Society 258; Assisted BF in electrical experiments 271, 278, 285, 301
House, George, brought first customer to BF's print shop 84
House of Commons 398
House of Representatives, population prerequisite established at Constitutional Convention 9
Howe, Richard, sent BF Cook's *Voyage to the Pacific Ocean* at request of Admiralty 350
How to Secure Houses &c. from Lightning, instructions on lightning rod in *Poor Richard's Almanack* 316–317
Hubbard, Elbert 31, 111
Huey, Joseph 321
Hume, David, advice to from BF on security from "mischiefs of lightning" 322
Hydrodynamics 377

I

Ignorance, should be frankly admitted to gain knowledge 300
Independence Hall 2, 403, 404; Featured on Bicentennial Medal with BF 207
Independence Mall 405
Independence National Historical Park 403
Independence Square 403
Indian corn (maize) BF on 372–373
Inflammations, treated with spirit 122
Ingenhousz, Jan 18, 132, 194, 215, 350, 351; BF wrote on military possibilities of balloons 358; Invited by BF to Philadelphia to do experiments together 397
Inoculation (smallpox) 186–190, 195
Inventors, injustice to 327–328
Invisible College, later Royal Society 125

J

James, London letter-founder, theory about dry-belly-ache 196
James's Print Shop (London), BF saw printers cast type there 80
James, William, gave up Fletcherism 165
Jansenist movement, influenced BF to adopt methods of logic 41
Jardin du Roi 310
Jay, John 6, 353
Jefferson, Thomas 7, 17, 45, 48, 171, 222, 372, 400; On BF's influence with French 47; Value of BF conversation 94; Studied under William Small, brought to U.S. by BF 383; Said BF as a policy never contradicted 395
Jeffries, John, with Blanchard ballooned across English Channel first 359
Johnson, Samuel 61, 123–124, 160, 166, 229, 393
Jones, John Paul, planned sea strategy with BF in France 223
Jorgenson (*See* Mott and Jorgenson)
Journal of Paris, BF's daylight saving satire addressed to 369
Judas Maccabeus (Handel) 230
Junto, founded by BF 83, 142, 245, 252, 269, 273, 346, 400–401, 403; Organization and activities 145–161; Origin of name 148; Junto membership questions 151; Queries for 153–154; Junto role in BF's Library Company 245–246; New Junto called Society for the Promotion of Useful Knowledge 261

K

Kames, Lord Henry Home, BF wrote him of a preference for Scotch tunes 229

Keimer, Samuel 57, 60, 83, 84, 214; Employed BF in his Philadelphia print shop 55; BF confounded with Socratic method 59

Keith, Sir William, Governor of Pennsylvania, 58, 60, 157

Kew Palace, George III ordered pointed lightning rods removed 327

King George's War (War of the Austrian Succession) 158

Kinnersley, Ebenezer, assisted BF electrical experiments 9, 218, 219, 271–274, 308, 315, 318

Kirchgessner, Marianne, glass harmonica virtuoso 234

Kiss, electrical, BF electrical recreation 279–280

Kite experiment 68, 291, 312–314, 342; Construction 313; BF lightning-electricity theory proven 314

Koenig, Frederick, coinventor with Bauer of steam press 384

Kubie, Lawrence 331

L

Lafayette, Marquis de, supported Mesmer 198

Laissez-faire theory 371

Lasting Revolution (science) 381–389

Lavoisier, Antoine Laurent 158, 198, 270, 382, 387

Lawrence, D.H. 108, 111; Criticism of BF and American way 333–338

League of Nations 142

Leather Apron Club, Junto so-called by Philadelphia merchants 147, 157

Leçons de Physique (Abbé Nollet) 295

Ledru, associate of Mesmer 200

Lee, Arthur, commissioner to France with BF and Silas Deane 7

Leonora Prohaska (Johann Duncker), Beethoven glass harmonica composition featured 228

Le Roy, Jean-Baptiste, French physicist member of Mesmer commission with BF 199; Defended BF electrical experiments 311; BF letter regretted not having French balloon for personal transport 359; BF letter on death

and taxes 404

Le Roy, Julien-David, BF wrote Maritime Observations to 18

Le Sage et la Goutte (Madame Brillon) verses to BF 168

Lettsom, Dr., Fothergill's biographer 308

Le Veillard, Louis 12; Urged BF to continue *Autobiography* 398

Leviticus 59; Inscription on Liberty Bell 405

Lexington-Concord 221

Leyden Jar 276, 304, 313; BF experimented with 281–284; Charging and discharging (BF terminology) 286

Liberty Bell 404, 405; Inscription from *Leviticus* 405 Peking Hanging Bell 405; Tsar Kolokol (Moscow) Bell 405

Library Company of Philadelphia, first subscription library in America 27, 83, 262; Began at Junto 245–246; BF list of books for 248; BF inscription for new building 251

Lightning 290; Considered same as electricity by BF 293; Behavior 294–295; Research since BF 298; Types and characteristics 298–299; Pointed lightning rod to guard against 301–303; Illustration of experiment 303; Use of experiment to prove BF correct 311; BF kite experiment 312–314; Electric bell operated 314; Paper to reassure Parisians about lightning and lightning rod 323

Lightning Rod 113, 267, 309; BF's contribution 273; BF predicted effectiveness 301–302; Instructions to Collinson in 1753 Almanac for construction and placement 316; Superstitions against 318–321; Attack by churchmen 318–319; Reverend Prince accused rod of causing earthquakes 319; Came to symbolize enlightenment, learning 320, 321; Construction details 322; Explanation for Parisians 323; Royal Society lightning rod committee 315, 324, 325

Lining, John, scientific correspondence with BF 121; BF on evap-

oration 121; BF letter concerning
relationship of lightning and
electricity 295; BF account of
knocking men down with charge
from Leyden jars 296–297
Linnaeus 25, 204, 259, 310
Little Journeys (Elbert Hubbard)
31
Little machines 126
Locke, John 40–46, 48, 147, 150, 256,
328, 371, 386; Theories of govern-
ment 43; Importance of experi-
ence and experiment 43
Logan, Deborah 371
Logan, George, was told Smith
consulted BF, Price &c. for
Wealth of Nations 371
Logan, James 57, 245, 246–247, 259,
285, 286, 289, 355; Translated
Cato Major, published by BF
88, 244; Interest in magic squares
171–176; Assisted with books for
Library Company 249
Logic: or the Art of Thinking
(Arnauld and Nicole), influenced
BF 41
London Chronicle, BF defense of
agriculture published in 372, 391
London Hope 61
London Journal, quoted on freedom
of speech in Silence Dogood
letter 189
Long Arm, BF invention 375–377,
378
Lopez, Claude-Anne, BF
biographer, Paris years 200
Louis XV 275; Amusement when
electricity caused monks to jump
276; Saw BF electrical experi-
ment succeed 311
Louis XVI 171; Appointed BF to
Mesmer investigation commission
199; Received private report of
Mesmerism's effect on women
200
Loyola, Ignatius 110
Lucas, F.L., English view of BF 160
Ludolff, Christian, used electricity
to ignite materials 342
Luther, Martin 34

M
Macaulay, Thomas Babington 73
Macbeth (Shakespeare) 294
Macclesfield, George Parker,
President of Royal Society when

BF became member 342
Madeira wine 263, 290, 291, 355,
394, 395
Madison, James 3, 12, 13, 338
Magical pictures 289
Magic squares and circles 171–176;
Utility in developing mathemat-
ical skills 172; BF square of 8
173; BF square of 16 174; BF
magic circle 175
Magna Charta 11
Maize (*See* Indian Corn)
Maria Theresa 158, 179
Marie Antoinette, received BF at
Versailles 158 BF demonstrated
electricity for 179; Glass harmon-
ica lessons 234
Maritime observations 18; Illustra-
tions 20–21
Marly, site in France where BF's
lightning theories were confirmed
311
Marriage of Heaven and Hell
(William Blake) 95
Marten-cap, BF standard article
of attire in France 394
Martin, David, painter 368
Masonic Lodges 12; Junto similar
in part 152
Materia medica 100
Materialism, BF blamed for its
prevalence in America 333
Mathematics 105–108, 172, 387
Mather, Cotton, Boston minister of
Second Congregational Church
58, 148, 192; Advised BF to stoop
to avoid bumps in life 59; *Essays
to do Good* 149; Inspiration for
Junto 148–150: Neighborhood
societies 149–150; Supported
smallpox inoculation 186–188;
Views on reason and science 319
Mather, Increase, founded first
scientific society in Boston 149
Mather, Samuel, son of Cotton
Mather, BF letter to on his
father's influence 149–150
Maugridge, William, member of
Junto 157
Maxwell, James Clerk 27
Mayflower 11
McHenry, James, delegate to the
Constitutional Convention from
Maryland 9
Mon Cher Papa (Claude-Anne
Lopez) 200

Mecom, Jane, sister of BF 338, 346, 347; BF letter on qualities desirable in a wife 162; BF on wooden shell worn to treat cancer 181; Recipe for Crown Soap 362, 398

Medical contributions of BF 180–206

Melody, analyzed by BF 230

Memorable Things of Socrates (Xenophon) 46

Meredith, Hugh, partner of BF 83, 214; Member of Junto 157

Meredith, Simon, father of Hugh Meredith, financed BF's printing business 83

Mesmer, Friedrich Anton 198–201, 236

Mesmerism, treatment described at Mesmer's clinic 199; BF tolerant judgment on 200–201; Erotic aspects of 200

Mickle, Samuel 88–89

Mifflin, Widow, house struck by lightning 294–295, 301

Miller, Joaquin 305

Miller, Merle 92

Millikan, Robert 27; Praised BF's contributions to electrical science 267–268, 279

Milton Street, (London) name given to former Grub Street 61

Minister Plenipotentiary, BF title in France 347, 349

Mirabeau, Comte 225

Mitchell, John, reported Royal Society laughter at BF's paper on sameness of lightning and electricity 308, 310

Molini, M., Parisian bookseller 374

Molyneux, Thomas, studied colds 190

Montagu, Lady Mary, enthusiast for inoculation 187

Montgolfier brothers, French balloon ascensionists 224, 345

Montgolfier, Joseph, ascension demonstration at Versailles 358

Morals of Chess, BF Bagatelle 169–170

Morris, Gouverneur, delegate to Constitutional Convention from Pennsylvania 8, 9

Morris, Robert 403

Morse, John T. Jr., BF biographer 87

Moschopoulus, Emanuel, early writer on magic squares 172

Mott and Jorgenson, BF editors 318, 355

Mozart, Wolfgang Amadeus 228, 242

Muller, Herbert J. 387

Muses 54, 244

Music 206–207, 227–238

Musschenbroek, established basis of condenser 276, 281

Mystical mathematics 107

N

National Academy of Sciences 27

Natural Philosophy, BF's preferred profession 4, 113, 116, 386

Nature and Necessity of a Paper Currency 155

Naumann, Johann Gottlieb, music for glass harmonica 207

Neale, Oliver, BF wrote to about swimming 69–70

Negative electricity 278–280

New-England Courant, began and published by James Franklin 38, 97, 102, 186, 211; BF acting editor when brother was jailed 188–189

New Printing-Office, BF print shop 84, 397, 399

Newton, A. Edward, efforts to acquire *Cato Major* from BF's press 244

Newton, Isaac 40, 44, 60, 63, 106, 147, 176, 265, 269, 273, 295, 305, 318, 328, 338, 342, 343, 346, 347, 348, 385, 386; Newton theories challenged 259

New York Times 378

Nicole, Pierre 41

Nimrod 102

Nollet, Abbé, electrical experimenter 305, 310, 326, 328; Shocked monks to amuse Louis XV 276; Predicted similarity of lightning and electricity in *Leçons de Physique* 295

Novum Organum Scientiarum (Francis Bacon), stressed reason in scientific investigations 388

Nye, Bill 230

O

Ocean luminescence, not electrical BF decided 300

Of Studies (Francis Bacon) 106

Oil on water, effect 359–361, 399
Old South Church (Boston) 32
One-fluid theory (electricity) 280
Osborne, Charles 59
O'Shaughnessy, Arthur William
Edgar 238
Outline of History (H.G. Wells) 255
Oxford College 343
Oxford English Dictionary 133, 389
Oxygen (dephlogisticated air),
discovered by Priestley 382

P

Pagin, M., violin virtuoso, BF
played glass harmonica for 237
Paine, Thomas 5, 352
Palmer, Samuel, employed BF in
London 61
Pamela (Samuel Richardson),
first novel published in America
88, 244
Paper currency, BF supported 155
Paralytics, BF treated with
electricity 197
Parisians, BF paper written to
reassure about lightning rods 323
Parsons, William, member of Junto
157; Among first members of
American Philosophical Society
258
Parton, James, BF biographer 62;
Noted BF's devotion to fresh
air 204
Pas trop gouverner, economic
precept against excessive govern-
ment 371
Passamaquoddy, Bay of 400
Passy, location of BF's Paris
home 167, 212, 224; Became
scientific crossroads 350, 355
Pasteur, Louis 27, 186
Peattie, Donald Culross 115
Pemberton, James, with Rush
founded anti-slavery society 191
Penn, John, considered BF an
enemy 261
Penn, Thomas, opposed BF's
Plain Truth and Freemen
Proposals, 285, 371
Penn, William, founder of Pennsyl-
vania 50, 57, 171, 241, 246–247,
261; Suggested forming "a small
junto" 148
Pennsylvania Gazette 44, 87, 97,
99–112, 146, 264, 356, 378; Colds
190; Front page of first BF issue

214; Earthquakes 249; BF proposal for military force 284–285;
Behavior of lightning 294–295;
Kite experiment reported 316;
Readers asked to notify BF of
lightning phenomena 323
Pennsylvania Hospital 157, 179,
202–204; BF inscription for
cornerstone 203
*Pennsylvania Society for Promo-
ting the Abolition of Slavery*,
BF chairman at eighty-one 396
Pennsylvanian Fireplace 113, 126–
139, 232, 269, 333, 378; BF
refused to profit from financially
129; Assembly instructions and
illustrations 134–135, 216–217
Perkins, John
BF letter to on penchant for
making theories 195; BF letter to
on waterspouts and whirlwinds
361–364
Perno, Abbé, added keys to glass
harmonica 234
Philadelphia 49–57; Called Athens
of America 53, 245; Population
in 1723 53
Philadelphia Academy, proposed
by BF 252–254, 260; BF
specifications for 253–254
Philadelphia Bicentennial Agency
207
Philadelphia Contributionship,
first fire insurance company 128
Philadelphia Library (*See* Library
Company of Philadelphia)
Philadelphia Society for Promoting
Agriculture 372
Philomath 334
Philosophy 119–120
Piccinni, composer, neighbor of
BF at Passy 228
Picnic, electrical 290
Pierce, William, delegate to Consti-
tutional Convention from Georgia
3, 5
Pierian spring 147
Plain Speaking (Merle Miller),
Truman on BF 92
Plain Truth, BF pamphlet urged
self-defense 157–158, 284, 285,
352, 371
Planck, Max Karl Ernst 268
Plato 106–108
Pliny the Elder 360–361
Pointed Rodders 324–327

Points, electrical 277
Political arithmetician 137
Political, Miscellaneous, and Philosophical Pieces 346; Frontispiece of BF in edition 347
Polly Baker, BF hoax, 177–178, 291, 306, 307, 334
Poor Richard's Almanack 4, 53, 54, 73, 88, 106, 160, 167, 260, 269, 291, 329, 333, 334, 405; Seeds of maxims in Josiah Franklin's house 32–33; Lightning rod instructions 316; *The Way to Wealth* 333–338
Pope, Alexander 147
Popular Party, supported by BF 261
Port Royal, Jansenist community 41
Positive electricity 278–280
Postmaster of Pennsylvania, BF position 256
Potts, Stephen, member of Junto 157
Poverty, ways to handle 391
Powder (scented), used in eighteenth century to combat fleas 393
Price, Richard 251, 371; BF wrote to about balloon flights 353–354
Pride, BF warned against it in science 351
Priestley, Joseph 7, 55, 180, 192, 270, 272, 350, 356, 379, 382, 384, 388, 394; BF offered Prudential Algebra to help him make decision 108–109; BF letter on scientific sharing 137; Details of kite experiment 313–314; Immigration to America because of BF 385
Prince, Reverend, thought lightning rods caused earthquakes 319
Principles of Trade (George Whately) 371
Pringle, Sir John 201, 205; BF visited hospital with him to study lead poisoning 196; BF reported his electrical treatments 197–198; As Royal Physician and President of Royal Society 327
Printer, BF claimed as his profession 354; Standing apology for 104
Printing press, used by BF as boy 211

Printing techniques used by BF 103, 355
Print shop, ideal university for BF 37
Proas 19
Proposals Relating to the Education of Youth in Pennsylvania, first step toward University of Pennsylvania 252–254
Proprietary Party, opposed by BF 261
Proprietor of Pennsylvania 285
Prudential algebra, technique of decision-making BF sent Priestley 108–109
Puckeridge (Pockrich), Richard, preceded BF using musical glasses 231
Purfleet, Board of Ordnance magazines, origin of lightning rod controversy 324–325

Q
Quartet for strings, composed by BF 229

R
Race Street (Philadelphia), where BF moved to have better surroundings for science 164, 274
Ralph, James 59, 63
Randolph, Edmund, delegate to Constitutional Convention from Virginia 5
Raulet, prior at Marly 311
Ray, Catherine (*See* Greene, Catherine)
Read, Deborah (*See* Franklin, Deborah)
Read, Jimmy, bookseller relative of BF 163
Read, John, father of Deborah Franklin 55
Reason, emphasized by Bacon as essential for scientific investigations 387, 388
Religio Medici (Sir Thomas Browne) 228
Reprisal, ship took BF to France 223
Republic (Plato), quoted in *Gazette* on usefulness of mathematics 107
Resolution, ship of Captain Cook 349
Reynolds, Sir Joshua 212
Rhoads, Samuel, among first members of American Philosophical

Society 258

Richardson, Samuel, his *Pamela* first novel published in America 88, 244

Rikhman, G., killed doing BF iron rod experiment 314

Rittenhouse, David 262, 400

Rivarol, Antoine de, called lightning rod sign of learning 320

Roberts, Hugh, BF reported to on hospital visits 204, 401

Robertson, John, on Royal Society lightning rod committee, 324–326

Robespierre, Maximilian de, unsuccessfully defended man accused of blasphemy for lightning rod on house rented from canon 320

Robin Hood's Songs 104

Rockefeller, John D. 165

Rodney, Admiral George 356

Rogers, James, house struck by lightning 295, 301

Rogers, John, Deborah Read's absent husband, presumed but not proven dead 79, 86

Romance in G, Beethoven composition for glass harmonica 228

Roosevelt, Franklin 166

Rose, Aquila 51, 55

Ross, Betsy 403

Ross, George 403

Ross, John, husband of Betsy Ross 403

Round Rodders 324–327

Rousseau, Jean Jacques 45, 140

Royal Academy of Art (London) 212

Royal Academy of Sciences (Paris) 199; D'Alibard reported to when BF theories were proved by experiment at Marly 311; Meeting place of Voltaire and BF 345–346; BF paper on Aurora Borealis 346

Royal Society of London 27, 55, 64, 286, 305, 311, 342, 347, 351, 361, 395; BF contacted through Peter Collinson 255; BF membership on council 125; Junto agenda patterned after that of the Royal Society 152; American Philosophical Society similar 256–257; BF electrical papers read 308; BF on lightning rod committee 315, 324–327; Copley Medal award to

BF 343–344; Sponsor of Captain Cook's voyages 348

Rozier, Pilatre de, he and D'Arlandes were first balloon passengers 358

Rump Parliament 148

Rush, Benjamin, founder with Pemberton of anti-slavery society, BF corresponded with on colds 191–192, 198, 201

Russell, Bertrand 107

S

Salem witch trials 149

Salts, medicinal use 42

Saturday Evening Post 355

Saunders, Richard (See *Poor Richard's Almanack*)

Scheme of Employment for the Twenty-four Hours of a Natural Day 115

Scholastics 386, 387

Schuylkill River 49, 290

Scientific method, establishment of 44

Scientific Revolution 382

Scientific truth, property of mankind 123

Scull, Nicholas, member of Junto 157

Seashells (Appalachians) 374

Second Treatise on Government (Locke) 43

Self-reliance vs. specialization 96

Shackleton, Ernest 348

Shakespeare, William 294, 337

Shelley, Percy Bysshe 56, 294

Shipley, William 159

Shooting stars, called "Shoots" by BF 366

Sign of the George Tavern 128

Sign of the Three Mariners 54

Silence Dogood, BF letters in *New-England Courant* 38, 97, 102, 211, 252, 291, 334; Description of birth at sea 39; Temple of learning dream reported 39; Quoted *London Journal* on freedom of speech 189

Simpson, Professor, corresponded with BF on temperature phenomena 120

Slavery, BF opposition on humanitarian and economic grounds 370; Chaired society for abolition 396

Sloane, Sir Hans 63, 64

Small, Alexander, given BF treatment for gout 361

Small, William, BF influenced his immigration to America 383

Smith, Adam 371

Smith, Logan Pearsall 246–247

Smoky chimneys, causes and cures 18, 130, 132, 194; BF illustration 215

Soap (*See* Crown Soap)

Society for Promotion of Useful Knowledge 261

Socrates 15, 46, 90, 94, 395

Socratic method, adopted by BF 46, 93

Soho Engineering Works (Birmingham, England), Watt steam engines made there 382

Solon et Sophocle (Solon and Sophocles), meeting of Voltaire and BF so described 345–346

Sonneck, O.G. 237

Sorts (printing), BF made own 80, 124

Soulavie, Abbé, 306, 346, 410; BF praised his method of basing conclusions on observed facts 388–389

Sparks, Jared, salvaged BF papers 226

Spectator (Addison and Steele), style for BF 41, 150, 151, 152, 166

Spencer, Dr. Archibald, his demonstration and equipment inspired BF electrical experiments 270

Stamp Act 398

State House (Philadelphia) (*See* Independence Hall)

Steam engine 382, 383

Steele, Richard 41, 150

Stevenson, Margaret, BF's landlady in London 72

Stevenson, Mary 134

Stevenson, Polly, BF corresponded with about science 118; Sunlight on snow experiment 119; Playful reference to cantharides by BF 120

Stifelius, BF sought to surpass his square of sixteen 173–175

Story of Civilization (Will and Ariel Durant) 267

Strahan, William, London publisher and correspondent with BF 163; Angry BF letter to him because of war 221

String quartet, composed by BF 229

Stuber, Dr. 305–306

Swift, Jonathan 60

Swift, Lindsay 335

Swimming, studied as science by BF 67–72

Syng, Philip, assisted BF electrical experiments 271

Systema Vegetabilium (Linnaeus) 25

T

Tailorshop (London) BF papers found there used as patterns 226

Tea, helped start Revolution, BF critical of cost 220

Tea Act of 1773 191

Ternary of Paradoxes (Walter Charleton), first used word electricity 275

Thales of Miletus 274

Theory of Relativity 365

Thevenot, BF used his swimming manual 68–69

Thomson, Sir Joseph 267, 280, 324

Thoreau, Henry David 360

Thundergust, usually negative electricity 315

Times (London), first newspaper printed with steam power 384

Timothée, Louis, America's first librarian 238, 247

Tomaschek, Johann, music for glass harmonica 207

Tonic bath 167, 202

Toolmaking animal, BF definition of man 124

Transactions of the Royal Society 306; Published abstract of BF paper on lightning and electricity 310

Transactions, scientific reports published by American Philosophical Society 262

Treaty of Peace with Britain 353

Truman, Harry, thought BF *Autobiography* guide to best use of time 92–93, 331

Tsar Kolokol Bell (Moscow) 405

Turgot, Anne-Robert-Jacques 225

Twain, Mark 329, 394

Two Cheers for Democracy (E.M. Forster) 110

U

Unforgotten Years (Logan
Pearsall Smith) 246–247
Union, club patterned on Junto 156
Union Fire Company, fire-fighting
group formed by BF 127, 157
United Nations 142
University of Pennsylvania 252–255,
262; Started as Philadelphia
Academy, founded by BF 252–254
Urban, Sylvanus, pseudonym of
Edward Cave 308

V

Van Doren, Carl, BF biographer
26, 87, 258–259, 312, 332; Newton
and BF names in Royal Society
guest book 348; Description of
BF in Paris 368
Vaughan, Benjamin, BF letter on
excessive influence of others 170;
Dry-belly-ache 195–196; BF on
nature of fire 280
Vegetarianism, tried by BF 54–55
Venerate the Plough (motto of
Philadelphia Society for Pro-
moting Agriculture) 372
Ventilation 192, 204, 378, 390
Vergennes, Charles Gravier, French
foreign minister, BF sought
money from for American cause
220
Versailles, Court of 353, 358
Versailles Peace Treaty 141
Vesuvius 274
Vine, club patterned on Junto 156
Virginian (Owen Wister) 51
Virtues, list used by BF as guide 90
Voltaire 2, 45, 267; Meeting with
BF 345–346
Von Kleist, E. 276, 341
Voyage to the Pacific Ocean
(Captain James Cook), sent to
BF by Admiralty in gratitude for
granting safe passage 350

W

Wagner, Richard 230
Walter rotary press 384
Wanamaker 334
War of the Austrian Succession
(King George's War) 158
Washington, George 3, 6, 7, 9, 11,
12, 13, 223, 225, 338, 351–352,
372, 403; BF left him Crabtree
walking-stick 399–400; Sent letter
of praise to BF 402
Washington's chair, BF saw a
rising sun on it at Constitutional
Convention 11–12
Washington Square 403
Waterspouts 362–365
Watson, Joseph 59
Watson, William, electrical
experimenter 276, 328; Confirmed
BF positive and negative electric-
ity in report to Royal Society
305; Abstracted BF electrical
pamphlet for Royal Society 309,
310; Member with BF of light-
ning rod committee for Royal
Society 324–326; Proved existence
of electrical circuit 341
Watt, James 382–383, 385
Watts, John, employed BF in
London 61
The Way to Wealth 73, 335, 336,
337, 338
Wealth of Nations (Adam Smith)
371
Webb, Benjamin, letter from BF
on doing good with little money
172, 263
Webb, George, member of Junto 157
Webster, Noah, BF suggested
question mark at start of printed
sentence 415
Wedderburn, Alexander 395
Weems, Mason, BF biographer 385
Wells, H.G. 255
West, Benjamin, President of
Royal Academy after Reynolds
212
Whately, George, London
economist, BF wrote to him about
bifocals 367; Author of *Principles
of Trade* 371; BF letter antici-
pated pleasures of eternity 400
*What it is, or, How I Became
Young at Sixty* (Horace
Fletcher) 165
Whirlwinds 362–365; Illustration
363
Whistle, The, BF Bagatelle 66, 287
Whitehead, Alfred North 386
Widow Pratt's Tavern 128
Wilcox, John, London bookseller,
loaned books to BF 63
Will and Testament of BF 399
Willett, William, proposed
"Summer Time" daylight savings
in Britain 370

William and Mary College,
Honorary degree to BF 342, 383
Williams, Jonathan 17; BF sent
details of Long Arm 375–376
Wilson, Benjamin 312; On lightning
rod committee of Royal Society
324–326; Supported round rods
against majority, was backed by
George III 326–327
Wilson, James, read BF's speeches
at Constitutional Convention 3,
4–8, 338
Wilson, Woodrow 139, 141, 145
Winkler, German scientist 295
Winthrop, John, Harvard Professor,
received BF letter on magic
square and circle 176; Studied
transit of Venus for American
Philosophical Society 262;
Supported lightning rods 319
Wister, Owen 51
Wooten, James 378
Wordsworth, William 29

Work, BF's pleasure 161–162
World of Washington Irving
(Van Wyck Brooks) 241
Wren, Christopher 343
Wright, Edward, reported French
success with BF electrical exper-
iments to Royal Society 311
Wright, Wilbur 15
Wygate, John, fellow printer in
London 69
Wyndham, Sir William,
employed BF to teach sons to
swim 69, 72

X
Xenophon 46

Y
Yale College, awarded Master of
Arts to BF 35, 342
Yale, Elihu, book gift started Yale
35